DEPARTMENT OF THE TREASURY
WASHINGTON, D.C.

SECRETARY OF THE TREASURY

A Message from the Secretary

The annual Financial Report of the U.S. Government provides the public a comprehensive overview of the Government's current financial position, as well as critical insight into our long term fiscal outlook. The Fiscal Year 2015 Financial Report reflects that the Nation's finances continue to benefit from the strengthening economy.

Since President Obama took office seven years ago, the Nation has made considerable progress in coming back from the worst recession since the Great Depression, and this Administration's agenda continues to improve the Nation's finances. Throughout the country, businesses are adding jobs, and wages and salaries have increased. The unemployment rate has been cut in half since peaking in 2009, and more Americans have access to affordable health care than ever before. And in the face of headwinds in the global economy, the world is counting on the continued strength of the U.S. economy.

In Fiscal Year 2015, the Nation's economic gains contributed to increased revenue and reduced the deficit by $44.5 billion. The Government's net operating cost decreased by more than a third from last year. And the Government's estimated long-term fiscal gap continues to be reduced by the provisions of the Affordable Care Act of 2010, Budget Control Act of 2011, and the American Taxpayer Relief Act of 2013. These and other measures have put our country on solid fiscal footing for the next decade, securing us the time necessary to address our longer-term challenges.

To keep on the path of long-term fiscal sustainability, we must make important investments in education, infrastructure, and innovation that keep our economy strong, and we must create new opportunities so that our growth is broadly shared by all Americans. Through these efforts, I am confident that we can lay the foundation for durable economic growth and broadly shared prosperity.

Jacob J. Lew
February 25, 2016

This page is intentionally blank.

Contents

List of Social Insurance Charts

This page is intentionally blank.

CITIZEN'S GUIDE

FINANCIAL
REPORT
OF THE
UNITED STATES
GOVERNMENT

Citizen's Guide to the Fiscal Year 2015
Financial Report of the United States Government

The Citizen's Guide to the Fiscal Year 2015 *Financial Report* of the U.S. Government (*Financial Report*) summarizes the U.S. Government's current financial position and condition and discusses key financial topics, including fiscal sustainability. This Guide and the *Financial Report* are produced by the U.S. Department of the Treasury in coordination with the Office of Management and Budget (OMB) of the Executive Office of the President. The Secretary of the Treasury, Director of OMB, and Comptroller General of the United States at the Government Accountability Office believe that the information discussed in this Guide is important to all Americans.

Where We Are Now

Comparing the Budget and the Financial Report

Together, the **Budget of the United States Government** (*Budget*) and the **Financial Report of the U.S. Government** *(Financial Report)* present complementary perspectives on the Government's financial position and condition.

- The *Budget* is the Government's primary financial planning and control tool. It accounts for past Government receipts and spending, and presents the President's proposed receipt and spending plan. The *Budget* focuses on *receipts*, or cash received by the U.S. Government (*Government*) and *outlays*, or payments made by the Government to the public. An excess of receipts over outlays is called a budget *surplus*; an excess of outlays over receipts is called a budget *deficit*.

- The *Financial Report* focuses on the Government's costs and revenues (what went out and what came in), assets and liabilities (what it owns and owes), and other important financial information. The *Financial Report* compares the Government's *revenues* (amounts earned, but not necessarily collected), with its *costs* (amounts incurred, but not necessarily paid) to derive net operating cost.

Chart 1 compares the Government's budget deficit (receipts vs. outlays) and net operating cost (revenues vs. costs) for Fiscal Years (FY) 2011-2015. During FY 2015:

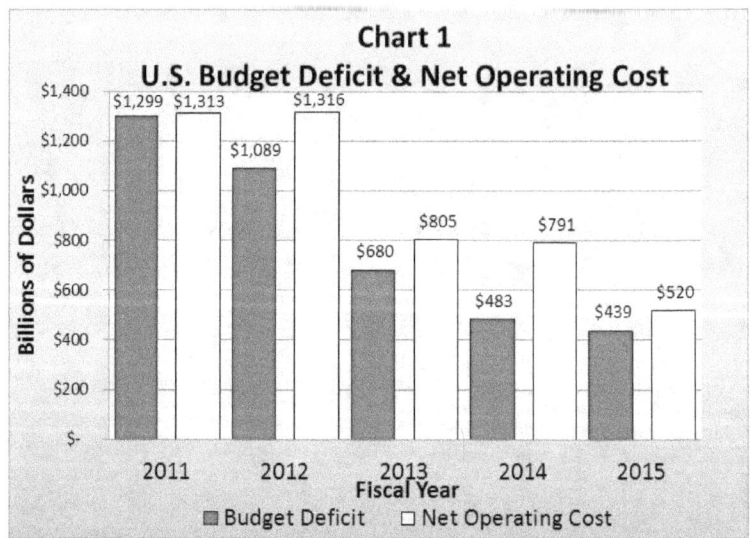

- A $227.9 billion increase in receipts more than offset a $183.4 billion increase in outlays to reduce the budget deficit by $44.5 billion (about 9 percent) to $438.9 billion.

- Net operating cost decreased $271.6 billion or 34.3 percent to $519.7 billion, due largely to a $267.9 billion increase in tax and other revenues, which more than offset a slight $21.8 billion increase in net cost.

- The $80.8 billion difference between the budget deficit and net operating cost is primarily due to accrued costs (incurred but not necessarily paid) associated with increases in estimated federal employee and veteran benefits liabilities and certain other liabilities that are included in net operating cost, but not the budget deficit.

What Went Out and What Came In

The Government's "bottom line" net operating cost (revenue less net cost of Government operations with some adjustments) of $519.7 billion in FY 2015 is calculated as follows:

- Starting with total gross costs of $4.3 trillion, the government subtracts earned program revenues (e.g., Medicare premiums, national park entry fees, and postal service fees) and adjusts the balance for gains or losses from changes in actuarial assumptions used to estimate future liabilities for federal employee and veterans benefits to derive its net cost of $3.9 trillion, a slight increase of $21.8 billion or 0.6 percent from FY 2014. This net increase is the combined effect

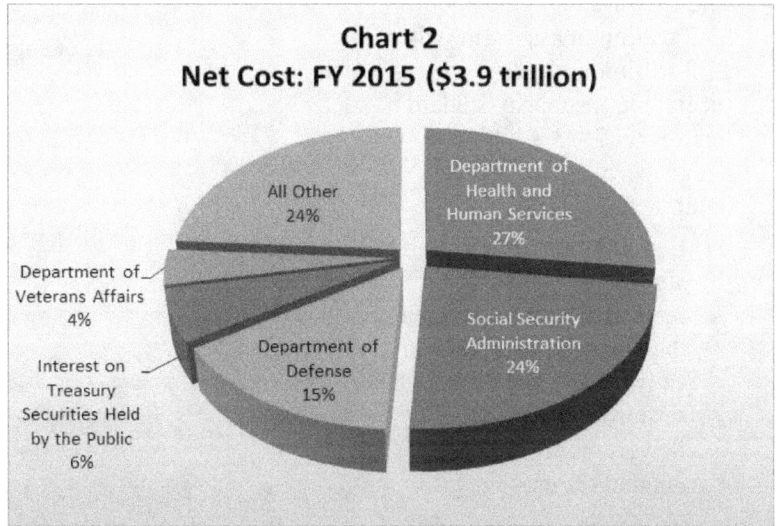

of many offsetting increases and decreases across the Government. For example:

  o The Department of Health and Human Services (HHS) and the Social Security Administration (SSA) experienced net cost increases of $78.0 billion and $38.3 billion, respectively, largely due to increases in benefit expenses from the social insurance programs administered by those agencies (e.g., Medicare, Social Security). Net costs at the Department of Defense (DOD) decreased by $88.7 billion due largely to decreases in costs for future military retirement and health care benefits. Chart 2 shows that the largest shares of the Government's total FY 2015 net cost came from HHS, SSA, and DOD.

  o The Department of Energy's net costs increased $19.9 billion due mostly to changes in environmental and other liability estimates, while the Department of Education's net costs decreased $11.4 billion due largely to decreases in loan program costs and increases in interest earned on loans.

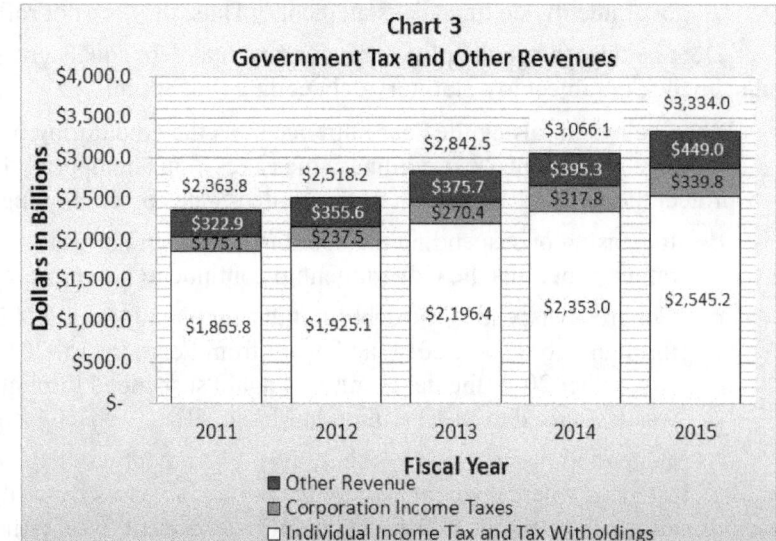

- The Government deducts tax and other revenues from its net cost (with some adjustments) to derive its "bottom line" net operating cost of $519.7 billion, a decrease of $271.6 billion from FY 2014. From Chart 3, total Government tax and other revenues grew by $267.9 billion or 8.7 percent to more than $3.3 trillion for FY 2015.

  o This increase can be attributed to a stronger economy and growth in wages and salaries.

  o Together, individual income tax and tax withholdings, and corporation taxes accounted for about 86.5 percent of total revenues in FY 2015. Other revenues include excise and unemployment taxes, and customs duties.

What We Own and What We Owe

Chart 4 summarizes what the Government owns in assets and what it owes in liabilities. As of September 30, 2015:

- The Government held about $3.2 trillion in assets (mostly $1.2 trillion in net loans receivable (primarily student loans) and $893.9 billion in net property, plant, and equipment).

  o Beyond these assets, other significant Government resources not reported on the balance sheet include stewardship assets, natural resources, and the Government's power to tax and set monetary policy.

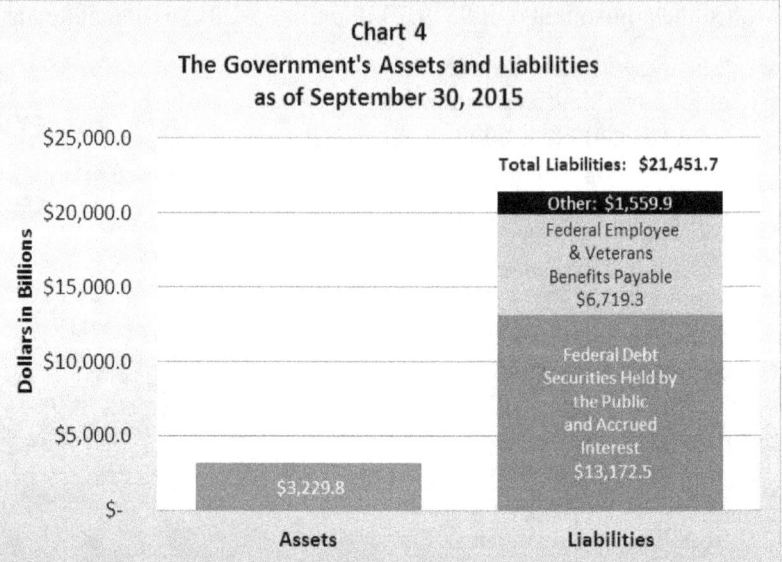

- Total liabilities ($21.5 trillion) consist mostly of: (1) $13.2 trillion in federal debt securities held by the public and accrued interest and (2) $6.7 trillion in federal employee and veteran benefits payable.

  o The "public" consists of individuals, corporations, state and local governments, Federal Reserve Banks, foreign governments, and other entities outside the federal government.

- The Government also reports about $5.1 trillion of intragovernmental debt outstanding, which arises when one part of the Government borrows from another.

  o For example, Government funds (e.g., Social Security and Medicare trust funds) typically must invest excess annual receipts in Treasury-issued federal debt securities, creating trust fund assets and Treasury liabilities. These amounts are included in the financial statements of investing agencies and Treasury, respectively, but offset each other when consolidated into the governmentwide financial statements. Thus, they are not reflected in Chart 4.

Debt held by the public plus intragovernmental debt equals gross federal debt, which, with some adjustments, is subject to a statutory debt ceiling ("debt limit").

- When delays in raising the debt limit occur, as they did during both fiscal years 2014 and 2015, Treasury implements "extraordinary measures," on a temporary basis, to enable the Government to protect the full faith and credit of the United States by continuing to pay the Nation's bills.

  o Increasing or suspending the debt limit does not increase spending or authorize new spending; rather, it permits the Government to continue to honor pre-existing commitments.

  o Congress suspended the debt limit during FY 2014 and FY 2015: from October 17, 2013 through February 7, 2014; and again from February 15, 2014 through March 15, 2015. In November 2015, the debt limit was again suspended through March 15, 2017. The debt limit was last raised to $18.1 trillion in March 2015.

As budget deficits continue to occur, the Government will have to continue to borrow from the public. Instances where the debt held by the public increases faster than the economy for extended periods can pose challenges to the sustainability of current fiscal policy.

Considering key macroeconomic indicators can help place the discussion of the Government's financial results in a broader context. During FY 2015, the economy continued to grow, job growth accelerated, and the unemployment rate declined. These and other economic and financial developments are discussed in greater detail in the *Financial Report*.

Where We Are Headed

An important purpose of this Guide and the *Financial Report* is to help citizens understand current fiscal policy and the importance and magnitude of policy reforms necessary to make it sustainable. A sustainable policy is one where the ratio of debt held by the public to Gross Domestic Product (GDP) (the debt-to-GDP ratio) is stable or declining over the long term. GDP measures the size of the Nation's economy in terms of the total value of all final goods and services that are produced in a year. Considering financial results relative to GDP is a useful indicator of the economy's capacity to sustain the Government's many programs.

To determine if current fiscal policy is sustainable, the projections discussed in this Guide assume current policy will continue indefinitely and draw out the implications for the growth of the debt-to-GDP ratio.[1] The projections are therefore neither forecasts nor predictions. As policy changes are enacted, actual financial outcomes will be different than those projected.

Receipts, Spending, and the Debt

Chart 5 shows historical and current policy projections for receipts, non-interest spending by major category, and total spending expressed as a percent of GDP.

- The difference between the receipts and non-interest spending shares of GDP (the primary deficit-to-GDP ratio) grew rapidly in 2009 due to the financial crisis, the recession, and the policies pursued to combat both. The ratio remained high from 2010 to 2012, despite shrinking in each successive year, and fell significantly in 2013 and 2014.

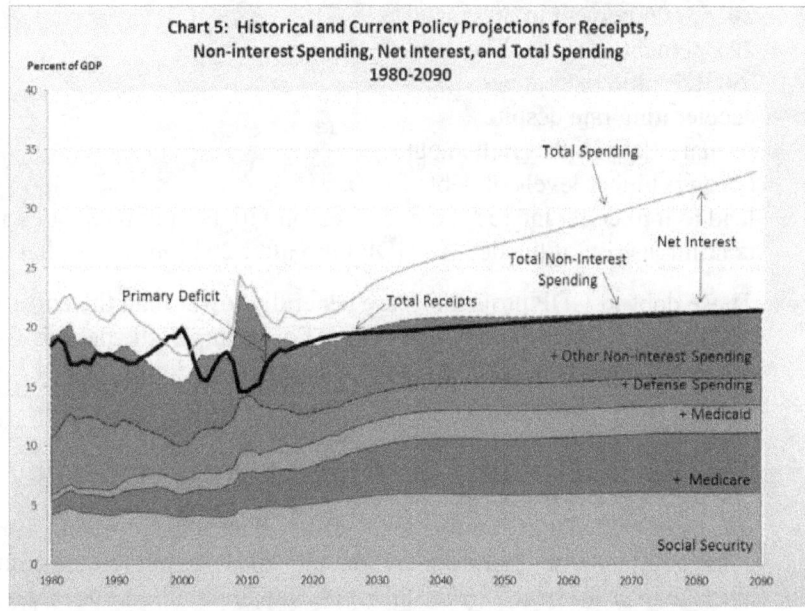

Chart 5: Historical and Current Policy Projections for Receipts, Non-interest Spending, Net Interest, and Total Spending 1980-2090

- The primary deficit is projected to shrink in the next few years as spending limits called for in the Budget Control Act (BCA) continue and the economy continues to recover, becoming a surplus starting in 2019 that peaks at 0.5 percent of GDP in 2024.

- After 2025, however, increased spending for Social Security and health programs[2] due to the continued retirement of the baby boom generation and increases in the price of health care services is expected to cause primary surpluses to steadily deteriorate and become a primary deficit starting in 2028 that reaches 1.0 percent of GDP by 2038. After 2038, the age composition of the population is expected to stabilize and the pace of health care

---

[1] Current policy in the projections is based on current law, but includes extension of certain policies that expire under current law but are routinely extended or otherwise expected to continue.

[2] The 2015 Medicare Trustees Report projects that the Hospital Insurance (HI) Trust Fund will remain solvent until 2030 (unchanged from last year's report). Under current law, tax revenue would be sufficient to pay 86 percent of estimated HI cost in 2030 and 84 percent by 2089. As for Social Security, under current law, the Old-Age, Survivors, and Disability Insurance (OASDI) Trust Fund reserves, considered on a theoretical combined basis, are projected to be depleted in 2034 (one year later than shown in last year's Financial Report), at which time the projected share of scheduled benefits payable from trust fund income is 79 percent, declining to 73 percent in 2089. The Disability Insurance (DI) Trust Fund alone was expected to deplete by the end of 2016, at which time 81 percent of scheduled benefits would be payable. However, the impending depletion of the DI Trust Fund was circumvented by the passage of the Bipartisan Budget Act of 2015, which reallocated a portion of the payroll tax rate from the Old Age Survivors Insurance Trust Fund to the DI Trust Fund. This reallocation is expected to ensure full payment of disability benefits into 2022. The projections assume full Social Security and Medicare benefits are paid after the corresponding trust funds are exhausted. See http://www.ssa.gov/oact/trsum/index.html pp 3, 10, 11

price increases is expected to slow, causing the primary deficit to gradually decrease and become a primary surplus in 2085 that reaches 0.1 percent of GDP in 2090.

o   In these projections, the Affordable Care Act (ACA)[3] provision of health insurance subsidies and expanded Medicaid coverage boost federal spending, and other ACA provisions significantly reduce per-beneficiary Medicare cost growth.

o   Overall, the ACA is projected to substantially reduce the growth rate of federal expenditures for Medicare over the next 75 years. However, as noted in the *Financial Report*, there is uncertainty about the extent to which the ACA's provisions will result in reduced health care cost growth. Even if those provisions work as intended and as assumed in these projections, Chart 5 still shows a persistent gap between projected receipts and total spending.

The primary deficit projections in Charts 5 and 6 (left axis), along with those for interest rates and GDP, determine the debt-to-GDP ratio projections shown in Chart 6 (right axis).

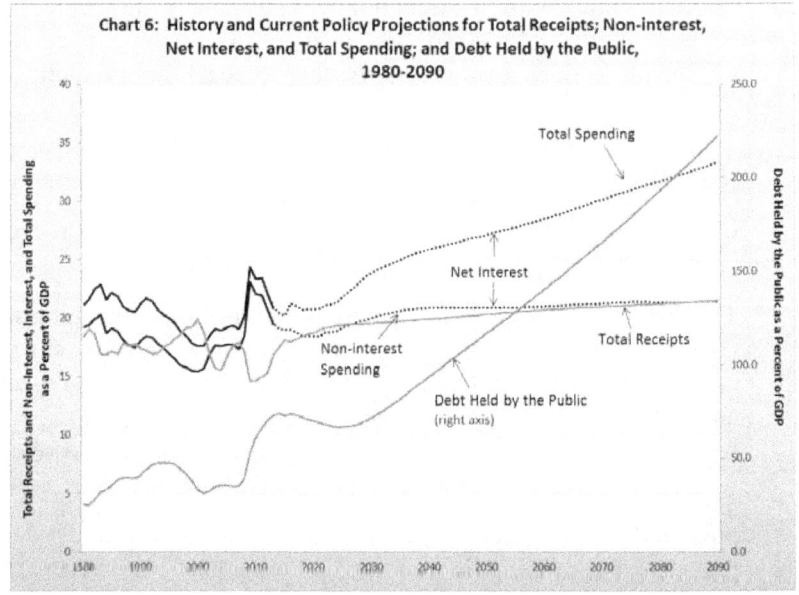

Chart 6: History and Current Policy Projections for Total Receipts; Non-interest, Net Interest, and Total Spending; and Debt Held by the Public, 1980-2090

-   The debt-to-GDP ratio was 74 percent at the end of FY 2015, and under the long-term fiscal projections of current policy is projected to be 67 percent in 2025, 106 percent in 2045, and 223 percent in 2090. The debt-to-GDP ratio rises at an accelerating rate despite primary deficits that flatten out because higher levels of debt lead to higher net interest expenditures, and higher net interest expenditures lead to higher debt. The continuous rise of the debt-to-GDP ratio after 2025 indicates that current policy is unsustainable.

-   These debt-to-GDP projections are generally lower than the corresponding projections in both the FY 2014 and FY 2013 *Financial Reports*. For example, the debt-to-GDP projection for 2088 (the final projection year for the 2013 report) is 217 percent in this year's *Financial Report*, was 315 percent in the FY 2014 *Financial Report*, and was 277 percent in the FY 2013 *Financial Report*.[4]

The Fiscal Gap and the Cost of Delaying Policy Reform

-   It is estimated that preventing the debt-to-GDP ratio from rising over the next 75 years would require some combination of spending reductions and receipt increases that amount to 1.2 percent of GDP on average over the next 75 years, 0.9 percentage points smaller than the 2.1 percent estimate in 2014.

-   The timing of changes to non-interest spending and receipts that close this "75-year fiscal gap" has important implications for the well-being of future generations.

o   For example, relative to a policy that begins immediately, if action is delayed by 10 years, it is estimated that the magnitude of reforms necessary to close the 75-year fiscal gap will increase by about 25 percent; if action is delayed by 20 years, the magnitude of reforms necessary will increase by nearly 60 percent.

---

[3] The ACA refers to P.L. 111-148, as amended by P.L. 111-152. The ACA expands health insurance coverage, provides health insurance subsidies for low-income individuals and families, includes many measures designed to reduce health care cost growth, and significantly reduces Medicare payment rates relative to the rates that would have occurred in the absence of the ACA. (See Note 23 and the Required Supplementary Information section of the *Financial Report*, and the 2014 Medicare Trustees Report for more information).

[4] See the Required Supplementary Information section of the FY 2014 Financial Report of the U.S. Government for more information about changes from the long term fiscal projections for FY 2014.

○　Future generations are harmed by a policy delay of this sort because the higher the primary surpluses are during their lifetimes, the greater is the difference between the taxes they pay and the programmatic spending from which they benefit.

Conclusion

- The Government took significant steps towards fiscal sustainability by enacting the ACA in 2010, the BCA in 2011, and the American Taxpayer Relief Act (ATRA) in 2013. The ACA holds the prospect of lowering long-term per beneficiary spending growth for Medicare and Medicaid, the BCA significantly curtails discretionary spending, and ATRA increased revenues. Together, these three laws substantially reduce the estimated long-term fiscal gap.

- But even with these laws, the Government's debt-to-GDP ratio is projected to remain relatively flat over the next ten years, and then commence a continuous rise over the remaining projection period and beyond if current policy is kept in place. This trend implies that current policy is not sustainable.

- Subject to the important caveat that changes in policy are not so abrupt that they slow continued economic growth, the sooner policies are put in place to avert these trends, the smaller the revenue increases and/or spending decreases will need to be to return the Government to a sustainable fiscal path.

The Nation By The Numbers

The *Financial Report* provides the President, Congress, and the American people a comprehensive view of how the Government is managing taxpayer dollars. It discusses the Government's financial position and condition, its revenues and costs, assets and liabilities, and other responsibilities and commitments, as well as important financial issues that affect the nation and its citizens both now and in the future. The table on the following page presents several key indicators of the Government's financial position and condition, which are summarized in this Guide and discussed in greater detail in the *Financial Report*.

The Government Accountability Office's (GAO) audit report on the U.S. Government's consolidated financial statements can be found beginning on page 239 of the full *Financial Report*. For the reasons discussed below, GAO was prevented from expressing (disclaimed) an opinion on these consolidated financial statements. GAO disclaimed an opinion on the 2015 Statement of Long-Term Fiscal Projections; the 2015, 2014, 2013, 2012, and 2011 Statements of Social Insurance (SOSI); and the 2015 and 2014 Statements of Changes in Social Insurance Amounts because of significant uncertainties (discussed in Note 23 in the *Financial Report*) primarily related to the achievement of projected reductions in Medicare cost growth and certain other limitations. In addition, GAO disclaimed an opinion on the remaining FY 2015 and 2014 financial statements in the *Financial Report* due to certain material financial reporting control weaknesses and other limitations on the scope of its work.

NATION BY THE NUMBERS
A Snapshot of
The Government's Financial Position & Condition

Dollars in Billions		2015		2014
Gross Costs	$	**(4,253.7)**	$	**(4,251.4)**
Less: Earned Revenue	$	375.6	$	417.9
Gain/(Loss) from Changes in Assumptions	$	19.3	$	(3.5)
Net Cost	$	**(3,858.8)**	$	**(3,837.0)**
Less: Total Tax and Other Revenues	$	**3,334.0**	$	**3,066.1**
Unmatched Transactions and Balances[1]	$	5.1	$	(20.4)
Net Operating Cost	$	**(519.7)**	$	**(791.3)**
Assets:	$	**3,229.8**	$	**3,065.3**
Less: Liabilities, comprised of:				
Debt Held By the Public & Accrued Interest	$	(13,172.5)	$	(12,833.6)
Federal Employee & Veteran Benefits	$	(6,719.3)	$	(6,672.6)
Other	$	(1,559.9)	$	(1,259.8)
Total Liabilities	$	**(21,451.7)**	$	**(20,766.0)**
Net Position (Assets Less Liabilities)	$	**(18,221.9)**	$	**(17,700.7)**
Sustainability Measures:				
Social Insurance Net Expenditures[2]	$	(41,487)	$	(41,916)
Total Non-Interest Net Expenditures[3]	$	(4,100)	$	(4,700)
Sustainability Measures as Percent of Gross Domestic Product (GDP)[4]:				
Social Insurance Net Expenditures		(3.7%)		(4.0%)
Non-Interest Spending Less Receipts		(0.3%)		(0.4%)
Budget Results				
Unified Budget Deficit	$	**(438.9)**	$	**(483.4)**

1 Reflects adjustments made to bring certain accounts into balance for such items as restatements and errors in federal agency reporting and unreconciled intragovernmental transactions and balances among agencies.

2 Source: Statement of Social Insurance. Amounts equal present value of projected revenues and expenditures for scheduled benefits over the next 75 years of certain benefit programs that are referred to as Social Insurance (e.g., Social Security, Medicare). Amounts represent 'open group' population (all current and future beneficiaries). These amounts are not considered liabilities on the balance sheet.

3 Source: Statement of Long-Term Fiscal Projections. Represents the 75-year projection of the federal government's receipts less non-interest spending.

4 GDP values used represent the average of 75-year present value of nominal GDP for 2015 and 2014 based on the Social Security and Medicare Trustees Reports.

Find Out More

The *2015 Financial Report of the United States Government* and other information about the nation's finances are available at:

- U.S. Department of the Treasury, http://www.fiscal.treasury.gov/fsreports/rpt/finrep/fr/fr_index.htm ;
- OMB's Office of Federal Financial Management, http://www.whitehouse.gov/omb/financial/index.html; and
- GAO, http://www.gao.gov/financial.html.

MANAGEMENT'S DISCUSSION AND ANALYSIS

Introduction

The Fiscal Year (FY) *2015 Financial Report of the United States Government (Financial Report)* provides the President, Congress, and the American people with a comprehensive view of the federal government's finances, i.e., its financial position and condition, its revenues and costs, assets and liabilities, and other obligations and commitments. The *Financial Report* also discusses important financial issues and significant conditions that may affect future operations, including the need to achieve fiscal sustainability over the medium and long term.

Pursuant to 31 U.S.C. § 331(e)(1), the Department of the Treasury (Treasury), in cooperation with the Office of Management and Budget (OMB), must submit an audited (by the Government Accountability Office or GAO) financial statement for the preceding fiscal year, covering all accounts and associated activities of the executive branch of the United States Government[1] – the central component of the *Financial Report* – to the President and Congress no later than six months after the September 30 fiscal year end. To encourage timely and relevant reporting, OMB accelerated both individual agency and governmentwide reporting deadlines.

The *Financial Report* is prepared from the audited financial statements of specifically designated federal agencies, including the Cabinet departments and many smaller, independent agencies (see organizational chart on the next page). As it has for the past eighteen years, GAO issued a "disclaimer" of opinion on the accrual-based, consolidated financial statements for the fiscal years ended September 30, 2015 and 2014. GAO also issued disclaimers of opinion on the 2015 Statement of Long-Term Fiscal Projections (SLTFP); the 2015, 2014, 2013, 2012 and 2011 Statements of Social Insurance (SOSI); and the 2015 and 2014 Statement of Changes in Social Insurance Amounts (SCSIA). A disclaimer of opinion indicates that sufficient information was not available for the auditors to determine whether the reported financial statements were fairly presented in accordance with Generally Accepted Accounting Principles (GAAP). In FY 2015, 33[2] of the 39 most significant agencies earned unmodified opinions on their financial statement audits.[3]

The FY 2015 *Financial Report* consists of:
- Management's Discussion and Analysis (MD&A), which provides management's perspectives on and analysis of information presented in the *Financial Report*, such as financial and performance trends;
- Principal financial statements and the related notes to the financial statements;
- Required Supplementary Information (RSI), Required Supplementary Stewardship Information (RSSI), and Other Information; and
- GAO's audit report.

In addition, a Citizen's Guide is included to provide the American taxpayer with a quick reference to the key issues in the *Financial Report* and an overview of the Government's financial position and condition.

Mission & Organization

The Government's fundamental mission is derived from the Constitution: *"...to form a more perfect union, establish justice, insure domestic tranquility, provide for the common defense, promote the general welfare and secure the blessings of liberty to ourselves and our posterity."* Congress authorizes and agencies implement programs as missions and initiatives evolve over time in pursuit of key public services and objectives, such as providing for national defense, promoting affordable health care, fostering income security, boosting agricultural productivity, providing veterans benefits and services, facilitating commerce, supporting housing and the

---

[1] The Government Management Reform Act of 1994 has required such reporting, covering the executive branch of the Government, beginning with financial statements prepared for FY 1997. Treasury and OMB have elected to include certain financial information on the legislative and judicial branches in consolidated financial statements as well.

[2] The 32 agencies include the Department of Health and Human Services, which received disclaimers of opinion on its 2015, 2014, 2013, 2012, and 2011 SOSI and on its 2015 and 2014 SCSIA.

[3] The Federal Deposit Insurance Corporation (FDIC), the National Credit Union Administration (NCUA), and the Farm Credit System Insurance Corporation (FCSIC) are among the 39 significant entities. However, because these entities operate on a calendar year basis (December 31 year-end), their 2015 audits are not yet complete. Statistic reflects 2014 audit results for these organizations. In addition, neither the Defense Security Cooperation Agency (DSCA) nor the General Fund of the U.S. Government were subject to audit for FY 2015.

transportation systems, protecting the environment, contributing to the security of energy resources, and helping States provide education. Exhibit 1 provides an overview of how the U.S. Government (Government) is organized.

Exhibit 1

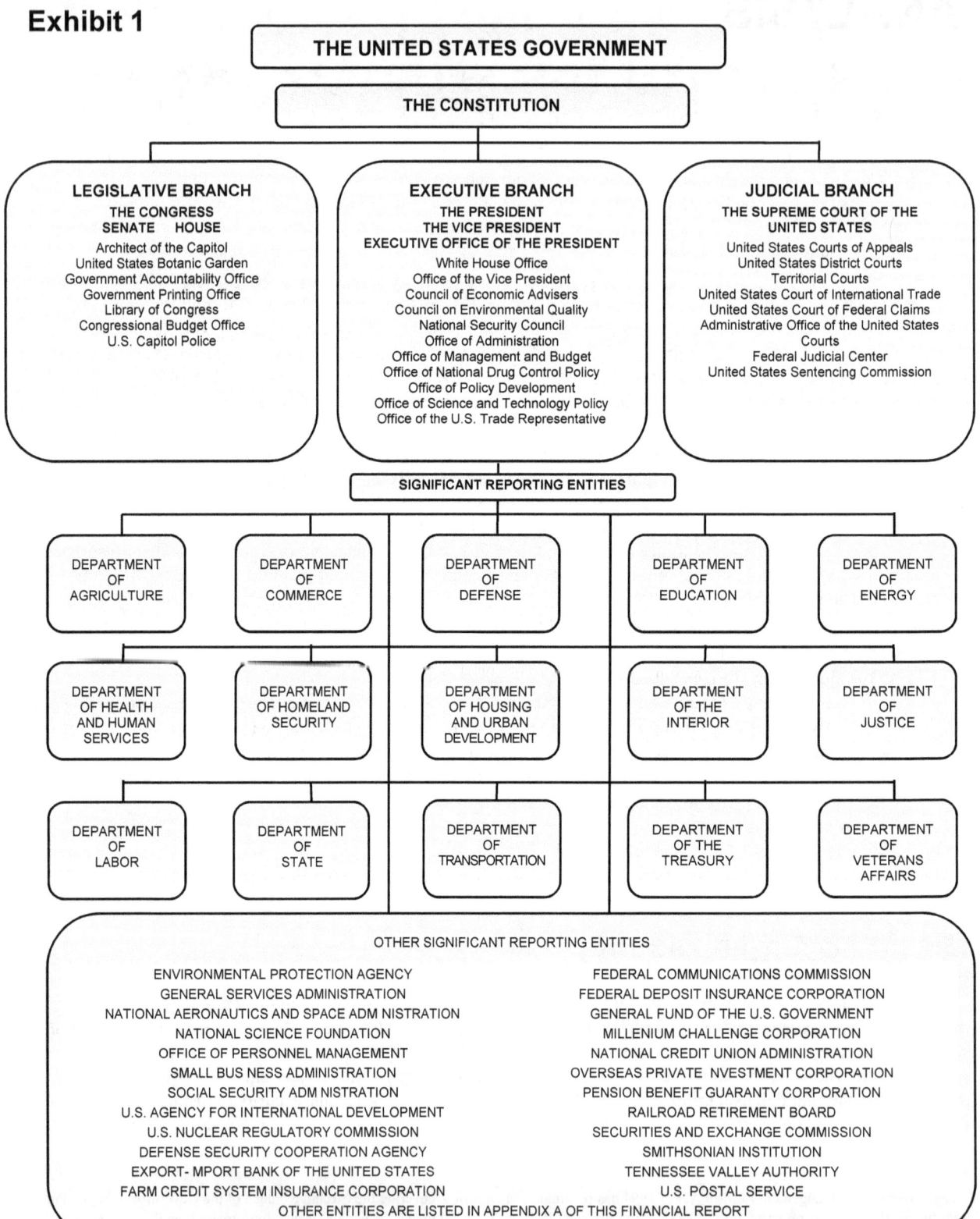

The Government's Financial Position and Condition

A complete assessment of the Government's financial or fiscal condition requires analysis of historical results, projections of future revenues and expenditures, and an assessment of the Government's long-term fiscal sustainability. This *Financial Report* discusses the Government's financial position at the end of the fiscal year, explains how and why the financial position changed during the year, and provides insight into how the Government's financial condition may change in the future.

Table 1 The Federal Government's Financial Position and Condition					
Dollars in Billions	2015	2014	Increase / (Decrease)		
			$	%	
FINANCIAL MEASURES					
Gross Cost	$ (4,253.7)	$ (4,251.4)	$ 2.3	0.1%	
Less: Earned Revenue	$ 375.6	$ 417.9	$ (42.3)	(10.1%)	
Gain/(Loss) from Changes in Assumptions	$ 19.3	$ (3.5)	$ 22.8	651.4%	
Net Cost[1]	$ (3,858.8)	$ (3,837.0)	$ 21.8	0.6%	
Less: Tax and Other Revenues	$ 3,334.0	$ 3,066.1	$ 267.9	8.7%	
Unmatched Transactions & Balances	$ 5.1	$ (20.4)	$ (25.5)	(125%)	
Net Operating Cost[2]	$ (519.7)	$ (791.3)	$ (271.6)	(34.3%)	
Assets[3]:					
Cash & Other Monetary Assets	$ 305.1	$ 264.9	$ 40.2	15.2%	
Loans Receivable, Net	$ 1,216.0	$ 1,125.7	$ 90.3	8.0%	
Inventories & Related Property, Net	$ 320.6	$ 318.4	$ 2.2	0.7%	
Property, Plant & Equipment, Net	$ 893.9	$ 878.3	$ 15.6	1.8%	
Other	$ 494.2	$ 478.0	$ 16.2	3.4%	
Total Assets	$ 3,229.8	$ 3,065.3	$ 164.5	5.4%	
Liabilities[3]:					
Federal Debt Held by the Public & Accrued Interest	$ (13,172.5)	$ (12,833.6)	$ 338.9	2.6%	
Federal Employee & Veterans Benefits	$ (6,719.3)	$ (6,672.6)	$ 46.7	0.7%	
Other	$ (1,559.9)	$ (1,259.8)	$ 300.1	23.8%	
Total Liabilities	$ (21,451.7)	$ (20,766.0)	$ 685.7	3.3%	
Net Position (Assets minus Liabilities)	$ (18,221.9)	$ (17,700.7)	$ 521.2	2.9%	
SUSTAINABILITY MEASURES					
Social Insurance Net Expenditures[4]:					
Social Security (OASDI)	$ (13,440)	$ (13,330)	$ 110	0.8%	
Medicare (Parts A, B, & D)	$ (27,940)	$ (28,483)	$ (543)	(1.9%)	
Other	$ (108)	$ (103)	$ 5	4.6%	
Total Social Insurance Net Expenditures	$ (41,487)	$ (41,916)	$ (429)	(1.0%)	
Total Noninterest Spending Less Receipts[5]	$ (4,100)	$ (4,700)	$ (600)	(12.8%)	
BUDGET DEFICIT					
Unified Budget Deficit[6]	$ (438.9)	$ (483.4)	$ (44.5)	(9.2%)	

1 Source: Statements of Net Cost.

2 Source: Statements of Operations and Changes in Net Position.

3 Source: Balance Sheet.

4 Source: Statements of Social Insurance (SOSI). Amounts equal estimated present value of projected revenues and expenditures for scheduled benefits over the next 75 years of certain 'Social Insurance' programs (Social Security, Medicare Parts A, B, & D, Railroad Retirement - Black Lung is projected through 2040). Amounts reflect 'Open Group' totals (all current and projected program participants during the 75-year projection period).

5 Represents the 75-year projection of the federal government's receipts less non-interest spending as reported in the Statement of Long-Term Fiscal Projections.

6 Source: Final Monthly Treasury Statement (as of 9/30/2015 and 9/30/2014).

Note: Totals may not equal sum of components due to rounding.

Table 1 on the previous page and the following summarize the federal government's financial position:

- The Government's gross costs stayed essentially flat, increasing by only $2.3 billion or 0.1 percent to $4.3 trillion. Deducting $375.6 billion in revenues earned for goods and services provided to the public (e.g., Medicare premiums, national park entry fees, and postal service fees) and deducting $19.3 billion in net gains from changes in assumptions (e.g., interest rates, inflation, disability claims rates) results in the Government's net cost of $3.9 trillion in FY 2015 a slight increase of $21.8 billion or 0.6 percent from FY 2014.

- Tax and other revenues increased $267.9 billion or 8.7 percent to $3.3 trillion, which, when offset against the Government's net cost, with some adjustment for unmatched transactions and balances, results in a "bottom line" net operating cost of $519.7 billion for FY 2015, a decrease of more than a third ($271.6 billion or 34.3 percent) from FY 2014.

- Comparing total 2015 Government assets of $3.2 trillion to total liabilities of $21.5 trillion (comprised mostly of $13.2 trillion in federal debt held by the public and accrued interest payable[4], and $6.7 trillion of federal employee and veterans benefits payable) yields a negative net position of $18.2 trillion.

- The sum of debt held by the public excluding accrued interest ($13.1 trillion), and intragovernmental debt ($5.1 trillion) equals gross federal debt, which, with some adjustments, is subject to the statutory debt limit. As of September 30, 2015, the Government's total debt subject to the debt limit was $18.1 trillion. Congress suspended the debt limit from February 15, 2014 through March 15, 2015 (P.L. 113-83), after which Treasury began implementing "extraordinary measures" on a temporary basis, which were still in effect as of September 30, 2015, to enable the Government to protect the full faith and credit of the United States Government by continuing to pay the Nation's bills. On November 2, 2015, Congress again suspended the debt limit, this time through March 15, 2017 (P.L. 114-74).

This *Financial Report* also contains information about potential impacts on the Government's future financial condition. Under federal accounting rules, social insurance spending as reported in the Statement of Long-Term Fiscal Projections; and social insurance expenditures, as reported in the Statement of Social Insurance (SOSI) are not considered liabilities of the Government. They can, however, provide a valuable perspective on the sustainability of the Government's fiscal path:

- Total projected spending, including other major programs (e.g., defense, Medicaid, and education) and tax revenues provide another perspective of the Government's projected fiscal condition. Over the next 75 years, under current policy, the present value (PV) of the Government's total non-interest spending (including its social insurance programs) is projected to exceed the PV of total receipts by $4.1 trillion.

- The SOSI compares the actuarial present value[5] of the Government's projected expenditures for scheduled benefits for Social Security, Medicare Parts A, B and D, and other social insurance programs over 75 years[6] to a subset of the revenues[7] supporting these programs. For 2015, these projected expenditures exceeded projected revenues by about $41.5 trillion, a $429 billion decrease from 2014 social insurance projections.

The Government's current financial position and long-term financial condition can be evaluated both in dollar terms and in relation to the economy as a whole. Gross Domestic Product (GDP) measures the size of the nation's economy in terms of the total value of all final goods and services that are produced in a year. Considering financial results relative to GDP is a useful indicator of the economy's capacity to sustain the Government's many programs. For example:

- The unified budget deficit (i.e., including the consolidated receipts and outlays from federal funds and the Social Security Trust Fund) decreased from $483.4 billion or 2.8 percent of GDP in FY 2014 to $438.9 billion (the lowest since 2007) or 2.5 percent of GDP in FY 2015, the lowest deficit-to-GDP level since

---

[4] On the Government's balance sheet, debt held by the public and accrued interest payable consists of Treasury securities, net of unamortized discounts and premiums, and accrued interest payable. The "public" consists of individuals, corporations, state and local governments, Federal Reserve Banks, foreign governments, and other entities outside the federal government.

[5] Present values recognize that a dollar paid or collected in the future is worth less than a dollar today because a dollar today could be invested and earn interest. To calculate a present value, future amounts are thus reduced using an assumed interest rate, and those reduced amounts are summed.

[6] The Black Lung Program is projected through September 30, 2040.

[7] Social Security is funded by the payroll taxes and revenue from taxation of benefits. Medicare Part A is funded by the payroll taxes, revenue from taxation of benefits, and premiums that support those programs. Medicare Parts B and D are primarily financed by general revenues and premiums. By accounting convention, general revenues transferred to Medicare Parts B and D are eliminated in consolidation at the governmentwide level and, as such, are not included in the SOSI.

2007 and less than the average of the last 40 years. The deficit-to-GDP ratio has declined by about three-quarters since 2009 – the fastest sustained deficit reduction since just after World War II.[8]

- The budget deficit is primarily financed through borrowing from the public. As of September 30, 2015, debt held by the public, excluding accrued interest, was $13.1 trillion (about 74 percent of GDP).

- The projected $41.5 trillion net present value excess of expenditures over receipts over 75 years for the programs reported in the 2015 SOSI represents about 3.7 percent of the present value of GDP over 75 years. The excess of total projected non-interest spending over receipts of $4.1 trillion discussed in the 'Statement of Long Term Fiscal Projections' represents 0.3 percent of GDP over 75 years. As discussed in this *Financial Report*, these projections can, in turn, have a significant impact on projected debt as a percent of GDP.

Fiscal Year 2015 Financial Statement Audit Results

For FY 2015, GAO issued a nineteenth consecutive disclaimer of audit opinion on the accrual-based, governmentwide financial statements. In addition, GAO issued disclaimers of opinion on the 2015 Statement of Long-Term Fiscal Projections (SLTFP); the 2015, 2014, 2013, 2012 and 2011 SOSI; and the 2015 and 2014 SCSIA. The SOSI, SCSIA, and SLTFP disclaimers stem from significant uncertainties (discussed in Note 23, Social Insurance), primarily related to the achievement of projected reductions in Medicare cost growth and certain other limitations.

Twenty-one of the 24 agencies required to issue audited financial statements under the Chief Financial Officers (CFO) Act received unmodified audit opinions, as did 12 of 15 additional significant reporting agencies (see Appendix A).[9]

The Governmentwide Reporting Entity

This *Financial Report* includes the financial status and activities of the executive, legislative, and judicial branches of the federal government. The legislative and judicial branches are not required by law to submit financial statement information to Treasury; however, these branches provided cash and a significant amount of accrual basis financial information to include in the

Table 2: FY 2015 CFO Act Financial Statement Audit Results	
Chief Financial Officers (CFO) Act Agency	Audit Opinion
Department of Agriculture (USDA)	Disclaimer
Department of Commerce (DOC)	Unmodified
Department of Defense (DOD)	Disclaimer
Department of Education (Education)	Unmodified
Department of Energy (DOE)	Unmodified
Department of Health and Human Services (HHS)[1]	Unmodified
Department of Homeland Security (DHS)	Unmodified
Department of Housing and Urban Development (HUD)	Disclaimer
Department of the Interior (DOI)	Unmodified
Department of Justice (DOJ)	Unmodified
Department of Labor (DOL)	Unmodified
Department of State (State)	Unmodified
Department of Transportation (DOT)	Unmodified
Department of the Treasury (Treasury)	Unmodified
Department of Veterans Affairs (VA)	Unmodified
Agency for International Development (USAID)	Unmodified
Environmental Protection Agency (EPA)	Unmodified
General Services Administration (GSA)	Unmodified
National Aeronautics and Space Administration (NASA)	Unmodified
National Science Foundation (NSF)	Unmodified
Nuclear Regulatory Commission (NRC)	Unmodified
Office of Personnel Management (OPM)	Unmodified
Small Business Administration (SBA)	Unmodified
Social Security Administration (SSA)	Unmodified

[1] Received disclaimer of opinion on Statement of Social Insurance and Statement of Changes in Social Insurance Amounts

Financial Report. Appendix A lists the organizations and agencies (entities) included in the U.S. Government's consolidated reporting entity for the *Financial Report*, as well as some entities not included in the reporting entity.

A number of entities and organizations are excluded due to the nature of their operations, including the Federal Reserve System (considered to be an independent central bank under the general oversight of Congress), all fiduciary funds, and Government-Sponsored Enterprises (GSEs), including the Federal Home Loan Banks, the Federal National Mortgage Association (Fannie Mae), and the Federal Home Loan Mortgage Corporation (Freddie Mac). Following U.S. GAAP for federal entities, the Government has not consolidated into its financial statements the assets, liabilities, or results of operations of any financial organization or commercial entity in which Treasury holds either a direct, indirect, or beneficial majority equity investment. Under Statement of Federal Financial

---

[8] Final Monthly Treasury Statement (as of September 30, 2015 and 2014), 10/15/15 press release – Joint Statement of Treasury Secretary Jacob J. Lew and OMB Director Shaun Donovan on Budget Results for Fiscal Year 2015

[9] The 21 agencies include the Department of Health and Human Services, which received disclaimers of opinions on its 2015, 2014, 2013, 2012, and 2011 SOSI and its 2015 and 2014 SCSIA.

Accounting Concepts (SFFAC) No. 2, these entities meet the criteria of paragraph 50 and do not appear in the Federal Budget section "Federal Programs by Agency and Account." As such, these entities are not consolidated into the financial reports of the Government. However, the values of the investments in and any related liabilities to such entities are presented on the balance sheet. Appendix A includes a list of the agencies and entities contributing to this *Financial Report*.[10]

The following pages contain a more detailed discussion of the Government's financial results for FY 2015, the budget, the economy, the debt, and a long-term perspective about fiscal sustainability, including the Government's ability to meet its social insurance benefits obligations. The information in this *Financial Report*, when combined with the Budget of the U.S. Government, collectively presents information on the Government's financial position and condition.

Accounting Differences Between The Budget and the Financial Report

Each year, the Administration issues two reports that detail the Government's financial results: the *Budget of the U.S. Government (Budget)*, prepared primarily on a "cash basis", and which provides a plan for future initiatives and the resources needed to support them, as well as prior year fiscal and performance results; and this *Financial Report*, which provides the President, Congress, and the American people a broad, comprehensive overview of the cost on an "accrual basis" of the Government's operations, the sources used to finance them, its balance sheet, and the overall financial outlook.

Treasury generally prepares the financial statements in this *Financial Report* on an accrual basis of accounting as prescribed by U.S. GAAP for federal entities.[11] These principles are tailored to the Government's unique characteristics and circumstances. For example, agencies prepare a uniquely structured "Statement of Net Cost," which is intended to present net Government resources used in its operations. Also, unique to Government is the preparation of separate statements to reconcile differences and articulate the relationship between the budget and financial accounting results.

Budget of the U.S. Government	Financial Report of the U.S. Government
Prepared primarily on a "*cash basis*"	Prepared on an "*accrual and modified cash basis*"
• Initiative-based and prospective: focus on current and future initiatives planned and how resources will be used to fund them. • Receipts ("cash in"), taxes and other collections recorded when received. • Outlays ("cash out"), largely recorded when payment is made.	• Agency-based and retrospective – prior and present resources used to implement initiatives. • Revenue: Tax revenue (more than 90 percent of total revenue) recognized on modified cash basis (see Financial Statement Note 1.B). Remainder recognized when earned, but not necessarily received. • Costs: recognized when incurred, but not necessarily paid.

---

[10] Since programs are not administered at the governmentwide level, performance goals and measures for the federal government, as a whole, are not reported here. The outcomes and results of those programs are addressed at the individual agency level and can be found in each agency's financial report. Go to www.performance.gov for more information about Government performance.

[11] Under U.S. GAAP, most U.S. Government revenues are recognized on a 'modified cash' basis, or when they become measurable. The Statement of Social Insurance presents the present value of the estimated future revenues and expenditures for scheduled benefits over the next 75 years for the Social Security, Medicare, Railroad Retirement programs; and through September 30, 2040 for the Black Lung program. The Statement of Long-Term Fiscal Projections presents the present value of the projected future receipts and non-interest spending for the federal government.

Budget Deficit vs. Net Operating Cost

The Government's primarily cash-based[12] budget deficit decreased nearly $44.5 billion (about 9 percent) from approximately $483.4 billion in FY 2014 to about $438.9 billion in FY 2015 (the lowest since 2007) due to higher receipts that more than offset an increase in outlays in FY 2015. The $227.9 billion (7.5 percent) increase in receipts can be attributed to a stronger economy. Growth in wages and salaries made collections of individual and payroll taxes strong throughout the year. Corporation income tax collections also increased in FY 2015 due to growth in taxable profits. Outlays increased $184 billion (5 percent) due to the net effect of: (1) spending increases for Social Security, Medicare, and Medicaid, along with lower dividend receipts from the GSEs, Fannie Mae and Freddie Mac (recorded as offsets to spending), partially offset by (2) spending decreases in the Departments of Agriculture, Defense, Housing and Urban Development, and Labor, among other agencies.[13] The Government's largely accrual-based net operating cost also decreased by $271.6 billion, or 34.3 percent, from $791.3 billion to $519.7 billion during FY 2015. As explained below, net operating costs are affected by both changes in revenues and costs.

Table 3: Net Operating Cost vs. Budget Deficit				
Dollars in Billions		2015		2014
Net Operating Cost	$	(519.7)	$	(791.3)
Change in:				
Federal Employee and Veterans Benefits Payable	$	46.7	$	134.3
Environmental and Disposal Liabilities	$	42.5	$	20.0
Property, Plant, and Equipment, Net[1]	$	(15.6)	$	18.4
Yearend Upward/(Downward) Credit Reform Subsidy Reestimates, Net[2]	$	(26.8)	$	22.9
Other Liabilities	$	38.6	$	7.3
Other, Net	$	(4.6)	$	105.0
Subtotal - Net Difference:	$	80.8	$	307.9
Budget Deficit	$	(438.9)	$	(483.4)

1 Net effect of: capitalized fixed assets, depreciation expense, and asset disposals and revaluations

2 Net effect of: yearend upward/(downward) credit reform subsidy reestimates and effect of prior year (upward)/downward credit reform subsidy reestimates.

The budget deficit is measured as the excess of outlays, or payments made by the Government, over receipts, or cash received by the Government. Net operating cost, on an accrual basis, is the excess of costs (what the Government has incurred, but has not necessarily paid) over revenues (what the Government has collected and expects to collect, but has not necessarily received). Net operating cost typically exceeds the budget deficit due largely to the inclusion of cost accruals associated with increases in estimated liabilities for the Government's postemployment benefit programs for its military and civilian employees and veterans. Similarly, the difference between the budget deficit and net operating cost can also be affected by changes in certain asset valuations, such as investments, and in other liabilities, such as estimated insurance and guarantee program liabilities. The longer-term estimated costs of these programs are included in the Government's net operating cost, calculated on an accrual basis as described above, but are not included in the largely cash-based budget deficit. In addition, the costs of certain assets, such as property plant and equipment, are recorded in the budget as outlays when purchased but are capitalized as assets and included in net operating cost as depreciation expense (an accrual cost) as they are used over the useful life of the asset. Significant changes in the Government's net operating cost, including those related to the aforementioned longer-term estimated costs, are discussed in the next section.

The *Reconciliation of Net Operating Cost and Unified Budget Deficit Statement*, Table 3 summarizes how the Government's net operating cost as reported in the primarily accrual-based financial statements relates to the more widely-known and primarily cash-based budget deficit. Table 3 shows how many of the elements described above contribute to the $80.8 billion net difference between the Government's budget deficit and net operating cost for FY 2015, the majority of which is attributable to: (1) a $46.7 billion net increase in liabilities for Federal employee and veteran benefits payable, and (2) a $42.5 billion increase in environmental and disposal liabilities. These and most of the other "Change in" amounts summarized in Table 3 affect net operating cost, but not the budget deficit.

---

[12] Interest outlays on Treasury debt held by the public are recorded in the budget when interest accrues, not when the interest payment is made. For federal credit programs, outlays are recorded when loans are disbursed, in an amount representing the present value cost to the Government (excluding administrative costs), or the credit subsidy cost. Credit programs record cash payments to and from the public in non-budgetary financing accounts.

[13] 10/15/15 press release -- Joint Statement of Treasury Secretary Jacob J. Lew and OMB Director Shaun Donovan on Budget Results for Fiscal Year 2015.

The Government's Net Position: "Where We Are"

The Government's financial position and condition have traditionally been expressed through the *Budget*, focusing on surpluses, deficits, and debt. However, this primarily cash-based discussion of the Government's net outlays (deficit) or net receipts (surplus) tells only part of the story. The Government's accrual-based net position, (the difference between its assets and liabilities), and its "bottom line" net operating cost (the difference between its revenues and costs) are also key financial indicators.

Costs and Revenues: "What Went Out & What Came In"

The Government's *Statement of Operations and Changes in Net Position*, much like a corporation's income statement, shows the Government's "bottom line" and its impact on net position (i.e., assets net of liabilities). To derive the Government's "bottom line" net operating cost, the *Statement of Net Cost* first shows how much it costs to operate the federal government, recognizing expenses when incurred, regardless of when payment is made (accrual basis). It shows the derivation of the Government's *net cost* or the net of: (1) gross costs, or the costs of goods produced and services rendered by the Government, (2) the earned revenues generated by those goods and services during the fiscal year, and (3) gains or losses from changes in actuarial assumptions used to estimate certain liabilities. This amount, in turn, is offset against the Government's taxes and other revenue reported in the *Statement of Operations and Changes in Net Position* to calculate the "bottom line" or *net operating cost*. [14]

Table 4: Gross Cost, Revenues, Net Cost, and Net Operating Cost					
Dollars in Billions	2015	2014	Increase / (Decrease) $	%
Gross Cost	$ (4,253.7)	$ (4,251.4)	$ 2.3	0.1%
Less: Earned Revenue	$ 375.6	$ 417.9	$ (42.3)	(10.1%)
Gain/(Loss) from Changes in Assumptions	$ 19.3	$ (3.5)	$ 22.8	651.4%
Net Cost	$ (3,858.8)	$ (3,837.0)	$ 21.8	0.6%
Less: Tax and Other Revenues	$ 3,334.0	$ 3,066.1	$ 267.9	8.7%
Unmatched Transactions and Balances	$ 5.1	$ (20.4)	$ (25.5)	(125%)
Net Operating Cost	$ (519.7)	$ (791.3)	$ (271.6)	(34.3%)

Table 4 shows that the Government's "bottom line" net operating cost decreased by more than a third, from $791.3 billion in FY 2014 to $519.7 billion in FY 2015. This $271.6 billion or 34.3 percent decrease is largely attributable to a $267.9 increase in tax and other revenues that more than offset a slight net increase in net cost amounts across agencies over the past fiscal year as summarized in the following.

Gross Cost and Net Cost

The *Statement of Net Cost*, starts with the Government's total gross costs of $4.3 trillion, subtracts revenues earned for goods and services provided (e.g., Medicare premiums, national park entry fees, and postal service fees), and adjusts the balance for gains or losses from changes in actuarial assumptions used to estimate certain liabilities, including federal employee and veterans benefits to derive its net cost of $3.9 trillion, a slight $21.8 billion or 0.6 percent increase over FY 2014.

Typically, the annual change in the Government's net cost is impacted by a variety of offsetting increases and decreases across agencies. For example offsetting change in net cost during FY 2015 included:

- an $88.7 billion decrease at DOD due largely to decreases in costs for future military retirement and health care benefits, largely driven by plan amendments, changes in actuarial assumptions, and other actuarial gains and losses. Specifically, these changes from actuarial assumptions resulted in a $27.5 billion gain (cost decrease) at DOD. Across the government, the net gain from changes in actuarial assumptions associated with the Government's civilian and military benefits programs amounted to $19.3 billion in FY 2015 as compared to a $3.5 billion loss in FY 2014, resulting in a $22.8 billion combined decrease in net cost. Agencies administering these types of programs employ a complex series of assumptions, including but not limited to interest rates, beneficiary eligibility, life expectancy, medical cost levels, compensation levels, disability claims rates, and cost of living to make annual actuarial projections of their long-term benefits liabilities. In addition to DOD, the Department of Veterans Affairs (VA) ($13.0 billion gain) and

---

[14] As shown in Table 4, net operating cost includes an adjustment for unmatched transactions and balances, which represent unreconciled differences in intragovernmental activity and balances between Federal agencies. These amounts are described in greater detail in the Other Information section of this *Financial Report*.

the Office of Personnel Management (OPM) ($17.1 billion loss) reported significant gains and losses, respectively from changes in these assumptions for FY 2015;

- $78.0 billion and $38.3 billion net cost increases at the Department of Health and Human Services (HHS) and the Social Security Administration (SSA), respectively, primarily due to cost increases of the benefits programs that these agencies administer (HHS – Medicare and Medicaid programs, SSA – Old Age Survivors and Disability Insurance (OASDI) programs);

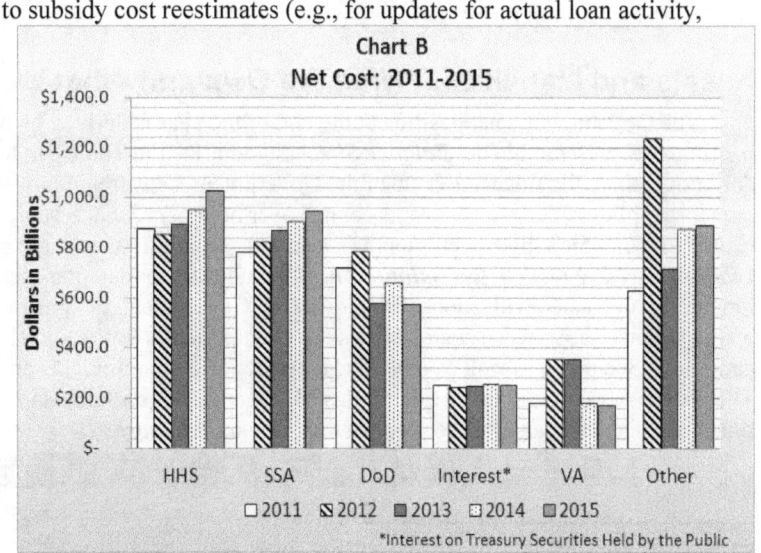

Chart A
Net Cost: FY 2015 ($3.9 trillion)

- a $19.9 billion cost increase at the Department of Energy, largely associated with changes in environmental and other liability estimates[15];

- an $11.6 billion cost decrease at the Department of Housing and Urban Development (HUD) due largely to subsidy cost reestimates by the Federal Housing Administration (FHA) and a decline in interest expenses for insurance and mortgage programs and funds[16]; and

- an $11.4 billion cost decrease at the Department of Education (Education), primarily due to a combination of decreases in gross costs related to subsidy cost reestimates (e.g., for updates for actual loan activity, changes and updates to loan program interest and discount rates) for Education's largest loan programs, and increases in earned or exchange revenues (interest earned on loans).[17]

Chart A shows the composition of the Government's net cost. In FY 2015, nearly two-thirds of total net cost came from DOD, the Social Security Administration (SSA), and the Department of Health and Human Services (HHS). These three agencies have consistently incurred the largest agency shares of the Government's total net cost in recent years (Chart B). As indicated above, HHS and SSA net costs

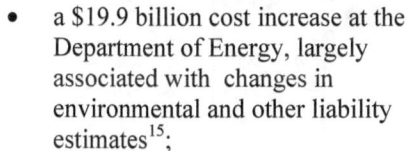

Chart B
Net Cost: 2011-2015

□2011 ▨2012 ■2013 ▢2014 ▥2015

*Interest on Treasury Securities Held by the Public

for FY 2015 ($1,029.5 billion and $944.7 billion, respectively) are attributable to major social insurance programs administered by these agencies. The *Statement of Long-Term Fiscal Projections (SLTFP)*, the *Statement of Social Insurance* (SOSI), and the related analysis and discussion included in this *Financial Report*, discuss the projected future revenues, expenditures, and sustainability of federal government programs in general and of social insurance programs in particular in greater detail. DOD net costs of $573.6 billion relate primarily to operations, readiness, and support; personnel; research; procurement; and retirement and health benefits. Chart A shows that the Department of Veterans Affairs (VA) as well as interest on debt held by the public contributed an additional combined 10 percent, and the other agencies included in the Government's FY 2015 Statement of Net Cost accounted for a combined 24 percent of the Government's total net cost for FY 2015.

---

[15] Department of Energy FY 2015 Agency Financial Report, p. 23

[16] Department of Housing and Urban Development FY 2015 Agency Financial Report, p. 35

[17] Department of Education FY 2015 Agency Financial Report, pp. 32-36

Tax and Other Revenues - Getting to the "Bottom Line"

As noted earlier, tax and other revenues from the ***Statement of Operations and Changes in Net Position*** are deducted from total net cost to derive the Government's "bottom line" net operating cost. Chart C shows that increases in each of the three taxes and other revenue categories shown - individual income tax and withholdings, corporation income taxes, and other revenue - combined to increase total Government tax and other revenues by $267.9 billion or 8.7 percent to nearly $3.3 trillion for FY 2015. This change is primarily attributed to an overall improvement in individual and corporation income tax collections.[18] As noted in the earlier discussion of budget receipts, these increases largely stem from a stronger economy and growth in wages and salaries. Earned revenues from Table 4 are not considered "taxes and other revenue" and, thus, are not shown in Chart C. Individual income tax and tax withholdings and corporation income taxes accounted for about 76 percent and 10 percent of total revenue, respectively in FY 2015; other revenues from Chart C include excise taxes, unemployment taxes, and customs duties.

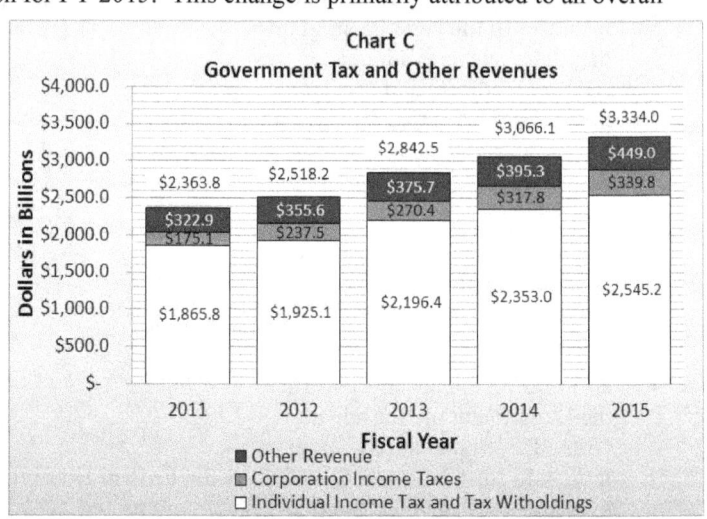

As previously shown in Table 4, the increase in tax and other revenues more than offset the slight increase in net cost, resulting in a net operating cost decrease of more than one-third ($271.6 billion or 34.3 percent) from $791.3 billion for FY 2014 to $519.7 billion for FY 2015.

Assets and Liabilities: "What We Own and What We Owe"

The Government's net position at the end of the year is derived by netting the Government's assets against its liabilities, as presented in the ***Balance Sheet*** (summarized in Table 5). It is important to note that the balance sheet does not include the financial value of the Government's sovereign powers to tax, regulate commerce, and set monetary policy. It also excludes its control over nonoperational resources, including national and natural resources, for which the Government is a steward. In addition, as is the case with the ***Statement of Operations and Changes in Net Position***, the ***Balance Sheet*** includes a separate presentation of the portion of net position related to funds from dedicated collections. Moreover, the Government's exposures are broader than the liabilities presented on the balance sheet, when such items as the Government's future social insurance exposures (namely, Medicare and Social Security), as well as other fiscal projections, commitments and contingencies, are taken into account. These exposures are discussed later in this Management Discussion and Analysis (MD&A) section as well as in the financial statements and RSI sections of this *Financial Report*.

Table 5: Assets and Liabilities				
Dollars in Billions	**2015**	**2014**	**Increase / (Decrease) $**	**%**
Assets				
Cash & Other Monetary Assets	$ 305.1	$ 264.9	$ 40.2	15.2%
Loans Receivable, Net	$ 1,216.0	$ 1,125.7	$ 90.3	8.0%
Inventories & Related Property, Net	$ 320.6	$ 318.4	$ 2.2	0.7%
Property, Plant & Equipment, Net	$ 893.9	$ 878.3	$ 15.6	1.8%
Other	$ 494.2	$ 478.0	$ 16.2	3.4%
Total Assets	**$ 3,229.8**	**$ 3,065.3**	**$ 164.5**	**5.4%**
Less: Liabilities, comprised of:				
Federal Debt Held by the Public & Accrued Interest	$ (13,172.5)	$ (12,833.6)	$ 338.9	2.6%
Federal Employee & Veteran Benefits	$ (6,719.3)	$ (6,672.6)	$ 46.7	0.7%
Other	$ (1,559.9)	$ (1,259.8)	$ 300.1	23.8%
Total Liabilities	**$(21,451.7)**	**$(20,766.0)**	**$ 685.7**	**3.3%**
Net Position (Assets Minus Liabilities)	**$(18,221.9)**	**$(17,700.7)**	**$ 521.2**	**2.9%**

---

[18] <u>Department of the Treasury FY 2015 Agency Financial Report</u>, **p. 27**

Assets – "What We Own"

As of September 30, 2015, the Government held about $3.2 trillion in assets, an increase of $164.5 billion (5.4 percent). The Government's assets are comprised mostly of net loans receivable ($1.2 trillion) and net property, plant, and equipment ($893.9 billion).[19] From Note 4, the Department of Education's (Education's) Federal Direct Student Loan Program accounted for $880.6 billion (72.4 percent) of total net loans receivable. Education's direct student loan program receivables balances have more than doubled since FY 2011 largely due to increased direct loan disbursements, attributable to the continued effect of 2010 legislation requiring a transition for new loans from guaranteed student loans to full direct lending by Education.[20]

Liabilities – "What We Owe"

As indicated in Table 5 and Chart D, of the Government's $21.5 trillion in total liabilities, the largest liability is federal debt securities held by the public and accrued interest, the balance of which increased $338.9 billion (2.6 percent) to $13.2 trillion as of September 30, 2015.

The other major component of the Government's liabilities is federal employee and veteran benefits payable (i.e., the Government's pension and other benefit plans for its military and civilian employees), which increased $46.7 billion (0.7 percent) during FY 2015, to $6.7 trillion. OPM administers the largest civilian pension plan, covering nearly 2.7 million current employees and 2.6 million annuitants and survivors. The military pension plan covers about 2.1 million current military personnel (including active service, reserve, and National Guard) and approximately 2.8 million retirees and annuitants.

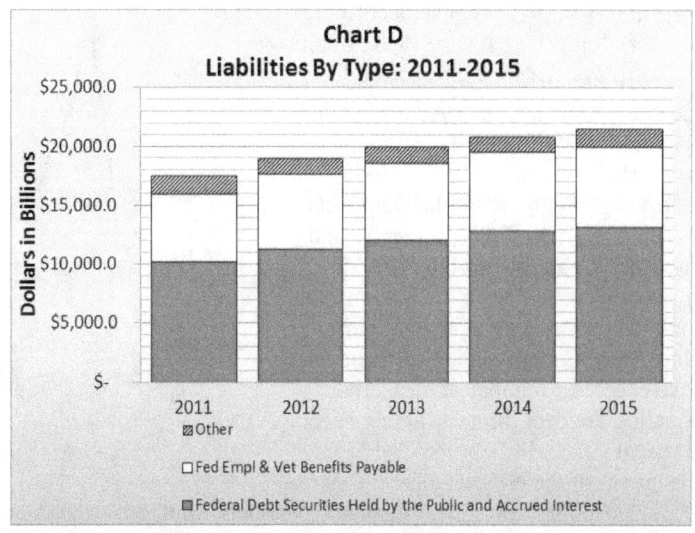

Chart D
Liabilities By Type: 2011-2015

☒ Other
☐ Fed Empl & Vet Benefits Payable
▤ Federal Debt Securities Held by the Public and Accrued Interest

Federal Debt

The unified budget surplus or deficit is the difference between total federal spending and receipts (e.g., taxes) in a given year. The Government borrows from the public (increases federal debt levels) to finance deficits. During a budget surplus (i.e., when receipts exceed spending), the Government typically uses those excess funds to reduce the debt held by the public. *The Statement of Changes in Cash Balance from Unified Budget and Other Activities* reports how the annual unified budget surplus or deficit relates to the federal government's borrowing and changes in cash and other monetary assets. It also explains how a budget surplus or deficit normally affects changes in debt balances.

The Government's publicly-held debt, or federal debt held by the public, and accrued interest, which is reported on the Government's balance sheet as a liability, is comprised of Treasury securities, such as bills, notes, and bonds, net of unamortized discounts and premiums; and accrued interest payable. The "public" consists of individuals, corporations, state and local governments, Federal Reserve Banks, foreign governments, and other entities outside the federal government. Federal debt held by the public and accrued interest totaled $13.2 trillion as of September 30, 2015. As indicated above, budget surpluses have typically resulted in borrowing reductions, and budget deficits have conversely yielded borrowing increases. However, the Government's debt operations are generally much more complex. Each year, trillions of dollars of debt mature and new debt is issued to take its place. In FY 2015, new borrowings were $7.0 trillion (decrease from FY 2014) and repayments of maturing debt held by the public were $6.7 trillion (slight increase from FY 2014).

In addition to debt held by the public, the Government has about $5.1 trillion in intragovernmental debt outstanding, which arises when one part of the Government borrows from another. It represents debt issued by the

---

[19] For financial reporting purposes, other than multi-use heritage assets, stewardship assets are not recorded as part of Property, Plant, and Equipment. Stewardship assets are comprised of stewardship land and heritage assets. Stewardship land consists of public domain land (e.g., national parks, wildlife refuges). Heritage assets include national monuments and historical sites that among other characteristics are of historical, natural, cultural, educational, or artistic significance. See Note 25 – Stewardship Land and Heritage Assets.

[20] With the enactment of the SAFRA Act, which was included as part of the Health Care and Education Reconciliation Act of 2010 (HCERA) (Pub. L. 111-152), beginning in July 2010, no new loans were originated under the Federal Family Education Loan (FFEL) Program (FY 2015 Federal Student Aid Financial Report). See also: U.S. Department of Education FY 2015 Agency Financial Report p. 30.

Treasury and held by Government accounts, including the Social Security ($2.8 trillion) and Medicare ($261.6 billion) trust funds. Intragovernmental debt is primarily held in Government trust funds in the form of special nonmarketable securities by various parts of the Government. Laws establishing Government trust funds generally require excess trust fund receipts (including interest earnings) over disbursements to be invested in these special securities. Because these amounts are both liabilities of the Treasury and assets of the Government trust funds, they are eliminated as part of the consolidation process for the governmentwide financial statements (see Note 11). When those securities are redeemed, e.g., to pay Social Security benefits, the Government will need to obtain the resources necessary to reimburse the trust funds. The sum of debt held by the public and intragovernmental debt

equals gross federal debt, which (with some adjustments), is subject to a statutory ceiling (i.e., the debt limit). At the end of FY 2015, debt subject to the statutory limit (DSL) was $18.1 trillion.

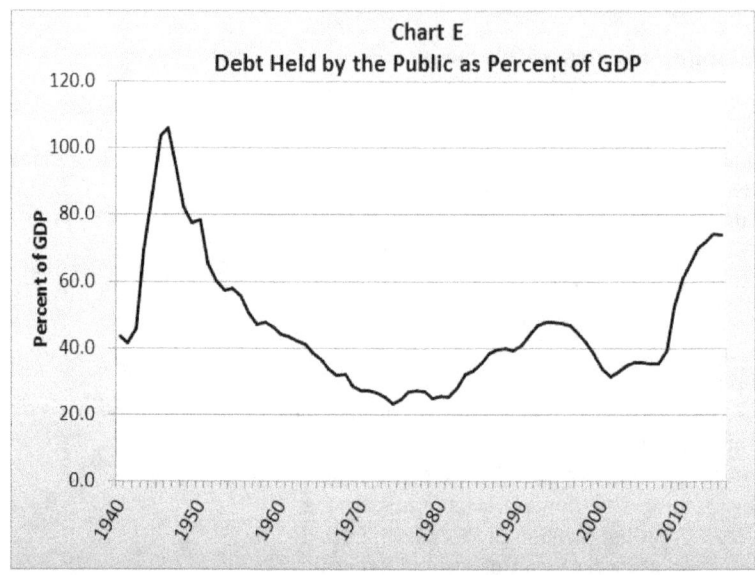

Prior to 1917, Congress approved each debt issuance. In 1917, to facilitate planning in World War I, Congress established a dollar ceiling for federal borrowing. With the Public Debt Act of 1941 (Public Law 77-7), Congress and the President set an overall limit of $65 billion on Treasury debt obligations that could be outstanding at any one time. Since then, Congress and the President have enacted a number of measures affecting the debt limit, including several in recent years. In February 2013, enactment of the No Budget, No Pay Act

of 2013 (Public Law 113-3) suspended the debt limit, enabling the debt to increase as needed through May 18, 2013. In accordance with provisions of the Act, the debt limit was reinstated on May 19, 2013 at a level of $16.7 trillion. Because the new debt limit was set at the level of then outstanding debt, Treasury began implementing "extraordinary measures", on a temporary basis, which were still in effect on September 30, 2013, to keep the DSL under the statutory limit. On October 17, 2013, P.L. 113-46 again suspended the debt limit, this time through February 7, 2014, after which the limit was re-instated at a level of $17.212 trillion. P.L. 113-83 again suspended the debt limit, this time from February 15, 2014 through March 15, 2015. On March 16, 2015, Treasury again implemented extraordinary measures, on a temporary basis, which were still in effect on September 30, 2015, to keep the DSL under the statutory limit of $18.1 trillion.[21] Most recently, in November 2015, the Bipartisan Budget Act of 2015 (P.L. 114-74) again suspended the debt limit through March 15, 2017. It is important to note that increasing or suspending the debt limit does not increase spending or authorize new spending; rather, it permits the United States to continue to honor pre-existing commitments to its citizens, businesses, and investors domestically and around the world.

The federal debt held by the public measured as a percent of GDP (debt-to-GDP ratio) (Chart E) compares the country's debt to the size of its economy, making this measure sensitive to changes in both. Over time, the debt-to-GDP ratio has varied widely. For most of the nation's history, the debt-to-GDP ratio has tended to increase during wartime and decline during peacetime. That pattern continued to hold following World War II until the 1970s. As shown in Chart E, wartime spending and borrowing had pushed the debt-to-GDP ratio to an all-time high of 106 percent in 1946, but it decreased rapidly in the post-war years, falling to 79 percent by 1950, 44 percent in 1960, and the postwar low point of 23 percent in 1974. Since then, the ratio has increased, growing rapidly from the mid-1970s until the early 1990s. In the 1990s, strong economic growth and fundamental fiscal decisions, including measures to reduce the federal deficit and implementation of binding "Pay As You Go" (PAYGO) rules, generated a significant decline in the debt-to-GDP ratio over the course of the 1990s, from a peak of 48 percent in 1993-1995, to

---

[21] A delay in raising the statutory debt limit existed as of September 30, 2015. When delays in raising the statutory debt limit occur, Treasury often must deviate from its normal debt management operations and take a number of extraordinary measures to meet the Government's obligations as they come due without exceeding the debt limit. Extraordinary measures taken by Treasury during the period of March 16, 2015, through September 30, 2015 resulted in federal debt securities not being issued to certain federal government accounts. As a result of Treasury securities not being issued to: the Government Securities Fund (G Fund) of the Thrift Savings Plan (TSP) , Treasury reported miscellaneous liabilities in the amount of $204.6 billion that represent uninvested principal of and related interest for the G Fund that would have been reported as Federal Debt Securities Held by the Public and Accrued Interest had there not been a delay in raising the statutory debt limit as of September 30, 2015, and had the securities been issued. In addition, uninvested principal of and related interest for the Civil Service Retirement and Disability Fund and the Postal Service Retiree Health Benefits Fund that would have been reported as intragovernmental debt totaled $146.1 billion. See Note 11, Federal Debt Securities Held by the Public and Accrued Interest and Note 16, Other Liabilities.

31 percent in 2001. During the last decade, much of this progress was undone as PAYGO rules were allowed to lapse, significant tax cuts were implemented, entitlements were expanded, and spending related to defense and homeland security increased. By September 2008, the debt-to-GDP ratio was 39 percent of GDP. The extraordinary demands of the last economic and fiscal crisis and the consequent actions taken by the federal government, combined with slower economic growth in the wake of the crisis, pushed the debt-to-GDP ratio up to 74.4 percent as of September 30, 2014, but the ratio declined slightly during FY 2015 to 73.8 percent despite a slight increase in borrowing to finance the deficit.[22]

The Economy in Fiscal Year 2015

A review of the nation's key macroeconomic indicators can help place the discussion of the Government's financial results in a broader context. As summarized in Table 6, the economy continued to expand at a moderate pace during FY 2015. Employment rose steadily and the unemployment rate declined during the fiscal year to its lowest level in more than seven years.

Table 6: National Economic Indicators*		
	FY 2015	FY 2014
Real GDP Growth	2.2%	2.9%
Residential Investment Growth	9.4%	0.5%
Average monthly payroll job change (thousands)	227	226
Unemployment rate (percent, end of period)	5.1%	6.0%
Consumer Price Index (CPI)	0.0%	1.7%
CPI, excluding food and energy	1.9%	1.7%
Treasury constant maturity 10-year rate (end of period)	2.06%	2.52%
Moody's Baa bond rate (end of period)	5.35%	4.81%

* Some FY2014 data may differ from the FY2014 *Financial Report* due to updates and revisions.

Real (i.e., inflation-adjusted) GDP expanded 2.2 percent during FY 2015, slowing from the 2.9 percent increase recorded over the four quarters of FY 2014. The moderation in the pace of expansion was due in part to a deterioration in the net export deficit. Growth of consumer spending accelerated during FY 2015 to 3.2 percent, and the recovery in the housing sector picked up sharply, with residential fixed investment increasing by 9.4 percent, compared with a rise of 0.5 percent during FY 2014. Growth of nonresidential fixed investment slowed to a 2.2 percent advance during FY 2015 from 7.6 percent during the previous fiscal year.

Labor market conditions improved further during FY 2015. The economy added 2.7 million nonfarm payroll jobs during the course of the fiscal year, matching the number of jobs added during FY 2014. On a monthly basis, nonfarm payroll employment rose at an average rate of 227,000 jobs per month, close to the average monthly increase of 226,000 during FY 2014. The number of unemployed persons fell from 9.3 million in September 2014 to 7.9 million in September 2015. The unemployment rate declined 0.9 percentage points, from 6.0 percent in September 2014 to 5.1 percent in September 2015. At the end of FY 2015, the unemployment rate was 4.9 percentage points lower than the peak of 10.0 percent, reached in October 2009.

Inflation remained low during FY 2015. The consumer price index (CPI) was flat during FY 2015, reflecting sharply lower energy prices and slower growth of food prices. Consumer price inflation was 1.7 percent during FY 2014. Underlying core inflation (the CPI excluding food and energy) was 1.9 percent during FY 2015, compared with 1.7 percent during the previous fiscal year.

Growth of real disposable (i.e., after-tax) personal income accelerated during FY 2015, reflecting lower inflation. The level of corporate profits fell 5.1 percent during FY 2015, compared with a gain of 5.8 percent during the previous fiscal year.

---

[22] Joint Statement of OMB Director, Shaun Donovan and Treasury Secretary, Jacob Lew.

The Long-Term Fiscal Outlook: "Where We Are Headed"

While the Government's immediate priority is to ensure that the economic expansion is sustained, there are longer-term fiscal challenges that must ultimately be addressed. The Government took potentially significant steps towards a sustainable fiscal policy by enacting the Affordable Care Act (ACA)[23] in 2010, the Budget Control Act (BCA) in 2011, and the American Taxpayer Relief Act (ATRA) in 2013. The ACA holds the prospect of lowering long-term per-beneficiary spending growth for Medicare and Medicaid, the BCA significantly curtails discretionary spending, and ATRA increases revenues. Together, these three laws substantially reduce the estimated long-term fiscal gap. However, persistent growth of health care costs the retirement of the "baby boom" generation[24], increasing longevity, and lower birth rates will make it increasingly difficult to fund critical social programs, including Medicare, Medicaid, and Social Security.

Pursuant to federal accounting standards, this FY 2015 *Financial Report* introduces a **Statement of Long-Term Fiscal Projections** as a basic financial statement and a related Note Disclosure (Note 24). This statement, note disclosure, and additional related information had previously appeared collectively in the *Financial Report* as Required Supplementary Information (RSI). The Statement displays the present value of 75-year projections of the federal government's receipts and non-interest spending[25] for FY 2015 and FY 2014 (see Table 1). Additional information about these projections may be found in Note 24 and the RSI section of this *Financial Report*.

Fiscal Sustainability

An important purpose of the *Financial Report* is to help citizens understand current fiscal policy and the importance and magnitude of policy reforms necessary to make it sustainable. A sustainable policy is one where the debt-to-GDP ratio is stable or declining over the long term.

To determine if current fiscal policies are sustainable, the projections of the deficit and debt discussed here assume current policy (i.e., current law, with certain adjustments, such as extension of expiring policies that are expected to continue)[26] will continue indefinitely and draw out the implications for the growth of debt held by the public as a share of GDP. The projections are therefore neither forecasts nor predictions. As policy changes are enacted, actual financial outcomes will be different than those projected.

The projections in this *Financial Report* indicate that current policy is not sustainable. As discussed below, if current policy is left unchanged, the debt-to-GDP ratio is projected to fall about 6 percentage points over the next decade before commencing a steady rise to 223 percent in 2090 and is expected to rise continuously thereafter. Preventing the debt-to-GDP ratio from rising over the next 75 years is estimated to require some combination of spending reductions and revenue increases that amount to 1.2 percent of GDP over the period. While this estimate of the "75-year fiscal gap" is highly uncertain, it is nevertheless nearly certain that current fiscal policies cannot be sustained indefinitely.

It is important to address the Government's fiscal imbalances soon. Delaying action increases the magnitude of spending reductions and/or revenue increases necessary to stabilize the debt-to-GDP ratio. For example, it is estimated that the magnitude of reforms necessary to close the 75-year fiscal gap is about 25 percent larger if reforms are delayed by just ten years, and nearly 60 percent larger if reform is delayed 20 years.

The estimates of the cost of policy delay in this *Financial Report* assume policy does not affect GDP or other economic variables. Delaying fiscal adjustments for too long raises the risk that growing federal debt would increase interest rates, which would, in turn, reduce investment and ultimately economic growth. However, abrupt and poorly designed deficit reduction could also be counterproductive for the economy, particularly if it takes the form of reducing investments in infrastructure, education, or innovation that are essential for robust longer-term economic growth.

---

[23] P.L. 111-148, as amended by P.L. 111-152. The ACA expands health insurance coverage, provides health insurance subsidies for low-income individuals and families, includes many measures designed to reduce health care cost growth, and reduces the annual increases in Medicare payment rates.

[24] Refers to the segment of the population born during the post-World War II era during which time birth rates in the U.S. were higher than normal.

[25] For the purposes of the Statement of Long-Term Fiscal Projections and this analysis, spending is defined in terms of outlays. In the context of federal budgeting, spending can either refer to: (1) budget authority – the authority to commit the government to make a payment; (2) obligations – binding agreements that will result in either immediate or future payment; or (3) outlays, or actual payments made.

[26] Current policy in the projections is based on current law, but includes certain adjustments, such as extension of certain policies that expire under current law but are routinely extended or otherwise expected to continue (e.g., reauthorization of the Supplemental Nutrition Assistance Program).

The Primary Deficit, Interest, and Debt

The primary deficit – the difference between non-interest spending and receipts – is the only determinant of the debt-to-GDP ratio that the Government controls directly. (The other determinants are interest rates and growth in GDP). Chart F shows receipts, non-interest spending, and the difference – the primary deficit – expressed as a share of GDP (primary deficit-to-GDP ratio). The primary deficit-to-GDP ratio grew rapidly in 2009 due to the financial crisis and the recession and the policies pursued to combat both. The ratio remained high from 2010 to 2012 despite shrinking in each successive year, and fell significantly in 2013 and 2014. The primary deficit is projected to shrink in the next few years as discretionary spending limits called for in the BCA continue and the economy continues to recover, becoming a primary surplus in 2019 that peaks at 0.5 percent of GDP in 2024. After 2025, however, increased spending for Social Security and health programs due to the ongoing retirement of the baby boom generation and increases in the price of health care services is expected to cause the primary surplus to steadily deteriorate and become a primary deficit starting in 2028 that reaches 1.0 percent of GDP by 2038. After 2039, the age composition of the population is stable and the pace of health care price increases slows, causing the primary deficit to gradually decrease and become a primary surplus in 2085 that reaches 0.1 percent of GDP in 2090.

Receipts as a share of GDP fell substantially in 2009 and 2010 and remained low in 2011 and 2012 because of the recession and tax reductions enacted as part of the American Recovery and Reinvestment Act of 2009 (ARRA) and the Tax Relief, Unemployment Insurance Reauthorization, and Job Creation Act of 2010. The share rose to 18.1 percent in 2015, exceeding its 30-year average due to continued economic growth and the higher tax rates

enacted under the ATRA. After 2020, receipts are projected to grow slightly more rapidly than GDP as increases in real incomes cause more taxpayers and a larger share of income to fall into the higher individual income tax brackets.

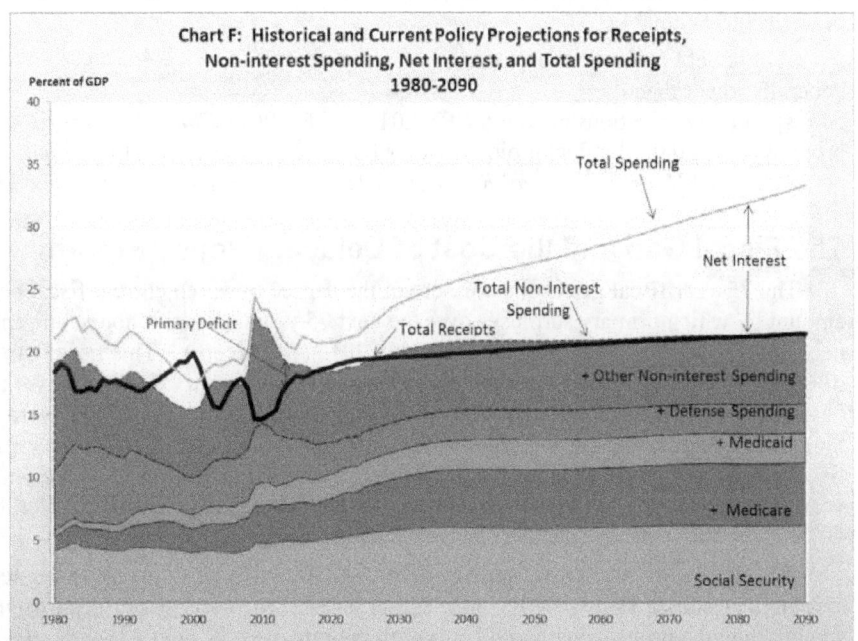

Chart F: Historical and Current Policy Projections for Receipts, Non-interest Spending, Net Interest, and Total Spending 1980-2090

Non-interest spending as a share of GDP is projected to stay at or below its current level of about 19 percent until 2027, and to then rise gradually to 20.9 percent of GDP by 2040 and 21.4 percent of GDP in 2090. The reductions in the non-interest spending share of GDP over the next few years are mostly due to the expected reductions in spending for overseas contingency operations, caps on discretionary spending, and the automatic spending cuts mandated by the BCA; the subsequent increases are principally due to faster growth in Medicare, Medicaid, and Social Security spending (see Chart F). The aging of the baby boom generation over the next 25 years is projected to increase the Social Security, Medicare, and Medicaid spending shares of GDP by about 1.1 percentage points, 1.6 percentage points, and 0.4 percentage points, respectively. After 2040, the Social Security spending share of GDP gradually declines, returns to 2040 levels in 2060, and then increases slightly, while the combined Medicare and Medicaid spending share of GDP continues to increase, albeit at a slower rate, due to projected increases in health care costs. The ACA provision of health insurance subsidies and expanded Medicaid coverage boost federal spending, and other ACA provisions significantly reduce per-beneficiary Medicare cost growth. On net, the ACA is projected to substantially reduce the growth rate of Medicare expenditures over the next 75 years. However, as discussed in Note 23, these projections are subject to much uncertainty about the ultimate effects the ACA will have on health care cost growth.

The primary deficit-to-GDP projections in Charts F and G (left axis), along with projections for interest rates, determine the debt-to-GDP ratio projections shown in Chart G (right axis). That ratio was 74 percent at the end of FY 2015 and under the long-term fiscal projections of current policy is projected to be 67 percent in 2025, 106 percent in 2045, and 223 percent in 2090. The debt-to-GDP ratio rises at an accelerating rate despite primary deficits that flatten out because higher levels of debt lead to higher net interest expenditures, and higher net interest expenditures lead to higher debt.[27] The continuous rise of the debt-to-GDP ratio after 2025 indicates that current policy is unsustainable.

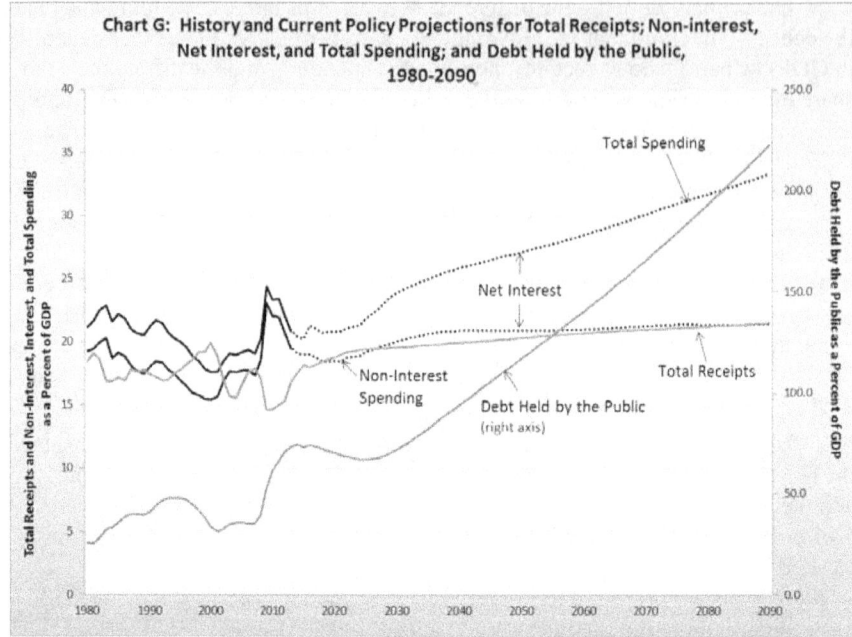

These debt projections are generally lower than the corresponding projections in both the FY 2014 and FY 2013 *Financial Reports*. For example, the debt-to-GDP projection for 2088 (the final projection year for the 2013 report) is 217 percent in this year's *Financial Report*, 315 percent in the FY 2014 *Financial Report*, and 277 percent in the FY 2013 *Financial Report*.[28]

The Fiscal Gap and the Cost of Delaying Policy Reform

The 75-year fiscal gap is one measure of the degree to which current fiscal policy is unsustainable. It is the amount by which primary surpluses over the next 75 years must rise above current policy levels in order for the debt-to-GDP ratio in 2090 to equal its level in 2015 (74 percent). This fiscal gap is estimated to equal 1.2 percent of GDP. It is the difference between the average level of primary surpluses over the next 75 years that would result in the 2090 debt-to-GDP ratio equaling its 2015 level (0.9 percent), and the average level of primary surpluses over the next 75 years under current policies (-0.3 percent, i.e., primary deficits averaging 0.3 percent). The 75-year fiscal gap is 6.1 percent as large as the 75-year present value of projected receipts and 6.0 percent as large as the 75-year present value of non-interest spending, and is 0.9 percentage points smaller than the 2.1 percent estimate in 2014.

It is noteworthy that preventing the debt-to-GDP ratio from rising over the next 75 years requires that primary surpluses be substantially positive on average. This is true because projected GDP growth rates are, on average, smaller than the projected government borrowing rate over the next 75 years. The implication is that debt would grow faster than GDP if primary surpluses were zero on average. For example, if the primary surplus was precisely zero in every year, then debt would grow at the rate of interest in every year, which would be faster than GDP growth.

Table 7 illustrates the cost of delaying policy to close the fiscal gap by comparing three policies that begin on different dates. The first policy begins immediately and calls for increasing primary surpluses by 1.2 percent of GDP in every year between 2016 and 2090. This is accomplished by invoking some combination of spending reductions and revenue

Table 7	
Costs of Delaying Fiscal Reform	
Period of Delay	**Change in Average Primary Surplus**
No Delay: Reform in 2016...............	1.2 percent of GDP between 2016 and 2090
Ten Years: Reform in 2026..............	1.5 percent of GDP between 2026 and 2090
Twenty Years: Reform in 2036........	1.9 percent of GDP between 2036 and 2090

Note: Amounts represent the change in the average primary surplus over the specified period necessary to yield the current year debt-to-GDP ratio Reforms occurring in 2015, 2025, and 2035 from the 2014 Financial Report were 2 1, 2 5, and 3 1 percent

---

[27] The change in debt each year is also affected by certain transactions not included in the unified budget deficit, such as changes in Treasury's cash balances and the nonbudgetary activity of Federal credit financing accounts. These transactions are assumed to hold constant at about 0.4 percent of GDP each year, with the same effect on debt as if the primary deficit was higher by that amount.

[28] See the Required Supplementary Information section of the FY 2014 Financial Report of the U.S. Government for more information about changes from the long term fiscal projections for FY 2013.

increases that amount to 1.2 percent of GDP in every year over the 75-year projection period. The second policy in Table 7 begins in 2026. Because the same fiscal consolidation must be compressed into ten fewer years, this policy change is more abrupt, calling for primary surplus increases amounting to 1.5 percent of GDP in every year between 2026 and 2090. Similarly, if debt is allowed to accumulate unabated for 20 years, then closing the 75-year fiscal gap would require even more abrupt primary surplus increases amounting to 1.9 percent of GDP in every year between 2036 and 2090. The differences between the primary surplus boost starting in 2026 and 2036 (1.5 and 1.9 percent of GDP, respectively) and the primary surplus boost starting in 2016 (1.2 percent of GDP) is a measure of the additional burden policy delay would impose on future generations. Future generations are harmed by a policy delay of this sort because the higher the primary surplus is during their lifetimes the greater the difference is between the taxes they pay and the programmatic spending from which they benefit.

Conclusion

The Government took potentially significant steps towards a sustainable fiscal policy by enacting the ACA in 2010, the BCA in 2011, and ATRA in 2013. The ACA holds the prospect of lowering long-term per-beneficiary spending growth for Medicare and Medicaid, the BCA significantly curtails discretionary spending, and ATRA increases revenues. Together, these three laws substantially reduce the estimated long-term fiscal gap. But even with these laws, the debt-to-GDP ratio is projected to remain relatively flat over the next ten years and then commence a continuous rise over the remaining projection period and beyond if current policies are kept in place. This trend implies that current policies are not sustainable. Subject to the important caveat that changes in policy are not so abrupt that they slow continued economic growth, the sooner policies are put in place to avert these trends, the smaller the revenue increases and/or spending decreases will need to be to return the Government to a sustainable fiscal path over the long term.

While this *Financial Report's* projections of expenditures and receipts under current policy are highly uncertain, it is nevertheless nearly certain that current policy cannot be sustained indefinitely.

These and other issues concerning fiscal sustainability are discussed in further detail in Note 24 and the RSI section of this *Financial Report*.

Social Insurance

The preceding analysis of the Government's long-term fiscal projections considered Government receipts and spending as a whole. The Statement of Social Insurance (SOSI) provides a more focused perspective of the Government's "social insurance" programs: Social Security, Medicare, Railroad Retirement, and Black Lung.[29] For these programs, the SOSI reports: (1) the actuarial present value of all future program revenue (mainly taxes and premiums) - excluding interest - to be received from or on behalf of current and future participants; (2) the estimated future scheduled expenditures to be paid to or on behalf of current and future participants; and (3) the difference between (1) and (2). Amounts reported in the SOSI and in the RSI section in this *Financial Report* are based on each program's official actuarial calculations. By accounting convention, the transfers of general revenues are eliminated in the consolidation of the SOSI at the governmentwide level and as such, the general revenues that are used to finance Medicare Parts B and D are not included in these calculations even though the expenditures on these programs are included. For the FY 2015 and 2014 SOSI, the amounts eliminated totaled $24.8 trillion and $24.7 trillion, respectively. SOSI programs and amounts are included in the broader fiscal sustainability analysis in the previous section, although on a slightly different basis (as described in Note 24).

The SOSI provides perspective on the Government's long-term estimated exposures and costs for social insurance programs. While these expenditures are not considered Government liabilities, they do have the potential to become expenses and liabilities in the future, based on the continuation of the social insurance programs' provisions contained in current law. The social insurance trust funds account for all related program income and expenses. Medicare and Social Security taxes, premiums, and other income are credited to the funds; fund disbursements may only be made for benefit payments and program administrative costs. Any excess revenues are invested in special non-marketable U.S. Government securities at a market rate of interest. The trust funds represent the accumulated value, including interest, of all prior program surpluses, and provide automatic funding authority to pay for future benefits.

---

[29] The Black Lung Benefits Act (BLBA) provides for monthly payments and medical benefits to coal miners totally disabled from pneumoconiosis (black lung disease) arising from their employment in or around the nation's coal mines. See http://www.dol.gov/owcp/regs/compliance/ca_main.htm

Table 8: Social Insurance Future Expenditures in Excess of Future Revenues				
Dollars in Billions	2015	2014	Increase / (Decrease)	
			$	%
Open Group (Net):				
Social Security (OASDI)	$ (13,440)	$ (13,330)	$ 110	0.8%
Medicare (Parts A, B, & D)	$ (27,940)	$ (28,483)	$ (543)	(1.9%)
Other	$ (108)	$ (103)	$ 5	4.6%
Total Social Insurance Expenditures, Net (Open Group)	**$ (41,487)**	**$ (41,916)**	$ (429)	(1.0%)
Total Social Insurance Expenditures, Net (Closed Group)	**$ (58,257)**	**$ (56,680)**	$ 1,578	2.8%
Social Insurance Net Expenditures as a % of Gross Domestic Product (GDP)*				
Open Group				
Social Security (OASDI)	(1.1%)	(1.3%)		
Medicare (Parts A, B, & D)	(2.7%)	(2.9%)		
Other	0.0%	0.0%		
Total (Open Group)	**(3.7%)**	**(4.0%)**		
Total (Closed Group)	**(5.2%)**	**(5.4%)**		

Source: Statement of Social Insurance (SOSI). Amounts equal estimated present value of projected revenues and expenditures for scheduled benefits over the next 75 years of certain 'Social Insurance' programs (e.g., Social Security, Medicare). 'Open Group' totals reflect all current and projected program participants during the 75-year projection period. 'Closed Group' totals reflect only current participants.

* GDP values used are from the 2015 & 2014 Social Security and Medicare Trustees Reports and represent the present value of GDP over the 75-year projection period. As the GDP used for Social Security and Medicare differ slightly in the Trust Fund Reports, the two values are averaged to estimate the 'Other' and Total Net Social Insurance Expenditures as % of GDP.

Note - some totals may not equal sum of components due to rounding.

Table 8 summarizes amounts reported in the SOSI, showing that net social insurance expenditures are projected to be $41.5 trillion over 75 years as of January 1, 2015 for the "Open Group," a decrease of $429 billion over net expenditures of $41.9 trillion projected in the 2014 *Financial Report*.[30] The 2015 amounts reported for Medicare reflect current law[31] and the 2014 amounts reflect the "projected baseline scenario" for Part B.[32]

Table 9 on the following page summarizes the principal reasons for the changes in projected social insurance amounts during 2015 and 2014. The following briefly summarizes the significant changes for the current valuation (as of January 1, 2015) as disclosed in Note 23, Social Insurance. See Note 23 for additional information.

---

[30] 'Closed' Group and 'Open' Group differ by the population included in each calculation. From the SOSI, the 'Closed' Group includes: (1) participants who have attained eligibility and (2) participants who have not attained eligibility. The 'Open' Group adds future participants to the 'Closed' Group. See 'Social Insurance' in the Required Supplementary Information section in this *Financial Report* for more information.

[31] The Medicare Access and CHIP Reauthorization Act (MACRA) of 2015 permanently replaces the sustainable growth rate (SGR) formula, which was used to determine payment updates under the Medicare physician fee schedule with specified payment updates through 2025. The changes specified in MACRA also establish differential payment updates starting in 2026 based on practitioners' participation in eligible alternative payment models; payments are also subject to adjustments based on the quality of care provided, resource use, use of certified electronic health records, and clinical practice improvement.

[32] The projected baseline scenario includes the assumption that the current-law physician updates will be legislatively overridden and that physician updates that were required at the time of publication of the 2014 Medicare Trustees Report will be 0.6 percent each year starting with 2016. (2014 Medicare Trustees Report, p. 8/footnote 5)

Table 9: Changes in Social Insurance Projections		
Dollars in Billions	2015	2014
Net Present Value (NPV) - Open Group		
(Beginning of the Year)	$ (41,916)	$ (39,698)
Changes In:		
Valuation Period	$ (1,858)	$ (1,769)
Demographic data and assumptions	$ (249)	$ (54)
Economic data and assumptions[1]	$ (146)	$ (605)
Law or policy	$ (23)	$ 29
Methodology and programmatic data[1]	$ 671	$ (90)
Economic and other healthcare assumptions[2]	$ 3,221	$ (318)
Change in projection base[2]	$ (1,187)	$ 589
Net Change in Open Group measure	$ 429	$ (2,218)
NPV - Open Group (End of the Year)	$ (41,487)	$ (41,916)

1 Relates to SSA.
2 Relates to HHS.
Note - totals may not equal sum of components due to rounding.

- Change in valuation period: This change replaces a small negative net cash flow for 2014 and replaces it with a much larger negative net cash flow for 2089. As a result, the present value of the estimated future net cash flows decreased (became more negative) by $1.9 trillion.

- Changes in economic and other healthcare assumptions: The assumption changes, specific to the Medicare projections, included, but were not limited to: for the current valuation (beginning on January 1, 2015), the only change to the ultimate economic assumption was that the ultimate real wage differential is assumed to be 1.17 percent in the current valuation period, compared to 1.13 percent in the prior valuation period. The higher wage differential assumption is more consistent with recent experience and expectations of slower growth in employer sponsored group health insurance premiums from the Centers for Medicare and Medicaid Services (CMS) Office of the Actuary. Because these premiums are not subject to the payroll tax, slower growth in these premiums means that a greater share of employee compensation will be in the form of wages that are subject to the payroll tax.

  o Otherwise, the ultimate economic assumptions for the current valuation are the same as those for the prior valuation. However, the starting economic values, and the way these values transition to the ultimate assumptions, were changed: (1) the ratio of average taxable earnings to the average wage averages about 0.6 percentage points higher during the long-range period compared to the previous valuation; and (2) the projected suspense file contains fewer wage items, which is consistent with having fewer workers (many of whom are undocumented immigrants) with wages on the suspense file and more of these workers with earnings in the underground economy, compared to the previous valuation.

  o The following health care assumptions, specific to the Medicare projections, were changed in the current valuation: (1) lower long-range growth rate assumptions; (2) utilization rate assumptions for inpatient hospital services were decreased; (3) lower assumed hospice spending; (4) higher assumed enrollment in Medicare Advantage plans where benefits are more costly; and (5) introduction of high-cost specialty drugs used to treat hepatitis C.

  The net impact of these changes increased (made less negative) the present value of the estimated future cash flows by $3.2 trillion. For Part A, these changes resulted in an increase to the present value of future expenditures and income, with an overall increase in the estimated future net cash flow. For Parts B and D, these changes decreased the present value of estimated future expenditures (and also income).

- Change in projection base: Actual income and expenditures in 2014 were different than what was anticipated when the 2014 Trustees Report projections were prepared. Medicare Part A income was slightly lower and expenditures were slightly higher than anticipated, based on actual experience. Part B total income and expenditures were also higher than estimated based on actual experience. For Part D, actual income and expenditures were both higher than prior estimates. The net impact of the Part A, B, and D projection base changes is a decrease in the estimated future net cash flow. Actual experience of the Medicare Trust Funds between January 1, 2014 and January 1, 2015 is incorporated in the current valuation and is slightly more than projected in the prior valuation. These changes had an overall net effect of decreasing (making more negative) the estimated future net cash flows by $1.2 trillion.

Projected net expenditures for Medicare Parts A and B declined significantly between FY 2009 and FY 2010 reflecting provisions of the ACA. As reported in Note 23, there continues to be uncertainty about whether the projected cost savings and productivity improvements will be sustained in a manner consistent with the projected cost growth over time. Note 23 includes an alternative projection to illustrate the uncertainty of projected Medicare costs. As indicated earlier, GAO disclaimed opinions on the 2015, 2014, 2013, 2012 and 2011 SOSI because of these significant uncertainties.

Costs as a percent of GDP of both Medicare and Social Security, which are analyzed annually in the Medicare and Social Security Trustees' Reports, are projected to increase substantially through 2035 because: (1) the number of beneficiaries rises rapidly as the baby-boom generation retires and (2) the lower birth rates that have persisted since the baby boom cause slower growth in the labor force and GDP.[33] According to the Medicare Trustees' Report, spending on Medicare is projected to rise from its current level of approximately 3.5 percent of GDP to 5.6 percent in 2040 and to 6.0 percent in 2089.[34] The Hospital Insurance (HI) Trust Fund is now expected to remain solvent until 2030, (unchanged from last year's report). Under current law, scheduled HI tax revenue would be sufficient to pay 86 percent of HI costs after depletion in 2030 and then gradually increasing to 84 percent by 2089.

As for Social Security, combined spending is projected to increase gradually from its current level of 4.9 percent of GDP to about 6.0 percent by 2035, declining to 5.9 percent by 2050 and rises to 6.2 percent by 2089. The Social Security Trustees' Report indicates that annual OASDI income, considered on a theoretical basis, including interest on trust fund assets, will exceed annual cost and trust fund assets will increase every year until 2020, at which time it will be necessary to begin drawing down on trust fund assets to cover part of expenditures until asset reserves become depleted in 2034 (one year later than indicated in last year's Report). Continuing tax income would be sufficient to pay 79 percent of scheduled benefits in 2034 and 73 percent of scheduled benefits in 2089. The Disability Insurance (DI) Trust Fund alone was expected to deplete much sooner, by the end of 2016. However, the impending depletion of the DI Trust Fund was circumvented by the passage of the Bipartisan Budget Act of 2015, which reallocated a portion of the payroll tax rate from the Old Age Survivors Insurance (OASI) Trust Fund to the DI Trust Fund. This reallocation is expected to ensure full payment of disability benefits into 2022.[35] The projections assume that full Social Security and Medicare benefits are paid after the corresponding trust fund assets are depleted.

As noted earlier, it is apparent that these programs are on a fiscally unsustainable path (as was previously discussed and as noted in the Trustees' Reports). Additional information from the Trustees Reports may be found in the RSI section of this *Financial Report*.

---

[33] 2015 Annual Trustees Reports on Social Security and Medicare (Summary), pp. 3, 9-10.

[34] Percent of GDP amounts are expressed in gross terms (including amounts financed by premiums and state transfers).

[35] 2015 Annual Trustees Reports on Social Security and Medicare (Summary), pp. 3, 9-10.

Systems, Controls, and Legal Compliance

Systems

As federal agencies demonstrate success in obtaining opinions on their audited financial statements, the federal government continues to face challenges in implementing financial systems that meet federal requirements. The number of CFO Act agencies reporting lack of substantial compliance with one or more of the three Section 803(a) requirements of the Federal Financial Management Improvement Act (FFMIA) was 10 in both FY 2015 and FY 2014, and the number of auditors reporting lack of substantial compliance with one or more of the three Section 803(a) FFMIA requirements was 12 in FY 2015 and 11 in FY 2014. These results underscore the importance of current initiatives to standardize the financial management practices across the federal government.

Controls

Federal managers have a fundamental responsibility to develop and maintain effective internal controls. Effective internal controls help to ensure that programs are managed with integrity and resources are used efficiently and effectively through three objectives: effective and efficient operations, reliable financial reporting, and compliance with applicable laws and regulations. The safeguarding of assets is a subcomponent of each objective.

In response to major management challenges to agency mission and goals, agencies are increasingly recognizing the importance and utility of Enterprise Risk Management (ERM) as a tool for identifying, assessing, mitigating, managing and preparing for risk. Effectively implemented, ERM contributes to improved decision-making, adopting a proactive rather than a reactive approach towards risk. ERM has the potential to change the perception that internal controls are limited to just compliance and financial reporting. Instead, internal controls can play a key tool to address management challenges that cut across multiple agency functions. ERM is currently practiced in both the private and public sectors as well as internationally, with examples in governments of the United Kingdom, Canada, and Japan, among others. In an effort to improve taxpayers' trust in government and prepare for future challenges, OMB has promoted ERM best practices across agencies. The upcoming update to OMB Circular No. A-123 will further explain and highlight ERM.

The Office of Management and Budget (OMB) Circular No. A-123, *Management's Responsibility for Internal Control,* is the policy document that implements the requirements of 31 U.S.C. 3512 (c), (d) (commonly known as the Federal Managers' Financial Integrity Act or FMFIA). Circular No. A-123 primarily focuses on providing agencies with a framework for assessing and managing risks more strategically and effectively. The Circular is currently being revised to reflect changes incorporated in GAO's recently updated Standards for Internal Control in the federal government. The revised Circular will be available to the Agencies in the near future. The Circular contains multiple appendices that address, at a more detailed level, one or more of the objectives of effective internal control. Appendix A provides a methodology for agency management to assess, document, test, and report on internal controls over financial reporting. Appendix B requires agencies to maintain internal controls that reduce the risk of fraud, waste, and error in Government charge card programs. Appendix C implements the Requirements for Effective Estimation and Remediation of Improper Payments. Appendix D defines new requirements for determining compliance with the FFMIA and will contribute to efforts to reduce the cost, risk, and complexity of financial system modernizations.

The total number of reported material weaknesses for the CFO Act agencies was 40 and 35 for FYs 2015 and 2014, respectively. Effective internal controls are a challenge not only at the agency level, but also at the governmentwide level. GAO reported that at the governmentwide level, material weaknesses resulted in ineffective internal control over financial reporting. While progress is being made at many agencies and across the Government in identifying and resolving internal control deficiencies, continued diligence and commitment are needed.

The Department of Health and Human Services (HHS) and the Department of the Treasury (Treasury) each have responsibilities for ensuring payment accuracy in programs created under the Affordable Care Act. Performing comprehensive risk assessments is critical to establishing an effective program for achieving payment accuracy in future years. In FY 2015, both Departments finalized plans for and began to perform comprehensive improper payment risk assessments to determine areas that might affect Advance Premium Tax Credit (APTC), Premium Tax Credit (PTC), Cost-sharing Reduction and Basic Health Plan payment accuracy. Both Departments are leveraging non-profit contractors known as Federally Funded Research and Development Centers (FFRDC) for the risk assessments, which will facilitate interagency coordination and provide a complete assessment of risk that takes into account activities by the Marketplaces created under the ACA, HHS and the Internal Revenue Service. An update on the status and preliminary results of the FFRDC supported risk assessments will be reported in the FY 2016 Agency Financial Reports (AFR). In addition, both Departments have established internal controls to provide for effective program operations, reliable financial reporting, and compliance with laws and regulations.

Legal Compliance

Federal agencies are required to comply with a wide range of laws and regulations, including appropriations, employment, health and safety, and others. Responsibility for compliance primarily rests with agency management. Compliance is addressed as part of agency financial statement audits. Agency auditors test for compliance with selected laws and regulations related to financial reporting. Certain individual agency audit reports contain instances of noncompliance. None of these instances were material to the governmentwide financial statements. However, GAO reported that its work on compliance with laws and regulations was limited by the material weaknesses and scope limitations discussed in its report.

Financial Management Progress and Priorities

Since the passage of the CFO Act of 1990, the federal financial community has made important strides in instilling strong accounting and financial reporting practices. For FY 2015, 21 of the 24 CFO Act agencies obtained an opinion from the independent auditors on their financial statements, three agencies received disclaimers[36]. In addition, 40 auditor-identified material weaknesses were reported in FY 2015, an approximately 30 percent decline from the material weaknesses that were identified in the early 2000s (see Table 10 on the following page). An increasing number of federal agencies have initiated and sustained disciplined and consistent financial reporting operations, implemented effective internal controls around financial reporting, and have successfully integrated transaction processing and accounting records. These efforts have resulted in improved results on financial statement audits. However, weaknesses in basic financial management practices and other limitations continue to prevent three of the CFO Act agencies, and the Government as a whole, from achieving an audit opinion.

Today, accountability means providing transparent information to the public about where and how federal dollars are being spent. It means protecting against fraud. It means avoiding wasteful or excessive use of taxpayer funds. It means ensuring that the federal government is not only responsible stewards of taxpayer dollars, but frugal stewards as well, looking for every opportunity to save money and create greater efficiencies.

The federal government has come a long way since the passage of the CFO Act in 1990. Today, the federal financial management community is focused on three important improvement initiatives:

- Improving the quality, utility, and transparency of financial information;
- Protecting against waste, fraud, and abuse; and
- Helping agencies maximize the impact of their limited financial resources.

---

[36] The 21 agencies include HHS, which received a clean opinion on all statements except the Statement of Social Insurance and the Statement of Changes in Social Insurance, both of which received a disclaimer of opinion.

Table 10: Auditor-Reported Material Weaknesses: FY 2015					
Agency	Beginning	New	Resolved	Consolidated	Ending
Department of Agriculture (USDA)	2	0	0	0	2
Department of Commerce (DOC)	0	0	0	0	0
Department of Defense (DOD)	13	0	0	0	13
Department of Education (Education)	0	0	0	0	0
Department of Energy (DOE)	0	0	0	0	0
Department of Health and Human Services (HHS)	1	0	0	0	1
Department of Homeland Security (DHS)	4	0	1	0	3
Department of Housing and Urban Development (HUD)	8	3	2	0	9
Department of the Interior (DOI)	1	2	1	0	2
Department of Justice (DOJ)	0	0	0	0	0
Department of Labor (DOL)	0	1	0	0	1
Department of State (State)	0	0	0	0	0
Department of Transportation (DOT)	1	0	0	0	1
Department of the Treasury (Treasury)	1	0	0	0	1
Department of Veterans Affairs (VA)	1	3	0	0	4
Agency for International Development (USAID)	1	0	0	0	1
Environmental Protection Agency (EPA)	1	0	0	0	1
General Services Administration (GSA)	1	0	1	0	0
National Aeronautics and Space Administration (NASA)	0	0	0	0	0
National Science Foundation (NSF)	0	0	0	0	0
Nuclear Regulatory Commission (NRC)	0	0	0	0	0
Office of Personnel Management (OPM)	0	1	0	0	1
Small Business Administration (SBA)	0	0	0	0	0
Social Security Administration (SSA)	0	0	0	0	0
Totals	35	10	5	0	40

Improve the Quality, Utility, and Transparency of Federal Financial Information

DATA Act

The Digital Accountability and Transparency Act of 2014 (DATA Act), signed on May 9, 2014, sets forth a clear vision for the future of Federal spending transparency. The Act amended the Federal Funding Accountability and Transparency Act of 2006 (FFATA) by requiring that all federal spending be displayed on a website in searchable, downloadable, and machine-readable format. This data includes obligations, outlays, budgetary authority, unobligated balances, and other budgetary resources for each appropriations account. It also expands federal award reporting previously required under FFATA. In May 2015, OMB and Treasury issued financial data definition standards and policy guidance outlining the first set of DATA Act implementation requirements. By 2017, all agencies must report this data to a centralized website and adhere to the data standards and guidance issued by OMB and Treasury. Posting this financial information will allow spending comparisons across and within agencies that have never been possible before as well as unlock spending data for use by the public.

Since the DATA Act was signed into law, OMB and Treasury have been partnering to lead governmentwide implementation. They have established a robust governance structure with representatives from agencies and functional communities fostering collaboration on data standards, policy changes, USAspending.gov improvements, and agency implementation. The implementation plan was developed to be collaborative, iterative, incremental, and agile, with a data centric focus. This approach sets the foundation for future success with shorter term and intermediate deliverables.

USAspending.gov

USAspending.gov was established to provide clear information on federal award spending. Continuing to improve the quality, utility and transparency of this federal spending information is a foundational Administration commitment to open government, as identified in the U.S. Government's National Action Plan for Open Government. To continue its efforts to improve the quality of spending data, OMB and Treasury will issue additional policy guidance to adjust USAspending.gov reporting requirements and procedures pursuant to the DATA Act.

To align our federal spending and financial management transparency efforts, the Administration has transferred responsibility for USAspending.gov from the General Services Administration (GSA) to Treasury. In March 2015, Treasury released a new version of USAspending.gov with improved search capabilities and visualizations of data. Treasury's leadership in executing a governmentwide vision for spending transparency enables the federal government to move forward in achieving the objective of making spending data more useful, accurate, and timely – consistent with the agency's other work through financial reporting, work on improper payments, among other priority areas.

Moving forward, in concert with Treasury, OMB will continue to collaborate with federal and non-federal stakeholders to evolve the Administration's governmentwide spending transparency framework to effectively provide the public with transparent information about how taxpayer dollars are being spent.

Protect Against Waste, Fraud, and Abuse

Improper Payments

Addressing improper payments is a central component of the Administration's overall efforts to eliminate waste, fraud, and abuse. When the President took office in 2009, the improper payment error rate was 5.42 percent, an all-time high. Since then, the Administration, working together with Congress, has made progress by strengthening accountability and transparency through annual reviews by agency Inspectors General, and expanded requirements for high-priority programs. As a result of this concerted effort, in FY 2013 the Administration reported an improper payment rate of 3.53 percent. In FY 2014 and FY 2015, the governmentwide improper payment rate was 4.02 percent and 4.39 percent, which corresponds to an improper payment dollar amount of $124.6 billion[37] and $136.9 billion, respectively.[38] The Medicare Fee for Service (FFS) program continues to account for the largest portion of the government-wide total in FY 2015, whereas Earned Income Tax Credit (EITC) and Medicaid combined, account for approximately a third of the government-wide total. In addition, agencies recovered roughly $20 billion in overpayments through the payment recapture audits and other methods in FY 2015.

Prior to FY 2015 reporting, agencies were required to categorize their improper payment estimates based on three categories of improper payments: (1) documentation and administrative errors; (2) authentication and medical necessity errors; and (3) verification errors. However, those categories proved to be limited and not necessarily applicable to most programs. Therefore, OMB—in consultation with agencies—developed new improper payment categories. FY 2015 marked the first year of the new OMB reporting requirement for root causes reporting as shown in Chart H. Approximately $45 billion of the government-wide improper payments in FY 2015 are caused by insufficient documentation. A lack of supporting documentation could be a situation where there is a lack of supporting documentation necessary to verify the accuracy of a payment identified in the improper payment testing sample such as a program not having the documentation to support a beneficiary's eligibility for a benefit. Approximately $31 billion of the government-wide improper payments in FY 2015 were caused by the inability to authenticate eligibility. The inability to authenticate eligibility is a situation in which an improper payment is made because the agency is unable to authenticate eligibility criteria such as no database or other

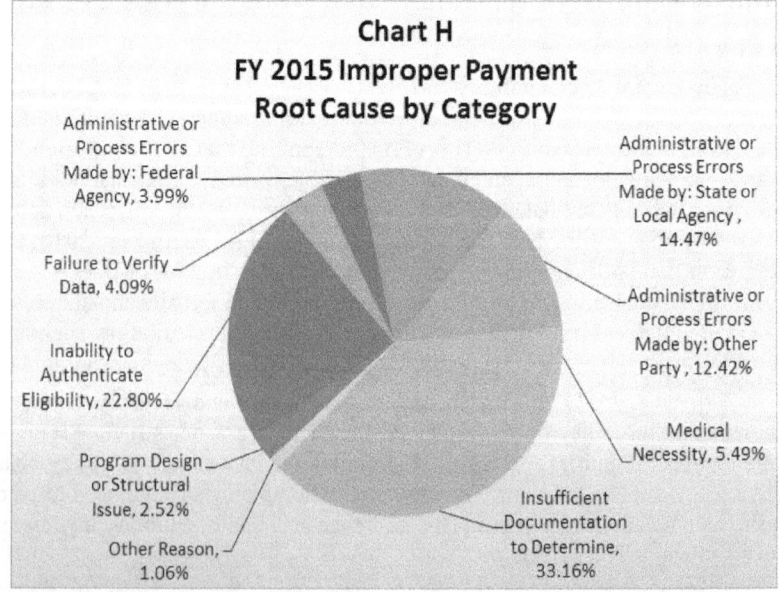

Chart H
FY 2015 Improper Payment
Root Cause by Category

Administrative or Process Errors Made by: Federal Agency, 3.99%

Failure to Verify Data, 4.09%

Inability to Authenticate Eligibility, 22.80%

Program Design or Structural Issue, 2.52%

Other Reason, 1.06%

Administrative or Process Errors Made by: State or Local Agency, 14.47%

Administrative or Process Errors Made by: Other Party, 12.42%

Medical Necessity, 5.49%

Insufficient Documentation to Determine, 33.16%

---

[37] Due to updates made in some agencies FY 2015 AFRs to reflect their prior year estimates the new revised estimate for FY 2014 is $124.6 billion compared to the $124.7 billion FY 2014 estimate previously reported.

[38] DOD's Commercial Payments were first included in the government-wide rate in FY 2013. When the DOD commercial payments are excluded from the government-wide figures the FY 2015 rate is 4.82 percent.

resource exist to help the agency make a determination of eligibility or statutory constraints exist preventing a program from being able to access the information that would help prevent the improper payment. This additional detail behind the root causes of improper payments provides more granularity on improper payment estimates and will be used to inform more effective corrective actions and more focused strategies for reducing improper payments.

The Administration continues to use the Budget to build on congressional and Administration action to reduce improper payments. For example, the President's FY 2016 and 2017 Budget included a number of program integrity proposals aimed at reducing improper payments and improving government efficiency. The FY 2016 proposals included a robust package of Medicare and Medicaid program integrity proposals, strategic reinvestment in the Internal Revenue Service (IRS), and an equally robust package of Social Security program integrity proposals, in addition to many other proposals for other programs also aimed at reducing improper payments. The President's FY 2017 Budget also includes a number of new program integrity proposals.

The Government is also advancing data analytics and improved technologies to prevent improper payments before they happen. In doing so, as part of the President's Do Not Pay Initiative, the Administration established a Do Not Pay System of Records at Treasury and launched data informed insights reports for agencies to improve their payment accuracy and program integrity. OMB's and Treasury's combined work with agencies to implement the Do Not Pay Initiative, outlined in Section 5 of IPERIA, and OMB Memorandum 13-20, Protecting Privacy while Reducing Improper Payments with the Do Not Pay List, has catalyzed agencies to improve their payment business operations, reduce improper payments, and incorporate multiple databases and analytics resources as they verify entity eligibility for awards or payments. Agencies have reported over $2 billion of improper payments stopped through the Do Not Pay initiative and other efforts in FY 2014, as identified in OMB's report to Congress transmitted on December 4, 2015. The Administration looks forward to continued work with Congress on Administration priorities including the sharing of death data from states to prevent improper payments to the deceased while maintaining privacy to ensure program integrity and payment accuracy.

Combating improper payments within the federal government is a top priority for the Administration and it will continue to explore new and innovative ways to address the problem. Each dollar paid in error represents a loss of public resources, and this Administration is committed to reducing waste, fraud, and abuse and continuing to improve payment accuracy with every tool at its disposal.

Improving Grants Management

On December 19, 2014, 28 federal awarding agencies adopted final guidance to better target risk and reduce waste, fraud, and abuse (2 CFR Part 200—Uniform Administrative Requirements, Cost Principles, And Audit Requirements for Federal Awards). The culmination of a three-year collaborative effort across federal agencies and its non-federal partners, the rule effectively implements OMB guidance on grant-making across the 28 federal agencies. This effort streamlined eight existing OMB Circulars on financial management into one consolidated set of guidance in the CFR, reduced the total volume of financial management regulations for federal grants and other assistance by 75 percent, and reduced administrative burdens and risk of waste, fraud, and abuse for the approximately $600 billion awarded annually in federal financial assistance.

Specifically, the revised policies emphasize risk-based decision making to reduce administrative burden and waste, fraud, and abuse by:

- Eliminating duplicative and conflicting guidance;
- Focusing on performance over compliance for accountability;
- Encouraging efficient use of information technology and shared services;
- Providing for consistent and transparent treatment of costs;
- Limiting allowable costs to make the best use of federal resources;
- Setting standard business processes using data definitions;
- Encouraging non-federal entities to have family-friendly policies;
- Strengthening oversight; and
- Targeting audit requirements on risk of waste, fraud, and abuse.

The Council on Financial Assistance Reform (COFAR) has established metrics, as outlined in the OMB issued Memorandum M-14-17, Metrics for Uniform Guidance, that will measure the effectiveness of the new policies and is working with federal and non-federal stakeholders to develop additional training and outreach resources. The administrative metrics for the base year are published on the COFAR website at https://cfo.gov/cofar/.

To help with the implementation of the Uniform Guidance during the initial year of applicability, OMB has issued a set of technical corrections to the Uniform Guidance and developed a set of Frequently Asked Questions that provide additional instructions and clarifications to the provisions in the Uniform Guidance (https://cfo.gov/wp-content/uploads/2015/09/9.9.15-Frequently-Asked-Questions.pdf)

In July 2015, OMB published final guidance for reporting and use of information concerning recipient integrity and performance for inclusion in the Uniform Guidance (http://www.gpo.gov/fdsys/pkg/FR-2015-07-22/pdf/2015-17753.pdf). This guidance requires federal awarding agencies to use the Federal Awardee Performance and Integrity Information System (FAPIIS) to implement the requirements of Section 872 of the Duncan Hunter National Defense Authorization Act as applicable to grants. The requirements are effective for federal assistance awarded on or after January 1, 2016.

Help Agencies Maximize the Impact of their Limited Financial Resources

FedStat/Benchmarking

Over the course of this Administration, OMB has used regular data-driven management reviews to advance many of its most important shared priorities. Through implementation of the GPRA Modernization Act of 2010 and the President's Management Agenda, these reviews have led to a number of tangible improvements in the effectiveness and efficiency of individual agencies and the Government as a whole, and OMB will continue that work through ongoing PortfolioStat, Benchmarking, and Strategic Review engagements.

The federal government's efforts to improve government efficiency aim to increase the quality and value of core administrative operations and enhance productivity to achieve cost savings or cost avoidance. Establishing cost and quality benchmarks for these operations have helped to develop tools for the federal government to measure performance in key mission-support areas, including human resources, financial management, acquisition, information technology, and real property.

During FY 2015, OMB designed and launched the "FedStat" review to bring these efforts and other emerging priorities into focus in a cohesive discussion of opportunities with the CFO Act agencies for improved performance and risk mitigation that will more closely align with the Budget process and inform program management and administration. OMB met with agencies to discuss data-driven evidence on shared challenges across the government, to identify potential areas for agency sub-component improvement, and to explore opportunities to pursue cross-agency solutions, including policies, processes, and leading practices of excellence for broader application.

In support of the President's Management Agenda, agency implementation of these action items will improve agency management of mission-support functions and mission delivery, identify potential Budget, legislative, or other proposals early to inform the development of the FY 2017 Budget, as appropriate, and inform the FY 2016 FedStat process with a meaningful data-driven decision making process that supports each agency's mission.

Improving Effectiveness and Efficiency in Financial Operations and Systems

The Administration continues to make significant progress in the effort to minimize the costs and risks associated with agency financial systems modernization. While in the past the use of shared services was limited to smaller agencies, in FY 2015, cabinet-level agencies took steps to realize the benefit of shared service agreements. For example, in the Government's largest shared service arrangement to date, the Department of Housing and Urban Development (HUD) successfully transitioned many of its core financial management functions—as well as select administrative and human-resource functions— to Treasury, with other cabinet-level agencies expected to follow.

In February 2015, OMB commissioned a study to identify possibilities to improve the management of mission support shared services. The study confirmed that to improve performance and efficiency throughout government, reform is required in the way the government delivers and oversees its shared service initiatives. As a result of this study, a new cross-governmental Shared Services Governance Board (SSGB), led by OMB, was established to serve as the decision-making body for the shared services ecosystem. A Unified Shared Services Management (USSM) office was also established within the GSA to serve as an integration body for the ecosystem, working across functions, providers and consumers to enable the delivery of high-quality, high-value shared services. Led by the SSGB and USSM, stakeholders from across the government will work together to manage and oversee mission-support shared services with an initial scope of acquisitions, financial management, human resources, travel and information technology.

In addition, OMB published OMB Memorandum M-15-19, Improving Government Efficiency and Saving Taxpayer Dollars Through Electronic Invoicing, which directs agencies to transition to electronic invoicing for appropriate federal procurements by the end of FY 2018. The Government is the largest single purchaser of goods and services in the United States, processing over 19 million invoices each year. Approximately 40 percent of these invoices are processed using electronic invoicing with the remaining using a mix of electronic and manual processes that provide little visibility to businesses and can result in tax dollars being used for late payment fees rather than to support critical agency missions. The move to electronic invoicing can addresses cash flow issues for businesses, particularly small businesses, while also reducing administrative burden and costs to taxpayers.

Driving Real Property Efficiencies through Better Data and Data Analytics

The federal domestic building inventory is diverse and contains 300,000 buildings requiring approximately $21 billion of annual operation and maintenance expenditures, including approximately $6.8 billion of annual lease costs. Within the inventory, there are opportunities to realize cost savings by utilizing space more efficiently and reducing the portfolio. In 2013, the "Freeze the Footprint" Policy (OMB Management Procedures Memorandum 2013-02) was issued, requiring agencies to freeze their real property footprint. Agencies reduced their federal domestic office and warehouse space by 22 million square feet in FY 2013 and FY 2014. To improve the quality of federal real property data in annual PARs or AFRs, agencies were required to validate and report "Freeze the Footprint" square footage and associated operations and maintenance costs in their 2014 and 2015 financial statements. The final compliance year for the "Freeze the Footprint" policy was FY 2015, and that year's portfolio reduction will be released in April, 2016.

In FY 2015, the Government issued the National Strategy for the Efficient Use of Real Property (Strategy) and implementing policy– the Reduce the Footprint (RTF) policy. The Strategy provides a framework for agencies to measure the efficiency of their real property portfolios to identify and prioritize efficiency actions to reduce portfolio size. The RTF policy requires agencies to set annual portfolio reduction targets to help implement identified efficiency improvements and to implement an office space design standard to ensure office space is designed for efficiency. Over time, the Strategy and RTF policy will improve utilization of government-owned buildings to reduce reliance on leasing, lower the number of excess and underutilized properties, and improve the cost effectiveness and efficiency of the federal real property portfolio.

For the first time, the RTF policy requires that agencies reduce the size of the federal real property portfolios to improve program efficiency, and agencies have developed and finalized their first ever five year RTF reduction Plans to implement the policy. The agencies' RTF Plans target an aggregate reduction of 60 million square feet (SF) over the Plans' five year (FY 2016 – FY 2020) implementation time period. The magnitude of the targeted 60 million square feet reduction indicates the Strategy and RTF policy will be effective tools to improve the efficiency of the government's real property portfolio. Agencies will update their RTF Plans and annual reduction targets in March of each year with the goal of increasing the magnitude of targeted reductions year-over-year as agencies' ability to fully utilize the policies matures. The agencies' FY 2017 – FY 2021 RTF Plans are due in March, 2016.

To support increased reduction targets, the GSA and OMB have developed a new management tool within the Federal Real Property Profile (FRPP) database that enables agencies to fully analyze their portfolios. The new management tool uses the real property performance metrics developed through the President's Management Agenda to measure the performance of agencies' portfolios and thereby enable the identification and prioritization efficiency opportunities. The management tool, combined with the improved FRPP data quality that will result from the implementation of GSA's forthcoming technical guidance that establishes mandatory FRPP data validation and verification requirements, will enhance agencies' ability to implement data driven decision making to develop their annual RTF reduction targets. Focusing policy on reducing the portfolio, improving the quality of FRPP data through mandatory data validation and verification procedures, and the broad use of the new FRPP management tool will support higher RTF square foot reduction targets and efficiency gains in future years.

Conclusion

The federal government has seen significant progress in financial management since the passage of the CFO Act more than 20 years ago. Yet significant challenges remain. The issues that the federal government faces today require our financial managers to move beyond the status quo and to generate a higher return on investment for our financial management activities. The steps outlined above leverage the tools and capacities in place today, and refocus energies on critical and emerging priorities – cutting wasteful spending, improving the efficiency of our operations and information technology, and laying a foundation for data quality and collaboration as the federal government enters a new era of transparency and open government.

Additional Information

This *Financial Report's* Appendix contains the names and websites of the significant Government entities included in the *Financial Report's* financial statements. Details about the information in this *Financial Report* can be found in these entities' financial statements included in their Performance and Accountability and Agency Financial Reports. This *Financial Report*, as well as those from previous years, is also available at the Treasury, OMB, and GAO websites at: http://www.fiscal.treasury.gov/fsreports/fs_reports_publications.htm; http://www.whitehouse.gov/omb/financial/index.html; and http://www.gao.gov/financial.html, respectively. Other related Government publications include, but are not limited to the:

- *Budget of the United States Government,*
- *Treasury Bulletin,*
- *Monthly Treasury Statement of Receipts and Outlays of the United States Government,*
- *Monthly Statement of the Public Debt of the United States,*
- *Economic Report of the President*, and
- *Trustees' Reports* for the Social Security and Medicare Programs.

Limitations of the Financial Statements

The principal financial statements have been prepared to report the financial position and results of operations of the federal government, and the financial condition and changes in financial condition of its social insurance programs, and the federal government's projected long-term trends in receipts, spending, and debt, pursuant to the requirements of 31 U.S.C. § 331(e)(1). These statements are in addition to the financial reports used to monitor and control budgetary resources that are prepared from the same books and records.

U.S. GOVERNMENT ACCOUNTABILITY OFFICE

441 G St. N.W.   Comptroller General
Washington, DC 20548   of the United States

February 25, 2016

The President
The President of the Senate
The Speaker of the House of Representatives

The federal government reported a unified budget deficit of approximately $439 billion for fiscal year 2015, a decrease of about $45 billion from fiscal year 2014. However, the federal government continues to face an unsustainable long-term fiscal path. To operate as effectively and efficiently as possible and to make difficult decisions to address the federal government's fiscal challenges, Congress, the administration, and federal managers must have ready access to reliable and complete financial and performance information—both for individual federal entities and for the federal government as a whole. Our report on the U.S. government's consolidated financial statements underscores that much work remains to improve federal financial management, and these improvements are urgently needed.

Our audit report on the U.S. government's consolidated financial statements is enclosed. In summary, we found the following:

- Certain material weaknesses[1] in internal control over financial reporting and other limitations on the scope of our work resulted in conditions that prevented us from expressing an opinion on the accrual-based consolidated financial statements as of and for the fiscal years ended September 30, 2015, and 2014.[2] About 34 percent of the federal government's reported total assets as of September 30, 2015, and approximately 19 percent of the federal government's reported net cost for fiscal year 2015 relate to three Chief Financial Officers (CFO) Act agencies—the Department of Defense (DOD), the Department of Housing and Urban Development, and the U.S. Department of Agriculture—that received disclaimers of opinion on their fiscal year 2015 financial statements.

- Significant uncertainties (discussed in Note 23 to the consolidated financial statements), primarily related to the achievement of projected reductions in Medicare cost growth, and a material weakness in internal control over financial reporting, prevented us from expressing

---

[1]A material weakness is a deficiency, or a combination of deficiencies, in internal control over financial reporting such that there is a reasonable possibility that a material misstatement of the entity's financial statements will not be prevented, or detected and corrected, on a timely basis. A deficiency in internal control exists when the design or operation of a control does not allow management or employees, in the normal course of performing their assigned functions, to prevent, or detect and correct, misstatements on a timely basis.
[2]The accrual-based consolidated financial statements as of and for the fiscal years ended September 30, 2015, and 2014, consist of the (1) Statements of Net Cost, (2) Statements of Operations and Changes in Net Position, (3) Reconciliations of Net Operating Cost and Unified Budget Deficit, (4) Statements of Changes in Cash Balance from Unified Budget and Other Activities, and (5) Balance Sheets, including the related notes to these financial statements. Most revenues are recorded on a modified cash basis.

an opinion on the sustainability financial statements,[3] which consist of the 2015 Statement of Long-Term Fiscal Projections (a new comprehensive basic financial statement that provides information on the federal government's long-term financial condition); the 2015, 2014, 2013, 2012, and 2011 Statements of Social Insurance; and the 2015 and 2014 Statements of Changes in Social Insurance Amounts.[4] About $27.9 trillion, or 67.0 percent, of the reported total present value of future expenditures in excess of future revenue presented in the 2015 Statement of Social Insurance relates to Medicare programs reported in the Department of Health and Human Services' (HHS) 2015 Statement of Social Insurance, which received a disclaimer of opinion.

- Material weaknesses resulted in ineffective internal control over financial reporting for fiscal year 2015.

- Material weaknesses and other scope limitations discussed in our audit report limited our tests of compliance with selected provisions of applicable laws, regulations, contracts, and grant agreements for fiscal year 2015.

Overall, significant progress has been made in improving federal financial management since the enactment of key federal financial management reforms in the 1990s. Importantly, almost all of the 24 CFO Act agencies received unmodified ("clean") opinions on their respective entities' fiscal year 2015 financial statements, up from 6 CFO Act agencies that received clean audit opinions in 1996. In addition, accounting and financial reporting standards have continued to evolve to provide greater transparency and accountability over the federal government's operations, financial condition, and fiscal outlook. Further, the preparation and audit of individual federal entities' financial statements have identified numerous deficiencies, leading to corrective actions to strengthen federal entities' internal controls, processes, and systems.

However, since the federal government began preparing consolidated financial statements 19 years ago, three major impediments continued to prevent us from rendering an opinion on the federal government's accrual-based consolidated financial statements over this period: (1) serious financial management problems at DOD that have prevented its financial statements from being auditable, (2) the federal government's inability to adequately account for and reconcile intragovernmental activity and balances between federal entities, and (3) the federal government's ineffective process for preparing the consolidated financial statements.

DOD has consistently been unable to receive an audit opinion on its financial statements. Following years of unsuccessful financial improvement efforts, the DOD Comptroller established the Financial Improvement and Audit Readiness (FIAR) Directorate to develop, manage, and implement a strategic approach for addressing internal control weaknesses and for achieving auditability, and to integrate those efforts with other improvement activities, such as the

---

[3]As required by the Statement of Federal Financial Accounting Standards No. 36, "Reporting Comprehensive Long-Term Fiscal Projections for the U.S. Government," as amended, the federal government presents a new basic financial statement, the Statement of Long-Term Fiscal Projections, for fiscal year 2015, along with the related notes, as part of the consolidated financial statements. The Statement of Long-Term Fiscal Projections presents for all the activities of the federal government, the present value of projected receipts and noninterest spending under current policy without change, the relationship of these amounts to projected gross domestic product, and changes in the present value of projected receipts and noninterest spending from the prior year. The unaudited Statement of Long-Term Fiscal Projections for the fiscal year ended September 30, 2014, is presented for comparison purposes and was not subject to audit.

[4]Statements of Social Insurance are presented for the current year and each of the 4 preceding years in accordance with U.S. generally accepted accounting principles. Also, the sustainability financial statements do not interrelate with the accrual-based consolidated financial statements.

department's business systems modernization efforts. DOD's current FIAR strategy and methodology focus on two priorities—budgetary information and asset accountability—with an overall goal of having its department-wide financial statements audit ready by September 30, 2017.[5] Because budgetary information is widely and regularly used for management, one of DOD's highest interim priorities is to improve its budgetary information and processes underlying its Statement of Budgetary Resources (SBR).

Based on difficulties encountered in preparing for an audit of the SBR, DOD made a significant change to its FIAR Guidance that limited the scope of the first-year SBR audits for all DOD components.[6] As outlined in the November 2014 FIAR Plan Status Report and the November 2013 revised FIAR Guidance, the scope of initial SBR audits beginning in fiscal year 2015 is to focus on current-year budget activity, to be reported on a Schedule of Budgetary Activity (SBA).[7] This is intended to be an interim step toward achieving the audit of multiple-year budget activity required for an audit of the SBR. In making this strategic change, DOD officials concluded—based on the difficulties encountered in obtaining documentation for prior year transactions on the U.S. Marine Corps SBR audit—that the most effective path to an audit of the SBR would be to start with reporting and auditing only current-year activity for fiscal year 2015 appropriations and expanding subsequent audits to include current-year appropriations and prior appropriations going back to fiscal year 2015. Consequently, certain DOD components—including the Army, Navy, and Air Force—underwent their first SBA audits for fiscal year 2015. Independent public accountants (IPA) issued disclaimers of opinion[8] on the Army's and the Air Force's fiscal year 2015 SBAs and identified material weaknesses in internal control at both Army and Air Force. Army and Air Force management have generally concurred with the findings in the respective IPA reports and stated that they will develop and execute corrective actions to address the IPAs' recommendations. The Navy's SBA audit is ongoing and the report is expected to be issued February 29, 2016. In its November 2015 FIAR Plan Status Report, DOD reported that the Army, Navy, and Air Force will again undergo SBA audits for fiscal year 2016. In addition, with regard to meeting its goal of having its financial statements audit ready department-wide by September 30, 2017, the department has not, among other things, fully developed the details of its strategy for consolidating individual component financial statements into department-wide financial statements, including eliminating intragovernmental transactions.

---

[5]Section 1003 of the National Defense Authorization Act for Fiscal Year 2010, Pub. L. No. 111-84, 123 Stat. 2190, 2439-41 (Oct. 28, 2009), made the development and maintenance of the FIAR Plan a statutory requirement. Under the act, the FIAR Plan must describe specific actions to be taken and the costs associated with ensuring that DOD's financial statements are validated as ready for audit by September 30, 2017. In addition, section 1005 of the National Defense Authorization Act for Fiscal Year 2013, Pub. L. No. 112-239, 126 Stat. 1632, 1904-05 (Jan. 2, 2013), enacted a requirement for DOD's FIAR Plan to describe specific actions to be taken and the costs associated with ensuring that one of DOD's financial statements, the Statement of Budgetary Resources, would be validated as ready for audit by September 30, 2014, but DOD has acknowledged that it did not meet this target date. More recently, section 1003 of the National Defense Authorization Act for Fiscal Year 2014, Pub. L. No. 113-66, 127 Stat. 672, 842 (Dec. 26, 2013) (reprinted in 10 U.S.C. § 2222 note), mandated an audit of DOD's fiscal year 2018 financial statements and that the audit results be submitted to Congress by March 31, 2019.

[6]The FIAR Guidance was first issued by the DOD Comptroller in May 2010 and provides a standardized methodology for DOD components to follow for achieving financial management improvements and auditability. The DOD Comptroller periodically updates this guidance.

[7]Unlike the SBR, which reflects multiple-year budget activity, the SBA reflects the balances and associated activity related only to funding from fiscal year 2015 forward. As a result, the SBAs exclude unobligated and unexpended amounts carried over from funding prior to fiscal year 2015 as well as information on the status and use of such funding (e.g., obligations incurred and outlays) in fiscal year 2015 and thereafter.

[8]The Army's IPA issued its opinion on January 15, 2016, and the Air Force's IPA issued its opinion on November 20, 2015.

Various efforts are also under way to address the other two major impediments to an audit of the consolidated financial statements. For example, during fiscal year 2015, the Department of the Treasury (Treasury) continued to actively work with significant federal entities[9] to resolve differences in intragovernmental activity and balances between federal entities through its quarterly scorecard process.[10] This process highlights differences requiring the entities' attention, identifies differences that need to be resolved through a formal dispute resolution process,[11] and reinforces the entities' responsibilities to resolve intragovernmental differences. Treasury also began developing policies and procedures over accounting for and reporting all significant activity and balances of the General Fund of the U.S. Government (General Fund),[12] and began reconciling the activity and balances between the General Fund and federal entity trading partners. Further, over the past few years, Treasury has implemented new systems to collect certain additional data from entities and to compile the consolidated financial statements and new or enhanced procedures to address certain internal control deficiencies detailed in our previously issued report.[13] To help address the magnitude of the issues in these areas, it will be important that Treasury continues to improve its systems and continues to ensure that it has appropriate personnel. It will also be important that Treasury and the Office of Management and Budget (OMB) further enhance their corrective action plans to include certain key elements, such as (1) sufficient information on how progress on interim actions would be monitored and (2) outcome measures for assessing the effectiveness of the corrective actions. In addition to continued leadership by Treasury and OMB, strong and sustained commitment by federal entities is critical to fully address these issues.

The material weaknesses underlying these three major impediments continued to (1) hamper the federal government's ability to reliably report a significant portion of its assets, liabilities, costs, and other related information; (2) affect the federal government's ability to reliably measure the full cost, as well as the financial and nonfinancial performance of certain programs and activities; (3) impair the federal government's ability to adequately safeguard significant assets and properly record various transactions; and (4) hinder the federal government from having reliable financial information to operate in an efficient and effective manner.

In addition to the material weaknesses referred to above, we identified three other material weaknesses. These are the federal government's inability to (1) determine the full extent to which improper payments[14] occur and reasonably assure that appropriate actions are taken to

---

[9]OMB and Treasury have identified 39 federal entities that are significant to the U.S. government's fiscal year 2015 consolidated financial statements, including the 24 CFO Act agencies. See *Treasury Financial Manual*, vol. I, part 2, ch. 4700, for a listing of the 39 entities.

[10]For each quarter, Treasury produces a scorecard for each significant entity that reports various aspects of the entity's intragovernmental differences with its trading partners, including the composition of the differences by trading partner and category. Entities are expected to resolve, with their respective trading partners, the differences identified in their scorecards.

[11]When an entity and its respective trading partner cannot resolve an intragovernmental difference, the entity must request Treasury to resolve the dispute. Treasury will review the dispute and issue a decision on how to resolve the difference, which the entities must follow.

[12]The General Fund is a component of Treasury's central accounting function. It is a stand-alone reporting entity that comprises the activities fundamental to funding the federal government (e.g., issued budget authority, cash activity, and debt financing activities).

[13]GAO, *Management Report: Improvements Needed in Controls over the Processes Used to Prepare the U.S. Consolidated Financial Statements*, GAO-15-630 (Washington, D.C.: July 30, 2015).

[14]When excluding DOD's Defense Finance and Accounting Service Commercial Pay program, federal entity-reported estimates of improper payments totaled $136.7 billion in fiscal year 2015, an increase from the revised prior year estimate of $124.6 billion. This increase was mostly attributable to an increased error rate in HHS's Medicaid program.

reduce them, (2) identify and resolve information security control deficiencies and manage information security risks on an ongoing basis, and (3) effectively manage its tax collection activities. Additional details concerning these material weaknesses and their effect on the accrual-based consolidated financial statements and on the management of federal government operations are presented in our audit report. Until the problems outlined in our audit report are adequately addressed, they will continue to have adverse implications for the federal government and American taxpayers.

The federal government reported a net operating cost of about $519.7 billion for fiscal year 2015 compared to the approximately $791 billion reported for fiscal year 2014. Increases in reported taxes and certain other revenues were primarily responsible for the decrease in net operating cost. The reported unified budget deficit of approximately $439 billion for fiscal year 2015 was down from the approximately $483 billion reported for fiscal year 2014. The federal government's reported assets totaled about $3.2 trillion as of September 30, 2015, which was about $165 billion greater than the amount reported as of September 30, 2014. Its reported liabilities totaled about $21.5 trillion as of September 30, 2015, which was about $686 billion greater than the amount reported as of September 30, 2014. Most of the net increase in the federal government's reported assets was due to student loans made by the Department of Education. The net increase in liabilities was due primarily to a net increase in federal debt held by the public and the liability for restoration of federal debt principal and interest to the Federal Thrift Savings Plan.[15] As of September 30, 2015, federal debt held by the public totaled about 74 percent of gross domestic product (GDP). Additional details regarding the above-noted fluctuations and the federal government's financial condition can be found in the Management's Discussion and Analysis section of the *Fiscal Year 2015 Financial Report of the United States Government* (*2015 Financial Report*).

Importantly, there are risks that certain factors could affect the federal government's financial condition in the future, including the following:

- The Pension Benefit Guaranty Corporation's (PBGC) financial future is uncertain because of long-term challenges related to PBGC's governance and funding structure. PBGC's liabilities exceeded its assets by over $76 billion as of September 30, 2015—an increase of over $14 billion from the end of fiscal year 2014. PBGC reported that it is subject to further losses if plan terminations that are considered reasonably possible occur.

- In 2008, during the financial crisis, the federal government placed the Federal National Mortgage Association (Fannie Mae) and the Federal Home Loan Mortgage Corporation (Freddie Mac) under conservatorship and entered into preferred stock purchase agreements with these government-sponsored enterprises (GSE) to help ensure their financial stability. The agreements with the GSEs could affect the federal government's financial position. As of September 30, 2015, the federal government continued to report about $106 billion of investments in the GSEs, which is net of about $88 billion in valuation losses. Cash dividends paid by the GSEs to Treasury under the agreements totaled $20.4 billion and

---

[15]Due to delays in raising the debt limit, Treasury deviated from its normal debt management operations and took a number of extraordinary actions, consistent with relevant laws and regulations, from March 16, 2015 through September 30, 2015, to avoid exceeding the debt limit. Many extraordinary actions taken by Treasury during fiscal year 2015 resulted in federal debt securities not being issued to certain federal government accounts. As a result of securities not being issued to the Government Securities Investment Fund (G-Fund) of the Thrift Savings Plan, a liability was reported that represents uninvested principal and related interest for the G-Fund that would have been reported as federal debt held by the public had there not been a delay in raising the debt limit as of September 30, 2015, and had the securities been issued.

$72.5 billion during fiscal years 2015 and 2014, respectively. Although Treasury does not believe that any further draws by the GSEs are probable, the reported maximum remaining contractual commitment to the GSEs, if needed, is $258.1 billion. Importantly, the ultimate role of the GSEs in the mortgage market could affect the financial condition of the Federal Housing Administration, which in the past expanded its lending role in distressed housing and mortgage markets.

- The U.S. Postal Service (USPS) continues to be in a serious financial crisis as it has reached its borrowing limit of $15 billion and finished fiscal year 2015 with a reported net loss of $5.1 billion.

Every 2 years, GAO provides Congress with an update on its High-Risk Series, which highlights federal entities and program areas that are at high risk due to their vulnerabilities to fraud, waste, abuse, and mismanagement or are most in need of broad reform. We issued our most recently updated High-Risk Series on February 11, 2015.[16] GAO's High-Risk Series includes most of the above-noted issues, such as DOD financial management, information security, USPS's business model, the PBGC insurance programs, and the financial regulatory system for housing finance. Another area included in the High-Risk Series that could affect the federal government's financial condition in the future is the Internal Revenue Service's (IRS) enforcement of tax laws, including reducing the net tax gap—the difference between taxes owed and taxes paid—which was last estimated to be $385 billion.[17]

While the near-term outlook has improved, the comprehensive long-term fiscal projections presented in the Statement of Long-Term Fiscal Projections, and related information in Note 24 and in the unaudited Required Supplementary Information section of the *2015 Financial Report*, show that absent policy changes, the federal government continues to face an unsustainable long-term fiscal path. In the near term, the projections in the *2015 Financial Report* show the primary deficit continuing to decline from the recent historic highs. However, these projections do not reflect legislation enacted subsequent to September 30, 2015, which, in order to achieve certain national priorities and goals, causes deficits to increase in the near term.[18] Over the long term, the imbalance between spending and revenue that is built into current law and policy is projected to lead to continued growth of debt held by the public as a share of GDP. This situation—in which debt grows faster than GDP—means that the current federal fiscal path is unsustainable.

Under these projections, spending for the major health and retirement programs will increase in coming decades more rapidly than GDP as more members of the baby boom generation become eligible for benefits. These projections, with regard to Social Security and Medicare, are based on the same assumptions underlying the information presented in the Statement of Social Insurance and assume that the provisions enacted in the Patient Protection and Affordable Care Act, as amended (ACA) designed to slow the growth of Medicare costs are sustained and remain effective throughout the projection period.[19] They also reflect the effects of the Medicare Access and CHIP Reauthorization Act of 2015 (MACRA), which, among other

---

[16]GAO, *High-Risk Series: An Update*, GAO-15-290 (Washington, D.C.: Feb. 11, 2015).
[17]IRS last estimated the gross tax gap of $450 billion in 2012 for tax year 2006.
[18]The 2015 Statement of Long-Term Fiscal Projections is based on current policy as of September 30, 2015. This is prior to the enactment of the Bipartisan Budget Act of 2015 and the Consolidated Appropriations Act, 2016; therefore, the projections do not reflect the effects of these two statutes. Management notes that neither statute is expected to have a material effect on the long-term fiscal projections in its report.
[19]ACA, Pub. L. No. 111-148, 124 Stat. 119 (Mar. 23, 2010), as amended by the Health Care and Education Reconciliation Act of 2010, Pub. L. No. 111-152, 124 Stat. 1029 (Mar. 30, 2010).

things, revised the methodology for determining physician payment rates.[20] If, however, the Medicare cost containment measures and physician payment rate methodology are not sustained over the long term—concerns expressed by the Trustees of the Medicare trust funds, the Centers for Medicare & Medicaid Services' (CMS) Chief Actuary, the Congressional Budget Office, and others—spending on federal health care programs will grow more rapidly than assumed in the projections.

GAO also prepares long-term federal fiscal simulations, using different sets of assumptions which continue to show debt held by the public rising as a share of GDP.[21] Under GAO's Alternative simulation,[22] using the CMS Office of the Actuary's alternative health care cost projections, future spending in excess of receipts would be greater and debt held by the public as a share of GDP would grow more quickly than the projections in the *2015 Financial Report*. Under the Alternative simulation, debt held by the public will surpass its historic high (106 percent in 1946) by 2031.

Both the projections in the *2015 Financial Report* and our long-term simulations follow the spending limits enacted in the Balanced Budget and Emergency Deficit Control Act of 1985 (BBEDCA), as amended.[23] Under these limits, discretionary spending will continue to decline as a share of the economy and within the next 5 years will be lower as a share of GDP than any level seen in the last 50 years. At the same time, the projections in the *2015 Financial Report* show revenues rising in the near term as the economy continues to recover. Our long-term simulations show revenues rising in some years and declining in others in the near term.

Debt held by the public as a share of GDP, however, remains well above the post-war historical average of 43 percent since 1946. At the end of fiscal year 2015, debt held by the public reached about 74 percent of GDP—the second highest (after fiscal year 2014, when it was slightly higher) it has been as a share of GDP since 1950. Debt held by the public at these high levels could limit the federal government's flexibility to address emerging issues and unforeseen challenges, such as another economic downturn or large-scale disaster. Further, our past work has also identified a variety of fiscal exposures—responsibilities, programs, and activities that

---

[20]MACRA, Pub. L. No. 114-10, title I, § 101, 129 Stat. 87, 89 (Apr. 16, 2015), repealed the sustainable growth rate (SGR) formula for calculating annual updates to Medicare reimbursement payment rates to physicians and certain nonphysician medical providers and established an alternative set of annual updates.

[21]GAO, *Fiscal Outlook: Federal Fiscal Outlook* (2016) (Washington, D.C.: 2016), accessed February 17, 2016, http://www.gao.gov/fiscal_outlook/federal_fiscal_outlook/overview.

[22]Our 2016 Alternative simulation, the most recent one available as of the date of our audit report, incorporates the CMS Office of the Actuary's 2015 alternative projections for health care cost growth, which assume certain cost controls are not maintained over the long term. Our Alternative simulation also assumes that tax provisions that are scheduled to expire, such as the credit for construction of energy-efficient new homes, are extended. In the Alternative simulation, discretionary spending follows the caps established in the Balanced Budget and Emergency Deficit Control Act of 1985, as amended, but not the lower caps triggered by the automatic enforcement procedures.

[23]The Budget Control Act of 2011 (BCA) amended BBEDCA, imposing discretionary spending limits for fiscal years 2012 through 2021 to reduce projected spending by about $1 trillion. Pub. L. No. 112-25, 125 Stat. 240 (Aug. 2, 2011). BCA also established the Joint Select Committee on Deficit Reduction (Joint Committee), which was tasked with proposing legislation to reduce the deficit by at least an additional $1.2 trillion through fiscal year 2021. The Joint Committee did not report a proposal, and Congress and the President did not enact legislation. This triggered the sequestration process in section 251A of BBEDCA. Section 251A, as amended by the BCA, required (1) a sequestration for fiscal year 2013 and (2) annual downward adjustments to discretionary spending limits and sequestration of direct spending from fiscal years 2014 through 2021. BBEDCA has been amended several times since August 2011, including most recently by the Bipartisan Budget Act (BBA) of 2015, which increased discretionary spending limits for fiscal years 2016 and 2017. The BBA of 2015 also extended the sequestration of direct spending through fiscal year 2025 and made other changes to direct spending and revenue. Pub. L. No. 114-74, §§ 101, 102, 129 Stat. 584, 585-87 (Nov. 2, 2015). GAO's long-term simulations reflect the effects of the BBA of 2015.

explicitly or implicitly expose the federal government to future spending.[24] Fiscal exposures vary widely as to source, extent of the government's legal commitment, and magnitude. Over the past decade, some fiscal exposures have grown because of events and trends and the government's response to them. Increased attention to these fiscal exposures will be important for understanding risks to the federal fiscal outlook and enhancing oversight of federal resources.

As we have previously reported, the debt limit does not restrict Congress's ability to enact spending and revenue legislation that affects the level of federal debt or otherwise constrain fiscal policy; it restricts Treasury's authority to borrow to finance the decisions already enacted by Congress and the President.[25] The United States benefits from the confidence investors have that debt backed by the full faith and credit of the United States will be honored. Because Treasury securities are viewed as one of the safest assets in the world, they are broadly held by individuals—often in pension funds or mutual funds—and by institutions and central banks for use in everyday transactions. Treasury securities are also the cheapest and one of the most widely used forms of collateral for financial transactions. In many ways, U.S. Treasury securities are the underpinning of the world financial system. As we have also previously reported, delays in raising the debt limit can create uncertainty in the Treasury market. To avoid such uncertainty and the disruption to the Treasury market that it creates, as well as to help inform the fiscal policy debate in a timely way, we have suggested that Congress should consider ways to better link decisions about the debt limit with decisions about spending and revenue at the time those decisions are made.[26] In our July 2015 report on the debt limit, we discussed several potential approaches to delegating borrowing authority that would both achieve this link and minimize disruptions to the market.[27]

The Digital Accountability and Transparency Act of 2014 (DATA Act) holds great promise for improving the transparency and accountability of federal spending data by providing consistent, reliable, and complete data on federal spending and for helping decision makers in addressing the federal government's fiscal challenges. However, in order to fully and effectively implement the DATA Act, the federal government will need to address complex policy and technical issues. Central among these are defining and developing common data elements across multiple reporting areas and standing up the necessary supporting systems and processes to enable reporting of the federal spending data required by the DATA Act. Since the act was signed into law in May 2014, OMB and Treasury have made progress using a variety of outreach approaches to address questions and obtain feedback from federal and nonfederal stakeholders, but as was reported in January 2016, more complete and timely guidance is needed to ensure effective implementation.[28]

———————————

Our audit report on the U.S. government's consolidated financial statements would not be

---

[24]GAO, *Fiscal Outlook: Federal Fiscal Outlook (2016),* accessed February 17, 2016, http://www.gao.gov/fiscal_outlook/federal_fiscal_outlook/overview#t=3, and *Fiscal Exposures: Improving Cost Recognition in the Federal Budget*, GAO-14-28 (Washington, D.C.: Oct. 29, 2013).

[25]GAO, *Debt Limit: Analysis of 2011-2012 Actions Taken and Effect of Delayed Increase on Borrowing Costs*, GAO-12-701 (Washington, D.C.: July 23, 2012), and *Debt Limit: Delays Create Debt Management Challenges and Increase Uncertainty in the Treasury Market*, GAO-11-203 (Washington, D.C.: Feb. 22, 2011).

[26]GAO-12-701 and GAO-11-203.

[27]GAO, *Debt Limit: Market Response to Recent Impasses Underscores Need to Consider Alternative Approaches*, GAO-15-476 (Washington, D.C.: July 9, 2015).

[28]GAO, *DATA Act: Data Standards Established, but More Complete and Timely Guidance Is Needed to Ensure Effective Implementation*, GAO-16-261 (Washington, D.C.: Jan. 29, 2016).

possible without the commitment and professionalism of inspectors general throughout the federal government who are responsible for annually auditing the financial statements of individual federal entities. We also appreciate the cooperation and assistance of Treasury and OMB officials, as well as the federal entities' chief financial officers. We look forward to continuing to work with these individuals, the administration, and Congress to achieve the goals and objectives of federal financial management reform.

Our audit report begins on page 239. Our guide to the *Financial Report of the United States Government (Financial Report)* is intended to help those who seek to obtain a better understanding of the *Financial Report* and is available on GAO's website at www.gao.gov.[29] In addition, the website includes a guide to understanding the differences between accrual and generally cash-based budget measures and provides a useful perspective on the different purposes that cash and accrual measures serve in providing a comprehensive picture of the federal government's fiscal condition today and over time.[30]

Our audit report was prepared under the direction of Robert F. Dacey, Chief Accountant, and J. Lawrence Malenich, Director, Financial Management and Assurance. If you have any questions, please contact me on (202) 512-5500 or them on (202) 512-3406.

Gene L. Dodaro
Comptroller General
of the United States

cc: The Majority Leader of the Senate
       The Minority Leader of the Senate
       The Majority Leader of the House of Representatives
       The Minority Leader of the House of Representatives

---

[29]GAO, *Understanding the Primary Components of the Annual Financial Report of the United States Government,* GAO-09-946SP (Washington, D.C.: September 2009).
[30]See http://www.gao.gov/special.pubs/longterm/deficit/, which is based on information in GAO, *Understanding Similarities and Differences between Accrual and Cash Deficits,* GAO-07-117SP (Washington, D.C.: December 2006). In January 2007 and 2008, we issued updates to this guide for fiscal years 2006 and 2007; see GAO-07-341SP (Washington, D.C.: January 2007) and GAO-08-410SP (Washington, D.C.: January 2008).

This page is intentionally blank.

Financial Statements of the United States Government for the Years Ended September 30, 2015, and 2014

The consolidated financial statements of the United States Government (Government) were prepared using U.S. generally accepted accounting principles (GAAP). The consolidated financial statements include the accrual-based financial statements and the sustainability financial statements, which are discussed in more detail below, and the related notes to the consolidated financial statements. Collectively, the accrual-based financial statements, the sustainability financial statements, and the notes represent basic information that is deemed essential for the consolidated financial statements to be presented in conformity with GAAP.

ACCRUAL-BASED FINANCIAL STATEMENTS

The accrual-based financial statements present historical information on what the federal government owns (assets) and owes (liabilities) at the end of the year, what came in (revenues) and what went out (net costs) during the year, and how accrual-based net operating costs of the federal government reconcile to the budget deficit and changes in its cash balances during the year. The following sections discuss each of the accrual-based financial statements.

Statements of Net Cost

These statements present the net cost of the Government operations for fiscal years 2015 and 2014, including the operations related to funds from dedicated collections (funds financed by specifically identified revenues, often supplemented by other financing sources, which remain available over time). The Government's fiscal year begins October 1 and ends September 30. Costs and earned revenues are categorized on the Statement of Net Cost by significant entity, providing greater accountability by showing the relationship of the agencies' net cost to the governmentwide net cost. Costs and earned revenues are presented in this *Financial Report* by significant entity on an accrual basis, while the budget presents costs and revenues by outlays and receipts, generally on a cash basis. The focus of the budget of the United States is by agency. Budgets are prepared, defended, and monitored by agency. In reporting by agency, we are assisting the external users in assessing the budget integrity, operating performance, stewardship, and systems and controls of the Government.

These statements contain the following four components:

- Gross cost—is the full cost of all the departments and entities excluding (gain)/loss from changes in assumptions. These costs are assigned on a cause-and-effect basis, or reasonably allocated to the corresponding entities.
- Earned revenue—is exchange revenue resulting from the Government providing goods and services to the public at a price.
- (Gain)/loss from changes in assumptions—is the gain or loss from changes in long-term assumptions used to measure the liabilities reported for federal civilian and military employee pensions, other post-employment benefits, and other retirement benefits, including veterans' compensation.
- Net cost—is computed by subtracting earned revenue from gross cost, adjusted by the (gain)/loss from changes in assumptions.

Individual agency net cost amounts will differ from the agency's financial statements primarily because of allocations of Office of Personnel Management (OPM) benefit program costs and intragovernmental eliminations, as adjusted for buy/sell cost, buy/sell revenues, and imputed costs. Because of its specific function, most of the costs originally associated with OPM have been allocated to their user agencies for governmentwide reporting purposes. The remaining costs for OPM on the Statements of Net Cost are the administrative operating costs, the expenses from prior costs from health and pension plan amendments, and the actuarial gains and losses, if applicable. With regard to intragovernmental buy/sell costs and related revenues, the amounts recognized by each agency are added to, and subtracted from, respectively, the individual agency non-federal net cost amounts. Because of the specific functions of the General Services Administration (GSA), as the primary provider of goods and services to federal agencies, once GSA's net cost is adjusted for its intragovernmental buy/sell costs and related revenues, the remaining costs for GSA on the Statements of Net Cost are its administrative operating costs. In addition, the intragovernmental imputed costs recognized for the receipt of goods and services, financed in whole or part by the providing agencies, are added to the individual agency non-federal net cost amounts. The interest on securities issued by the Department of the Treasury (Treasury) and held by the public is reported on Treasury's financial statements, but, because of its importance and the dollar amounts involved, it is reported separately in these statements.

Statements of Operations and Changes in Net Position

These statements report the results of Government operations, net operating costs, which include the results of operations for funds from dedicated collections. They include non-exchange revenues, which are generated from transactions that do not require a Government entity to give value directly in exchange for the inflow of resources. The Government does not "earn" the non-exchange revenue. These are generated principally by the Government's sovereign power to tax, levy duties, and assess fines and penalties. These statements also include the net cost reported in the Statement of Net Cost. They further include certain adjustments and unreconciled transactions that affect the net position.

Revenue

Inflows of resources to the government that the government demands or that it receives by donations are identified as non-exchange revenue. The inflows that it demands include individual income tax and tax withholdings, excise taxes, corporation income taxes, unemployment taxes, custom duties, and estate and gift taxes. The non-exchange revenue is recognized when collected and adjusted for the change in net measurable and legally collectable amounts receivable.

Individual income tax and tax withholdings include Federal Insurance Contributions Act (FICA)/Self-Employment Contributions Act (SECA) taxes and other taxes.

Excise taxes consist of taxes collected for various items, such as airline tickets, gasoline products, distilled spirits and imported liquor, tobacco, firearms, and other items.

Other taxes and receipts include Federal Reserve Banks (FRBs) earnings, tax related fines, penalties and interest, and railroad retirement taxes.

Miscellaneous earned revenues consist of earned revenues received from the public with virtually no associated cost. These revenues include rents and royalties on the Outer Continental Shelf Lands resulting from the leasing and development of mineral resources on public lands.

Generally, funds from dedicated collections are financed by specifically identified revenues, provided to the government by non-federal sources, often supplemented by other financing sources, which remain available over time. These specifically identified revenues and other financing sources are required by statute to be used for designated activities, benefits or purposes, and must be accounted for separately from the Government's general revenue. See Note 21—Funds from Dedicated Collections for detailed information.

Intragovernmental interest represents interest earned from the investment of surplus dedicated collections, which finance the deficit spending of all other fund's non-dedicated operations. These investments are recorded as intragovernmental debt holdings and are included in Note 11—Federal Debt Securities Held by the Public and Accrued Interest, in the table titled Intragovernmental Debt Holdings: Federal Debt Securities Held as Investments by Government Accounts. These interest earnings and the associated investments are eliminated in the consolidation process.

Net Cost of Government Operations

The net cost of Government operations—gross cost (including gains/losses from changes in assumptions) less earned revenue—flows through from the Statements of Net Cost. The net cost associated with funds from dedicated collections activities is separately reported and starting in fiscal year 2015, the intragovernmental net cost associated with funds from dedicated collections is separately reported.

Intragovernmental Transfers

Intragovernmental transfers reflect budgetary and other financing sources for funds from dedicated collections, excluding financing sources related to non-exchange revenues, intragovernmental interest, and miscellaneous revenues. These intragovernmental transfers include appropriations, transfers, and other financing sources. These amounts are labeled as "other changes in fund balance" in Note 21—Funds from Dedicated Collections. Some transfers reflect amounts required by statute to be transferred from the General Fund of the U.S. Government (General Fund) to funds from dedicated collections. For Supplementary Medical Insurance (SMI), transfers from the General Fund financed 75 percent of 2015 program costs to both Part B and D.

Unmatched Transactions and Balances

Unmatched transactions and balances are adjustments needed to bring the change in net position into balance due primarily to unreconciled intragovernmental differences. See Note 1.S—Unmatched Transactions and Balances for detailed information.

The unmatched transactions and balances are included in net operating cost to make the sum of net operating costs and prior period adjustments for the year equal to the change in the net position balance.

Net Operating Cost

The net operating cost equals revenue less net cost of Government operations (that flows from the Statement of Net Cost) adjusted by unmatched transactions and balances (see Note 1.S).

Net Position, Beginning of Period

The net position, beginning of period, reflects the amount reported on the prior year's balance sheet as of the end of that fiscal year. The net position for funds from dedicated collections is shown separately.

Prior-period adjustments are revisions to the beginning net position presented on the prior year financial statements due to corrections of material errors or certain changes in accounting principles. See Note 18—Prior Period Adjustments for detailed information.

Net Position, End of Period

The net position, end of period, reflects the amount as of the end of the fiscal year. The net position for funds from dedicated collections is separately shown.

Reconciliations of Net Operating Cost and Unified Budget Deficit

These statements reconcile the results of operations (net operating cost) on the Statements of Operations and Changes in Net Position (SOCNP) to the unified budget deficit. The premise of the reconciliation is that the accrual and budgetary accounting basis share transaction data.

Receipts and outlays in the budget are measured primarily on a cash basis and differ from the accrual basis of accounting used in the *Financial Report*. Refer to Note 1.B—Basis of Accounting and Revenue Recognition for details. These statements begin with the net results of operations (net operating cost) and report activities where the basis of accounting for the components of net operating cost and the unified budget deficit differ.

Components of Net Operating Cost Not Part of the Budget Deficit

This information includes the operating components, such as the changes in benefits payable for veterans, military and civilian employees, environmental and disposal liabilities, and depreciation expense, not included in the budget results.

Components of the Budget Deficit Not Part of Net Operating Cost

This information includes the budget components, such as capitalized fixed assets (that are recorded as outlays in the budget when purchased and reflected in net operating cost through depreciation expense over the useful life of the asset) and increases in other assets that are not included in the operating results.

Statements of Changes in Cash Balance from Unified Budget and Other Activities

The primary purpose of these statements is to report how the annual unified budget deficit relates to the change in the Government's cash and other monetary assets, as well as debt held by the public. It explains why the unified budget deficit normally would not result in an equivalent change in the Government's cash and other monetary assets.

These statements reconcile the unified budget deficit to the change in cash and other monetary assets during the fiscal year. They also serve to explain how the budget deficits were financed. A budget deficit is the result of outlays (expenditures) exceeding receipts (revenue) during a particular fiscal year.

The budget deficit is primarily financed through borrowings from the public. Other transactions, such as the payment of interest on debt held by the public, also require cash disbursements and are not part of the deficit. Additionally, the budget deficit includes certain amounts that are recognized in the budget, but will be disbursed in a future period, or are adjustments that did not affect the cash balance. These amounts include interest accrued on debt issued by Treasury and held by the public, as well as subsidy expense related to direct and guaranteed loans.

These statements show the adjustments for non-cash outlays included in the budget, and items affecting the cash balance not included in the budget, to explain the change in cash and other monetary assets.

Balance Sheets

The balance sheets show the Government's assets, liabilities, and net position. When combined with stewardship information, this information presents a more comprehensive understanding of the Government's financial position. The net position for funds from dedicated collections is shown separately.

Assets

Assets included on the balance sheets are resources of the Government that remain available to meet future needs. The most significant assets that are reported on the balance sheets are loans receivable, net; property, plant, and equipment (PP&E), net; inventories and related property, net; and cash and other monetary assets. There are, however, other significant resources available to the Government that extend beyond the assets presented in these balance sheets. Those resources include Stewardship Land and Heritage Assets in addition to the Government's sovereign powers to tax and set monetary policy.

Liabilities and Net Position

Liabilities are obligations of the Government resulting from prior actions that will require financial resources. The most significant liabilities reported on the balance sheets are federal debt securities held by the public and accrued interest, and federal employee and veteran benefits payable. Liabilities also include environmental and disposal liabilities, benefits due and payable, as well as insurance and guarantee program liabilities.

As with reported assets, the Government's responsibilities, policy commitments, and contingencies are much broader than these reported balance sheet liabilities. They include the social insurance programs reported in the Statements of Social Insurance and disclosed in the Required Supplementary Information (RSI)—Social Insurance section, fiscal long-term projections of non-interest spending reported in the Statement of Long-Term Fiscal Projections, and a wide range of other programs under which the Government provides benefits and services to the people of this Nation, as well as certain future loss contingencies.

The Government has entered into contractual commitments requiring the future use of financial resources and has unresolved contingencies where existing conditions, situations, or circumstances create uncertainty about future losses. Commitments and contingencies that do not meet the criteria for recognition as liabilities on the balance sheets, but for which there is at least a reasonable possibility that losses have been incurred, are disclosed in Note 19—Contingencies and Note 20—Commitments.

The collection of certain taxes and other revenue is credited to the corresponding funds from dedicated collections that will use these funds to meet a particular Government purpose. If the collections from taxes and other sources exceed the payments to the beneficiaries, the excess revenue is invested in Treasury securities or deposited in the General Fund; therefore, the trust fund balances do not represent cash. An explanation of the trust funds for social insurance is included in Note 21—Funds from Dedicated Collections. That note also contains information about trust fund receipts, disbursements, and assets.

Due to its sovereign power to tax and borrow, and the country's wide economic base, the Government has unique access to financial resources through generating tax revenues and issuing federal debt securities. This provides the Government with the ability to meet present obligations and those that are anticipated from future operations, and are not reflected in net position.

The net position is the residual difference between assets and liabilities and is the cumulative results of operations since inception. For detailed components that comprise the net position, refer to the section "Statement of Operations and Changes in Net Position."

SUSTAINABILITY FINANCIAL STATEMENTS

The sustainability financial statements comprise the Statement of Long-Term Fiscal Projections, covering all federal government programs, and the Statement of Social Insurance and the Statement of Changes in Social Insurance Amounts, covering social insurance programs (Social Security, Medicare, Railroad Retirement, and Black Lung programs). The sustainability financial statements are designed to illustrate the relationship between projected receipts and expenditures if current policy is continued over a 75 year time horizon. For this purpose, the projections assume that scheduled social insurance benefit payments would continue after related trust funds are projected to be exhausted, contrary to current law, and that debt could continue to rise indefinitely without severe economic consequences. The sustainability financial statements are intended to help citizens understand current policy and the importance and magnitude of policy reforms necessary to make it sustainable.

By accounting convention, the Statement of Social Insurance does not include projected general revenues that, under current law, would be used to finance the remainder of the expenditures in excess of revenues for Medicare Parts B and D reported in the Statement of Social Insurance. The Statement of Long-Term Fiscal Projections includes all revenues (including general revenues) of the federal government.

Statements of Long-Term Fiscal Projections

The new statement of Long-Term Fiscal Projections in 2015 is intended to assist readers of the government's financial statements in assessing the financial condition of the federal government and how the government's financial condition has changed (improved or deteriorated) during the year and may change in the future. It is also intended to assist readers in assessing whether future budgetary resources of the Government will likely be sufficient to sustain public services and to meet obligations as they come due, assuming that current policy for federal government public services and taxation is continued without change.

The Statements of Long-Term Fiscal Projections display the present value of 75-year projections by major category of the Federal Government's receipts and non-interest spending. These projections show the extent to which future receipts of the Government exceed or fall short of the Government's non-interest spending. The projections are presented both in terms of present value dollars and in terms of present value dollars as a percent of present value Gross Domestic Product (GDP). Unaudited fiscal year 2014 projections from last year's *Financial Report* are included for comparison. The projections are on the basis of policies currently in place and are neither forecasts nor predictions. These projections are consistent with the projections for Social Security and Medicare presented in the Statements of Social Insurance and are based on the same economic and demographic assumptions as underlie the Statements of Social Insurance. Note 24, Long-Term Fiscal Projections, further explains the methods used to prepare these projections and provides additional information such as the fiscal gap. Unaudited required supplementary information further assesses the sustainability of current fiscal policy and provides results based on alternative assumptions to those used in the basic statement.

As discussed further in Note 24, a sustainable policy is one where the ratio of debt held by the public to GDP (the debt-to-GDP ratio) is stable or declining over the long term. GDP measures the size of the Nation's economy in terms of the total value of all final goods and services that are produced in a year. Considering financial results relative to GDP is a useful indicator of the economy's capacity to sustain the Government's many programs.

Statements of Social Insurance and Changes in Social Insurance Amounts

The Statements of Social Insurance provide estimates of the status of the most significant social insurance programs: Social Security, Medicare, Railroad Retirement, and Black Lung. They are administered by the Social Security Administration (SSA), U.S. Department of Health and Human Services (HHS), the Railroad Retirement Board (RRB), and the Department of Labor (DOL), respectively. The estimates are actuarial present values[1] of the projections and are based on the economic and demographic assumptions representing the trustees' reasonable estimates as set forth in the relevant Social Security and Medicare trustees' reports as well as in the agency financial reports of HHS, SSA, and DOL (Black Lung) and in the relevant agency performance and accountability report for the RRB. The basis for the projections has changed since last year due to the enactment of the Medicare Access and CHIP Reauthorization Act (MACRA) of 2015. This law repealed the sustainable growth rate (SGR) formula that set physician fee schedule payments, which were usually modified and replaced it with specified payment updates for physicians. In last year's report, the income, expenditures, and assets for Medicare Part B reflected the *projected baseline* scenario, which assumed an override of the SGR payment provisions and an increase in the physician fee schedule equal to the average of the most recent 10 years of SGR overrides (through March 2015) or 0.6 percent. Since the new legislation has replaced the SGR system with specified payment updates for physicians, the projections in this year's report are based on the continuation of program provisions contained in current law, with one exception in regard to payment reductions that would result from the projected depletion of the Social Security and Medicare Hospital Insurance (Part A) Trust Funds; under current law, payments would be reduced to levels that could be covered by incoming tax and premium revenues when the Social Security and Medicare Hospital Insurance (Part A) Trust Funds are depleted.

The magnitude and complexity of social insurance programs, coupled with the extreme sensitivity of projections relating to the many assumptions of the programs, produce a wide range of possible results. In preparing the Statements of Social Insurance, Government management considers and selects assumptions and data that it believes provide a reasonable basis for the assertions in the statements. However, because of the large number of factors that affect the Statements of Social

---

[1] Present values recognize that a dollar paid or collected in the future is worth less than a dollar today, because a dollar today could be invested and earn interest. To calculate a present value, future amounts are thus reduced using an assumed interest rate, and those reduced amounts are summed.

Insurance plus the fact that such assumptions are inherently subject to substantial uncertainty (arising from the likelihood of future events, significant uncertainties, and contingencies), there will be differences between the estimates in the Statements of Social Insurance and the actual results, and those differences may be material. Note 23—Social Insurance describes the social insurance programs, reports long-range estimates that can be used to assess the financial condition of the programs, and explains some of the factors that impact the various programs. The Statements of Changes in Social Insurance Amounts reconcile the change between the current valuation period and the prior valuation period.

United States Government
Statement of Net Cost
for the Year Ended September 30, 2015

(In billions of dollars)	Gross Cost	Earned Revenue	Subtotal	(Gain)/Loss from Changes in Assumptions	Net Cost
Department of Health and Human Services	1,130.9	101.3	1,029.6	(0.1)	1,029.5
Social Security Administration	945.0	0.3	944.7	-	944.7
Department of Defense...	646.6	45.5	601.1	(27.5)	573.6
Interest on Treasury Securities Held by the Public	250.8	-	250.8	-	250.8
Department of Veterans Affairs....................................	186.9	4.8	182.1	(13.0)	169.1
Department of Agriculture...	147.7	9.1	138.6	-	138.6
Department of the Treasury...	146.0	29.3	116.7	-	116.7
Office of Personnel Management	104.9	20.3	84.6	17.1	101.7
Department of Transportation.......................................	76.1	0.8	75.3	-	75.3
Department of Energy...	76.5	4.6	71.9	-	71.9
Department of Homeland Security................................	60.2	12.1	48.1	4.1	52.2
Department of Labor...	45.8	-	45.8	-	45.8
Department of Education	71.3	26.6	44.7	-	44.7
Defense Security Cooperation Agency	38.8	-	38.8	-	38.8
Department of Housing and Urban Development	32.7	1.5	31.2	-	31.2
Department of Justice...	32.3	1.7	30.6	-	30.6
Department of State...	30.2	4.3	25.9	0.1	26.0
National Aeronautics and Space Administration.........	19.8	0.2	19.6	-	19.6
Department of the Interior...	19.2	2.7	16.5	-	16.5
Pension Benefit Guaranty Corporation	23.7	8.0	15.7	-	15.7
Railroad Retirement Board	10.3	3.4	12.9	-	12.9
U.S. Agency for International Development.................	12.7	0.1	12.6	-	12.6
Federal Communications Commission	9.6	0.3	9.3	-	9.3
Department of Commerce...	12.3	3.2	9.1	-	9.1
Environmental Protection Agency................................	9.3	0.7	8.6	-	8.6
National Science Foundation	7.0	-	7.0	-	7.0
U.S. Postal Service...	73.8	67.9	5.9	-	5.9
Millennium Challenge Corporation...............................	0.8	-	0.8	-	0.8
Smithsonian Institution...	0.8	-	0.8	-	0.8
U.S. Nuclear Regulatory Commission	1.0	0.8	0.2	-	0.2
Farm Credit System Insurance Corporation................	-	0.2	(0.2)	-	(0.2)
Overseas Private Investment Corporation	(0.1)	0.1	(0.2)	-	(0.2)
General Services Administration...................................	0.3	0.6	(0.3)	-	(0.3)
National Credit Union Administration	-	0.3	(0.3)	-	(0.3)
Securities and Exchange Commission	1.5	2.0	(0.5)	-	(0.5)
Small Business Administration.....................................	(0.5)	0.4	(0.9)	-	(0.9)
Tennessee Valley Authority	9.8	10.9	(1.1)	-	(1.1)
Export-Import Bank of the United States	(0.6)	1.3	(1.9)	-	(1.9)
Federal Deposit Insurance Corporation......................	(6.5)	8.6	(15.1)	-	(15.1)
All other entities	20.8	1.7	19.1	-	19.1
Total...	4,253.7	375.6	3,878.1	(19.3)	3,858.8

The accompanying notes are an integral part of these financial statements.

United States Government
Statement of Net Cost
for the Year Ended September 30, 2014

(In billions of dollars)	Gross Cost	Earned Revenue	Subtotal	(Gain)/Loss from Changes in Assumptions	Net Cost
Department of Health and Human Services	1,029.5	78.1	951.4	0.1	951.5
Social Security Administration	906.8	0.4	906.4	-	906.4
Department of Defense	716.9	61.5	655.4	6.9	662.3
Interest on Treasury Securities Held by the Public	260.0	-	260.0	-	260.0
Department of Veterans Affairs	207.4	4.3	203.1	(22.1)	181.0
Department of Agriculture	150.5	9.3	141.2	-	141.2
Department of the Treasury	182.9	79.9	103.0	-	103.0
Office of Personnel Management	85.3	19.5	65.8	21.3	87.1
Department of Transportation	77.2	0.9	76.3	-	76.3
Department of Energy	57.0	5.0	52.0	-	52.0
Department of Homeland Security	58.1	10.3	47.8	(1.3)	46.5
Department of Labor	53.6	-	53.6	-	53.6
Department of Education	80.9	24.8	56.1	-	56.1
Defense Security Cooperation Agency	34.9	-	34.9	-	34.9
Department of Housing and Urban Development	44.4	1.6	42.8	-	42.8
Department of Justice	33.0	1.7	31.3	-	31.3
Department of State	30.6	3.8	26.8	(1.4)	25.4
National Aeronautics and Space Administration	18.4	0.2	18.2	-	18.2
Department of the Interior	18.7	2.4	16.3	-	16.3
Pension Benefit Guaranty Corporation	38.5	11.2	27.3	-	27.3
Railroad Retirement Board	13.9	5.6	8.3	-	8.3
U.S. Agency for International Development	11.7	-	11.7	-	11.7
Federal Communications Commission	9.3	0.4	8.9	-	8.9
Department of Commerce	12.0	3.2	8.8	-	8.8
Environmental Protection Agency	8.9	0.5	8.4	-	8.4
National Science Foundation	7.2	-	7.2	-	7.2
U.S. Postal Service	73.6	66.9	6.7	-	6.7
Millennium Challenge Corporation	1.0	-	1.0	-	1.0
Smithsonian Institution	0.7	-	0.7	-	0.7
U.S. Nuclear Regulatory Commission	1.0	0.8	0.2	-	0.2
Farm Credit System Insurance Corporation	-	0.2	(0.2)	-	(0.2)
Overseas Private Investment Corporation	(0.3)	0.1	(0.4)	-	(0.4)
General Services Administration	0.7	0.6	0.1	-	0.1
National Credit Union Administration	(1.2)	0.1	(1.3)	-	(1.3)
Securities and Exchange Commission	1.4	1.9	(0.5)	-	(0.5)
Small Business Administration	(0.3)	0.4	(0.7)	-	(0.7)
Tennessee Valley Authority	10.5	11.1	(0.6)	-	(0.6)
Export-Import Bank of the United States	1.1	1.1	-	-	-
Federal Deposit Insurance Corporation	(4.4)	8.8	(13.2)	-	(13.2)
All other entities	20.0	1.3	18.7	-	18.7
Total	4,251.4	417.9	3,833.5	3.5	3,837.0

The accompanying notes are an integral part of these financial statements.

United States Government
Statement of Operations and Changes in Net Position
for the Year Ended September 30, 2015

(In billions of dollars)	Funds other than those from Dedicated Collections (Combined)	Funds from Dedicated Collections (Note 21) (Combined)	Eliminations	Consolidated
		2015		
Revenue (Note 17):				
Individual income tax and tax withholdings	1,521.1	1,024.1	-	2,545.2
Corporation income taxes	339.8	-	-	339.8
Excise taxes	44.2	57.5	-	101.7
Unemployment taxes...	-	49.1	-	49.1
Customs duties	33.6	-	-	33.6
Estate and gift taxes..	19.1	-	-	19.1
Other taxes and receipts	165.6	37.3	-	202.9
Miscellaneous earned revenues..........................	38.8	3.8	-	42.6
Intragovernmental interest..................................	-	108.4	(108.4)	-
Total Revenue..	2,162.2	1,280.2	(108.4)	3,334.0
Net Cost of Government Operations:				
Net cost...	2,300.4	1,558.4	-	3,858.8
Intragovernmental net cost.................................	(7.2)	7.2	-	-
Intragovernmental interest..................................	108.4	-	(108.4)	-
Total net cost..	2,401.6	1,565.6	(108.4)	3,858.8
Intragovernmental transfers...............................	(335.2)	335.2	-	-
Unmatched transactions and balances (Note 1.S)	5.1	-	-	5.1
Net operating (cost)/revenue..............................	(569.5)	49.8	-	(519.7)
Net position, beginning of period	(20,898.3)	3,197.6	-	(17,700.7)
Prior period adjustments–changes in accounting principles (Note 18 and 21)	(1.8)	0.3	-	(1.5)
Net operating (cost)/revenue..............................	(569.5)	49.8	-	(519.7)
Net position, end of period................................	(21,469.6)	3,247.7	-	(18,221.9)

The accompanying notes are an integral part of these financial statements.

United States Government
Statement of Operations and Changes in Net Position
for the Year Ended September 30, 2014

(In billions of dollars)	Funds other than those from Dedicated Collections (Combined)	Funds from Dedicated Collections (Note 21) (Combined)	Eliminations	Consolidated
		2014		
Revenue (Note 17):				
Individual income tax and tax withholdings	1,374.0	979.0	-	2,353.0
Corporation income taxes	317.8	-	-	317.8
Excise taxes	38.6	56.3	-	94.9
Unemployment taxes...	-	52.6	-	52.6
Customs duties	32.9	-	-	32.9
Estate and gift taxes...	19.3	-	-	19.3
Other taxes and receipts	125.8	50.8	-	176.6
Miscellaneous earned revenues..........................	14.0	5.0	-	19.0
Intragovernmental interest..................................	-	113.8	(113.8)	-
Total Revenue...	1,922.4	1,257.5	(113.8)	3,066.1
Net Cost of Government Operations:				
Net cost...	2,333.2	1,503.8	-	3,837.0
Intragovernmental interest..................................	113.8	-	(113.8)	-
Total net cost..	2,447.0	1,503.8	(113.8)	3,837.0
Intragovernmental transfers.............................	(299.9)	299.9	-	-
Unmatched transactions and balances (Note 1.S)	(20.4)	-	-	(20.4)
Net operating (cost)/revenue.............................	(844.9)	53.6	-	(791.3)
Net position, beginning of period	(20,053.0)	3,143.7	-	(16,909.3)
Prior period adjustments–changes in accounting principles (Note 18 and 21)	(0.4)	0.3	-	(0.1)
Net operating (cost)/revenue..............................	(844.9)	53.6	-	(791.3)
Net position, end of period.................................	(20,898.3)	3,197.6	-	(17,700.7)

The accompanying notes are an integral part of these financial statements.

United States Government
Reconciliations of Net Operating Cost and Unified Budget Deficit
for the Year Ended September 30, 2015, and 2014

(In billions of dollars)	2015	2014
Net operating cost	(519.7)	(791.3)
Components of net operating cost not part of the budget deficit:		
Increase/(Decrease) in liability for military employee benefits (Note 12):		
Military pension liabilities	(1.9)	40.9
Military health liabilities	(29.3)	12.9
Other military benefits	(1.7)	(0.9)
Liability for military employee benefits	(32.9)	52.9
Increase/(Decrease) in liability for veteran's compensation (Note 12)	11.5	32.3
Increase/(Decrease) in liabilities for civilian employee benefits (Note 12):		
Civilian pension liabilities	39.8	37.3
Civilian health liabilities	27.2	10.1
Other civilian benefits	1.1	1.7
Liabilities for civilian employee benefits	68.1	49.1
Increase/(Decrease) in environmental and disposal liabilities (Note 13):		
Energy's environmental and disposal liabilities	40.0	19.6
All others' environmental and disposal liabilities	2.5	0.4
Environmental and disposal liabilities	42.5	20.0
Property, plant, and equipment depreciation expense	54.5	67.7
Property, plant, and equipment disposals and revaluations	(15.6)	4.8
Increase/(Decrease) in benefits due and payable	22.3	17.3
Increase/(Decrease) in insurance and guarantee program liabilities	9.3	28.3
Increase/(Decrease) in other liabilities	38.6	7.3
(Increase)/Decrease in deposit fund balances	(19.1)	(0.8)
Increase/(Decrease) in accounts payable	(0.7)	2.8
(Increase)/Decrease in net accounts and taxes receivable	(13.8)	(0.8)
Agencies year-end upward/(downward) credit reform subsidy re-estimates	(2.3)	24.5
Unrealized Valuation Loss/(Gain) on investments in Government-Sponsored Enterprises (GSEs)	(10.5)	44.4
Components of the budget deficit not part of net operating cost:		
Capitalized property, plant, and equipment:		
Department of Defense	(24.9)	(27.7)
All other agencies	(29.6)	(26.4)
Total capitalized property, plant, and equipment	(54.5)	(54.1)
Effect of prior year agencies (upward)/downward credit reform subsidy re-estimates	(24.5)	(1.6)
(Increase)/Decrease in inventory	(2.2)	(7.3)
(Increase)/Decrease in debt and equity securities	11.0	(7.6)
(Increase)/Decrease in other assets	(2.9)	-
Credit reform and other loan activities	4.9	13.1
All other reconciling items	(2.9)	15.6
Unified budget deficit	(438.9)	(483.4)

The accompanying notes are an integral part of these financial statements.

United States Government
Statements of Changes in Cash Balance from Unified Budget and Other Activities
for the Years Ended September 30, 2015, and 2014

(In billions of dollars)	2015		2014	
Unified budget deficit	(438.9)		(483.4)	
Adjustments for Noncash Outlays Included in the budget:				
Interest accrued by Treasury on debt held by the public	245.4		255.5	
Agencies year-end credit reform subsidy re-estimates	26.8		(22.9)	
Subsidy (income) (Note 4)	(20.1)		(10.3)	
Subtotal		252.1		222.3
Items Affecting the Cash Balance Not Included in the budget:				
Net Transactions from financing activity:				
Borrowings from the public	7,037.5		7,475.8	
Repayment of debt held by the public	(6,700.6)		(6,672.0)	
Agency securities	0.1		(1.2)	
Deposit fund balances	20.5		0.3	
Effect of Uninvested principal from the Thrift Savings Plan (TSP) G Fund on Financing Activity	203.2		(119.9)	
Subtotal		560.7		683.0
Transactions from monetary and other activity:				
Interest paid by Treasury on debt held by the public	(243.5)		(252.9)	
Net loan receivable and equity investments activity	(102.2)		(104.3)	
Holdings of special drawing rights	(2.9)		(1.8)	
Other	14.9		(4.3)	
Subtotal		(333.7)		(363.3)
Cash and other monetary assets: (Note 2)				
Increase in Cash and other monetary assets		40.2		58.6
Balance, beginning of period		264.9		206.3
Balance, end of period		305.1		264.9

For budgetary purposes, the effect of the year-end downward re-estimates (reduction of net outlays) and upward re-estimates (increase of net outlays) is not recognized until the subsequent fiscal year.

The accompanying notes are an integral part of these financial statements.

United States Government
Balance Sheets
as of September 30, 2015, and 2014

(In billions of dollars)	2015	2014
Assets:		
Cash and other monetary assets (Note 2)	305.1	264.9
Accounts and taxes receivable, net (Note 3)	117.8	104.0
Loans receivable, net (Note 4)	1,216.0	1,125.7
Inventories and related property, net (Note 5)	320.6	318.4
Property, plant and equipment, net (Note 6)	893.9	878.3
Debt and equity securities (Note 7)	104.4	115.4
Investments in government-sponsored enterprises (Note 8)	106.3	95.8
Other assets (Note 9)	165.7	162.8
Total assets	3,229.8	3,065.3
Stewardship land and heritage assets (Note 25)		
Liabilities:		
Accounts payable (Note 10)	68.3	69.0
Federal debt securities held by the public and accrued interest (Note 11)	13,172.5	12,833.6
Federal employee and veteran benefits payable (Note 12)	6,719.3	6,672.6
Environmental and disposal liabilities (Note 13)	411.6	369.1
Benefits due and payable (Note 14)	213.9	191.6
Insurance and guarantee program liabilities (Note 15)	177.5	168.2
Loan guarantee liabilities (Note 4)	36.3	52.8
Other liabilities (Note 16)	652.3	409.1
Total liabilities	21,451.7	20,766.0
Contingencies (Note 19) and Commitments (Note 20)		
Net Position:		
Funds from Dedicated Collections (Note 21)	3,247.7	3,197.6
Funds other than those from Dedicated Collections	(21,469.6)	(20,898.3)
Total net position	(18,221.9)	(17,700.7)
Total liabilities and net position	3,229.8	3,065.3

The accompanying notes are an integral part of these financial statements.

United States Government
Statements of Long-Term Fiscal Projections (Note 24)
Present Value of 75 Year Projections as of September 30, 2015 and 2014[1]

	Dollars in Trillions			Percent of GDP[2]		
	2015	2014 (unaudited)	Change	2015	2014 (unaudited)	Change
Receipts:						
Social Security Payroll Taxes.......................	52.4	47.9	4.5	4.4	4.3	0.1
Medicare Payroll Taxes...............................	17.4	16.1	1.3	1.5	1.4	0.0
Individual Income Taxes.............................	127.8	117.1	10.7	10.7	10.5	0.2
Other Receipts...	43.5	42.5	1.1	3.6	3.8	(0.2)
Total Receipts...	241.2	223.6	17.6	20.2	20.0	0.1
Non-interest Spending:						
Social Security...	70.0	65.5	4.5	5.9	5.9	0.0
Medicare Part A[3].....................................	24.0	23.0	1.1	2.0	2.1	0.0
Medicare Parts B & D[4].............................	28.7	27.8	0.9	2.4	2.5	(0.1)
Medicaid..	27.3	26.0	1.3	2.3	2.3	0.0
Other Mandatory.......................................	36.8	31.1	5.7	3.1	2.8	0.3
Defense Discretionary...............................	28.6	26.9	1.6	2.4	2.4	0.0
Non-defense Discretionary.........................	30.0	28.1	1.8	2.5	2.5	0.0
Total Non-interest Spending.......................	245.3	228.4	17.0	20.5	20.4	0.1
Non-interest Spending less Receipts............	4.1	4.7	(0.6)	0.3	0.4	(0.1)

[1] 75-year present value projections for 2015 are as of 9/30/2015 for the period FY 2016-2090; projections for 2014 are as of 9/30/2014 for he period FY 2015-2089.

[2] The 75-year present value of nominal Gross Domestic Product (GDP), which drives the calculations above is $1,196.3 trillion starting in FY 2016, and was $1,117.2 trillion starting in FY 2015.

[3] Represents portions of Medicare supported by payroll taxes.

[4] Represents portions of Medicare supported by general revenues. Consistent with the President's Budget, outlays for Parts B & D are presented net of premiums.

Totals may not equal the sum of components due to rounding.

The accompanying notes are an integral part of these financial statements.

United States Government
Statements of Social Insurance (Note 23)
Present Value of Long-Range (75 Years, except Black Lung) Actuarial Projections

(In billions of dollars)	2015	2014	2013	2012	2011
Federal Old-age, Survivors and Disability Insurance (Social Security):[14]					
Revenue (Contributions and Dedicated Taxes) from:					
Participants who have attained eligibility age (age 62 and over)	1,166	984	908	847	726
Participants who have not attained eligibility age	27,791	25,391	24,591	22,703	20,734
Future participants	26,580	24,594	23,419	21,649	20,144
All current and future participants	55,537	50,969	48,918	45,198	41,603
Expenditures for Scheduled Future Benefits for:					
Participants who have attained eligibility age (age 62 and over)	(12,833)	(11,852)	(11,021)	(9,834)	(8,618)
Participants who have not attained eligibility age	(45,276)	(42,419)	(40,591)	(37,753)	(34,042)
Future participants	(10,867)	(10,028)	(9,600)	(8,890)	(8,100)
All current and future participants	(68,976)	(64,299)	(61,212)	(56,477)	(50,760)
Present value of future expenditures in excess of future revenue	(13,440)[1]	(13,330)[2]	(12,294)[3]	(11,278)[4]	(9,157)[5]
Federal Hospital Insurance (Medicare Part A):[14]					
Revenue (Contributions and Dedicated Taxes) from:					
Participants who have attained eligibility age (age 65 and over)	382	332	301	302	262
Participants who have not attained eligibility age	9,134	8,398	8,147	7,929	7,581
Future participants	8,386	7,812	7,744	7,367	7,260
All current and future participants	17,902	16,542	16,192	15,598	15,104
Expenditures for Scheduled Future Benefits for:					
Participants who have attained eligibility age (age 65 and over)	(3,803)	(3,484)	(3,422)	(3,369)	(2,023)
Participants who have not attained eligibility age	(14,494)	(14,117)	(14,629)	(14,919)	(12,887)
Future participants	(2,792)	(2,764)	(2,913)	(2,891)	(2,546)
All current and future participants	(21,089)	(20,365)	(20,964)	(21,179)	(18,356)
Present value of future expenditures in excess of future revenue	(3,187)[1]	(3,823)[2]	(4,772)[3]	(5,581)[4]	(3,252)[5]
Federal Supplementary Medical Insurance (Medicare Part B):[14]					
Revenue (Premiums) from:					
Participants who have attained eligibility age (age 65 and over)	898	763	701	635	570
Participants who have not attained eligibility age	4,633	4,548	4,073	3,826	3,651
Future participants	998	1,145	944	884	865
All current and future participants	6,529	6,456	5,718	5,344	5,086
Expenditures for Scheduled Future Benefits for:					
Participants who have attained eligibility age (age 65 and over)	(3,637)	(3,171)	(2,887)	(2,646)	(2,343)
Participants who have not attained eligibility age	(16,818)	(17,003)	(15,075)	(14,303)	(13,489)
Future participants	(3,540)	(4,137)	(3,415)	(3,211)	(3,108)
All current and future participants	(23,995)	(24,311)	(21,377)	(20,159)	(18,940)
Present value of future expenditures in excess of future revenue [6]	(17,466)[1]	(17,856)[2]	(15,659)[3]	(14,815)[4]	(13,854)[5]

Totals may not equal the sum of components due to rounding.

The accompanying notes are an integral part of these financial statements.

United States Government
Statements of Social Insurance (Note 23), continued
Present Value of Long-Range (75 Years, except Black Lung) Actuarial Projections

(In billions of dollars)	2015	2014	2013	2012	2011
Federal Supplementary Medical Insurance (Medicare Part D):[14]					
Revenue (Premiums and State Transfers) from:					
Participants who have attained eligibility age (age 65 and over)	251	209	184	179	173
Participants who have not attained eligibility age	1,814	1,596	1,491	1,510	1,608
Future participants...	804	703	665	661	703
All current and future participants..	2,869	2,508	2,340	2,349	2,484
Expenditures for Scheduled Future Benefits for:					
Participants who have attained eligibility age (age 65 and over)	(887)	(775)	(722)	(694)	(695)
Participants who have not attained eligibility age	(6,424)	(5,928)	(5,871)	(5,866)	(6,438)
Future participants...	(2,845)	(2,609)	(2,617)	(2,568)	(2,817)
All current and future participants..	(10,156)	(9,312)	(9,211)	(9,128)	(9,950)
Present value of future expenditures in excess of future revenue [6] ...	(7,287)[1]	(6,804)[2]	(6,871)[3]	(6,778)[4]	(7,466)[5]
Railroad Retirement:					
Revenue (Contributions and Dedicated Taxes) from:					
Participants who have attained eligibility	8	8	7	7	6
Participants who have not attained eligibility	66	63	60	56	46
Future participants...	79	78	79	78	65
All current and future participants..	153	149	146	141	117
Expenditures for Scheduled Future Benefits for:					
Participants who have attained eligibility	(131)	(126)	(123)	(119)	(109)
Participants who have not attained eligibility	(97)	(97)	(96)	(95)	(86)
Future participants...	(35)	(34)	(34)	(34)	(28)
All current and future participants..	(263)	(257)	(253)	(248)	(223)
Present value of future expenditures in excess of future revenue [7] ...	(110)[1]	(108)[2]	(107)[3]	(107)[4]	(106)[5]
Black Lung (Part C):					
Present value of future revenue in excess of future expenditures [8] ...	2 [9]	5 [10]	5 [11]	5 [12]	5 [13]
Total present value of future expenditures in excess of future revenue ...	(41,487)	(41,916)	(39,698)	(38,554)	(33,830)

Totals may not equal the sum of components due to rounding.

The accompanying notes are an integral part of these financial statements.

United States Government
Statements of Social Insurance (Note 23), continued
Present Value of Long-Range (75 Years, except Black Lung) Actuarial Projections

(In billions of dollars)	2015	2014	2013	2012	2011
Social Insurance Summary[14]					
Participants who have attained eligibility age:					
Revenue (e.g., contributions and dedicated taxes)	2,705	2,296	2,101	1,970	1,737
Expenditures for scheduled future benefits	(21,291)	(19,408)	(18,175)	(16,662)	(14,688)
Present value of future expenditures in excess of					
future revenue	(18,586)	(17,112)	(16,074)	(14,692)	(12,951)
Participants who have not attained eligibility age:					
Revenue (e.g., contributions and dedicated taxes)	43,438	39,996	38,362	36,024	33,620
Expenditures for scheduled future benefits	(83,109)	(79,564)	(76,262)	(72,936)	(66,942)
Present value of future expenditures in excess of					
future revenue	(39,671)	(39,568)	(37,900)	(36,912)	(33,322)
Closed-group - Total present value of future expenditures in					
excess of future revenue...	(58,257)	(56,680)	(53,974)	(51,604)	(46,272)
Future participants:					
Revenue (e.g., contributions and dedicated taxes)	36,847	34,332	32,851	30,639	29,037
Expenditures for scheduled future benefits	(20,077)	(19,567)	(18,575)	(17,589)	(16,594)
Present value of future revenue in excess of future					
expenditure	16,770	14,765	14,276	13,050	12,443
Open-group - Total present value of future expenditures in					
excess of future revenue...	(41,487)	(41,916)	(39,698)	(38,554)	(33,830)

[1] The projection period is 1/1/2015-12/31/2089 and the valuation date is 1/1/2015.
[2] The projection period is 1/1/2014-12/31/2088 and the valuation date is 1/1/2014.
[3] The projection period is 1/1/2013-12/31/2087 and the valuation date is 1/1/2013.
[4] The projection period is 1/1/2012-12/31/2086 and the valuation date is 1/1/2012.
[5] The projection period is 1/1/2011-12/31/2085 and the valuation date is 1/1/2011.
[6] These amounts represent the present value of the future transfers from the General Fund to the Supplementary Medical Insurance Trust Fund. These future intragovernmental transfers are included as income in both HHS' and the Centers for Medicare & Medicaid Services' Financial Reports but are not income from the governmentwide perspective of this report.
[7] These amounts do not include the present value of the financial interchange between the railroad retirement and social security systems, which is included as income in the Railroad Retirement Financial Report, but is not included from the governmentwide perspective of this report. (See discussion of Railroad Retirement Program in the unaudited required supplementary information section of this report).
[8] Does not include interest expense accruing on the outstanding debt.
[9] The projection period is 9/30/2015-9/30/2040 and the valuation date is 9/30/2015.
[10] The projection period is 9/30/2014-9/30/2040 and the valuation date is 9/30/2014.
[11] The projection period is 9/30/2013-9/30/2040 and the valuation date is 9/30/2013.
[12] The projection period is 9/30/2012-9/30/2040 and the valuation date is 9/30/2012.
[13] The projection period is 9/30/2011-9/30/2040 and the valuation date is 9/30/2011.
[14] Current participants for the Social Security and Medicare programs are assumed to be the "closed-group" of individuals who are at least 15 years of age at the start of the projection period, and are participating as either taxpayers, beneficiaries, or both.

Totals may not equal the sum of components due to rounding.

The accompanying notes are an integral part of these financial statements.

United States Government
Statement of Changes in Social Insurance Amounts
for the Year Ended September 30, 2015 (Note 23)

(In billions of dollars)	Social Security[1]	Medicare HI[1]	Medicare SMI[1]	Other[2]	Total
Net present value (NPV) of future revenue less future expenditures for current and future participants (the "open group") over the next 75 years, beginning of the year	(13,330)	(3,823)	(24,660)	(103)	(41,916)
Reasons for changes in the NPV during the year:					
Changes in valuation period	(560)	(202)	(1,094)	(2)	(1,858)
Changes in demographic data and assumptions	(103)	(35)	(108)	(3)	(249)
Changes in economic data and assumptions	(146)	-	-	-	(146)
Changes in law or policy	29	201	(253)	-	(23)
Changes in methodology and programmatic data	671	-	-	-	671
Changes in economic and other health care assumptions	-	755	2,466	-	3,221
Change in projection base	-	(83)	(1,104)	-	(1,187)
Net change in open group measure	(109)	636	(93)	(5)	429
Open group measure, end of year	(13,440)	(3,187)	(24,753)	(108)	(41,487)

Totals may not equal the sum of components due to rounding.

[1] Amounts represent changes between valuation dates 1/1/2014 and 1/1/2015.

[2] Includes Railroad Retirement changes between valuation dates 1/1/2014 and 1/1/2015 and Black Lung changes between 9/30/2014 and 9/30/2015.

The accompanying notes are an integral part of these financial statements.

United States Government
Statement of Changes in Social Insurance Amounts
for the Year Ended September 30, 2014 (Note 23)

(In billions of dollars)	Social Security[1]	Medicare HI[1]	Medicare SMI[1]	Other[2]	Total
Net present value (NPV) of future revenue less future expenditures for current and future participants (the "open group") over the next 75 years, beginning of the year	(12,294)	(4,772)	(22,530)	(102)	(39,698)
Reasons for changes in the NPV during the year:					
Changes in valuation period	(540)	(239)	(988)	(2)	(1,769)
Changes in demographic data and assumptions	235	(139)	(152)	2	(54)
Changes in economic data and assumptions	(604)	-	-	(1)	(605)
Changes in law or policy	(37)	108	(42)	-	29
Changes in methodology and programmatic data	(90)	-	-	-	(90)
Changes in economic and other health care assumptions	-	772	(1,090)	-	(318)
Change in projection base	-	447	142	-	589
Net change in open group measure	(1,036)	949	(2,130)	(1)	(2,218)
Open group measure, end of year	(13,330)	(3,823)	(24,660)	(103)	(41,916)

Totals may not equal the sum of components due to rounding.

[1] Amounts represent changes between valuation dates 1/1/2013 and 1/1/2014.

[2] Includes Railroad Retirement changes between valuation dates 1/1/2013 and 1/1/2014 and Black Lung changes between 9/30/2013 and 9/30/2014.

The accompanying notes are an integral part of these financial statements.

United States Government Notes to the Financial Statements for the Years Ended September 30, 2015, and 2014

Note 1. Summary of Significant Accounting Policies

A. Reporting Entity

This *Financial Report* includes the financial status and activities of the executive branch, the legislative branch, and the judicial branch of the government. The financial reporting period ends September 30 and is the same as used for the annual budget. The legislative and judicial branches are not required by law to submit financial statement information to Treasury; however, these branches provided cash and a significant amount of accrual basis financial information to include in the *Financial Report*. Appendix A of this report lists the organizations and agencies (entities) included in the U.S. Government's consolidated reporting entity for the *Financial Report,* as well as some entities not included in the reporting entity. Federal Accounting Standards Advisory Board's (FASAB) Statement of Federal Financial Accounting Concepts (SFFAC) No. 2, *Entity and Display*, provides criteria for determining which entities are included in the reporting entity. Such criteria are summarized in Appendix A. Also, as discussed further in Appendix A, certain entities are excluded from the *Financial Report* because they do not meet the criteria, such as the Thrift Savings Fund, or were specifically excluded from the consolidated reporting entity in accordance with SFFAC No. 2, such as the Board of Governors of the Federal Reserve System and bailout entities. Examples of bailout entities include the Federal Home Loan Mortgage Corporation (Freddie Mac) and Federal National Mortgage Association (Fannie Mae).

During fiscal year 2008, the government began a number of emergency economic measures relating to the economy that involved various financing programs. Key initiatives beginning in fiscal year 2008 involved programs concerning Fannie Mae and Freddie Mac (Government-Sponsored Enterprises [GSEs]), provision of a credit facility for GSEs and Federal Home Loan Banks, purchase of Mortgage-Backed Securities (MBSs) [see Note 1.H—Investments in Government-Sponsored Enterprises and Note 8—Investments in Government-Sponsored Enterprises].

Following U.S. Generally Accepted Accounting Principles (GAAP) for federal entities, the government has not consolidated into its financial statements the assets, liabilities, or results of operations of any financial organization or commercial entity in which Treasury holds either a direct, indirect, or beneficial equity investment. Even though some of the equity investments are significant, under SFFAC No. 2, these entities meet the criteria of paragraph 50 and do not appear in the federal budget section "Federal Programs by Agency and Account." As such, these entities are not consolidated into the financial reports of the government. However, the values of the investment in such entities are presented on the balance sheet.

Material intragovernmental transactions are eliminated in consolidation, except as described in the Other Information—Unmatched Transactions and Balances (see Note 1.S).

B. Basis of Accounting and Revenue Recognition

Consolidated Financial Statements

The consolidated financial statements of the Government were prepared using GAAP, primarily based on FASAB's Statement of Federal Financial Accounting Standards (SFFAS). The consolidated financial statements include accrual-based financial statements and sustainability financial statements, which are discussed in more detail below, and the related notes to the consolidated financial statements. Collectively, the accrual-based financial statements, the sustainability financial statements, and the notes represent basic information that is deemed essential for the financial statements and notes to be presented in conformity with GAAP.

Accrual-Based Financial Statements

The accrual-based financial statements were prepared under the following principles:

- Expenses are generally recognized when incurred.
- Non-exchange revenue, including taxes, duties, fines, and penalties, are recognized when collected and adjusted for the change in net measurable and legally collectible amounts receivable. Related refunds and other offsets, including those that are measurable and legally payable, are netted against non-exchange revenue.
- Exchange (earned) revenue is recognized when the government provides goods and services to the public for a price. Exchange revenue includes user charges such as admission to federal parks and premiums for certain federal insurance.

The basis of accounting used for budgetary purposes, which is primarily on a cash basis (unified budget deficit) and follows budgetary concepts and policies, differs from the basis of accounting used for the financial statements which follow U.S. GAAP. See the Reconciliations of Net Operating Cost and Unified Budget Deficit in the Financial Statements section.

Sustainability Financial Statements

The sustainability financial statements were prepared based on the projected present value of the estimated future revenue and estimated future expenditures, primarily on a cash basis, for a 75 year period. They include the Statement of Long-Term Fiscal Projections, covering all federal government programs, and the Statement of Social Insurance and the Statement of Changes in Social Insurance Amounts, covering social insurance programs (Social Security, Medicare, Railroad Retirement, and Black Lung programs). These estimates are based on economic as well as demographic assumptions presented in Notes 23 and 24. The sustainability financial statements are not forecasts or predictions. The sustainability financial statements are designed to illustrate the relationship between receipts and expenditures, if current policy is continued. For this purpose, the projections assume that scheduled social insurance benefit payments would continue after related trust funds are projected to be exhausted, contrary to current law, and that debt could continue to rise indefinitely without severe economic consequences.

By accounting convention, the Statement of Social Insurance does not include projected general revenues that, under current law, would be used to finance the remainder of the expenditures in excess of revenues for Medicare Parts B and D that is reported in the Statement of Social Insurance. The Statement of Long-Term Fiscal Projections includes all revenues (including general revenues) of the federal government.

New Standards Issued in Prior Years and Implemented in Current Year

Beginning in fiscal year 2015, the government implemented the requirements of new standards related to the reporting for: Deferred Maintenance and Repairs, Impairment of General Property, Plant, and Equipment Remaining in Use, and the presentation of Long-Term Projections as a basic financial statement. The new standards being implemented are:

- FASAB issued SFFAS No. 42, *Deferred Maintenance and Repairs, Amending SFFAS No. 6, 14, 29, and 32.* Among other things, SFFAS No. 42 replaces the definition, measurement, and reporting requirements for deferred maintenance and repairs established in SFFAS No. 6, *Accounting for Property, Plant, and Equipment* and rescinds the current governmentwide disclosures required for deferred maintenance established in SFFAS No. 32, *Consolidated Financial Report of the United States Government Requirements.* SFFAS No. 42 also requires the governmentwide financial statements to disclose as RSI a description of what constitutes deferred maintenance and repairs (DM&R) and how it was measured; amounts of DM&R for each major category of property, plant, and equipment; and a general reference to specific component entity reports for additional information.
- FASAB issued SFFAS No. 44, *Accounting for Impairment of General Property, Plant, and Equipment Remaining in Use* which provides accounting and reporting requirements for partial impairments of general property, plant, and

equipment (G-PP&E) remaining in use and construction work-in-process. SFFAS No. 44 requires description of what constitutes G-PP&E impairment, disclosure of related losses, and a reference to specific component entity reports for additional information.

- FASAB issued SFFAS No. 46, *Deferral of the Transition to Basic Information for Long-Term Projections; Amending SFFAS No. 36 and 45.* SFFAS No. 46 amends the effective date of the phased implementation first established in SFFAS No. 36, *Comprehensive Long-Term Projections for the U.S. Government* and later amended by SFFAS No. 45, *Deferral of the Transition to Basic Information for Long-Term Projections.* SFFAS No. 46 requires the presentation of the long-term projections for the government and related disclosures as basic information in fiscal year 2015.

New Standard Issued and Not Yet Implemented

FASAB issued the following new standard that is applicable to the *Financial Report*, but is not yet implemented at the governmentwide level for fiscal year 2015:

- In December 2014, FASAB issued SFFAS No. 47, *Reporting Entity.* SFFAS No. 47 establishes principles to identify organizations for which elected officials are accountable. The standard also guides preparers of general purpose federal financial reports in determining what organizations to report upon, whether such organizations are considered "consolidation entities" or "disclosure entities," and what information should be presented about those organizations. Generally, an organization is considered a consolidation entity if, based on assessment of the following characteristics as a whole, the organization: is financed through taxes and other non-exchange revenues, is governed by the Congress and/or President, imposes or may impose risks and rewards to the federal government, and provides goods and services on a non-market basis. A disclosure entity has a greater degree of autonomy with the federal government than a consolidation entity. To avoid obscuring information about these more autonomous organizations while still providing accountability, such organizations are to be disclosed rather than consolidated at the governmentwide level. The standard also requires information to be provided about related party relationships of such significance that it would be misleading to exclude information. SFFAS No. 47 is effective for periods beginning after September 30, 2017 and early implementation is not permitted.

C. Accounts and Taxes Receivable

Accounts receivable represent claims to cash or other assets from entities outside the government that arise from the sale of goods or services, duties, fines, certain license fees, recoveries, or other provisions of the law. Accounts receivable are reported net of an allowance for uncollectible amounts. An allowance is established when it is more likely than not the receivables will not be totally collected. The allowance method varies among the agencies in the government and is usually based on past collection experience and is re-estimated periodically as needed. Methods include statistical sampling of receivables, specific identification and intensive analysis of each case, aging methodologies, and percentage of total receivables based on historical collection.

Taxes receivable consist primarily of uncollected tax assessments, penalties, and interest when taxpayers have agreed or a court has determined the assessments are owed. Taxes receivable do not include unpaid assessments when taxpayers or a court have not agreed that the amounts are owed (compliance assessments) or the government does not expect further collections due to factors such as the taxpayer's death, bankruptcy, or insolvency (write-offs). Taxes receivable are reported net of an allowance for the estimated portion deemed to be uncollectible. The allowance for uncollectible amounts is based on projections of collectibles from a statistical sample of unpaid tax assessments.

D. Loans Receivable and Loan Guarantee Liabilities

Direct loans obligated and loan guarantees committed after fiscal year 1991 are reported based on the present value of the net cash flows estimated over the life of the loan or guarantee. The difference between the outstanding principal of the direct loans and the present value of their net cash inflows is recognized as a subsidy cost allowance. The present value of estimated net cash flows of the loan guarantees is recognized as a liability for loan guarantees.

The subsidy expense for direct or guaranteed loans disbursed during a fiscal year is the present value of estimated net cash flows for those loans or guarantees. A subsidy expense also is recognized for modifications made during the year to loans and guarantees outstanding and for re-estimates made as of the end of the fiscal year to the subsidy allowances or loan guarantee liability for loans and guarantees outstanding.

Direct loans obligated and loan guarantees committed before fiscal year 1992 are valued under two different methodologies within the government: the allowance-for-loss method and the present-value method. Under the allowance-for-loss method, the outstanding principal of direct loans is reduced by an allowance for uncollectible amounts; the liability for loan guarantees is the amount the agency estimates would more likely than not require future cash outflow to pay default claims. Under the present-value method, the outstanding principal of direct loans is reduced by an allowance equal to the difference between the outstanding principal and the present value of the expected net cash flows. The liability for loan guarantees is the present value of expected net cash outflows due to the loan guarantees.

E. Inventories and Related Property

Inventory is tangible personal property that is (1) held for sale, principally to federal agencies, (2) in the process of production for sale, or (3) to be consumed in the production of goods for sale or in the provision of services for a fee. SFFAS No. 3, *Accounting for Inventory and Related Property*, requires inventories held for sale and held in reserve for future sale within the government to be valued using either historical cost or latest acquisition cost (LAC). Historical cost methods include first-in-first-out, weighted average, and moving average. When LAC methods are used, the inventory is revalued periodically and an allowance account should be established for unrealized holding gains and losses.

The Department of Defense (DOD) values approximately 97 percent of resale inventory using the moving average cost method. Additionally, DOD reports the remaining 3 percent of resale inventories at an approximation of historical cost using latest acquisition cost adjusted for holding gains and losses to approximate the historical cost of resale inventory items remaining in its legacy system. The latest acquisition cost method is used because legacy inventory systems were designed for material management rather than accounting. Although these systems provide visibility and accountability over inventory items, they do not maintain historical cost data necessary to comply with SFFAS No. 3. DOD is continuing to transition inventories currently accounted for under the LAC methods, to be accounted for under the moving average cost methods. When using historical cost valuation, estimated repair costs reduce the value of inventory held for repair. Excess, obsolete, and unserviceable inventories are valued at estimated net realizable value. When LAC is used to value inventory held for sale, it is adjusted for holding gains and losses in order to approximate historical cost.

Related property includes commodities, seized monetary instruments, forfeited and foreclosed property, raw materials and work in process. Operating materials and supplies are valued at historical cost, LAC, and standard price using the purchase and consumption method of accounting. Operating materials and supplies that are valued at latest acquisition cost and standard pricing are not adjusted for holding gains and losses.

F. Property, Plant, and Equipment

Property, Plant and Equipment (PP&E) consists of tangible assets including buildings, equipment, construction in progress, internal use software, assets acquired through capital leases (including leasehold improvements), and other assets used to provide goods and services.

PP&E used in government operations are carried at acquisition cost, with the exception of some DOD equipment. In some instances, DOD equipment is valued at estimated historical costs, which are calculated using internal DOD records. To establish a baseline, DOD accumulated information relating to program funding and associated equipment, equipment useful life, program acquisitions, as well as disposals. The equipment baseline is updated using expenditure information and information related to acquisitions and disposals.

All PP&E is capitalized if the acquisition costs (or estimated acquisition cost for DOD) are in excess of capitalization thresholds that vary considerably between the federal entities. Depreciation and amortization expense applies to PP&E reported on the balance sheets except for land, unlimited duration land rights, and construction in progress. Depreciation and amortization are recognized using the straight-line method over the estimated useful lives of the assets. All PP&E are assigned useful lives depending on their category. The cost of acquisition, betterment, or reconstruction of all multi-use heritage assets is capitalized as general PP&E and is depreciated. Construction in progress is used for the accumulation of the cost of construction or major renovation of fixed assets during the construction period. The assets are transferred out of construction in progress when the project is substantially completed. Internal use software includes purchased commercial off-the-shelf software, contractor-developed software, and software internally developed.

SFFAS No. 44, *Accounting for Impairment of General Property, Plant and Equipment Remaining in Use*, requires the establishment of accounting and financial reporting standards for impairment of general PP& E remaining in use, except for internal use software. General PP&E is considered impaired when there is a significant and permanent decline in the service utility of PP& E or expected service utility for construction in progress and management has no reasonable expectation that the lost service utility will be replaced or restored. Existing processes and internal controls are expected to reasonably assure identification and communication of potential material impairments, such as those related to deferred maintenance and repairs.

For financial reporting purposes, other than multi-use heritage assets, stewardship assets are not recorded as part of PP&E. Stewardship Assets consist of public domain land (Stewardship Land) and Heritage Assets. Examples of stewardship land include national parks, wildlife refuges, national forests, and other lands of national and historical significance. Heritage assets include national monuments, and historical sites that among other characteristics are of historical, natural, cultural, educational, or artistic significance. Stewardship land and most heritage assets are considered priceless and irreplaceable, and as such they are measured in physical units with no financial value assigned to them. Some heritage assets have been designated as multi-use heritage assets, for example the White House, the predominant use of which is in government operations. For more details on stewardship assets, see Note 25—Stewardship Land and Heritage Assets.

G. Debt and Equity Securities

Debt and equity securities are classified as held-to-maturity, available-for-sale, and trading. Held-to-maturity debt and equity securities are reported at amortized cost, net of unamortized premiums and discounts. Available-for-sale debt and equity securities are reported at fair value. Trading debt and equity securities are reported at fair value.

H. Investments in Government-Sponsored Enterprises

The senior preferred stock and associated common stock warrants in GSEs are presented at their fair value. The annual valuation to estimate the asset's fair value incorporates various forecasts, projections, and cash flow analyses. These valuations are performed on the senior preferred stock and warrants and any changes in valuation, including impairment, are recorded and disclosed in accordance with SFFAS No. 7, *Accounting for Revenue and Other Financing Sources*. Since the valuation is an annual process, the changes in valuation of the senior preferred stock and warrants are deemed usual and recurring. Accordingly, changes in valuation are recorded as an exchange transaction which is either an expense or revenue. Since the costs of the senior preferred stock and warrants are reflected in exchange transactions, any change in valuation is also recorded as an exchange transaction.

The *Housing and Economic Recovery Act of 2008 (HERA)* established the Federal Housing Finance Agency (FHFA), which was created to enhance authority over the GSEs, and provide the Secretary of the Treasury with certain authorities to support the financial stability of the GSEs. In September 2008, Treasury entered into a Senior Preferred Stock Purchase Agreement (SPSPA) with each GSE. Based on U.S. GAAP, these commitments, predicated on the future occurrence of any stockholders' equity net deficits of the GSEs, at the end of any reporting quarter are potential liabilities of Treasury. The potential liabilities to the GSEs, if any, are assessed annually and recorded at the gross estimated amount. For more detailed information on investments in GSEs, refer to Note 8—Investments in Government-Sponsored Enterprises.

I. Federal Debt

Accrued interest on Treasury securities held by the public is recorded as an expense when incurred, instead of when paid. Certain Treasury securities are issued at a discount or premium. These discounts and premiums are amortized over the term of the security using an interest method for all long-term securities and the straight line method for short-term securities.

Treasury also issues Treasury Inflation-Protected Securities (TIPS). The principal for TIPS is adjusted daily over the life of the security based on the Consumer Price Index for all Urban Consumers (CPI-U).

J. Federal Employee and Veteran Benefits Payable

Generally, federal employee and veteran benefits payable are recorded during the time employee services are rendered. The related liabilities for defined benefit pension plans, veterans' compensation and burial benefits, post-retirement health benefits, and post-retirement life insurance benefits, are recorded at estimated present value of future benefits, less any estimated present value of future normal cost contributions. Normal cost is the portion of the actuarial present value of projected benefits allocated as an expense for employee services rendered in the current year. Actuarial gains and losses (as well as prior service cost, if any) are recognized immediately in the year they occur without amortization.

The Department of Veterans Affairs (VA) also provides certain veterans and/or their dependents with pension benefits, based on annual eligibility reviews, if the veteran died or was disabled for nonservice-related causes. The actuarial present value of the future liability for these VA pension benefits is a non-exchange transaction and is not required to be recorded on the Balance Sheet. These benefits are expenses when benefits are paid rather than when employee services are rendered.

The liabilities for Federal Employees' Compensation Act (workers compensation) benefits are recorded at estimated present value of future benefits for injuries and deaths that have already been incurred.

Gains and losses from changes in long-term assumptions used to estimate federal employee pensions, Other Retirement Benefits (ORB), and Other Postemployment Benefits (OPEB) liabilities are reflected separately on the Statement of Net Cost and the components of the expense related to federal employee pension, ORB, and OPEB liabilities are disclosed in Note 12—Federal Employee and Veteran Benefits Payable as prescribed by SFFAS No. 33. In addition, SFFAS No. 33 also provides a standard for selecting the discount rate assumption for present value estimates of federal employee pension, ORB, and OPEB liabilities.

K. Environmental and Disposal Liabilities

Environmental and disposal liabilities are recorded at the estimated current cost of removing, containing, treating, and/or disposing of radioactive waste, hazardous waste, chemical and nuclear weapons, as well as other environmental contaminations (including asbestos), assuming the use of current technology. Hazardous waste is a solid, liquid, or gaseous waste that, because of its quantity or concentration, presents a potential hazard to human health or the environment. Remediation consists of removal, decontamination, decommissioning, site restoration, site monitoring, closure as well as post-closure cost, treatment, and/or safe containment. Where technology does not exist to clean up radioactive or hazardous waste, only the estimable portion of the liability (typically monitoring and safe containment) is recorded.

L. Insurance and Guarantee Program Liabilities

Insurance and guarantee programs (such as Deposit Insurance Fund Program, Federal Crop Insurance Program and Benefit Pension Plans Program) provide protection to individuals or entities against specified risks except for those specifically covered by federal employee and veteran benefits, social insurance, and loan guarantee programs. Insurance and guarantee program funds are commonly held in revolving funds in the government and losses sustained by participants are paid from these funds. Many of these programs receive appropriations to pay excess claims and/or have authority to borrow from the Treasury. The values of insurance and guarantee program liabilities are particularly sensitive to changes in underlying estimates and assumptions. Insurance and guarantee programs with recognized liabilities in future periods (i.e., liabilities that extend beyond one year) are reported at their actuarial present value.

M. Deferred Maintenance and Repairs

Deferred maintenance and repairs are maintenance and repairs that were not performed when they should have been or scheduled maintenance and repairs that were delayed or postponed. Maintenance is the act of keeping fixed assets in acceptable condition, including preventative maintenance, normal repairs, and other activities needed to preserve the assets, so they continue to provide acceptable service and achieve their expected life. Maintenance and repairs exclude activities aimed at expanding the capacity of assets or otherwise upgrading them to serve needs different from those originally intended. Deferred maintenance and repairs expenses are not accrued in the Statements of Net Cost or recognized as liabilities on the Balance Sheet. However, deferred maintenance and repairs information is disclosed in the unaudited RSI section of this report. Please see unaudited RSI, Deferred Maintenance & Repairs for additional information including measurement methods.

N. Contingencies

Liabilities for contingencies are recognized on the Balance Sheet when both:
- A past transaction or event has occurred, and
- A future outflow or other sacrifice of resources is probable and measurable.

The estimated contingent liability may be a specific amount or a range of amounts. If some amount within the range is a better estimate than any other amount within the range, then that amount is recognized. If no amount within the range is a better estimate than any other amount, then the minimum amount in the range is recognized and the range is disclosed.

Contingent liabilities that do not meet the above criteria for recognition, but for which there is at least a reasonable possibility that a loss may be incurred, are disclosed in Note 19—Contingencies.

O. Commitments

In the normal course of business, the government has a number of unfulfilled commitments that may require the use of its financial resources. Note 20—Commitments describes the components of the government's actual commitments that are disclosed due to their nature and/or their amount. They include long-term leases, undelivered orders, and other commitments.

P. Social Insurance

A liability for social insurance programs (Social Security, Medicare, Railroad Retirement, Black Lung, and Unemployment) is recognized for any unpaid amounts currently due as of the reporting date. No liability is recognized for future benefit payments not yet due. For further information, see the unaudited RSI—Social Insurance section, and Note 23—Social Insurance.

Q. Funds from Dedicated Collections

Generally, funds from dedicated collections are financed by specifically identified revenues, provided to the government by non-federal sources, often supplemented by other financing sources that remain available over time. These specifically identified revenues and other financing sources are required by statute to be used for designated activities, benefits, or purposes, and must be accounted for separately from the government's general revenues. The three required criteria for a fund from dedicated collections are:
- A statute committing the government to use specifically identified revenues and/or other financing sources that are originally provided to the government by a non-federal source only for designated activities, benefits, or purposes;

- Explicit authority for the fund to retain revenues and/or other financing sources not used in the current period for future use to finance the designated activities, benefits, or purposes; and
- A requirement to account for and report on the receipt, use, and retention of the revenues and/or other financing sources that distinguishes the fund from the government's general revenues.

For more details on funds from dedicated collections, see Note 21—Funds from Dedicated Collections.

R. Related Party Transactions

Federal Reserve System

The Federal Reserve System (FR System) was created by Congress under the *Federal Reserve Act of 1913*. The FR System consists of the Federal Reserve Board of Governors (Board), the Federal Open Market Committee (FOMC), and the Federal Reserve Banks (FRBs). Collectively, the FR System serves as the nation's central bank and is responsible for formulating and conducting monetary policy, issuing and distributing currency (Federal Reserve Notes), supervising and regulating financial institutions, providing nationwide payments systems (including large-dollar transfers of funds, Automated Clearing House (ACH) operations, and check collection), providing certain financial services to federal agencies and fiscal principals, and serving as the U.S. government's bank. Monetary policy includes actions undertaken by the FR System that influence the availability and cost of money and credit as a means of helping to promote national economic goals. The FR System also conducts operations in foreign markets in order to counter disorderly conditions in exchange markets or to meet other needs specified by the FOMC to carry out its central bank responsibilities. The FR System is not included in the federal budget. It is considered an independent central bank, and its decisions are not ratified by the executive branch of the federal government.

The government interacts with the FRBs in a variety of ways, including the following:

- The FRBs serve as the government's fiscal agent and depositary, executing banking and other financial transactions on the government's behalf. The government reimburses the FRBs for these services, the cost of which is included on the Statements of Net Cost;
- The FRBs hold Treasury and other federal securities in the FRBs' System Open Market Account (SOMA) for the purpose of conducting monetary policy (Note 11—Federal Debt Securities Held by the Public and Accrued Interest);
- The FRBs hold gold certificates issued by the government in which the certificates are collateralized by gold (Note 2—Cash and Other Monetary Assets);
- The FRBs hold Special Drawing Rights (SDR) certificates issued by the government which are collateralized by SDRs (see Note 2—Cash and Other Monetary Assets); and,
- The FRBs are required by Board policy to transfer their excess earnings to the government, which are included in Other Taxes and Receipts on the Statements of Operations and Changes in Net Position.

The government also consults with the FR System on matters affecting the economy and certain financial stability activities (Note 4—Loans Receivable and Loan Guarantee Liabilities, Net). The above financial activities involving the government are accounted for and disclosed in the government consolidated financial statements. In accordance with SFFAC No. 2, *Entity and Display*, the FR System's assets, liabilities, and operations are not consolidated into the government's financial statements, and are, therefore, not a part of the reporting entity.

Federal Reserve System Structure

The Board is an independent organization governed by seven members who are appointed by the President and confirmed by the Senate. The full term of a Board member is 14 years, and the appointments are staggered so that one term expires on January 31 of each even-numbered year. The Board has a number of supervisory and regulatory responsibilities for institutions including, among others, state-chartered banks that are members of the FR System, bank holding companies, and savings and loan holding companies. In addition, the Board has general supervisory responsibilities for the 12 FRBs, and issues currency (Federal Reserve Notes) to the FRBs for distribution.

The FOMC is comprised of the seven Board members and five of the 12 FRB presidents, and is charged with formulating and conducting monetary policy primarily through open market operations (the purchase and sale of certain securities in the open market), the principal tool of national monetary policy. These operations affect the amount of reserve balances available to depository institutions, thereby influencing overall monetary and credit conditions. The 12 FRBs are chartered under the Federal Reserve Act, which requires each member bank to own the capital stock of its FRB. Supervision and control of each FRB is exercised by a board of directors, of which three are appointed by the Board of Governors of the FR System, and six are elected by their member banks.

The FRBs participate in formulating and conducting monetary policy, distribute currency and coin, and serve as fiscal agents for the government, other federal agencies, and fiscal principals. Additionally, the FRBs provide short-term loans to depository institutions and loans to participants in programs or facilities with broad-based eligibility in unusual and exigent circumstances when approved by the Board and the Treasury Secretary.

Federal Reserve System Assets and Liabilities

The FRBs hold Treasury and other securities in the SOMA for the purpose of conducting monetary policy. Treasury securities held by the FRBs totaled $1,845.3 billion and $1,919.4 billion at September 30, 2015 and 2014, respectively (Note 11—Federal Debt Securities Held by the Public and Accrued Interest). These assets are generally subject to the same market (principally interest-rate) and credit risks as other financial instruments. In the open market, the FR System purchases and sells Treasury securities as a mechanism for controlling the money supply.

The FRBs have deposit liabilities with Treasury and depository institutions. The FRBs issue Federal Reserve Notes, the circulating currency of the United States, which are collateralized by the Treasury securities and other assets held by the FRBs. Financial and other information concerning the FR System, including financial statements for the Board and the FRBs, may be obtained at http://www.federalreserve.gov.

FRB Residual Earnings Transferred to the Government

FRBs generate income from interest earned on securities, reimbursable services provided to federal agencies, and the provision of priced services to depository institutions, as specified by the *Monetary Control Act of 1980*. Although the FRBs generate earnings from carrying out open market operations (via the earnings on securities held in the SOMA account), their execution of these operations is for the purpose of accomplishing monetary policy rather than generating earnings. Each FRB is required by Board policy to transfer to the government its residual (or excess) earnings, after providing for the cost of operations, payment of dividends, and reservation of an amount necessary to equate surplus with paid-in capital. These residual earnings may vary due to, among other things, changes in the SOMA balance levels that may occur in conducting monetary policy. In the event of losses, or a substantial increase in capital, a FRB will suspend its payments to the U.S. Treasury until such losses or increases in capital are recovered through subsequent earnings. The FRB residual earnings of $96.5 billion and $99.2 billion for fiscal years ended September 30, 2015 and 2014, respectively, are reported as other taxes and receipts on the Statements of Operations and Changes in Net Position. Accounts and taxes receivables, net, includes a receivable for FRB's residual earnings which represents the earnings due to the General Fund as of September 30, but not collected by the General Fund until after the end of the month. As of September 30, 2015 and 2014, interest receivable on FRB's residual earnings are $0.3 billion and $1.7 billion, respectively (Note 3—Accounts and Taxes Receivables, Net).

Other Related Parties

The federal government, through the Federal Housing Finance Agency (FHFA) is the conservator for Fannie Mae and Freddie Mac. See Note 8—Investments in Government-Sponsored Enterprises.

The Secretary of Transportation has possession of two long term notes with the National Railroad Passenger Service Corporation (more commonly referred to as Amtrak). The first note is for $4 billion and matures in 2975 and the second note is for $1.1 billion and matures in 2082 with renewable 99 year terms. Interest is not accruing on these notes as long as the current financial structure of Amtrak remains unchanged. If the financial structure of Amtrak changes, both principal and accrued interest are due and payable. The Department of Transportation (DOT) does not record the notes in its financial statements since the notes, with maturity dates of 2975 and 2082, are considered fully uncollectible due to the lengthy terms and Amtrak's history of operating losses.

In addition, DOT has possession of all the preferred stock shares (109.4 million) of Amtrak. Congress, through DOT, has continued to fund Amtrak since approximately 1972; originally through grants, then, beginning in 1981, through the purchase of preferred stock, and then through grants again after 1997. The *Amtrak Reform and Accountability Act of 1997* changed the structure of the preferred stock by rescinding the voting rights with respect to the election of the Board of Directors and by eliminating the preferred stock's liquidation preference over the common stock. The Act also eliminated further issuance to DOT of preferred stock. DOT does not record the Amtrak preferred stock in its financial statements because, under the Corporation's current financial structure, the preferred shares do not have a liquidation preference over the common shares, the preferred shares do not have any voting rights, and dividends are neither declared nor in arrears.

In general, Amtrak is not a department, agency, or instrumentality of the government or DOT. However, the United States Supreme Court has held that, for the purposes of assessing certain constitutional issues, Amtrak is a governmental entity. The nine members of Amtrak's Board of Directors are appointed by the President and are subject to confirmation by the United States Senate. Once appointed, board members, as a whole, act independently without the consent of the government or any of its officers to set Amtrak policy, determine its budget, and decide operational issues. The Secretary of Transportation is statutorily appointed to the nine member board. Traditionally, the Secretary of Transportation has designated the FRA Administrator to represent the Secretary at Board meetings.

The Export-Import Bank of the United States (Ex-Im Bank) has contractual agreements with the Private Export Funding Corporation (PEFCO). PEFCO, which is owned by a consortium of private-sector banks, industrial companies, and financial services institutions, makes medium-term and long-term fixed-rate and variable-rate loans to foreign borrowers to purchase U.S.-made equipment when such loans are not available from traditional private sector lenders on competitive terms. Ex-Im Bank's credit and guarantee agreement with PEFCO extends through December 31, 2020. Through its contractual agreements with PEFCO, Ex-Im Bank exercises a broad measure of supervision over PEFCO's major financial management decisions, including approval of both the terms of individual loan commitments and the terms of PEFCO's long-term debt issues, and is entitled to representation at all meetings of PEFCO's board of directors, advisory board, and its exporters' council.

The contractual agreements provide that Ex-Im Bank will (1) guarantee the due and punctual payment of principal, as well as interest on export loans made by PEFCO and (2) guarantee the due and punctual payment of interest on PEFCO's long-term secured debt obligations when requested by PEFCO. Related to the amounts for Ex-Im Bank as shown in Note 4 - Loans Receivable and Loan Guarantee Liabilities, Net, these guarantees to PEFCO, aggregating $12.6 billion and $10.0 billion at September 30, 2015, and 2014, respectively, are included within the principal amounts guaranteed by the United States. The allowance related to these transactions is included within the guaranteed loan liability. Ex-Im Bank received fees for the agreements totaling $0.03 billion and $0.04 billion for fiscal years 2015 and 2014, respectively, which are included as earned revenue on the Statements of Net Cost.

S. Unmatched Transactions and Balances

The reconciliation of the change in net position requires that the difference between ending and beginning net position equals the difference between revenue and cost, plus or minus prior-period adjustments.

The unmatched transactions and balances are needed to bring the change in net position into balance. The primary factors affecting this out of balance situation are:
- Unmatched intragovernmental transactions and balances between federal agencies; and
- Errors and restatements in federal agencies' reporting.

Refer to the Other Information (unaudited) —Unmatched Transactions and Balances for detailed information.

T. Reclassifications

The fiscal year 2014 amounts related to the Troubled Asset Relief Program (TARP) direct loans and equity investments are no longer presented as a separate line on the Balance Sheet or separate note disclosure. For fiscal year 2015, TARP is included in the loans receivable line on the balance sheet and the all other programs line in the Note 4. Loans Receivable and Loan Guarantee Liabilities.

Certain amounts were reclassified in fiscal year 2015 and affect the fiscal year 2014 Statement of Net Cost. For fiscal year 2015, as stated in Appendix A of this report, the Foreign Military Financing Program and Foreign Military Sales Program were consolidated to create the Defense Security Cooperation Agency (DSCA). These two entities were previously identified as additional entities in Appendix A, but as a consolidated entity, DSCA is now being reported as a significant entity. As a result, DSCA is now separately identified on the Statement of Net Cost and its consolidated fiscal year 2014 net cost amounts were reclassified out of "All other entities."

U. Restatements

There were no material restatements to fiscal year 2014 reported amounts.

V. Fiduciary Activities

Fiduciary activities are the collection or receipt, as well as the management, protection, accounting, investment and disposition by the government of cash or other assets in which non-federal individuals or entities have an ownership interest that the government must uphold. Fiduciary cash and other fiduciary assets are not assets of the government and are not recognized on the Balance Sheet. See Note 22—Fiduciary Activities, for further information.

W. Use of Estimates

The government has made certain estimates and assumptions relating to the reporting of assets, liabilities, revenues, expenses, and the disclosure of contingent liabilities to prepare these financial statements. There are a large number of factors that affect these assumptions and estimates, which are inherently subject to substantial uncertainty arising from the likelihood of future changes in general economic, regulatory, and market conditions. As such, actual results will differ from these estimates and such differences may be material.

Significant transactions subject to estimates include loans and credit program receivables, federal employee and veteran benefits payable, credit reform subsidy costs, investments in GSEs, and other non-federal securities and related impairment, tax receivables, loan guarantees, depreciation, imputed costs, other actuarial liabilities, cost and earned revenue allocations, as well as contingencies and any related recognized liabilities.

The government recognizes the sensitivity of credit reform modeling to slight changes in some model assumptions and uses regular review of model factors, statistical modeling, and annual re-estimates to reflect the most accurate cost of the credit programs to the U.S. Government. *Federal Credit Reform Act of 1990* (FCRA) loan receivables and loan guarantees are disclosed in Note 4—Loans Receivable and Loan Guarantee Liabilities, Net.

The forecasted future cash flows used to determine credit reform amounts are sensitive to slight changes in model assumptions, such as general economic conditions, specific stock price volatility of the entities in which the government has an equity interest, estimates of expected default, and prepayment rates. Therefore, forecasts of future financial results have inherent uncertainty.

The GSE senior preferred stock purchase agreements (SPSPAs) provide that the government will fund the GSEs, if needed at the end of any quarter. The FHFA, acting as the conservator, determines whether the liabilities of either GSE, individually, exceed its respective assets. The annual valuation performed as of September 30 on the preferred stock and warrants comprising the Investments in GSEs line item on the Balance Sheets incorporates various forecasts, projections, and cash flow analyses to develop an estimate of the asset's fair value. A key input into the investment valuation for the senior preferred stock is the present value of the projected quarterly dividend payments, and a key input for the warrants is the market value of the shares of common stock of the GSEs which are traded on the over-the-counter (OTC) Bulletin Board. Treasury performs annual calculations, as of September 30, to assess the need for recording an estimated liability in accordance with SFFAS No. 5, *Accounting for Liabilities of The Federal Government,* related to the government's funding commitment to the GSEs under the SPSPAs. As part of the fiscal year 2015 assessment process, Treasury used 25-year financial forecasts prepared through year 2040 and 2039 in assessing if a contingent liability was required as of September 30, 2015 and 2014, respectively, to determine the implied amount of total liability. For more detailed information on investments in GSEs and the amended SPSPAs, see Note 8—Investments in Government-Sponsored Enterprises.

The government offers its employees' pension and other post-employment retirement benefits, as well as life and health insurance. The Office of Personnel Management administers the largest civilian plan and the Department of Defense and Department of Veterans Affairs administer the military plans. Generally the benefits payable are recorded during the time employee services are rendered. The related liabilities for defined benefit pension plans, veterans' compensation and burial benefits, post-retirement health benefits, life insurance benefits, and *Federal Employees' Compensation Act* benefits are recorded at estimated present value of future benefits, less any estimated present value of future normal cost contributions. See Note—12 Federal Employee and Veteran Benefits Payable for additional information.

X. Credit Risk

Credit risk is the potential, no matter how remote, for financial loss from a failure of a borrower or counterparty to perform in accordance with underlying contractual obligations. The government takes on credit risk when it makes direct loans or guarantees to non-federal entities, provides credits to foreign entities, or becomes exposed to institutions which engage in financial transactions with foreign countries.

The government also takes on credit risk related to committed, but undisbursed direct loans, funding commitments to GSEs, guarantee of money market funds, and other activities. These activities generally focus on the underlying problems in the credit markets. These programs were developed to provide credit where borrowers are not able to get access to credit with reasonable terms and conditions. Because these programs attempt to correct for a market imperfection, it can expose the Government to potential costs and losses. The extent of the risk assumed is described in more detail in the notes to the financial statements, and where applicable, is factored into credit reform models and reflected in fair value measurements.

Note 2. Cash and Other Monetary Assets

Cash and Other Monetary Assets as of September 30, 2015, and 2014

(In billions of dollars)	2015	2014
Unrestricted cash:		
Cash held by Treasury for governmentwide operations	193.3	153.2
Other	6.6	7.2
Restricted	26.1	21.5
Total cash	226.0	181.9
International monetary assets	58.5	66.0
Gold and silver	11.1	11.1
Foreign currency	9.5	5.9
Total cash and other monetary assets	305.1	264.9

Unrestricted cash includes cash held by Treasury for governmentwide operations (Operating Cash) and all other unrestricted cash held by the federal agencies. Operating Cash represents balances from tax collections, other revenue, federal debt receipts, and other various receipts net of cash outflows for budget outlays and other payments. Treasury checks outstanding are netted against Operating Cash until they are cleared by the Federal Reserve System. Other unrestricted cash not included in Treasury's Operating Cash balance includes balances representing cash, cash equivalents, and other funds held by agencies, such as undeposited collections, deposits in transit, demand deposits, amounts held in trust, and imprest funds. Operating Cash held by the Treasury increased by $40.1 billion (an increase of approximately 26 percent) in fiscal year 2015 due to Treasury's investment and borrowing decisions to manage the balance and timing of the Government's cash position.

Restrictions on cash are due to the imposition on cash deposits by law, regulation, or agreement. Restricted cash is primarily composed of cash held by the DSCA. The Foreign Military Sales Program - DSCA included $23.9 billion and $20.5 billion as of September 30, 2015, and 2014, respectively.

International monetary assets include the U.S. reserve position in the International Monetary Fund (IMF) and U.S. holdings of Special Drawing Rights (SDRs). The U.S. reserve position in the IMF is an interest-bearing claim on the IMF that includes the reserve asset portion of the financial subscription that the United States has paid in as part of its participation in the IMF as well as any amounts drawn by the IMF from a letter of credit made available by the United States as part of its financial subscription to the IMF. The IMF promotes international monetary cooperation and a stable payments system to facilitate growth in the world economy. Its primary activities are surveillance of members' economies, financial assistance, as appropriate, and technical assistance.

Only a portion of the U.S. financial subscription to the IMF is made in the form of reserve assets; the remainder is provided in the form of a letter of credit from the United States to the IMF. The balance available under the letter of credit totaled $49.6 billion and $47.6 billion as of September 30, 2015, and 2014 respectively. The U.S. reserve position in the IMF has a U.S. dollar equivalent of $9.4 billion and $14.7 billion as of September 30, 2015, and 2014, respectively.

The SDR is an international reserve asset created by the IMF to supplement the existing reserve assets of its members. These interest-bearing assets can be obtained by IMF allocations, transactions with IMF member countries, or in the form of interest earnings on SDR holdings and reserve positions in the IMF. U.S. SDR holdings are an interest-bearing asset of Treasury's Exchange Stabilization Fund (ESF). The total amount of SDR holdings of the United States was the equivalent of $50.3 billion and $53.2 billion as of September 30, 2015, and 2014, respectively.

The IMF allocates SDRs to its members in proportion to each member's quota in the IMF. *The SDR Act*, enacted in 1968, authorized the Secretary of the Treasury to issue SDR Certificates (SDRCs) to the Federal Reserve in exchange for dollars. The amount of SDRCs outstanding cannot exceed the dollar value of SDR holdings. The Secretary of the Treasury determines when Treasury will issue or redeem SDRCs. SDRCs outstanding totaled $5.2 billion as of September 30, 2015, and 2014, and are included in Note 16—Other Liabilities.

As of September 30, 2015, and 2014, other liabilities included $49.6 billion and $52.4 billion of interest-bearing liability to the IMF for SDR allocations. The SDR allocation item represents the cumulative total of SDRs distributed by the IMF to the United States in allocations. The United States has received no SDR allocations since 2009.

Gold is valued at the statutory price of $42.2222 per fine troy ounce. The number of fine troy ounces of gold was 261,498,927 as of September 30, 2015, and 2014. The market value of gold on the London Fixing was $1,114 and $1,217 per fine troy ounce as of September 30, 2015, and 2014, respectively. In addition, silver is valued at the statutory price of $1.2929 per fine troy ounce. The number of fine troy ounces of silver was 16,000,000 as of September 30, 2015, and 2014. The market value of silver on the London Fixing was $14.65 and $17.11 per fine troy ounce as of September 30, 2015, and 2014, respectively. Gold totaling $11.0 billion as of September 30, 2015, and 2014, was pledged as collateral for gold certificates issued and authorized to the FRBs by the Secretary of the Treasury. Gold certificates were valued at $11.0 billion as of September 30, 2015, and 2014, which are included in Note 16—Other Liabilities. Treasury may redeem the gold certificates at any time. Foreign currency is translated into U.S. dollars at the exchange rate at fiscal year-end. The foreign currency is maintained by the ESF and various U.S. federal agencies as well as foreign banks.

Note 3. Accounts and Taxes Receivable, Net

Accounts and Taxes Receivable as of September 30, 2015, and 2014

(In billions of dollars)	2015	2014
Accounts receivable:		
Gross accounts receivable	100.9	87.0
Allowance for uncollectible amounts	(27.4)	(26.0)
Accounts receivable, net	73.5	61.0
Taxes receivable:		
Gross taxes receivable	177.4	161.7
Allowance for uncollectible amounts	(133.1)	(118.7)
Taxes receivable, net	44.3	43.0
Total accounts and taxes receivable, net	117.8	104.0

Gross accounts receivable include related interest receivable of $3.7 billion and $5.0 billion as of September 30, 2015, and 2014, respectively.

Treasury comprises approximately 35.7 percent of the Government's reported accounts and taxes receivable, net, as of September 30, 2015. Refer to the financial statements of the Department of the Treasury, the Department of Health and Human Services, the Social Security Administration, the Department of Defense, the Department of Homeland Security, the Pension Benefit Guaranty Corporation, the Federal Communications Commission, the Department of Energy, the Federal Deposit Insurance Corporation, the Department of Veterans Affairs, and the Department of Labor for details on gross accounts and taxes receivable and the related allowance for uncollectible amounts. These agencies comprise 91.0 percent of the Government's accounts and taxes receivable, net, of $117.8 billion as of September 30, 2015.

Note 4. Loans Receivable and Loan Guarantee Liabilities, Net

Direct Loan and Defaulted Guaranteed Loan Programs as of September 30, 2015, and 2014

(In billions of dollars)	Face Value of Loans Outstanding		Long-term Cost of (Income from) Direct Loans and Defaulted Guaranteed Loans Outstanding		Loans Receivable, Net		Subsidy Expense (Income) for the Fiscal Year	
	2015	2014	2015	2014	2015	2014	2015	2014
Federal Direct Student Loans - Education	845.1	731.2	(35.5)	(47.4)	880.6	778.6	(0.9)	8.1
Federal Family Education Loans - Education	132.2	139.8	(2.5)	(3.1)	134.7	142.9	0.4	(2.0)
Electric Loans - USDA	47.9	51.2	2.0	2.2	45.9	49.0	(0.4)	(0.1)
Rural Housing Services - USDA	32.2	31.9	3.5	3.6	28.7	28.3	0.1	0.2
Export-Import Bank Loans	24.1	22.9	2.6	3.4	21.5	19.5	(0.3)	(0.5)
Housing and Urban Development Loans	23.1	18.1	6.9	5.5	16.2	12.6	(3.1)	(0.6)
Water and Environmental Loans - USDA	12.6	12.0	0.2	0.3	12.4	12.3	(0.1)	0.1
International Monetary Fund Program - Treasury	11.7	16.2	1.0	0.7	10.7	15.5	0.3	0.2
All other programs	81.7	84.7	16.4	17.7	65.3	67.0	1.5	(0.8)
Total direct loans and defaulted guaranteed loans	1,210.6	1,108.6	(5.4)	(17.1)	1,216.0	1,125.7	(2.5)	4.6

Loan Guarantees as of September 30, 2015, and 2014

(In billions of dollars)	Principal Amount of Loans Under Guarantee		Principal Amount Guaranteed by the United States		Loan Guarantee Liabilities		Subsidy Expense (Income) for the Fiscal Year	
	2015	2014	2015	2014	2015	2014	2015	2014
Federal Housing Administration Loans - HUD	1,292.1	1,290.6	1,178.1	1,185.7	16.1	33.5	(13.6)	(10.5)
Veterans Housing Benefit Programs - VA	453.9	389.3	117.4	101.5	9.9	8.9	0.5	0.4
Rural Housing Services - USDA ..	113.2	102.9	101.9	92.6	4.8	4.5	1.0	0.7
Small Business Loans - SBA	105.7	99.0	88.3	83.5	1.7	2.0	(1.3)	(1.3)
Export-Import Bank Guarantees ..	72.2	78.1	72.2	78.1	1.4	1.6	(0.2)	(0.3)
Israel Loan Guarantee Program - AID	10.5	10.5	10.5	10.5	1.0	1.0	-	-
Federal Family Education Loans - Education	219.7	241.6	215.1	236.5	-	-	(4.3)	(4.6)
All other guaranteed loan programs	45.5	42.8	40.4	38.3	1.4	1.3	0.3	0.7
Total loan guarantees	2,312.8	2,254.8	1,823.9	1,826.7	36.3	52.8	(17.6)	(14.9)

The Government has two types of loan programs: direct loans and loan guarantees. One major type of loan is direct loans such as the Department of Education's (Education) Federal Direct Student Loans. The second type is loan guarantee programs, such as the Department of Housing and Urban Development's (HUD's) Federal Housing Administration Loans program.

Direct loans and loan guarantee programs are used to promote the Nation's welfare by making financing available to segments of the population not served adequately by non-federal institutions, or otherwise providing for certain activities or investments. For those unable to afford credit at the market rate, federal credit programs provide subsidies in the form of direct loans offered at an interest rate lower than the market rate. For those to whom non-federal financial institutions are reluctant to grant credit because of the high risk involved, federal credit programs guarantee the payment of these non-federal loans and absorb the cost of defaults.

The amount of the long-term cost of post-1991 direct loans and loan guarantees outstanding equals the subsidy cost allowance for direct loans and the liability for loan guarantees as of September 30. The amount of the long-term cost of pre-1992 direct loans and loan guarantees equals the allowance for uncollectible amounts (or present value allowance) for direct loans and the liability for loan guarantees. The long-term cost is based on all direct loans and guaranteed loans disbursed in this fiscal year and previous years that are outstanding as of September 30. It includes the subsidy cost of these loans and guarantees estimated as of the time of loan disbursement and subsequent adjustments such as modifications, re-estimates, amortizations, and write-offs.

Net loans receivable includes related interest and foreclosed property. Foreclosed property is property that is transferred from borrowers to a federal credit program, through foreclosure or other means, in partial or full settlement of post-1991 direct loans or as a compensation for losses that the Government sustained under post-1991 loan guarantees. Please refer to the financial statements of the United States Department of Agriculture (USDA), VA, and HUD for significant detailed information regarding foreclosed property. The total subsidy expense/(income) is the cost of direct loans and loan guarantees recognized during the fiscal year. It consists of the subsidy expense/(income) incurred for direct and guaranteed loans disbursed during the fiscal year, for modifications made during the fiscal year of loans and guarantees outstanding, and for upward or downward re-estimates as of the end of the fiscal year of the cost of loans and guarantees outstanding. This expense/(income) is included in the Statements of Net Cost.

Loan Programs

The majority of the loan programs are provided by Education, HUD, USDA, Treasury, Small Business Administration (SBA), VA, Export-Import Bank and United States Agency for International Development (USAID). For significant detailed information regarding the direct and guaranteed loan programs listed in the tables above, please refer to the financial statements of the agencies.

Education has two major loan programs, authorized by Title IV of the *Higher Education Act of 1965 (HEA)*. The first program is the William D. Ford Federal Direct Student Loan Program, (referred to as the Direct Loan Program) that was established in fiscal year 1994. The Direct Loan Program offers four types of educational loans: Stafford, Unsubsidized Stafford, PLUS for parents and/or graduate or professional students, and consolidation loans. With this program, the Government makes loans directly to students and parents through participating institutions of higher education. Direct loans are originated and serviced through contracts with private vendors. Education disbursed approximately $142.2 billion in Direct Loans to eligible borrowers in fiscal year 2015 and approximately $134.0 billion in fiscal year 2014. The second program is the Federal Family Education Loan (FFEL) Program. This program was established in fiscal year 1965, and is a guaranteed loan program. Like the Direct Loan Program, it offers four types of loans: Stafford, Unsubsidized Stafford, PLUS for parents and/or graduate or professional students, and consolidation loans. The *Student Aid and Fiscal Responsibility Act (SAFRA)*, which was enacted as part of the *Health Care Education and Reconciliation Act of 2010* (Public Law 111-152), eliminated the authority to guarantee new FFEL after June 30, 2010. During fiscal year 2015, Education net loans receivable increased by $102.0 billion, largely the result of increased Direct Loan Program disbursements for new loan originations and FFEL consolidations, net of borrower principal and interest collections.

HUD's Federal Housing Administration (FHA) provides mortgage insurance to encourage lenders to make credit available to expand home ownership. FHA serves many borrowers that the conventional market does not serve adequately. This includes first-time homebuyers, minorities, low-income, and other underserved households to realize the benefits of home ownership. Borrowers obtain an FHA insured mortgage and pay an upfront premium as well as an annual premium to FHA. The proceeds from those premiums are used to fund FHA program costs, including claims on defaulted mortgages and holding costs, property management fees, property sales, and other associated costs.

In 2009, Congress passed the *Supplemental Appropriations Act of 2009* which authorized an increase in the U.S. quota in the IMF, as well as an increase in U.S. participation in the New Arrangements to Borrow, one of the IMF's supplemental borrowing arrangements. The legislation applied FCRA to both program increases and, thus, the program increases are treated as direct loans to the IMF.

USDA offers direct and guaranteed loans through credit programs in the Farm and Foreign Agricultural Services (FFAS) mission area through the Farm Service Agency (FSA), and the Commodity Credit Corporation (CCC), and in the Rural Development (RD) mission area. The FFAS delivers commodity, credit, conservation, disaster, and emergency assistance programs that help strengthen and stabilize the agricultural economy. The FSA offers direct and guaranteed loans to farmers who are temporarily unable to obtain private, commercial credit. Through this supervised credit offered by FSA, the goal is to graduate its borrowers to commercial credit. The CCC offers both credit guarantee and direct credit programs for buyers of U.S. exports, suppliers, and sovereign countries in need of food assistance. The RD provides affordable housing and essential community facilities to rural communities through its rural housing loan and grant programs. The Rural Utilities Program helps to improve the quality of life in rural America through a variety of loan programs for electric energy, telecommunications, and water and environmental projects.

The Export-Import Bank aids in financing and promoting U.S. exports. Loans and guarantees extended under the medium-term loan program typically have repayment terms of one to seven years, while loans and guarantees extended under the long-term loan program usually have repayment terms in excess of seven years. Generally, both the medium-term and long-term loan and guarantee programs cover up to 85 percent of the U.S. contract value of shipped goods.

The SBA provides guarantees that help small businesses obtain bank loans and licensed companies to make investments in qualifying small businesses. The SBA also makes loans to microloan intermediaries and provides a direct loan program that assists homeowners, renters and businesses to recover from disasters.

VA operates the following direct loan and loan guaranty programs: Vocational Rehabilitation and Employment, Home Loans, and Insurance. The VA Home Loans program is the largest of the VA loan programs. The Home Loans program provides loan guarantees and direct loans to veterans, service members, qualifying dependents, and limited non-veterans to purchase homes and retain homeownership with favorable market terms. During fiscal year 2015, the VA principal amount of loans under guarantee increased by $64.6 billion. This increase was primarily due to new loans under guarantee with a principal totaling $134.3 billion, partially offset by guaranteed loan terminations with a principal amount of $69.7 billion.

USAID's Israel Loan Guarantee Program guarantees the repayment of loans made from commercial sources that cover the costs for immigrants resettling to Israel from the former Soviet Union, Ethiopia, and other countries. As of fiscal year 2015, $6.8 billion in loan guarantees remains outstanding. The program also guarantees the repayment of loans that support

Israel's comprehensive economic plan to overcome economic difficulties and create conditions for higher and sustainable growth, of which $3.7 billion in loan guarantees remains outstanding as of September 30, 2015.

Note 5. Inventories and Related Property, Net

Inventories and Related Property, Net as of September 30, 2015, and 2014

(In billions of dollars)	Defense	All Others	Total	Defense	All Others	Total
		2015			2014	
Inventory purchased for resale	61.3	0.4	61.7	63.2	0.4	63.6
Inventory and operating material and supplies held for repair	79.6	1.5	81.1	60.8	1.4	62.2
Inventory—excess, obsolete, and unserviceable	1.4	-	1.4	0.5	-	0.5
Operating materials and supplies held for use	121.9	3.5	125.4	138.5	3.5	142.0
Operating materials and supplies held in reserve for future use	-	0.2	0.2	-	0.2	0.2
Operating materials and supplies-excess, obsolete, and unserviceable	2.0	-	2.0	2.4	-	2.4
Stockpile materials	0.4	52.8	53.2	0.3	50.8	51.1
Stockpile materials held for sale	-	-	-	0.2	0.1	0.3
Other related property	1.5	1.1	2.6	1.5	1.1	2.6
Allowance for loss	(6.4)	(0.6)	(7.0)	(5.9)	(0.6)	(6.5)
Total inventories and related property, net	261.7	58.9	320.6	261.5	56.9	318.4

Inventory purchased for resale is the cost or value of tangible personal property purchased by an agency for resale. As of September 30, 2015, DOD values approximately 97 percent of its resale inventory using the moving average cost (MAC) method. DOD reports the remaining 3 percent of resale inventories at an approximation of historical cost using LAC adjusted for holding gains and losses. The LAC method is used because DOD's legacy inventory systems do not maintain historical cost data. DOD improved its capability to distinguish between held for use and held for repair for operating materials and supplies which resulted in a major increase for inventory and operating material and supplies held for repair, and a decrease for operating materials and supplies held for use for fiscal year 2015. Please refer to the individual financial statements of DOD for significant detailed information regarding its inventories.

Inventory and operating materials and supplies held for repair are damaged inventory that require repair to make them suitable for sale (inventory) or is more economical to repair than to dispose of (operating materials and supplies). Excess, obsolete, and unserviceable inventory is reported at net realizable value. Inventory—excess, obsolete, and unserviceable consists of:

- Excess inventory that exceeds the demand expected in the normal course of operations and which does not meet management's criteria to be held in reserve for future sale.
- Obsolete inventory that is no longer needed due to changes in technology, laws, customs, or operations.
- Unserviceable inventory that is damaged beyond economic repair.

Operating materials and supplies held for use are tangible personal property to be consumed in normal operations. Operating materials and supplies held in reserve for future use are materials retained because they are not readily available in the market or because they will not be used in the normal course of operations, but there is more than a remote chance they will eventually be needed. DOD, which accounts for most of the reported operating materials and supplies held for use, uses LAC, MAC, and Standard Price and expenses a significant amount when purchased instead of when consumed.

Operating materials and supplies—excess, obsolete, and unserviceable consists of:

- Excess operating materials and supplies are materials that exceed the demand expected in the normal course of operations, and do not meet management's criteria to be held in reserve for future use.
- Obsolete operating materials and supplies are materials no longer needed due to changes in technology, laws, customs, or operations.
- Unserviceable operating materials and supplies are materials damaged beyond economic repair.

DOD, which accounts for most of the reported excess, obsolete, and unserviceable operating materials and supplies, revalues it to a net realizable value of zero through the allowance account. Please refer to the individual financial statements of DOD for significant detailed information regarding operating materials and supplies. Stockpile materials include strategic and critical materials held in reserve for use in national defense, conservation, or national emergencies due to statutory requirements; for example, nuclear materials and oil, as well as stockpile materials that are authorized to be sold. The majority of the amount reported by DOD is stockpile materials held for sale. The amount reported by others is stockpile materials held in reserve, with the majority of it being reported by the Department of Energy (DOE). Please refer to their financial statements for more information on stockpile materials.

Other related property consists of the following:

- Commodities include items of commerce or trade that have an exchange value used to stabilize or support market prices. Please refer to the financial statements of the USDA for detailed information regarding commodities.
- Seized monetary instruments are comprised only of monetary instruments that are awaiting judgment to determine ownership. The related liability is included in other liabilities. Other property seized by the Government, such as real property and tangible personal property, is not considered a Government asset. It is accounted for in agency property-management records until the property is forfeited, returned, or otherwise liquidated. Please refer to the financial statements of the Department of Justice (DOJ), Treasury, and the Department of Homeland Security (DHS) for detailed information regarding seized property.
- Forfeited property is comprised of monetary instruments, intangible property, real property, and tangible personal property acquired through forfeiture proceedings; property acquired by the Government to satisfy a tax liability; and/or unclaimed/abandoned merchandise. Please refer to the financial statements of DOJ, Treasury, and DHS for detailed information regarding forfeited property.
- Foreclosed property is comprised of assets received in satisfaction of a loan receivable or as a result of payment of a claim under a guaranteed or insured loan (excluding commodities acquired under price support programs). All properties included in foreclosed property are assumed to be held for sale. Please refer to the financial statements of USDA and HUD for detailed information regarding foreclosed property.

Note 6. Property, Plant, and Equipment, Net

Property, Plant, and Equipment as of September 30, 2015

(In billions of dollars)	Cost		Accumulated Depreciation/ Amortization		Net	
	Defense	All Others	Defense	All Others	Defense	All Others
Buildings, structures, and facilities	283.2	268.1	137.0	144.0	146.2	124.1
Furniture, fixtures, and equipment	1,010.6	169.6	584.0	110.0	426.6	59.6
Construction in progress	41.8	43.3	N/A	N/A	41.8	43.3
Land	10.9	12.8	N/A	N/A	10.9	12.8
Internal use software	12.0	32.6	8.4	19.5	3.6	13.1
Assets under capital lease	0.4	3.4	0.2	1.7	0.2	1.7
Leasehold improvements	0.5	9.9	0.2	5.7	0.3	4.2
Other property, plant, and equipment	0.4	10.3	-	5.2	0.4	5.1
Subtotal	1,359.8	550.0	729.8	286.1	630.0	263.9
Total property, plant, and equipment, net		1,909.8		1,015.9		893.9

Property, Plant, and Equipment as of September 30, 2014

(In billions of dollars)	Cost		Accumulated Depreciation/ Amortization		Net	
	Defense	All Others	Defense	All Others	Defense	All Others
Buildings, structures, and facilities	271.7	259.2	130.7	137.3	141.0	121.9
Furniture, fixtures, and equipment	992.0	166.2	571.6	105.4	420.4	60.8
Construction in progress	42.1	41.3	N/A	N/A	42.1	41.3
Land	10.8	12.6	N/A	N/A	10.8	12.6
Internal use software	11.8	28.5	8.4	16.4	3.4	12.1
Assets under capital lease	0.6	3.3	0.5	1.7	0.1	1.6
Leasehold improvements	0.5	9.4	0.2	5.0	0.3	4.4
Other property, plant, and equipment	0.8	9.5	-	4.8	0.8	4.7
Subtotal	1,330.3	530.0	711.4	270.6	618.9	259.4
Total property, plant, and equipment, net		1,860.3		982.0		878.3

See Note 25—Stewardship Land and Heritage Assets for additional information on multi-use heritage assets.

DOD comprises approximately 70.6 percent of the Government's reported property, plant, and equipment, net, as of September 30, 2015. Refer to the financial statements of DOD, DOE, the Tennessee Valley Authority (TVA), GSA, VA, the Department of the Interior (DOI), DHS, and the Department of State (DOS), for detailed information on the useful lives and related capitalization thresholds for property, plant, and equipment. These agencies comprise 90.8 percent of the Government's reported property, plant, and equipment net of $893.9 billion as of September 30, 2015.

Note 7. Debt and Equity Securities

Debt and Equity Securities as of September 30, 2015

(In billions of dollars)	Held-To-Maturity			Available-for-Sale			Trading Securities			
	Cost Basis	Unamortized Premium/ Discount	Net Invest-ment	Cost Basis	Unrealized Gain (Loss)	Fair Value	Cost Basis	Unrealized Gain (Loss)	Fair Value	Total
Debt Securities:										
Non-U.S. Government............	0.1	-	0.1	12.4	(0.7)	11.7	10.9	(0.8)	10.1	21.9
Corporate and other bonds....	-	-	-	-	-	-	11.3	-	11.3	11.3
Mortgage/asset backed..........	0.2	-	0.2	-	-	-	3.6	-	3.6	3.8
Commercial.............................	-	-	-	-	-	-	0.2	-	0.2	0.2
All other debt securities..........	-	-	-	-	-	-	3.5	-	3.5	3.5
Equity Securities:										
Unit trust................................	-	-	-	-	-	-	17.4	3.8	21.2	21.2
Common stocks......................	-	-	-	-	-	-	1.3	0.3	1.6	1.6
All other equity securities.......	0.1	-	0.1	-	-	-	2.5	(0.4)	2.1	2.2
Other......................................	3.7	-	3.7	-	-	-	11.1	0.4	11.5	15.2
Total debt and securities categorized as held-to-maturity, available-for-sale or trading.......................................	4.1	-	4.1	12.4	(0.7)	11.7	61.8	3.3	65.1	80.9
Total RRB debt and equity securities.................................										23.5
Total debt and equity securities.................................										104.4

Debt and Equity Securities as of September 30, 2014

| (In billions of dollars) | Held-To-Maturity | | | Available-for-Sale | | | Trading Securities | | | |
	Cost Basis	Unamortized Premium/ Discount	Net Investment	Cost Basis	Unrealized Gain (Loss)	Fair Value	Cost Basis	Unrealized Gain (Loss)	Fair Value	Total
Debt securities:										
Non-U.S. Government	0.2	-	0.2	19.0	(1.1)	17.9	11.4	(0.1)	11.3	29.4
Corporate and other bonds	-	-	-	-	-	-	10.6	0.6	11.2	11.2
Mortgage/asset backed	0.3	-	0.3	-	-	-	3.0	-	3.0	3.3
All other debt securities	-	-	-	-	-	-	2.6	(0.1)	2.5	2.5
Equity securities:										
Unit trust	-	-	-	-	-	-	15.3	5.7	21.0	21.0
Common stocks	-	-	-	-	-	-	2.0	0.6	2.6	2.6
All other equity securities	0.1	-	0.1	-	-	-	2.3	(0.2)	2.1	2.2
Other	3.6	-	3.6	-	-	-	14.2	0.2	14.4	18.0
Total debt and equity securities categorized as held-to-maturity, available-for-sale or trading	4.2	-	4.2	19.0	(1.1)	17.9	61.4	6.7	68.1	90.2
Total RRB debt and equity securities										25.2
Total debt and equity securities										115.4

Debt and Equity Securities as of September 30, 2015, and 2014

(In billions of dollars)	By Agency	
	2015	2014
Pension Benefit Guaranty Corporation	55.7	58.0
Railroad Retirement Board	23.5	25.2
Department of the Treasury	11.7	17.9
Tennessee Valley Authority	9.2	10.0
All other	4.3	4.3
Total securities and investments	104.4	115.4

These debt and equity securities do not include nonmarketable Treasury securities, which have been eliminated in consolidation. Held-to-maturity debt and equity securities are reported at amortized cost, net of unamortized discounts and premiums. Available-for-sale debt and equity securities are reported at fair value. Trading debt and equity securities are reported at fair value. The Pension Benefit Guaranty Corporation (PBGC) and the TVA invest primarily in fixed maturity and equity securities, classified as trading. PBGC reported gains related to trading securities still held as of September 30, 2015 and September 30, 2014 of $3.5 billion and $1.2 billion, respectively. TVA reported losses related to trading securities still held as of September 30, 2015 and September 2014 of $0.2 billion and $0.3 billion, respectively. Treasury invests primarily in fixed maturity and equity securities, classified as available-for-sale securities. Treasury's Exchange Stabilization Fund invests primarily in foreign fixed maturity debt, with a fair value of $11.7 billion and $17.9 billion as of September 30, 2015, and 2014, respectively. The National Railroad Retirement Investment Trust (NRRIT), on behalf of the RRB, manages and invests railroad retirement assets that are to be used to pay retirement benefits to the Nation's railroad workers under the Railroad Retirement Program. As an investment company, NRRIT is subject to different accounting standards that do not require the classifications presented above. NRRIT's total debt and equity securities are presented as a separate line item. Please refer to NRRIT's financial statements for more detailed information concerning this specific investment. The TVA balance includes $6.9 billion and $7.6 billion as of September 30, 2015, and 2014, respectively, for the Tennessee Valley Authority Retirement System. PBGC, NRRIT, Treasury and TVA base market values on the last sale of a listed security, on the mean of the "bid-and-ask" for nonlisted securities, or on a valuation model in the case of fixed income securities that are not actively traded. These valuations are determined as of the end of each fiscal year. Purchases and sales of securities are recorded on the trade date. Please refer to the individual financial statements of PBGC, NRRIT, Treasury, and TVA for more detailed information related to debt and equity securities. These agencies comprise 95.9 percent of the total reported debt and equity securities of $104.4 billion as of September 30, 2015.

Note 8. Investments in Government-Sponsored Enterprises

Congress established Fannie Mae and Freddie Mac as GSEs to support mortgage lending. A key function of the GSEs is to purchase mortgages and package those mortgages into securities, which are subsequently sold to investors, and guarantee the timely payment of principal and interest on these securities.

Leading up to the financial crisis, increasingly difficult conditions in the housing market challenged the soundness and profitability of the GSEs, thereby threatening to undermine the entire housing market. This led Congress to pass the HERA. This Act created the FHFA, with enhanced regulatory authority over the GSEs, and provided the Secretary of the Treasury with certain authorities intended to ensure the financial stability of the GSEs, if necessary. In September 2008, FHFA placed the GSEs under conservatorship and Treasury entered into a SPSPA with each GSE. These actions were taken to preserve the GSEs' assets, ensure a sound and solvent financial condition, and mitigate systemic risks that contributed to market instability.

The actions taken by Treasury, as authorized by section 1117 of HERA, thus far are temporary and are intended to provide financial stability. The purpose of Treasury's actions is to maintain the solvency of the GSEs so they can continue to fulfill their vital roles in the home mortgage market while the Administration and Congress determine what structural changes should be made to the housing finance system. Draws under the SPSPAs are designed to enable the GSEs to maintain a positive net worth. The SPSPAs were structured to ensure any draws result in an increased investment in the GSEs as further discussed below. Per SFFAC No. 2, *Entity and Display*, these entities meet the criteria of "bailed out" entities. Accordingly, the government has not consolidated them into the financial statements, but included disclosure of the relationship(s) with the bailed out entities and any actual or potential material costs or liabilities in the consolidated financial statements.

Senior Preferred Stock Purchase Agreements

Under the SPSPAs, Treasury initially received from each GSE: 1) 1,000,000 shares of non-voting variable liquidation preference senior preferred stock with a liquidation preference value of $1,000 per share and 2) a non-transferable warrant for the purchase, at a nominal cost, of 79.9 percent of common stock on a fully-diluted basis. The warrants expire on September 7, 2028. Under the August 2012 amendments to the SPSPAs, the quarterly dividend payment changed from a 10.0 percent per annum fixed rate dividend to an amount equivalent to the GSE's positive net worth above a capital reserve amount. The capital reserve amount was initially set at $3.0 billion for calendar year 2013, declined to $2.4 billion on January 1, 2014, and $1.8 billion on January 1, 2015, and will continue to decline by $600 million at the beginning of each calendar year until it reaches zero by calendar year 2018. The GSEs will not pay a quarterly dividend if their positive net worth is below the required capital reserve threshold.

Cash dividends of $20.4 billion and $72.5 billion were received during fiscal years ended September 30, 2015, and 2014, respectively. Dividends received in fiscal year 2014 were primarily attributable to a federal income tax benefit that was recognized in the earnings of one GSE in fiscal year 2014.

The SPSPAs, which have no expiration date, provide that Treasury will disburse funds to the GSEs if at the end of any quarter, the FHFA determines that the liabilities of either GSE exceed its assets. The maximum amount available to each GSE under this agreement was previously based on a formulaic cap which ended December 31, 2012, at which time, the maximum amount became fixed. Draws against the funding commitment of the SPSPAs do not result in the issuance of additional shares of senior preferred stock; instead the liquidation preference of the initial 1,000,000 shares is increased by the amount of the draw. There were no payments to the GSEs for the fiscal years ended September 30, 2015 and 2014.

Senior Preferred Stock and Warrants for Common Stock

In determining the fair value of the senior preferred stock and warrants for common stock, Treasury relied on the GSEs' public filings and press releases concerning their financial statements, as well as non-public, long-term financial forecasts, monthly summaries, quarterly credit supplements, independent research regarding preferred stock trading, independent research regarding the GSEs' common stock trading on the OTC Bulletin Board, discussions with each of the GSEs and FHFA, and other information pertinent to the fair valuations. Because of the nature of the senior preferred stock and warrants, which are not publicly traded and for which there is no comparable trading information available, the fair valuations rely on significant unobservable inputs that reflect assumptions about the expectations that market participants would use in pricing.

The fair value of the senior preferred stock considers the amount of forecasted dividend payments. The fair valuations assume that a hypothetical buyer would acquire the discounted dividend stream as of the transaction date. The fair value of the senior preferred stock increased at September 30, 2015 when compared to 2014 primarily reflecting higher forecasted

GSE earnings derived from guarantee fees, lower volatility and risk in the mortgage lending industry, and lower forecasted mortgage loan losses due to reduced credit risk assumed by the GSEs.

The fair value of the warrants is impacted by the nominal exercise price and the large number of potential exercise shares, the market trading of the common stock that underlies the warrants as of September 30, the principal market, and the market participants. Other factors impacting the fair value include, among other things, the holding period risk related directly to the assumption of the amount of time that it will take to sell the exercised shares without depressing the market. The fair value of the warrants increased at the end of fiscal year 2015 when compared to 2014 primarily due to increases in the market price of the underlying common stock of each GSE.

Contingent Liability to GSEs

As part of the annual process undertaken by Treasury, a series of long-term financial forecasts are prepared to assess as of September 30, the likelihood and magnitude of future draws to be required by the GSEs under the SPSPAs within the forecast time horizon. Treasury used 25-year financial forecasts prepared through 2040 and 2039 in assessing if a contingent liability was required as of September 30, 2015 and 2014, respectively. If future payments under the SPSPAs are deemed to be probable within the forecast time horizon, Treasury will estimate and accrue a contingent liability to the GSEs to reflect the forecasted equity deficits of the GSEs. This accrued contingent liability will be undiscounted and will not take into account any of the offsetting dividends that could be received, as the dividends, if any, would be owed directly to the General Fund. Such recorded accruals will be adjusted in subsequent years as new information develops or circumstances change.

Based on the annual assessment, Treasury estimated no probable future funding draws as of September 30, 2015 and 2014, and thereby accrued no contingent liability. As of September 30, 2015 and 2014, the maximum remaining contractual commitment to the GSEs for the remaining life of the SPSPAs was $258.1 billion. Refer to Note 20-Commitments for a full description of other commitments and risks.

Estimation Factors

Treasury's forecasts concerning the GSEs may differ from actual experience. Estimated senior preferred values and future draw amounts will depend on numerous factors that are difficult to predict including, but not limited to, changes in government policy with respect to the GSEs, the business cycle, inflation, home prices, unemployment rates, interest rates, changes in housing preferences, home financing alternatives, availability of debt financing, market rates of guarantee fees, outcomes of loan refinancings and modifications, new housing programs, and other applicable factors.

Regulatory Environment

To date, Congress has not approved a plan to address the future of the GSEs, and thus the GSEs continue to operate under the direction of their conservator, the FHFA, whose stated strategic goals for the GSEs are to: (1) maintain foreclosure prevention activities and credit availability to foster liquid, efficient, competitive, and resilient national housing finance markets; (2) reduce taxpayer risk through increasing the role of private capital in the mortgage market, and (3) build a new single-family securitization infrastructure.

The *Temporary Payroll Tax Cut Continuation Act of 2011* (TPTCCA) was funded by an increase of 10-basis points in the GSEs' guarantee fees which began in April 2012, and is effective through October 1, 2021. The increased fees are to be remitted to Treasury and not retained by the GSEs.

Accordingly, the increased fees do not affect the profitability of the GSEs. For fiscal years 2015 and 2014, the GSEs remitted to the Treasury the increased fees totaling $2.4 billion and $1.9 billion, respectively.

As of September 30, 2015, and 2014, GSEs investments consisted of the following:

Investments in GSEs as of September 30, 2015

(In billions of dollars)	Gross Investments	Cumulative Valuation Gain/(Loss)	Fair Value
Fannie Mae senior preferred stock	117.0	(61.7)	55.3
Freddie Mac senior preferred stock	72.1	(35.5)	36.6
Fannie Mae warrants common stock	3.1	6.2	9.3
Freddie Mac warrants common stock	2.3	2.8	5.1
Total investments in GSEs	194.5	(88.2)	106.3

Investments in GSEs as of September 30, 2014

(In billions of dollars)	Gross Investments	Cumulative Valuation Gain/(Loss)	Fair Value
Fannie Mae senior preferred stock	117.0	(64.3)	52.7
Freddie Mac senior preferred stock	72.1	(40.7)	31.4
Fannie Mae warrants common stock	3.1	4.6	7.7
Freddie Mac warrants common stock	2.3	1.7	4.0
Total investments in GSEs	194.5	(98.7)	95.8

Note 9. Other Assets

Other Assets as of September 30, 2015, and 2014

(In billions of dollars)	2015	2014
Advances and prepayments	108.1	106.6
Regulatory assets	22.4	21.1
FDIC receivable from resolution activity	13.9	15.2
Other	21.3	19.9
Total other assets	165.7	162.8

Advances and prepayments are assets that represent funds disbursed in contemplation of the future performance of services, receipt of goods, the incurrence of expenditures, or the receipt of other assets. These include advances to contractors and grantees, travel advances, and prepayments for items such as rents, taxes, insurance, royalties, commissions, and supplies.

The Federal Deposit Insurance Corporation (FDIC) has the responsibility for resolving failed institutions in an orderly and efficient manner. The resolution process involves valuing a failing institution, marketing it, soliciting and accepting bids for the sale of the institution, determining which bid is least costly to the insurance fund, and working with the acquiring institution through the closing process. FDIC records receivables for resolutions that include payments by the Deposit Insurance Fund to cover obligations to insured depositors, advances to receiverships and conservatorships for working capital, and administrative expenses paid on behalf of receiverships and conservatorships.

With regard to regulatory assets, the DOE's Power Marketing Authorities (PMAs) and the TVA record certain amounts as assets in accordance with Financial Accounting Standards Board (FASB) Accounting Standards Codification (ASC) Topic 980, *Regulated Operations*. The provisions of FASB ASC Topic 980 require that regulated enterprises reflect rate actions of the regulator in their financial statements, when appropriate. These rate actions can provide reasonable assurance of the existence of an asset, reduce or eliminate the value of an asset, or impose a liability on a regulated enterprise. In order to defer incurred costs under FASB ASC Topic 980, a regulated entity must have the statutory authority to establish rates that recover all costs, and those rates must be charged to and collected from customers. If the PMAs' or TVA's rates should become market-based, FASB ASC Topic 980 would no longer be applicable, and all of the deferred costs under that standard would be expensed. Other items included in "other" are purchased power generating capacity, deferred nuclear generating units, nonmarketable equity investments in international financial institutions, derivative assets, and the balance of assets held by the experience rated carriers participating in the Health Benefits and Life Insurance Program (pending disposition on behalf of OPM).

Note 10. Accounts Payable

Accounts Payable as of September 30, 2015, and 2014

(In billions of dollars)	2015	2014
Department of Defense	18.9	17.9
Department of Veterans Affairs	10.9	11.7
Department of Justice	6.3	5.9
Department of the Treasury	3.9	6.4
Department of Education	3.7	4.0
Department of Energy	3.7	1.5
Department of State	2.5	2.7
Department of Homeland Security	2.1	2.3
General Services Administration	2.0	2.1
Department of Agriculture	1.8	2.3
U.S. Postal Service	1.8	1.9
U.S. Agency for International Development	1.8	1.7
Tennessee Valley Authority	1.5	1.4
National Aeronautics and Space Administration	1.4	1.5
Department of the Interior	1.0	0.9
All other	5.0	4.8
Total accounts payable	68.3	69.0

Accounts payable includes amounts due for goods and property ordered and received, services rendered by other than federal employees, accounts payable for cancelled appropriations, and non-debt related interest payable.

Note 11. Federal Debt Securities Held by the Public and Accrued Interest

Federal Debt Securities Held by the Public and Accrued Interest

(In billions of dollars)	Balance September 30, 2014	Net Change During Fiscal Year 2015	Balance September 30, 2015	Average Interest Rate 2015	2014
Treasury securities (public):					
Marketable securities:					
Treasury bills	1,409.6	(54.4)	1,355.2	0.1%	0.1%
Treasury notes	8,160.2	205.8	8,366.0	1.8%	1.8%
Treasury bonds	1,534.1	154.1	1,688.2	4.7%	4.9%
Treasury inflation-protected securities (TIPS)	1,044.7	90.7	1,135.4	0.8%	0.9%
Treasury floating rate notes (FRN)	123.0	164.1	287.1	0.1%	0.1%
Total marketable Treasury securities	12,271.6	560.3	12,831.9		
Nonmarketable securities...............	513.4	(221.4)	292.0	2.5%	2.3%
Net unamortized premiums/(discounts)	(29.4)	(2.0)	(31.4)		
Total Treasury securities, net (public)	12,755.6	336.9	13,092.5		
Agency securities:					
Tennessee Valley Authority	23.6	0.1	23.7		
All other agencies	0.2	-	0.2		
Total agency securities, net of unamortized premiums and discounts	23.8	0.1	23.9		
Accrued interest payable	54.2	1.9	56.1		
Total federal debt securities held by the public and accrued interest	12,833.6	338.9	13,172.5		

Types of marketable securities:

Bills–Short-term obligations issued with a term of 1 year or less.

Notes–Medium-term obligations issued with a term of 2-10 years.

Bonds–Long-term obligations of more than 10 years.

TIPS–Term of more than 5 years.

FRN–Term of 2 years.

Federal debt securities held by the public outside the Government are held by individuals, corporations, state or local governments, FRBs, foreign governments, and other entities outside the federal government. The above table details Government borrowing primarily to finance operations and shows marketable and nonmarketable securities at face value less net unamortized premiums and discounts including accrued interest.

Securities that represent federal debt held by the public are issued primarily by the Treasury and include:

- Interest-bearing marketable securities (bills, notes, bonds, inflation-protected, and floating rate notes).
- Interest-bearing nonmarketable securities (government account series held by deposit and fiduciary funds, foreign series, state and local government series, domestic series, and savings bonds).
- Non-interest-bearing marketable and nonmarketable securities (matured and other).

Section 3111 of Title 31, United States Code (U.S.C.) authorizes the Secretary of the Treasury to use money received from the sale of an obligation and other money in the General Fund to buy, redeem, or refund, at or before maturity, outstanding bonds, notes, certificates of indebtedness, Treasury bills, or savings certificates of the Government.

Gross federal debt (with some adjustments) is subject to a statutory ceiling (i.e., the debt limit). Prior to 1917, Congress approved each debt issuance. In 1917, to facilitate planning in World War I, Congress and the President first enacted a statutory dollar ceiling for federal borrowing. With the *Public Debt Act of 1941* (Public Law 77-7), Congress and the President set an overall limit of $65 billion on Treasury debt obligations that could be outstanding at any one time; since then, Congress and the President have enacted a number of debt limit increases.

During fiscal years 2015 and 2014, Treasury faced multiple delays in raising the statutory debt limit that required it to depart from its normal debt management operations and to invoke legal authorities to avoid exceeding the statutory debt limit. During these periods, extraordinary measures taken by Treasury have resulted in federal debt securities not being issued to certain federal accounts. One such recent period occurred from May 20, 2013 through October 16, 2013. On October 17, 2013, the *Continuing Appropriations Act*, 2014 (Public Law No. 113-46) was enacted which temporarily suspended the statutory debt limit through February 7, 2014. On February 8, 2014, the debt limit was raised to $17,211.6 billion. A second occurred from February 10, 2014, through February 14, 2014. On February 15, 2014 Congress enacted the *Temporary Debt Limit Extension Act* (Public Law No. 113-83) which temporarily suspended the debt limit through March 15, 2015. On March 16, 2015, in accordance with Public Law No. 113-83, the statutory debt limit was raised to $18,113.0 billion. A third delay in raising the statutory debt limit occurred from March 16, 2015 through November 1, 2015. On November 2, 2015 Congress enacted the *Bipartisan Budget Act of 2015* (Public Law No. 114-74) which temporarily suspended the debt limit through March 15, 2017.

As of September 30, 2015, and 2014, debt subject to the statutory debt limit was $18,113.0 billion and $17,781.1 billion, respectively. The debt subject to the limit includes Treasury securities held by the public and Government guaranteed debt of federal agencies (shown in the table above) and intragovernmental debt holdings (shown in the following table). As noted above, a delay in raising the statutory debt limit existed as of September 30, 2015. Extraordinary measures taken by Treasury during the period of March 16, 2015 through September 30, 2015 resulted in federal debt securities not being issued to certain federal government accounts. See Note 16—Other Liabilities, Note 22—Fiduciary Activities and Note 26—Subsequent Events for additional information.

**Intragovernmental Debt Holdings: Federal Debt Securities
Held as Investments by Government Accounts as of September 30, 2015, and 2014**

(In billions of dollars)	Balance 2014	Net Change During Fiscal Year 2015	Balance 2015
Social Security Administration, Federal Old-Age and Survivors Insurance Trust Fund	2,712.8	53.8	2,766.6
Office of Personnel Management, Civil Service Retirement and Disability Fund	857.2	(125.9)	731.3
Department of Defense, Military Retirement Fund	483.1	47.9	531.0
Department of Defense, Medicare-Eligible Retiree Health Care Fund	200.4	5.4	205.8
Department of Health and Human Services, Federal Hospital Insurance Fund	202.2	(6.7)	195.5
Department of Health and Human Services, Federal Supplementary Medical Insurance Trust Fund	68.4	(2.3)	66.1
Federal Deposit Insurance Corporation, The Deposit Insurance Fund	48.8	11.3	60.1
Department of Energy, Nuclear Waste Disposal Fund	51.5	0.3	51.8
Office of Personnel Management, Postal Service Retiree Health Benefits Fund	48.5	(3.3)	45.2
Department of Labor, Unemployment Trust Fund	35.9	8.5	44.4
Office of Personnel Management, Employees Life Insurance Fund	43.2	0.8	44.0
Social Security Administration, Federal Disability Insurance Trust Fund	70.1	(28.5)	41.6
Office of Personnel Management, Employees Health Benefits Fund	23.6	(0.6)	23.0
Department of the Treasury, Exchange Stabilization Fund	22.6	(1.8)	20.8
Pension Benefit Guaranty Corporation Fund	17.4	1.1	18.5
Department of State, Foreign Service Retirement and Disability Fund	17.8	0.3	18.1
Department of Housing and Urban Development, FHA, Mutual Mortgage Insurance Capital Reserve Account	6.4	8.3	14.7
Department of Housing and Urban Development, Guarantees of Mortgage-Backed Securities Capital Reserve Account	-	12.8	12.8
Department of Transportation, Airport and Airway Trust Fund	12.8	(0.1)	12.7
National Credit Union Share Insurance Fund	11.0	0.6	11.6
All other programs and funds	105.4	5.8	111.2
Subtotal	5,039.1	(12.3)	5,026.8
Total net unamortized premiums/(discounts) for intragovernmental	67.8	7.5	75.3
Total intragovernmental debt holdings, net	5,106.9	(4.8)	5,102.1

Intragovernmental debt holdings represent the portion of the gross federal debt held as investments by government entities such as trust funds, revolving funds, and special funds. As noted above, the delay in raising the debt limit still existed as of September 30, 2015. As such, suspension of certain investments of the Civil Service Retirement and Disability Fund contributed to the decrease in the intragovernmental debt holdings balance for the fund.

Government entities that held investments in Treasury securities include trust funds that have funds from dedicated collections. For more information on funds from dedicated collections, see Note 21—Funds from Dedicated Collections. These intragovernmental debt holdings are eliminated in the consolidation of these financial statements.

Note 12. Federal Employee and Veteran Benefits Payable

Federal Employee and Veteran Benefits Payable as of September 30, 2015, and 2014

(In billions of dollars)	Civilian		Military		Total	
	2015	2014	2015	2014	2015	2014
Pension and accrued benefits	1,945.0	1,905.2	1,563.2	1,565.1	3,508.2	3,470.3
Veterans compensation and burial benefits	N/A	N/A	2,018.6	2,007.1	2,018.6	2,007.1
Post-retirement health and accrued benefits	364.0	336.8	731.2	760.5	1,095.2	1,097.3
Life insurance and accrued benefits	49.6	48.3	8.4	9.1	58.0	57.4
FECA benefits	28.1	28.3	8.3	8.8	36.4	37.1
Liability for other benefits	0.9	0.9	2.0	2.5	2.9	3.4
Total federal employee and veteran benefits payable	2,387.6	2,319.5	4,331.7	4,353.1	6,719.3	6,672.6

Change in Pension and Accrued Benefits

(In billions of dollars)	Civilian		Military		Total	
	2015	2014	2015	2014	2015	2014
Actuarial accrued pension liability, beginning of fiscal year	1,905.2	1,867.9	1,565.1	1,524.2	3,470.3	3,392.1
Pension expense:						
Normal costs	37.9	38.4	31.3	32.6	69.2	71.0
Interest on liability	75.9	77.2	66.6	64.9	142.5	142.1
Actuarial (gains)/losses (from experience)	(0.8)	(12.9)	(33.8)	(22.6)	(34.6)	(35.5)
Actuarial (gains)/losses (from assumption changes)	12.0	17.6	(9.4)	21.6	2.6	39.2
Other	0.3	-	-	-	0.3	-
Total pension expense	125.3	120.3	54.7	96.5	180.0	216.8
Less benefits paid	(85.5)	(83.0)	(56.6)	(55.6)	(142.1)	(138.6)
Actuarial accrued pension liability, end of fiscal year	1,945.0	1,905.2	1,563.2	1,565.1	3,508.2	3,470.3

Change in Post-Retirement Health and Accrued Benefits

(In billions of dollars)	Civilian		Military		Total	
	2015	**2014**	**2015**	**2014**	**2015**	**2014**
Actuarial accrued post-retirement health benefits liability, beginning of fiscal year....	336.8	326.7	760.5	747.6	1,097.3	1,074.3
Post-Retirement health benefits expense:						
Prior (and past) service costs from plan amendments or new plans......................	-	-	(21.2)	-	(21.2)	-
Normal costs	11.5	11.7	19.6	21.8	31.1	33.5
Interest on liability.......................................	14.3	14.2	33.0	33.3	47.3	47.5
Actuarial (gains)/losses (from experience)..	7.6	(3.1)	(22.5)	(8.0)	(14.9)	(11.1)
Actuarial (gains)/losses (from assumption changes)................................	8.8	1.3	(18.1)	(14.7)	(9.3)	(13.4)
Total post-retirement health benefits expense	42.2	24.1	(9.2)	32.4	33.0	56.5
Less claims paid..	(15.0)	(14.0)	(20.1)	(19.5)	(35.1)	(33.5)
Actuarial accrued post-retirement health benefits liability, end of fiscal year	364.0	336.8	731.2	760.5	1,095.2	1,097.3

The Government offers its employees retirement and other benefits, as well as health and life insurance. The liabilities for these benefits, which include both actuarial amounts and amounts due and payable to beneficiaries and health care carriers, apply to current and former civilian and military employees. Large fluctuations in actuarial amounts can result from changes in estimates to future outflows for benefits based on complex assumptions and cost models.

OPM administers the largest civilian plan. DOD and VA administers the largest military plans. Other significant pension plans with more than $10 billion in accrued benefits payable include those of the Coast Guard (DHS), Foreign Service (Department of State), TVA, and HHS's Public Health Service Commissioned Corps Retirement System. Please refer to the financial statements of the agencies listed for further details regarding their pension plans and other benefits.

Change in Civilian Life Insurance and Accrued Benefits

(In billions of dollars)	2015	2014
Actuarial accrued life insurance benefits liability, beginning of fiscal year	48.3	47.6
Life insurance benefits expense:		
New entrant expense...	0.3	0.2
Interest on liability	2.0	2.0
Actuarial (gains)/losses (from experience).......................................	(0.9)	(0.7)
Actuarial (gains)/losses (from assumption changes).......................	0.4	(0.2)
Total life insurance benefits expense...	1.8	1.3
Less costs paid...	(0.5)	(0.6)
Actuarial accrued life insurance benefits liability, end of fiscal year...............	49.6	48.3

Significant Long-Term Economic Assumptions Used in Determining Pension Liability and the Related Expense

| | Civilian | | | | Military | |
| | 2015 | | 2014 | | 2015 | 2014 |
	FERS	CSRS	FERS	CSRS		
Rate of interest	4.10%	3.70%	4.30%	3.90%	4.10%	4.30%
Rate of inflation	2.30%	2.30%	2.50%	2.50%	2.10%	2.40%
Projected salary increases	1.70%	1.70%	1.90%	1.90%	2.30%	2.50%
Cost of living adjustment	1.80%	2.30%	1.90%	2.50%	-	-

Significant Long-Term Economic Assumptions Used in Determining Post-Retirement Health Benefits and the Related Expense

| | Civilian | | Military | |
	2015	2014	2015	2014
Rate of interest	4.10%	4.30%	4.10%	4.30%
Single equivalent medical trend rate	5.30%	5.30%	4.56%	4.92%
Ultimate medical trend rate	3.90%	4.20%	4.85%	5.15%

Significant Long-Term Economic Assumptions Used in Determining Life Insurance Benefits and the Related Expense

| | Civilian | |
	2015	2014
Rate of interest	4.00%	4.20%
Rate of increase in salary	1.70%	1.90%

In accordance with SFFAS No. 33, *Pension, Other Retirement Benefits, and Other Postemployment Benefits: Reporting the Gains and Losses from Changes in Assumptions and Selecting Discount Rates and Valuation Dates,* agencies are required to separately present gains and losses from changes in long-term assumptions used to estimate liabilities associated with pensions, ORB, and OPEB on the Statement of Net Cost. SFFAS No. 33 also provides a standard for selecting the discount rate assumption for present value estimates of federal employee pension, ORB, and OPEB liabilities. Additionally, SFFAS No. 33 provides a standard for selecting the valuation date for estimates of federal employee pension, ORB, and OPEB liabilities that establishes a consistent method for such measurements. The SFFAS No. 33 standard for selecting discount rate assumption requires it be based on a historical average of interest rates on marketable Treasury securities consistent with the cash flows being discounted.

In fiscal year 2014, Treasury developed a new model and methodology for developing these rates to provide a sustainable, justifiable data resource for the affected agencies. As of July 2014, Treasury began releasing interest rate yield curve data using this new U.S. Department of the Treasury's Yield Curve for Treasury Nominal Coupon Issues (TNC yield curve), which is derived from Treasury notes and bonds. The TNC yield curve provides information on Treasury nominal coupon issues and the methodology extrapolates yields beyond 30 years through 100 years maturity. The TNC yield curve is used to produce a Treasury spot yield curve (a zero coupon curve), which provides the basis for discounting future cash flows.

The new method is based on methodology used to produce the High Quality Market (HQM) Yield Curve pursuant to the Pension Protection Act of 2006.[1] Generally, for FY 2014, the data from the new yield curve was implemented in full in one single year (i.e., replace the historical rate series used under the legacy method with those produced under the new TNC method).

Civilian Employees

Pensions

OPM administers the largest civilian pension plan, which covers substantially all full-time, permanent civilian federal employees. This plan includes two components of defined benefits, the Civil Service Retirement System (CSRS) and the Federal Employees' Retirement System (FERS). The basic benefit components of the CSRS and the FERS are financed and operated through the Civil Service Retirement and Disability Fund (CSRDF), a trust fund.

CSRDF monies are generated primarily from employees' contributions, agency contributions, payments from the General Fund, and interest on investments in Treasury securities.

The Federal Retirement Thrift Investment Board administers the TSP Fund. The TSP Fund investment options include two fixed income funds (the G and F Funds), three stock funds (the C, S, and I Funds) and five lifecycle funds (L 2050, L 2040, L 2030, L 2020, and L Income). The L Funds diversify participant accounts among the G, F, C, S, and I Funds, using professionally determined investment mixes (allocations) that are tailored to different time horizons. Treasury securities held in the G Fund are included in federal debt securities held by the public and accrued interest on the Balance Sheet. The G Fund held $0.0 billion and $183.7 billion in nonmarketable Treasury securities as of September 30, 2015, and 2014, respectively. The decrease in nonmarketable Treasury securities held in the G Fund relates to the delay in raising the debt limit. The Secretary of the Treasury has authority to take extraordinary measures to stay within the statutory debt limit imposed by Congress. One such measure involves the suspension of the issuance of securities to the G Fund if the issuance cannot be made without causing the debt limit to be exceeded. Please see Note 16 — Other Liabilities for additional information.

Post-Retirement Health Benefits

The post-retirement civilian health benefit liability is an estimate of the Government's future cost of providing post-retirement health benefits to current employees and retirees. Although active and retired employees pay insurance premiums under the Federal Employees Health Benefits Program (FEHB), these premiums cover only a portion of the costs. The OPM actuary applies economic assumptions to historical cost information to estimate the liability. The *Postal Accountability and Enhancement Act of 2006* (Postal Act of 2006) (Public Law No 109-435, Title VIII), made significant changes in the funding of future retiree health benefits for employees of the USPS, including the requirement for the USPS to make scheduled payments to the third Health Benefits Program (HBP) fund, the Postal Service Retiree Health Benefits (PSRHB) Fund. Public Law No. 109-435 requires the USPS to make scheduled payment contributions to the PSRHB Fund ranging from $5.4 billion to $5.8 billion per year from fiscal year 2007 through fiscal year 2016. (The fiscal year 2009 payment was subsequently reduced to $1.4 billion.) Thereafter, the USPS will make annual payments in the amount of the normal cost payment plus or minus an amount to amortize the unfunded liability or surplus. The Postal Service currently owes the PSRHB Fund: $11.1 billion for FY 2012 and $5.6 billion that was due for FY 2013. In addition, there was a $5.7 billion payment due for both FY 2014 and for FY 2015. As of September 30, 2015, the Postal Service has not indicated its intention regarding payment of the total $28.1 billion due. At this time, Congress has not taken further action on these payments due to the PSRHB from USPS. The cost for these annual payments, including any defaulted payments, along with all its other benefit program costs, are included in USPS' net cost in the consolidated Statements of Net Cost.

Life Insurance Benefits

One of the largest other employee benefits is the Federal Employee Group Life Insurance (FEGLI) Program. Employee and annuitant contributions and interest on investments fund a portion of this liability. The actuarial life insurance liability is the expected present value of future benefits to pay to, or on behalf of, existing FEGLI participants, less the expected present

---

[1] Treasury's HQM resource is available at: http://www.treasury.gov/resource-center/economic-policy/corp-bond-yield/Pages/Corp-Yield-Bond-Curve-Papers.aspx.

value of future contributions to be collected from those participants. The OPM actuary uses salary increase and interest rate yield curve assumptions that are generally consistent with the pension liability.

Workers' Compensation Benefits

The DOL determines both civilian and military agencies' liabilities for future workers' compensation benefits for civilian federal employees, as mandated by the Federal Employees' Compensation Act (FECA), for death, disability, medical, and miscellaneous costs for approved compensation cases, and a component for incurred, but not reported, claims. The FECA liability is determined annually using historical benefit payment patterns related to injury years to predict the future payments.

The actuarial methodology provides for the effects of inflation and adjusts historical payments to current year constant dollars by applying wage inflation factors (cost-of-living adjustments or COLA) and medical inflation factors (consumer price index-medical or CPIM) to the calculation of projected benefits.

In FY 2015, DOL refined the approach for selecting the COLA factors, CPIM factors, and discount rate by averaging the COLA rates, CPIM rates, and interest rates for the current and prior four years. The five-year averaging period used in FY 2015 reflects average historical rates without giving undue weight to recent past experience. In FY 2014, DOL selected the COLA and CPIM factors based on a one-year average.

The COLAs and CPIMs used in the projections for FY 2015 are listed below in the table. For the COLAs and CPIMs used in the projections for FY 2014, refer to the *Fiscal Year 2014 Financial Report of the U.S. Government.*

Fiscal Year	COLA	CPIM
2016	1.64%	2.94%
2017	1.47%	2.98%
2018	1.33%	3.09%
2019	1.43%	3.39%
2020+	1.65%	3.69%

DOL selected the interest rate assumptions whereby projected annual payments were discounted to present value based on the TNC Yield Curve to reflect the average duration of income payments and medical payments. For FY 2015, based on averaging the TNC Yield Curves for the current and prior four years, the average durations and interest rate assumptions were 14.9 years and 3.13% for income payments and 9.8 years and 2.50% for medical payments. For FY 2014, based on the TNC Yield Curve for one year, the average durations and interest rate assumptions were 15.1 years and 3.46% for income payments and 9.9 years and 2.86% for medical payments.

Military Employees (Including Veterans)

Pensions

The DOD Military Retirement Fund was established by Public Law (P.L.) 98-94 (currently Chapter 74 of Title 10, U.S.C.) and accumulates funds to finance, on an accrual basis, the liabilities of DOD military retirement and survivor benefit programs. The $1.9 billion decrease in the Military Retirement Pension liability is attributable to experience gains and assumption changes that offset the liability growth generated by benefit accruals (normal cost) and interest on the outstanding liability. Liabilities in the future will depend on expected changes due to interest and benefit accruals, future benefit changes, assumption changes, and actuarial experience.

This Fund receives income from three sources: monthly normal cost payments from the Services and Treasury to pay for the current years' service cost; annual payments from the Treasury to amortize the unfunded liability and pay for the increase in the normal cost attributable to Concurrent Receipt per Public Law 108-136; and investment income.

The military retirement system consists of a funded, noncontributory, defined benefit plan. It applies to military personnel (Departments of Army, Navy, Air Force, and the Marine Corps). This system includes non-disability retired pay, disability retired pay; survivor annuity programs, and Combat-Related Special Compensation. The Service Secretaries may approve immediate non-disability retired pay at any age with credit of at least 20 years of active duty service. Reserve retirees must be at least 60 years old and have at least 20 qualifying years of service before retired pay commences; however, in some cases, the age can be less than 60 if the reservist performs certain types of active service. P.L. 110-181 provides for a 90-day reduction in the reserve retirement age from age 60 for every 3 months of certain active duty service served within a fiscal year for service after January 28, 2008 (not below age 50). There is no vesting of benefits before non-disabled retirement. There are distinct non-disability benefit formulas related to four populations within the Military Retirement System: Final Pay, High-3, Career Status Bonus/Redux, and Bipartisan Budget Act of 2013 (Ryan/Murray) with subsequent amendments (BBA 2013). The date an individual enters the military determines which retirement system they would fall under and if they have the option to pick their retirement system. For more information on these benefits, see DOD's website http://www.dfas mil/retiredmilitary/plan/estimate.html.

Post-Retirement Health Benefits

Military retirees and their dependents are entitled to health care in military medical facilities if a facility can provide the needed care. The Military Retiree Health Benefits are post-retirement benefits DOD provides to non-Medicare-eligible military retirees and other eligible beneficiaries through private sector health care providers and DOD's medical treatment facilities. Prior to becoming Medicare eligible, military retirees and other eligible beneficiaries are entitled to participate in TRICARE (now managed by the Defense Health Agency)[2], which reimburses (net of beneficiary copay and deductible requirements) for the cost of health care from civilian providers. TRICARE options are available in indemnity, preferred provider organization, and health maintenance organization (HMO) designs.

Since fiscal year 2002, TRICARE, as second payer to Medicare, covers military retirees and other eligible beneficiaries after they become Medicare eligible. This TRICARE coverage for Medicare eligible beneficiaries requires that the beneficiary enroll in Medicare Part B (unless the beneficiary that is Medicare eligible is the spouse of an Active Duty Service Member) and is referred to as TRICARE for Life (TFL). Health care under TFL can be obtained from military medical facilities on an "as available" basis or from civilian providers. Military retiree health care actuarial liabilities are calculated annually using assumptions and actual experience. Trend assumptions include inpatient and outpatient care and prescriptions for both direct care and purchased services. Military retiree health care liability figures include costs incurred in military medical facilities, as well as claims paid to civilian providers and certain administrative costs. Costs paid to civilian providers are net of Medicare's portion of the cost.

10 U.S.C., Chapter 56 created the DOD Medicare-Eligible Retiree Health Care Fund (MERHCF), which became operative on October 1, 2002. The purpose of this fund is to account for the health benefits of Medicare-eligible military retirees, their dependents, and survivors who are Medicare eligible. The Fund receives revenues from three sources: interest earnings on MERHCF assets, Uniformed Services normal cost contributions, and Treasury contributions. The DOD Medicare-Eligible Retiree Health Care Board of Actuaries (the Board) approves the methods and assumptions used to calculate the per capita normal cost rates and the U.S. Treasury contribution, and the Secretary of Defense directs the Secretary of Treasury to make the payments. The MERHCF pays costs incurred in military medical facilities as well as claims for care provided by civilian providers under TFL administration costs associated with processing the TFL claims and capitated payments for coverage provided by U.S. Family Health Plans. The actuaries calculate the actuarial liabilities annually using assumptions and actual experience (e.g., mortality and retirement rates, direct care costs, purchased care).

Military post-retirement health and accrued benefits payable decreased $29.3 billion. The $29.3 billion decrease in military post-retirement health and accrued benefits was due primarily to the combined effect of plan changes -- including those associated with the 2015 National Defense Authorization Act, lower than expected historical costs, and a reduction in future assumed rates of healthcare cost increases.

In addition to the health care benefits for civilian and military retirees and their dependents, the VA also provides medical care to veterans on an "as available" basis, subject to the limits of the annual appropriations. In accordance with 38 CFR 17.36 (c), VA's Secretary makes an annual enrollment decision that defines the veterans, by priority, who will be treated for that fiscal year subject to change based on funds appropriated, estimated collections, usage, the severity index of enrolled veterans, and changes in cost. While VA expects to continue to provide medical care to veterans in future years, an estimate of such future benefits cannot be reasonably made. Accordingly, VA recognizes the medical care expenses in the period the medical care services are provided. For the fiscal years 2011 through 2015, the average medical care cost per year was $44.0 billion.

Veterans Compensation and Burial Benefits

---

[2] On October 1, 2013, the Department of Defense established the Defense Health Agency (DHA) to manage the activities of the Military Health System. These activities include those previously managed by TRICARE Management Activity (TMA), which was disestablished on the same date.

The Government compensates disabled veterans and their survivors. Veterans compensation is payable as a disability benefit or a survivor's benefit. Entitlement to compensation depends on the veteran's disabilities having been incurred in, or aggravated during, active military service; death while on duty; or death resulting from service-connected disabilities, if not on active duty.

Eligible veterans who die or are disabled from military service-related causes, as well as their dependents, receive compensation benefits. Also, veterans are provided with burial flags, headstones/markers, and grave liners for burial in a VA national cemetery or are provided a burial flag, headstone/marker and a plot allowance for burial in a private cemetery. These benefits are provided under 38 U.S.C., Part 2, Chapter 23 in recognition of a veteran's military service and are recorded as a liability in the period the requirements are met.

The liability for veterans' compensation and burial benefits payable is based on an actuarial estimate of future compensation and burial payments and increased by $11.5 billion in fiscal year 2015. The $11.5 billion increase in the Federal Employee and Veterans Benefits Liabilities is primarily attributable to interest on the outstanding liability, offset by benefits paid and the net effect of assumption changes. A smaller change in the estimate of backlogged claims contributed to the lower level of actuarial losses in FY 2015, relative to FY 2014.

Several significant actuarial assumptions were used in the valuation of compensation and burial benefits to calculate the present value of the liability. A liability was recognized for the projected benefit payments to: 1) those beneficiaries, including veterans and survivors, currently receiving benefit payments; 2) current veterans who will in the future become beneficiaries of the compensation program; and 3) a proportional share of those in active military service as of the valuation date who will become veterans in the future. Future benefit payments to survivors of those veterans in classes 1, 2, and 3 above are also incorporated into the projection. The projected liability does not include any administrative costs.

The veterans compensation and burial benefits liability is developed on an actuarial basis. It is impacted by interest on the liability balance, changes in experience, changes in actuarial assumptions, prior service costs, and amounts paid for costs included in the liability balance.

Change in Veterans Compensation and Burial Benefits

(In billions of dollars)	Compensation		Burial		Total	
	2015	**2014**	**2015**	**2014**	**2015**	**2014**
Actuarial accrued liability beginning of fiscal year	2,002.6	1,970.2	4.5	4.6	2,007.1	1,974.8
Current year expenses:						
Interest on the liability balance	85.9	82.7	0.2	0.2	86.1	82.9
Prior (and past) service costs from program amendments or new programs during the period	-	-	-	-	-	-
Actuarial (gain)/losses (from experience)	9.5	36.8	0.1	-	9.6	36.8
Actuarial (gain)/losses (from assumption changes)	(13.0)	(22.0)	-	(0.1)	(13.0)	(22.1)
Total current year expense	82.4	97.5	0.3	0.1	82.7	97.6
Less benefits paid	(71.0)	(65.1)	(0.2)	(0.2)	(71.2)	(65.3)
Actuarial accrued liability, end of fiscal year	2,014.0	2,002.6	4.6	4.5	2,018.6	2,007.1

Significant Economic Assumptions Used in Determining Veterans Compensation and Burial Benefits as of September 30, 2015, and 2014

	2015	2014
Rate of interest	4.08%	4.29%
Rate of inflation	2.44%	2.61%

Life Insurance Benefits

The largest veterans' life insurance programs consist of the following:

- National Service Life Insurance (NSLI) covers policyholders who served during World War II.
- Veterans' Special Life Insurance (VSLI) was established in 1951 to meet the insurance needs of veterans who served during the Korean Conflict and through the period ending January 1, 1957.
- Service-Disabled Veterans Insurance (S-DVI) program was established in 1951 to meet the insurance needs of veterans who received a service-connected disability rating.

The components of veteran life insurance liability for future policy benefits are presented below:

Veterans Life Insurance Liability as of September 30, 2015, and 2014

(In billions of dollars)	2015	2014
Insurance death benefits:		
NSLI	3.8	4.4
VSLI	1.3	1.4
S-DVI	0.6	0.6
Other	0.5	0.3
Total death benefits	6.2	6.7
Death benefit annuities	0.1	0.1
Disability income & waiver	0.8	0.8
Insurance dividends payable	1.3	1.4
Unearned premiums	-	0.1
Total veterans life insurance liability	8.4	9.1

Insurance dividends payable consists of dividends left on a deposit with VA, related interest payable, and dividends payable to policyholders.

The VA supervises Service members Group Life Insurance (SGLI) and Veterans Group Life Insurance programs that provide life insurance coverage to members of the uniformed armed services, reservists, and post-Vietnam Veterans as well as their families. All SGLI insureds are automatically covered under the Traumatic Injury Protection (TSGLI) program, which provides for insurance payments to Veterans who suffer a serious traumatic injury in service. VA has entered into a group policy with the Prudential Insurance Company of America to administer these programs.

Pension Benefits

The VA also provides certain veterans and/or their dependents with pension benefits, based on annual eligibility reviews, if the veteran died or was disabled for nonservice-related causes. VA pension benefits are recognized as a non-exchange transaction due to the nature of the VA pension plan. Therefore, the actuarial present value of these future benefits is not required to be recorded on the Balance Sheet. The projected amounts of future payments for pension benefits (presented for informational purposes only) as of September 30, 2015, and 2014, was $94.1 billion and $102.8 billion, respectively.

Note 13. Environmental and Disposal Liabilities

Environmental and Disposal Liabilities as of September 30, 2015, and 2014

(In billions of dollars)	2015	2014
Department of Energy:		
Environmental and disposal liabilities	339.8	299.8
Department of Defense:		
Environmental restoration	27.2	27.0
Disposal of weapon systems program	22.2	21.2
Environmental corrective other	6.7	6.2
Base realignment and closure	3.9	4.2
Total Department of Defense	60.0	58.6
All other agencies	11.8	10.7
Total environmental and disposal liabilities	411.6	369.1

During World War II and the Cold War, DOE (or predecessor agencies) developed a massive industrial complex to research, produce, and test nuclear weapons. This included nuclear reactors, chemical-processing buildings, metal machining plants, laboratories, and maintenance facilities that manufactured tens of thousands of nuclear warheads and conducted more than 1,000 nuclear tests.

At all sites where these activities took place, some environmental contamination occurred. This contamination was caused by the production, storage, and use of radioactive materials and hazardous chemicals, which resulted in contamination of soil, surface water, and groundwater. The environmental legacy of nuclear weapons production also includes thousands of contaminated buildings and large volumes of waste and special nuclear materials requiring treatment, stabilization, and disposal.

Estimated cleanup costs at sites for which there are no current feasible remediation approaches, such as the Nevada nuclear test site, are excluded from the estimates, although applicable stewardship and monitoring costs for these sites are included. DOE has not been required through regulation to establish remediation activities for these sites.

Estimating DOE's environmental cleanup liability requires making assumptions about future activities and is inherently uncertain. The future course of DOE's environmental cleanup and disposal will depend on a number of fundamental technical and policy choices, many of which have not been made. The sites and facilities could be restored to a condition suitable for any desirable use, or could be restored to a point where they pose no near-term health risks. Achieving the former conditions would have a higher cost but may (or may not) warrant the costs, or be legally required. The environmental and disposal liability estimates include contingency estimates intended to account for the uncertainties associated with the technical cleanup scope of the program.

DOE's environmental and disposal liabilities estimates are dependent on annual funding levels and achievement of work as scheduled. Congressional appropriations at lower than anticipated levels or unplanned delays in project completion would cause increases in life-cycle costs. DOE's environmental and disposal liabilities increased by $40 billion, which is primarily attributable to an increase of $35 billion in life-cycle adjustments in DOE's estimated cleanup cost liability across the Department, with the remaining $5 billion pertaining mainly to inflation. Updates to the environmental liability cost estimates due to life-cycle adjustments added numerous years to the life-cycle cleanup schedule.

DOE's environmental and disposal liabilities also include the estimated cleanup and post-closure responsibilities, including surveillance and monitoring activities, soil and groundwater remediation, and disposition of excess material for sites. The Department is responsible for the post-closure activities at many of the closure sites as well as other sites. The costs for these post-closure activities are estimated for a period of 75 years after the balance sheet date, i.e., through 2090 in fiscal year 2015 and through 2089 in fiscal year 2014. While some post-cleanup monitoring and other long-term stewardship activities post-2090 are included in the liability, there are others the Department expects to continue beyond 2090 for which the costs cannot reasonably be estimated.

A portion of DOE's environmental and disposal liabilities at various field sites includes anticipated costs for facilities managed by DOE's ongoing program operations which will ultimately require stabilization, deactivation, and decommissioning. The estimate is largely based upon a cost-estimating model. Site specific estimates are used in lieu of the cost-estimating model, when available. Cost estimates for ongoing program facilities are updated each year. For facilities newly contaminated since fiscal year 1997, cleanup costs allocated to future periods and not included in environmental and disposal liabilities amounted to $0.7 billion for both fiscal years 2015 and 2014.

Please refer to the financial statements of the DOE for significant detailed information regarding DOE's environmental and disposal liabilities, including cleanup costs.

DOD follows the Comprehensive Environmental Response, Compensation, and Liability Act (CERCLA), Superfund Amendments and Reauthorization Act, Resource Conservation and Recovery Act (RCRA) and other applicable federal or state laws to clean up contamination. The CERCLA and RCRA require the DOD to clean up contamination in coordination with regulatory agencies, current owners of property damaged by the Department, and third parties that have a partial responsibility for the environmental restoration. Failure to comply with agreements and legal mandates puts the DOD at risk of incurring fines and penalties.

DOD must restore active installations, installations affected by base realignment and closure, and other areas formerly used as Defense sites. DOD also bears responsibility for disposal of chemical weapons and environmental costs associated with the disposal of weapons systems (primarily nuclear powered aircraft carriers and submarines).

DOD uses engineering estimates and independently validated models to estimate environmental costs. The engineering estimates are used after obtaining extensive data during the remedial investigation/feasibility phase of the environmental project.

For general PP&E placed into service after September 30, 1997, DOD expenses associated environmental costs systematically over the life of the asset using two methods: physical capacity for operating landfills and life expectancy in years for all other assets. The Department expenses the full cost to clean up contamination for stewardship property, plant, and equipment at the time the asset is placed into service. DOD has expensed the costs for cleanup associated with general property, plant, and equipment placed into service before October 1, 1997, except for costs intended to be recovered through user charges; for those costs, DOD has expensed cleanup costs associated with that portion of the asset life that has passed since it was placed into service. DOD systematically recognizes the remaining cost over the remaining life of the asset. The unrecognized portion of the cleanup cost associated with general property, plant, and equipment is $3.1 billion for both fiscal years 2015 and 2014. Not all components of DOD are able to compile the necessary information for this disclosure, thus the amount reported may not accurately reflect DOD's total unrecognized costs associated with general property, plant, and equipment. DOD is implementing procedures to address these deficiencies.

DOD is unable to estimate and report a liability for environmental restoration and corrective action for buried chemical munitions and agents, because the extent of the buried chemical munitions and agents is unknown at this time. DOD is also unable to provide a complete estimate for the Formerly Utilized Sites Remedial Action Program. DOD has ongoing studies and will update its estimate as additional liabilities are identified. DOD has the potential to incur costs for restoration initiatives in conjunction with returning overseas Defense facilities to host nations. However, DOD is unable to provide a reasonable estimate at this time because the extent of required restoration is unknown.

Please refer to the financial statements of the DOD for further detailed information regarding DOD's environmental and disposal liabilities, including cleanup costs.

In addition, in accordance with Technical Bulletin 2006-1, agencies recorded an environmental and disposal liability for asbestos-related cleanup costs totaling $4.3 billion and $3.6 billion as of September 30, 2015, and 2014, respectively.

Note 14. Benefits Due and Payable

Benefits Due and Payable as of September 30, 2015, and 2014

(In billions of dollars)	2015	2014
Federal Old-Age and Survivors Insurance	66.1	62.9
Federal Supplementary Medical Insurance (Medicare Parts B and D)	37.9	31.9
Grants to States for Medicaid	36.8	32.3
Federal Hospital Insurance (Medicare Part A)	28.3	25.7
Federal Disability Insurance	27.1	25.8
Supplemental Security Income	5.3	5.2
Unemployment Insurance	1.1	1.0
All other benefits programs	11.3	6.8
Total benefits due and payable	213.9	191.6

Benefits due and payable are amounts owed to program recipients or medical service providers as of September 30 that have not been paid. HHS and the SSA administer the majority of the medical service programs and the DOL administers the Unemployment Insurance program. For a description of the programs, see Note 23—Social Insurance and the Unaudited Required Supplementary Information—Social Insurance section.

Note 15. Insurance and Guarantee Program Liabilities

Insurance and Guarantee Program Liabilities as of September 30, 2015, and 2014

(In billions of dollars)	2015	2014
Insurance and Guarantee Program Liabilities:		
Pension Benefit Guaranty Corporation - Benefit Pension Plans	161.1	146.9
Department of Agriculture - Federal Crop Insurance	8.3	7.3
Federal Deposit Insurance Corporation Funds	7.3	13.2
All other insurance and guarantee programs	0.8	0.8
Total insurance and guarantee program liabilities	177.5	168.2

PBGC insures pension benefits for participants in covered defined benefit pension plans. As a wholly-owned corporation of the government, PBGC's financial activity and balances are included in the consolidated financial statements of the government. However, under current law, PBGC's liabilities may be paid only from PBGC's assets and not from the General Fund or assets of the government in general. As of September 30, 2015, and 2014, PBGC had total liabilities of $164.0 billion and $151.6 billion, and its total liabilities exceeded its total assets by $76.3 billion and $61.8 billion, respectively. In addition, as discussed in Note 19—Contingencies, PBGC reported reasonably possible contingent losses of about $237.7 billion and $184.4 billion as of September 30, 2015, and 2014, respectively.

As of September 30, 2015, and 2014, $8.3 billion and $7.3 billion, respectively, pertain to the USDA's Federal Crop Insurance Program. The Federal Crop Insurance Program is administered by the Federal Crop Insurance Corporation, whose mission is to provide an actuarially sound risk management program to reduce agricultural producers' economic losses due to natural disasters.

Of the total FDIC amount as of September 30, 2015, and 2014, $0.5 billion and $1.9 billion, respectively, represents the recorded contingent liability and loss provision for institutions insured by the Deposit Insurance Fund that are likely to fail. In addition, $6.7 billion and $11.3 billion pertain to liabilities due to resolutions of failed or failing institutions and to pending depositor claims as of September 30, 2015, and 2014, respectively.

16. Other Liabilities

Other Liabilities as of September 30, 2015, and 2014
(In billions of dollars)

	2015	2014
Unearned revenue and assets held for others:		
Unearned fees for nuclear waste disposal (DOE) and other unearned revenue	67.2	50.6
Assets held on behalf of others	99.4	81.9
Subtotal	166.6	132.5
Employee-related liabilities:		
Accrued federal employees' wages and benefits	38.1	38.3
Selected DOE contractors' and D.C. employees' pension benefits	50.0	48.6
Subtotal	88.1	86.9
International monetary liabilities and gold certificates:		
Exchange Stabilization Fund	54.8	57.6
Gold certificates (see Note 2)	11.0	11.0
Subtotal	65.8	68.6
Subsidies and grants:		
Farm and other subsidies	5.5	9.8
Grant payments due to state and local governments and others	17.8	16.9
Subtotal	23.3	26.7
Miscellaneous liabilities:		
Legal and other contingencies	47.1	46.1
Non-federal power projects and capital lease liabilities, and disposal liabilities	11.1	13.1
Liability for restoration of federal debt principal and interest	204.6	-
Other miscellaneous	45.7	35.2
Subtotal	308.5	94.4
Total	652.3	409.1

Other liabilities represent liabilities that are not separately identified on the Balance Sheet and are presented on a comparative basis by major category.

Unearned Revenue and Assets Held for Others

The government recognizes a liability when it receives money in advance of providing goods and services or assumes custody of money belonging to others. The government's unearned revenue from fees DOE has collected from utility companies for the future cost of managing the disposal of nuclear waste is about $37.4 billion and $36.0 billion as of September 30, 2015, and 2014, respectively. Other unearned revenue includes USPS income for such things as prepaid postage, outstanding money orders, and prepaid P.O. Box rentals. Assets held on behalf of others include funds collected in advance, and undelivered Defense articles. DSCA holds $78.1 billion and $68.0 billion as of September 30, 2015, and 2014, respectively for articles and services for future delivery to foreign governments.

Employee-Related Liabilities

This category includes amounts owed to employees at year-end and actuarial liabilities for certain non-federal employees. Actuarial liabilities for federal employees and veteran benefits are included in Note 12–Federal Employee and Veteran Benefits Payable and are reported on another line on the Balance Sheet. The largest liability in the employee-related liabilities category is the amount owed at the end of the fiscal year to federal employees for wages and benefits (including accrued annual leave). In addition, DOE is liable to certain contractors for contractor employee pension and postretirement benefits, which is about $26.3 billion and $23.4 billion as of September 30, 2015 and 2014, respectively. Also, the government owed about $8.8 billion and $9.2 billion as of September 30, 2015, and 2014, for estimated future pension benefits of the District of Columbia's judges, police, firefighters, and teachers.

International Monetary Liabilities and Gold Certificates

Consistent with U.S. obligations in the IMF on orderly exchange arrangements and a stable system of exchange rates, the Secretary of the Treasury, with the approval of the President, may use the Exchange Stabilization Fund to deal in gold, foreign exchange, and other instruments of credit and securities.

Gold certificates are issued in nondefinitive or book-entry form to the Federal Reserve Bank of New York (FRBNY). The government's liability incurred by issuing the gold certificates, as reported on the Balance Sheet, is limited to the gold being held by the Department of the Treasury at the standard value established by law. Upon issuance of gold certificates to the FRBNY, the proceeds from the certificates are deposited into the operating cash of the U.S. Government. All of the Department of the Treasury's certificates issued are payable to the FRBNY.

Subsidies and Grants

The government supports the public good through a wide variety of subsidy and grant programs in such areas as agriculture, medical and scientific research, education, and transportation. USDA programs such as Conservation Reserve; grants, subsidies, and contributions; and payments to states account for the majority of the subsidies due, about $4.6 billion and $5.0 billion as of September 30, 2015 and 2014, respectively.

The government awards hundreds of billions of dollars in grants annually. These include project grants that are competitively awarded for agency-specific projects, such as HHS grants to fund projects to "enhance the independence, productivity, integration, and inclusion into the community of people with developmental disabilities." Other grants are formula grants, such as matching grants. Formula grants go to state governments for such things as education and transportation programs. These grants are paid in accordance with distribution formulas that have been provided by law or administrative regulations. Of the total liability reported for grants as of September 30, 2015, and 2014, DOT, Education, and HHS collectively owed their grantees about $12.6 billion and $12.3 billion, respectively. Refer to the financial statements and footnotes of the respective agencies for additional information.

Miscellaneous Liabilities

Some of the more significant liabilities included in this category are for (1) legal and other contingencies (see Note 19—Contingencies), (2) Bonneville Power Administration liability to pay annual budgets of several power projects for its electrical generating capacity, (3) payables due to the purchases of securities, and (4) other liabilities reported by Treasury as a result of the occurrence of a delay in raising the statutory debt limit as of September 30, 2015. When delays in raising the statutory debt limit occur, Treasury often must deviate from its normal debt management operations and take a number of extraordinary measures to meet the Government's obligations as they come due without exceeding the debt limit. Many extraordinary measures taken by Treasury during the period of March 16, 2015, through September 30, 2015, resulted in federal debt securities not being issued to certain federal government accounts. As a result of Treasury securities not being issued to the Government Securities Investment Fund (G Fund) of the Thrift Savings Plan (TSP), Treasury reported miscellaneous liabilities, as of September 30, 2015, in the amount of $204.6 billion that represent uninvested principal of and related interest for the TSP's G Fund that would have been reported in Note 11 – Federal Debt Securities Held by the Public and Accrued Interest had there not been a delay in raising the statutory debt limit as of September 30, 2015, and had the securities been issued. For further information related to the impact on TSP, see Note 22 – Fiduciary Activities and Note 26 – Subsequent Events.

In addition, many federal agencies reported relatively small amounts of miscellaneous liabilities that are not otherwise classified.

Note 17. Collections and Refunds of Federal Revenue

Collections of Federal Tax Revenue for the Year Ended September 30, 2015

(In billions of dollars)	Federal Tax Revenue Collections	Tax Year to Which Collections Relate			
		2015	2014	2013	Prior Years
Individual income tax and tax withholdings	2,799.1	1,790.8	954.6	28.3	25.4
Corporation income taxes	389.9	260.2	114.9	3.9	10.9
Excise taxes	102.8	79.9	22.8	0.1	-
Unemployment taxes	49.3	33.4	15.7	-	0.2
Customs duties	36.4	36.4	-	-	-
Estate and gift taxes	20.0	-	6.8	0.6	12.6
Railroad retirement taxes	6.4	5.0	1.4	-	-
Fines, penalties, interest, and other revenue	7.4	7.3	0.1	-	-
Subtotal	3,411.3	2,213.0	1,116.3	32.9	49.1
Less: amounts collected for non-federal entities	(0.4)				
Total	3,410.9				

Treasury is the Government's principal revenue-collecting agency. Collections of individual income and tax withholdings include FICA/SECA and individual income taxes. These taxes are characterized as non-exchange revenue.

Excise taxes, also characterized as non-exchange revenue, consist of taxes collected for various items, such as airline tickets, gasoline products, distilled spirits and imported liquor, tobacco, firearms, and others.

Federal Tax Refunds Disbursed for the Year Ended September 30, 2015

		Tax Year to Which Refunds Relate			
(In billions of dollars)	Refunds Disbursed	2015	2014	2013	Prior Years
Individual income tax and tax withholdings	351.4	30.7	290.0	23.6	7.1
Corporation income taxes	50.1	6.2	20.8	5.5	17.6
Excise taxes	1.1	0.4	0.6	0.1	-
Unemployment taxes	0.2	-	0.1	-	0.1
Customs duties	2.8	1.5	0.8	0.2	0.3
Estate and gift taxes	0.9	-	0.2	0.3	0.4
Total	406.5	38.8	312.5	29.7	25.5

Reconciliation of Revenue to Tax Collections for the Year Ended September 30, 2015, and 2014

(In billions of dollars)	2015	2014
Consolidated revenue per the Statement of Operations and Changes in Net Position	3,334.0	3,066.1
Tax refunds	406.5	375.2
Earned income tax and child tax credit imputed revenue	(80.7)	(81.6)
Other tax credits and accrual adjustments	(36.9)	(21.9)
Federal Insurance Contributions Act - Tax	20.1	19.8
Federal Reserve earnings	(96.5)	(99.2)
Nontax-related fines and penalties reported by agencies	(93.0)	(65.1)
Nontax-related earned revenue	(42.6)	(19.0)
Collections of federal tax revenue	3,410.9	3,174.3

Consolidated revenue in the SOCNP is presented on a modified cash basis, net of tax refunds, and includes other non-tax related revenue. Earned Income Tax Credit, Child Tax Credit, and other tax credits amounts (unaudited) are included in gross cost in the Statements of Net Cost. The Federal Insurance Contributions Act – Tax is included in the Individual income and tax withholdings line in the Collections of Federal tax revenue; however, it is not reported on the SOCNP as these collections are intragovernmental revenue and eliminated in consolidation. The table above reconciles total revenue to federal tax collections.

Collections of Federal Revenue for the Year Ended September 30, 2014

(In billions of dollars)	Federal Tax Revenue Collections	Tax Year to Which Collections Relate			
		2014	2013	2012	Prior Years
Individual income tax and tax withholdings	2,605.0	1,691.1	864.3	24.3	25.3
Corporation income taxes	353.1	252.9	87.9	1.2	11.1
Excise taxes	96.7	74.4	22.1	0.1	0.1
Unemployment taxes	52.7	27.1	15.3	10.2	0.1
Customs duties	34.2	34.2	-	-	-
Estate and gift taxes	20.2	-	7.0	0.9	12.3
Railroad retirement taxes	6.0	4.6	1.4	-	-
Fines, penalties, interest and other revenue	6.7	6.5	0.1	0.1	-
Subtotal	3,174.6	2,090.8	998.1	36.8	48.9
Less: amounts collected for non-federal entities	(0.3)				
Total	3,174.3				

Federal Tax Refunds Disbursed for the Year Ended September 30, 2014

(In billions of dollars)	Refunds Disbursed	Tax Year to Which Refunds Relate			
		2014	2013	2012	Prior Years
Individual income tax and tax withholdings	335.8	13.7	290.8	24.0	7.3
Corporation income taxes	35.3	4.4	10.9	6.7	13.3
Excise taxes	1.8	0.5	0.9	0.2	0.2
Unemployment taxes	0.1	-	0.1	-	-
Customs duties	1.3	0.7	0.3	0.1	0.2
Estate and gift taxes	0.9	-	0.2	0.5	0.2
Total	375.2	19.3	303.2	31.5	21.2

Note 18. Prior-Period Adjustments

Prior-Period Adjustments for the Year Ended September 30, 2015, and 2014

(In billions of dollars)	Changes to Net Position	
	2015	**2014**
Environmental Protection Agency	(1.3)	-
Department of Justice	(0.1)	(0.1)
Other prior-period adjustments	(0.1)	-
Total prior-period adjustments	(1.5)	(0.1)

During fiscal year 2015, several entities reported the prior-period adjustments line item. Environmental Protection Agency (EPA) changed its accounting treatment to record special accounts funds settlement proceeds as unearned revenue after determining that collections previously recorded as past costs were being used for future site cleanup. The effect is a $1.3 billion decrease in EPA's beginning net position.

For fiscal years 2015 and 2014, Department of Justice (DOJ) applied a change in accounting principle to certain components based on the implementation of their Financial Management Policy Memorandum (FMPM) 13-12, Capitalization of General Property, Plant, and Equipment and Internal Use Software. The primary impact of the policy change was an increase in the thresholds for capitalizing and reporting real property, including leasehold improvements, personal property, and internal use software. The change in accounting principle caused a $0.1 billion reduction in the overall PP&E balance for both fiscal years 2015 and 2014.

As discussed in Note 21 – Funds from Dedicated Collections, the Commodity Future Trading Commission erroneously did not report as a fund from dedicated collections for fiscal year 2014. This error was corrected in fiscal year 2015 and resulted in a prior-period adjustment amount of $0.3 billion.

Note 19. Contingencies

Financial Treatment of Loss Contingencies

Loss contingencies that are assessed to be at least reasonably possible are disclosed in this note. Loss contingencies involve situations where there is an uncertainty of a possible loss. The reporting of loss contingencies depends on the likelihood that a future event or events will confirm the loss or impairment of an asset or the incurrence of a liability. Terms used to assess the range for the likelihood of loss are probable, reasonably possible, and remote. Loss contingencies that are assessed as probable and measurable are accrued in the financial statements. Loss contingencies that are assessed as remote are not reported in the financial statements, nor disclosed in the notes. All other material loss contingencies are disclosed in this note. The following table provides criteria for how federal agencies are to account for loss contingencies, based on the likelihood of the loss and measurability.[3]

Likelihood of future outflow or other sacrifice of resources	Loss amount can be reasonably measured	Loss range can be reasonably measured	Loss amount or range cannot be reasonably measured
Probable Future confirming event(s) are more likely to occur than not.[4]	Accrue the liability. Report on Balance Sheet and Statement of Net Cost.	Accrue liability of the best estimate or (if there is no best estimate) minimum amount in loss range, and disclose nature of contingency and range of estimated liability.	Disclose nature of contingency and include a statement that an estimate cannot be made.
Reasonably possible Possibility of future confirming event(s) occurring is more than remote and less than likely.	Disclose nature of contingency and estimated loss amount.	Disclose nature of contingency and estimated loss range.	Disclose nature of contingency and include a statement that an estimate cannot be made.
Remote Possibility of future event(s) occurring is slight.	No disclosure.	No disclosure.	No disclosure.

---

[3] In addition, a third condition must be met to be a loss contingency: a past event or an exchange transaction must occur.

[4] For loss contingencies related to litigation, probable is defined as the future confirming event or events are more likely than not to occur, with the exception of pending or threatened litigation and unasserted claims. For the pending or threatened litigation and unasserted claims, the future confirming event or events are likely to occur.

The Government is subject to loss contingencies that include insurance and litigation cases. These loss contingencies arise in the normal course of operations and their ultimate disposition is unknown. Based on information currently available, however, it is management's opinion that the expected outcome of these matters, individually or in the aggregate, will not have a material adverse effect on the financial statements, except for the insurance and litigation described in the following section, which could have a material adverse effect on the financial statements.

Insurance Contingencies

At the time an insurance policy is issued, a contingency arises. The contingency is the risk of loss assumed by the insurer, that is, the risk of loss from events that may occur during the term of the policy. The Government has insurance contingencies that are reasonably possible in the amount of $239.1 billion as of September 30, 2015, and $186.4 billion as of September 30, 2014. The major programs are identified below:

- PBGC reported $237.7 billion and $184.4 billion as of September 30, 2015, and 2014, respectively, for the estimated aggregate unfunded vested benefits exposure to the PBGC for private-sector single-employer and multiemployer defined benefit pension plans that are classified as a reasonably possible exposure to loss. This increase is primarily due to the growth in the number of companies meeting the reasonably possible criteria for the single-employer program and the decrease in the interest rate used for valuing liabilities.
- FDIC reported $1.2 billion and $1.7 billion as of September 30, 2015, and 2014, respectively, for identified additional risk in the financial services industry that could result in additional loss to the DIF should potentially vulnerable insured institutions ultimately fail. Actual losses, if any, will largely depend on future economic and market conditions.

Deposit Insurance

Deposit insurance covers all types of deposit accounts such as checking, Negotiable Order of Withdrawal and savings accounts, money market deposit accounts, and certificates of deposit received at an insured bank, savings association, or credit union. The insurance covers the balance of each depositor's account and shares, dollar-for-dollar, up to the insurance limit, including principal and any accrued interest through the date of the insured financial institution's closing. As a result, the Government has the following exposure from federally-insured financial institutions:

- FDIC has estimated insured deposits of $6,420.0 billion as of September 30, 2015, and $6,131.9 billion as of September 30, 2014, for the DIF.
- National Credit Union Administration (NCUA) has estimated insured shares of $939.9 billion as of September 30, 2015, and $895.7 billion as of September 30, 2014, for the National Credit Union Share Insurance Fund.

Legal Contingencies

Legal contingencies as of September 30, 2015, and 2014, are summarized in the table below:

(In billions of dollars)	2015			2014		
	Accrued Liabilities [1]	Estimated Range of Loss for Certain Cases [2]		Accrued Liabilities [1]	Estimated Range of Loss for Certain Cases [2]	
		Lower End	Upper End		Lower End	Upper End
Legal contingencies:						
Probable	6.0	6.0	7.4	7.1	7.1	8.5
Reasonably possible..............	-	8.7	13.7	-	9.9	13.5

[1] Accrued liabilities are recorded and presented in the related line items of the Balance Sheet.

[2] Does not reflect the total range of loss; many cases assessed as reasonably possible of an unfavorable outcome did not include estimated losses that could be determined.

The Government is party to various administrative claims and legal actions brought against it, some of which may ultimately result in settlements or decisions against the Government.

Management and legal counsel have determined that it is "probable" that some of these actions will result in a loss to the Government and the loss amounts are reasonably measurable. The estimated liabilities for "probable" cases against the government are $6.0 billion and $7.1 billion as of September 30, 2015, and 2014, respectively, and are included in "Other Liabilities" on the Balance Sheet. For example, the U.S. Supreme Court decision in *Salazar v. Ramah Navajo Chapter*, dated June 18, 2012, is likely to result in additional claims against the Indian Health Service (IHS), which is a component within HHS. As a result of this decision, many tribes have filed claims. Some claims have been settled and others have been asserted but not yet settled.

There are also administrative claims and legal actions pending where adverse decisions are considered by management and legal counsel as "reasonably possible" with an estimate of potential loss or a range of potential loss. The estimated potential losses for such claims and actions range from $8.7 billion to $13.7 billion as of September 30, 2015, and from $9.9 billion to $13.5 billion as of September 30, 2014. For example, the Department of the Treasury's *American Recovery and Reinvestment Tax Act of 2009 (ARRA) Related Cases* are a number of cases that were filed in the U.S. Court of Federal Claims alleging that the U.S. government violated statutory and regulatory mandates to make proper payments to plaintiffs under ARRA, Section 1603, for having placed certain energy properties into service. The Department has determined there is a reasonably possible likelihood of unfavorable outcomes in some of the cases. The total alleged damages for these cases approximate $273 million.

Numerous litigation cases are pending where the outcome is uncertain or it is reasonably possible that a loss has been incurred and where estimates cannot be made. There are other litigation cases where the plaintiffs have not made claims for specific dollar amounts, but the settlement may be significant. The ultimate resolution of these legal actions for which the potential loss could not be determined may materially affect the U.S. government's financial position or operating results. An example of a specific case is summarized below:

- In the case, *Starr International Co., Inc. v. United States*, the plaintiff, an American International Group, Inc. (AIG) shareholder that brought on behalf of two classes of shareholders, alleges that the U.S. government violated the Fifth Amendment to the United States Constitution by illegally exacting or taking property without just compensation. One class, the Credit Agreement Class, claimed that the Fifth Amendment was violated when a majority share of AIG's equity and voting rights was conveyed in connection with an $85 billion loan to AIG during the 2008 financial crisis. Starr also asserted a Fifth Amendment violation on behalf of the second class, the Reverse Stock Split Shareholder Class, alleging that a June 2009 reverse split of AIG's common stock constituted a taking of the common stockholders' asserted right to a shareholder vote on whether to approve a reverse split of AIG's common stock. The U.S. Court of Federal Claims held that the Credit Agreement Shareholder Class prevails on liability, but recovers no damages, and that the Reverse Stock Split Shareholder class does not prevail on liability or damages.

Both the Plaintiff and the United States have appealed. The Government is unable to determine the likelihood of an unfavorable outcome or make an estimate of potential loss at this time.

Environmental and Disposal Contingencies

Environmental and disposal contingencies as of September 30, 2015, and 2014, are summarized in the table below:

| (In billions of dollars) | 2015 | | | 2014 | | |
| | Accrued Liabilities [1] | Estimated Range of Loss for Certain Cases [2] | | Accrued Liabilities [1] | Estimated Range of Loss for Certain Cases [2] | |
		Lower End	Upper End		Lower End	Upper End
Environmental and disposal contingencies:						
Probable	25.9	25.9	26.0	23.1	22.9	23.1
Reasonably possible	-	0.7	1.0	-	0.7	0.7

[1] Accrued liabilities are recorded and presented in the related line items of the Balance Sheet.

[2] Does not reflect the total range of loss; many cases assessed as reasonably possible of an unfavorable outcome did not include estimated losses that could be determined.

The Government is subject to loss contingencies for a variety of environmental cleanup costs for the storage and disposal of hazardous material as well as the operations and closures of facilities at which environmental contamination may be present.

Management and legal counsel have determined that it is "probable" that some of these actions will result in a loss to the Government and the loss amounts are reasonably measurable. The estimated liabilities for these cases are $25.9 billion and $23.1 billion as of September 30, 2015, and 2014, respectively, and are included in "Other Liabilities" on the Balance Sheet. In accordance with the *Nuclear Waste Policy Act of 1982* (NWPA), DOE entered into contracts with more than 45 utilities in return for payment of fees established by the NWPA into the Nuclear Waste Fund. DOE agreed to begin disposal of spent nuclear fuel (SNF) by January 31, 1998. Because DOE has no facility available to receive SNF under the NWPA, it has been unable to begin disposal of the utilities' SNF as required by the contracts. Therefore, DOE is subject to SNF litigation for damages suffered by all utilities as a result of the delay in beginning disposal of SNF and also damages for alleged exposure to radioactive and/or toxic substances. Significant claims for partial breach of contract and a large number of class action and/or multiple plaintiff tort suits have been filed with estimated liability amounts of $23.7 billion and $22.6 billion as of September 30, 2015, and 2014, respectively.

Other Contingencies

DOT and HHS reported the following other contingencies:

- The Federal Highway Administration (FHWA) preauthorizes states to establish construction budgets without having received appropriations from Congress for such projects. FHWA has authority to approve projects using advance construction under 23 U.S.C. 115(a). FHWA does not guarantee the ultimate funding to the states for these "Advance Construction" projects and does not obligate any funds for these projects. When funding becomes available to FHWA, the states can then apply for reimbursement of costs that they have incurred on such projects, at which time FHWA can accept or reject such requests. FHWA has pre-authorized $50.4 billion and $46.0 billion to the states to establish budgets for its construction projects for fiscal years ending September 30, 2015, and 2014, respectively. Congress has not provided appropriations for these projects and no liability is accrued in the DOT consolidated financial statements.
- Contingent liabilities have been accrued as a result of Medicaid audit and program disallowances that are currently being appealed by the states and for reimbursement of state plan amendments. The Medicaid amounts are $7.5 billion and $8.4 billion for fiscal years ending September 30, 2015, and 2014, respectively. In all cases, the funds have been returned to HHS. If the appeals are decided in favor of the states, HHS will be required to pay these

amounts. In addition, certain amounts for payment have been deferred under the Medicaid program when there is reasonable doubt as to the legitimacy of expenditures claimed by a state. There are also outstanding reviews of the state expenditures in which a final determination has not been made.

Treaties

The U.S. Government is a party to major treaties and other international agreements. These treaties and other international agreements address various issues including, but not limited to, trade, commerce, security, and arms that may involve financial obligations or give rise to possible exposure to losses. A comprehensive analysis to determine any such financial obligations or possible exposure to loss and their related effect on the consolidated financial statements of the U.S. Government has not yet been performed.

Note 20. Commitments

Long-Term Operating Leases as of September 30, 2015, and 2014

(In billions of dollars)	2015	2014
General Services Administration	23.9	24.4
U.S. Postal Service	7.1	6.8
Department of State	1.5	1.4
Department of Defense	1.1	0.7
Department of Health and Human Services	1.1	0.9
Department of the Treasury	0.6	0.6
Department of Transportation	0.5	0.6
Department of Agriculture	0.5	0.8
Other operating leases	3.1	2.2
Total long-term operating leases	39.4	38.4

The government has entered into contractual commitments that require future use of financial resources. It has significant amounts of long-term lease obligations and undelivered orders. Undelivered orders represent the value of goods and services ordered that have not yet been received.

The government has other commitments that may require future use of financial resources. For example, the government has callable subscriptions in certain Multilateral Development Banks (MDBs), which are international financial institutions that finance economic and social development projects in middle-income developing countries. Callable capital in the MDBs serve as a supplemental pool of resources that may be redeemed and converted into ordinary paid in shares, if the MDB cannot otherwise meet certain obligations through its other available resources. MDBs are able to use callable capital as backing to obtain favorable financing terms when borrowing from international capital markets. To date, there has never been a call on this capital at any MDBs and none are anticipated.

Undelivered Orders and Other Commitments as of September 30, 2015, and 2014

(In billions of dollars)	2015	2014
Undelivered Orders:		
Department of Defense	236.2	136.2
Department of the Treasury	169.6	164.4
Defense Security Cooperation Agency	136.4	160.9
Department of Education	124.9	130.2
Department of Transportation	108.7	107.8
Department of Health and Human Services	98.9	110.6
Department of Agriculture	40.3	43.6
Department of Housing and Urban Development	38.1	40.7
Department of Homeland Security	33.2	30.4
Department of Energy	22.5	25.5
Department of State	21.0	19.5
U.S. Agency for International Development	18.2	18.6
Department of Veterans Affairs	11.9	13.9
Federal Communications Commission	11.9	4.5
National Science Foundation	11.5	11.1
Department of Labor	9.2	9.8
All other agencies	32.3	35.7
Total undelivered orders	1,124.8	1,063.4
Other Commitments:		
GSE Senior Preferred Stock Purchase Agreement	250.1	258.1
Callable Capital Subscriptions for Multilateral Development Banks	112.3	102.3
Conservation Reserve Program	12.0	1.7
Agriculture Direct Loans and Guarantees	5.0	5.8
Fuel Purchase Obligations	4.9	5.3
Power Purchase Obligations	4.3	4.5
Other Purchase Obligations	2.8	2.8
Long-term Satellite and Systems	2.3	1.5
All other commitments	3.1	3.2
Total other commitments	404.8	385.2

Other Commitments and Risks

Undelivered Orders

DOD reported undelivered orders of $236.2 billion and $136.2 billion as of September 30, 2015, and 2014, respectively. The increase of $100 billion in FY 2015 was primarily caused by increased estimates in non-federal undelivered orders.

Commitments to GSEs

At September 30, 2015, the maximum remaining potential commitment to the GSEs for the remaining life of the SPSPAs was $258.1 billion, which was established on December 31, 2012. Refer to Note 8-Investments in Government-Sponsored Enterprises for a full description of the SPSPA agreements, related commitments, and contingent liability, if any, as well as additional information.

Terrorism Risk Insurance Program

The Terrorism Risk Insurance Act (TRIA), signed into law in November 2002, was originally enacted to address market disruptions resulting from terrorist attacks on September 11, 2001. Most recently, the Terrorism Risk Insurance Program Reauthorization Act of 2015 extended the Terrorism Risk Insurance Program (TRIA Program) until December 31, 2020. TRIA helps to ensure available and affordable commercial property and casualty insurance for terrorism risk, and simultaneously allows private markets to stabilize. The authority to pay claims under the TRIA Program is activated upon the certification of an "act of terrorism" by the Secretary of the Treasury in consultation with the Secretary of the U.S. Department of Homeland Security and the U.S. Attorney General. If a certified act of terrorism occurs, insurers may be eligible to receive reimbursement from the U.S. government for insured losses in connection with certified acts of terrorism resulting in more than $100 million in insured losses once a particular insurer has also satisfied its designated deductible amount. Insured losses above this amount will be shared between insurance companies and the U.S. government. TRIA includes both mandatory and discretionary authority for the Department of the Treasury to recoup federal payments made under the TRIA Program through policyholder surcharges under certain circumstances, and contains provisions designed to manage litigation arising from or relating to a certified act of terrorism. There were no claims under TRIA as of September 30, 2015 or 2014.

Conservation Reserve Program

The Conservation Reserve Program (CRP) was signed into law by Ronald Reagan in 1985. CRP is the largest private-lands conservation program in the United States. The program has improved water quality, reduced soil erosion, and increased habitat for endangered and threatened species. Through CRP, eligible participant's sign 10 to 15 year contracts to remove land from production in exchange for an annual rental payment. The participants also receive cost-share assistance for establishing conservation practices on the reserve acreage and additional incentive payments for adopting high-priority conservation measures. The Commodity Credit Corporation estimates that the maximum amount of future outlays for all existing CRP rental contracts over the contract terms, subject to funds availability and contract compliance, is approximately $12 billion.

Note 21. Funds from Dedicated Collections

Funds from Dedicated Collections as of September 30, 2015[1]

(In billions of dollars)	Federal Old-Age and Survivors Insurance Trust Fund	Federal Hospital Insurance Trust Fund (Medicare Part A)	Federal Disability Insurance Trust Fund	Federal Supplementary Medical Insurance Trust Fund (Medicare Parts B and D)	All Other Funds from Dedicated Collections	Total Funds from Dedicated Collections (Combined)
Assets:						
Cash and other monetary assets	-	-	-	-	59.2	59.2
Fund balance with Treasury	(0.1)	1.4	-	43.4	123.6	168.3
Investments in U.S. Treasury securities, net of unamortized premiums/discounts	2,766.6	195.5	41.6	66.1	207.0	3,276.8
Other federal assets	22.3	35.5	0.5	51.8	19.2	129.3
Non-federal assets	2.3	1.3	4.4	5.9	106.9	120.8
Total assets	2,791.1	233.7	46.5	167.2	515.9	3,754.4
Liabilities and net position:						
Due and payable to beneficiaries	66.2	28.3	27.5	37.9	6.7	166.6
Other federal liabilities	4.5	34.3	1.0	52.4	67.6	159.8
Other non-federal liabilities	-	0.6	-	0.6	179.1	180.3
Total liabilities	70.7	63.2	28.5	90.9	253.4	506.7
Total net position	2,720.4	170.5	18.0	76.3	262.5	3,247.7
Total liabilities and net position ..	2,791.1	233.7	46.5	107.2	515.9	3,754.4
Change in net position:						
Beginning net position	2,670.6	179.8	47.7	57.2	242.3	3,197.6
Prior-period adjustment	-	-	-	-	0.3	0.3
Beginning net position, adjusted ...	2,670.6	179.8	47.7	57.2	242.6	3,197.9
Investment revenue	92.2	8.4	2.4	2.4	3.0	108.4
Individual income taxes	672.2	237.7	114.2	-	-	1,024.1
Unemployment and excise taxes	-	-	-	-	106.6	106.6
Other taxes and receipts	-	0.6	-	3.0	33.7	37.3
Miscellaneous earned revenue	-	-	-	-	3.8	3.8
Other changes in fund balance (e.g., appropriations, transfers)	22.7	18.7	(2.0)	286.2	9.6	335.2
Total financing sources.................	787.1	265.4	114.6	291.6	156.7	1,615.4
Program gross costs and non-program expenses	737.3	278.4	144.3	344.5	198.7	1,703.2
Less: program revenue....................	-	(3.7)	-	(72.0)	(61.9)	(137.6)
Net cost..	737.3	274.7	144.3	272.5	136.8	1,565.6
Ending net position	2,720.4	170.5	18.0	76.3	262.5	3,247.7

[1] By law, certain expenses (costs), revenues, and other financing sources related to the administration of the above funds are not charged to the funds and are therefore financed and/or credited to other sources.

Funds from Dedicated Collections as of September 30, 2014[1]

(In billions of dollars)	Federal Old-Age and Survivors Insurance Trust Fund	Federal Hospital Insurance Trust Fund (Medicare Part A)	Federal Disability Insurance Trust Fund	Federal Supplementary Medical Insurance Trust Fund (Medicare Parts B and D)	All Other Funds from Dedicated Collections	Total Funds from Dedicated Collections (Combined)
Assets:						
Cash and other monetary assets	-	-	-	-	58.0	58.0
Fund balance with Treasury	(0.1)	0.7	(0.2)	18.4	119.5	138.3
Investments in U.S. Treasury securities, net of unamortized premiums/discounts	2,712.8	202.2	70.1	68.4	182.4	3,235.9
Other federal assets.......................	23.3	32.9	0.8	35.6	16.6	109.2
Non-federal assets..........................	2.2	1.2	4.2	5.4	112.8	125.8
Total assets	2,738.2	237.0	74.9	127.8	489.3	3,667.2
Liabilities and net position:						
Due and payable to beneficiaries	63.0	25.7	26.0	31.9	2.5	149.1
Other federal liabilities.....................	4.6	31.0	1.2	36.4	79.8	153.0
Other non-federal liabilities..............	-	0.5	-	2.3	164.7	167.5
Total liabilities	67.6	57.2	27.2	70.6	247.0	469.6
Total net position	2,670.6	179.8	47.7	57.2	242.3	3,197.6
Total liabilities and net position ...	2,738.2	237.0	74.9	127.8	489.3	3,667.2
Change in net position:						
Beginning net position	2,616.3	190.0	79.5	52.7	205.2	3,143.7
Prior period adjustment...................	-	-	-	-	0.3	0.3
Beginning net position, adjusted	2,616.3	190.0	79.5	52.7	205.5	3,144.0
Investment revenue	95.6	8.8	3.7	2.4	3.3	113.8
Individual income taxes	642.3	227.6	109.1	-	-	979.0
Unemployment and excise taxes	-	-	-	-	108.9	108.9
Other taxes and receipts..................	-	9.7	0.1	5.5	35.5	50.8
Miscellaneous earned revenue	-	-	-	-	5.0	5.0
Other changes in fund balance (e.g., appropriations, transfers)	18.0	10.5	(1.9)	247.9	25.4	299.9
Total financing sources................	755.9	256.6	111.0	255.8	178.1	1,557.4
Program gross cost and non-program expenses..	701.6	270.4	142.8	320.2	177.9	1,612.9
Less: program revenue...................	-	(3.6)	-	(68.9)	(36.6)	(109.1)
Net cost......................................	701.6	266.8	142.8	251.3	141.3	1,503.8
Ending net position	2,670.6	179.8	47.7	57.2	242.3	3,197.6

[1] By law, certain expenses (costs), revenues, and other financing sources related to the administration of the above funds are not charged to the funds and are therefore financed and/or credited to other sources.

Generally, funds from dedicated collections are financed by specifically identified revenues, often supplemented by other financing sources, provided to the government by non-federal sources, which remain available over time. These specifically identified revenues and other financing sources are required by statute to be used for designated activities, benefits, or purposes and must be accounted for separately from the government's general revenues. Funds from dedicated collections generally include trust funds, public enterprise revolving funds (not including credit reform financing funds), and special funds. Funds from dedicated collections specifically exclude any fund established to account for pensions, other retirement benefits, other postemployment or other benefits provided for federal employees (civilian and military). In the federal budget, the term "trust fund" means only that the law requires a particular fund be accounted for separately, used only for a specified purpose, and designated as a trust fund. A change in law may change the future receipts and the terms under which the fund's resources are spent. In the private sector, trust fund refers to funds of one party held and managed by a second party (the trustee) in a fiduciary capacity. The activity of funds from dedicated collections differs from fiduciary activities primarily in that assets within funds from dedicated collections are government-owned. For further information related to fiduciary activities, see Note 22—Fiduciary Activities.

Public enterprise revolving funds include expenditure accounts authorized by law to be credited with offsetting collections, mostly from the public, that are generated by and dedicated to finance a continuing cycle of business-type operations. Some of the financing for these funds may be from appropriations.

Special funds are federal funds dedicated by law for a specific purpose. Special funds include the special fund receipt account and the special fund expenditure account.

The tables above depict major funds from dedicated collections chosen based on their significant financial activity and importance to taxpayers. All other government funds from dedicated collections not shown separately are aggregated as "all other."

Total assets represent the unexpended balance from all sources of receipts and amounts due to the funds from dedicated collections, regardless of source, including related governmental transactions. These are transactions between two different entities within the government (for example, monies received by one entity of the government from another entity of the government).

The intragovernmental assets are comprised of fund balances with Treasury, investments in Treasury securities— including unamortized amounts, and other assets that include the related accrued interest receivable on federal investments. These amounts were eliminated in preparing the principal financial statements. The non-federal assets represent only the activity with individuals and organizations outside of the government.

Most of the assets within funds from dedicated collections are invested in intragovernmental debt holdings. The government does not set aside assets to pay future benefits or other expenditures associated with funds from dedicated collections. The cash receipts collected from the public for funds from dedicated collections are deposited in the General Fund, which uses the cash for general government purposes. Treasury securities are issued to federal agencies as evidence of its receipts. Treasury securities are an asset to the federal agencies and a liability to the U.S. Treasury and, therefore, they do not represent an asset or a liability in the *Financial Report*. These securities require redemption if a fund's disbursements exceeds its receipts. Redeeming these securities will increase the government's financing needs and require more borrowing from the public (or less repayment of debt), or will result in higher taxes than otherwise would have been needed, or less spending on other programs than otherwise would have occurred, or some combination thereof. See Note 11—Federal Debt Securities Held by the Public and Accrued Interest for further information related to the investments in federal debt securities.

Depicted below is a description of the major funds from dedicated collections shown in the above tables, which also identifies the government agencies that administer each particular fund. For detailed information regarding these funds from dedicated collections, please refer to the financial statements of the corresponding administering agencies. For information on the benefits due and payable liability associated with certain funds from dedicated collections, see Note 14—Benefits Due and Payable.

Federal Old-Age and Survivors Insurance Trust Fund

The Federal Old-Age and Survivors Insurance Trust Fund, administered by the SSA, provides retirement and survivors benefits to qualified workers and their families.

Payroll and self-employment taxes primarily fund the Federal Old-Age and Survivors Insurance Trust Fund. Interest earnings on Treasury securities, federal agencies' payments for the Social Security benefits earned by military and federal civilian employees, and Treasury payments for a portion of income taxes collected on Social Security benefits provide the fund with additional income. The law establishing the Federal Old-Age and Survivors Insurance Trust Fund and authorizing the depositing of amounts to the credit of the fund is set forth in 42 U.S.C. § 401.

Federal Hospital Insurance Trust Fund (Medicare Part A)

The Federal Hospital Insurance Trust Fund, administered by HHS, finances the Hospital Insurance Program (Medicare Part A). This program funds the cost of inpatient hospital and related care for individuals age 65 or older who meet certain insured status requirements, and eligible disabled people.

The Federal Hospital Insurance Trust Fund is financed primarily by payroll taxes, including those paid by federal agencies. It also receives income from interest earnings on Treasury securities, a portion of income taxes collected on Social Security benefits, and receipts from fraud and abuse control activities. Section 1817 of the *Social Security Act* established the Medicare Hospital Trust Fund.

Federal Disability Insurance Trust Fund

The Federal Disability Insurance Trust Fund provides assistance and protection against the loss of earnings due to a wage earner's disability in form of monetary payments. The SSA administers this fund.

Like the Federal Old-Age and Survivors Insurance Trust Fund, payroll taxes primarily fund the Federal Disability Insurance Trust Fund. The fund also receives income from interest earnings on Treasury securities, federal agencies' payments for the Social Security benefits earned by military and federal civilian employees, and Treasury payments for a portion of income taxes collected on Social Security benefits. The law establishing the Federal Disability Insurance Trust Fund and authorizing the depositing of amounts to the credit of the fund is set forth in 42 U.S.C. § 401.

Federal Supplementary Medical Insurance Trust Fund (Medicare Parts B and D)

The Federal Supplementary Medical Insurance Trust Fund, administered by HHS, finances the Supplementary Medical Insurance Program (Medicare Part B) and the Medicare Prescription Drug Benefit Program (Medicare Part D). These programs provide supplementary medical insurance for enrolled eligible participants to cover physician and outpatient services not covered by Medicare Part A and to obtain qualified prescription drug coverage, respectively. Medicare Part B financing is not based on payroll taxes; it is primarily based on monthly premiums, income from the General Fund, and interest earnings on Treasury securities. Medicare Supplementary Medical Insurance Trust Fund was established by Section 1841 of the *Social Security Act*.

Medicare Part D was created by the *Medicare Prescription Drug, Improvement, and Modernization Act of 2003* (Public Law No. 108-173). Medicare Part D financing is similar to Part B; it is primarily based on monthly premiums and income from the General Fund, not on payroll taxes. The fund also receives transfers from States. The law creating the Medicare prescription drug account within the Federal Supplementary Medical Insurance Trust Fund and authorizing the depositing of amounts to the credit of the fund is set forth in 42 U.S.C. § 1395w-116.

All Other Funds from Dedicated Collections

The government is responsible for the management of numerous funds from dedicated collections that serve a wide variety of purposes. The funds from dedicated collections presented on an individual basis in the above tables represent the majority of the government's net position attributable to funds from dedicated collections. All other activity attributable to funds from dedicated collections is aggregated in accordance with SFFAS No. 27, *Identifying and Reporting Funds from Dedicated Collections,* as amended by SFFAS No. 43, *Funds from Dedicated Collections: Amending Statement of Federal Financial Accounting Standards 27, Identifying and Reporting Earmarked Funds*. For the years ending September 30, 2015, and 2014, there were approximately 624 and 641 funds from dedicated collections, respectively. The funds from dedicated collections within the "all other" aggregate, along with the agencies that administer them, include the following:

- Land and Water Conservation Fund, Reclamation Fund, and Water and Related Resources Fund—administered by DOI.

- Exchange Stabilization Fund—administered by Treasury.
- Unemployment Trust Fund (UTF) and Black Lung Disability Trust Fund (BLDTF)—administered by DOL.
- Railroad Retirement Trust Fund—administered by RRB.
- National Flood Insurance Program—administered by DHS.
- Decommissioning and Decontamination Fund—administered by DOE.
- Government National Mortgage Association—administered by HUD.
- Highway Trust Fund and Airport and Airway Trust Fund—administered by DOT.
- Crime Victims Fund—administered by DOJ.
- Harbor Maintenance Trust Fund—administered by DOD.

In accordance with SFFAS No. 43, any funds established to account for pension, other retirement, or other post-employment benefits to civilian or military personnel are excluded from the reporting requirements related to funds from dedicated collections.

The Commodity Future Trading Commission erroneously did not report as a fund from dedicated collections for fiscal year 2014. This error was corrected in fiscal year 2015 and resulted in a prior-period adjustment of $0.3 billion.

Unemployment and Excise Taxes

Unemployment Taxes

The Unemployment Trust Fund (UTF), within the "all other" aggregate, represents all the unemployment tax revenues attributable to funds from dedicated collections shown on the consolidated Statement of Operations and Changes in Net Position.

UTF provides temporary assistance to workers who lose their jobs. The program is administered through a unique system of federal and state partnerships, established in federal law, but executed through conforming state laws by state officials. DOL administers the federal operations of the program.

Employer taxes provide the primary funding source for the UTF and constitute the largest portion of unemployment tax revenues attributable to funds from dedicated collections as shown on the consolidated Statement of Operations and Changes in Net Position. However, interest earnings on Treasury securities also provide income to the fund. For the years ending September 30, 2015, and 2014, UTF unemployment tax revenues were $49.1 billion and $52.6 billion, respectively. Appropriations have supplemented the fund's income during periods of high and extended unemployment. UTF was established under the authority of Section 904 of the *Social Security Act of 1935*.

Excise Taxes

There are 10 funds from dedicated collections within the "all other" aggregate that represent all of the dedicated excise tax revenue attributable to funds from dedicated collections shown on the consolidated Statement of Operations and Changes in Net Position. The Highway Trust Fund and the Airport and Airway Trust Fund, combined, represent more than 95 percent of all dedicated excise tax revenues. Both of these funds are administered by the DOT. For more information, please refer to DOT's financial statements.

The Highway Trust Fund was established to promote domestic interstate transportation and to move people and goods. The fund provides federal grants to states for highway construction, certain transit programs, and related transportation purposes. The Highway Trust Fund was created by the *Highway Revenue Act of 1956*. Funding sources include designated excise taxes on gasoline and other fuels, the initial sale of heavy trucks, and highway use by commercial motor vehicles. For the years ending September 30, 2015, and 2014, Highway Trust Fund excise tax revenues were $40.8 billion and $39.0 billion, respectively. As funds are needed for payments, the Highway Trust Fund corpus investments are liquidated and funds are transferred to the Federal Highway Administration, the Federal Transit Administration, or other DOT entities, for payment of obligations.

The Airport and Airway Trust Fund provides for airport improvement and airport facilities maintenance. It also funds airport equipment, research, and a portion of the Federal Aviation Administration's administrative operational support. The Airport and Airway Trust Fund was authorized by the *Airport and Airway Revenue Act of 1970*. Funding sources include:

- Taxes received from transportation of persons and property in the air, as well as fuel used in commercial and general aviation.
- International departure taxes.
- Interest earnings on Treasury securities.

For the years ending September 30, 2015, and 2014, Airport and Airway Trust Fund excise tax revenues were $14.3 billion and $13.5 billion, respectively.

Miscellaneous Earned Revenues

Miscellaneous earned revenues due to activity attributable to funds from dedicated collections primarily relate to royalties retained by various funds within DOI.

Note 22. Fiduciary Activities

Fiduciary activities are the collection or receipt, and the management, protection, accounting, investment and disposition by the Government of cash or other assets in which non-federal individuals or entities have an ownership interest that the Government must uphold. Fiduciary cash and other assets are not assets of the Government and are not recognized on the consolidated Balance Sheet. Examples of the Government's fiduciary activities include the Thrift Savings Plan (the Plan), which is administered by the Federal Retirement Thrift Investment Board, and the Indian Tribal and individual Indian Trust Funds, which are administered by the DOI.

Schedule of Fiduciary Net Assets as of September 30, 2015, and 2014

(In billions of dollars)	2015	2014
FRTIB-Thrift Savings Plan	427.3	416.1
Department of the Interior	5.1	5.1
All other	2.8	5.9
Total fiduciary net assets	435.2	427.1

In accordance with the requirements of SFFAS No. 31, *Accounting for Fiduciary Activities,* fiduciary investments in Treasury securities and fund balance with Treasury held by fiduciary funds are to be recognized on the Balance Sheet as debt held by the public and a liability for fiduciary fund balance with Treasury, respectively.

As of September 30, 2015, total fiduciary investments in Treasury securities and in non-Treasury securities are $209.5 billion and $243.1 billion, respectively. As of September 30, 2014, total fiduciary investments in Treasury securities and in non-Treasury securities were $187.1 billion and $241.9 billion, respectively. Refer to Note 11 – Federal Debt Securities Held by the Public and Accrued Interest for more information on the Treasury securities.

As of September 30, 2015, and 2014, the total fiduciary fund balance with Treasury is $1.2 billion and $1.0 billion, respectively. A liability for this fiduciary fund balance with Treasury is reflected as other miscellaneous liabilities in Note 16 - Other Liabilities.

As of September 30, 2015, and 2014, collectively, the fiduciary investments in Treasury securities and fiduciary fund balance with Treasury held by all Government entities represent $6.0 billion and $3.4 billion, respectively, of unrestricted cash included within cash held by Treasury for Governmentwide Operations shown in Note 2 - Cash and Other Monetary Assets.

Federal Retirement Thrift Investment Board (FRTIB)-Thrift Savings Plan

The TSP is administered by an independent Government agency, the FRTIB, which is charged with operating the TSP prudently and solely in the interest of the participants and their beneficiaries. Assets of the TSP are maintained in the Thrift Savings Fund.

The TSP is a retirement savings and investment plan for federal employees and members of the uniformed services. It was authorized by the United States Congress in the *Federal Employees' Retirement System Act of 1986*. The Plan provides federal employees and members of the uniformed services with a savings and tax benefit similar to what many private sector employers offer their employees under 401(k) plans. The Plan was primarily designed to be a key part of the retirement package (along with a basic annuity benefit and Social Security) for employees who are covered by FERS.

Federal employees, who are participants of FERS, the CSRS, or equivalent retirement systems, as provided by statute, and members of the uniformed services, are eligible to join the Plan immediately upon being hired. Generally, FERS employees are those employees hired on or after January 1, 1984, while CSRS employees are employees hired before January 1, 1984, who have not elected to convert to FERS. Each group has different rules that govern contribution rates. As of December 31, 2014, and 2013, there were approximately 4.8 million and 4.6 million participants in the TSP, respectively, with approximately 2.9 million contributing their own money. For further information about FRTIB and the TSP, please refer to the FRTIB website at http://www.frtib.gov.

As of September 30, 2015, and 2014, the TSP held $427.3 billion and $416.1 billion, respectively, in net assets, which included $0.0 billion and $183.7 billion, respectively, of U.S. Government Securities (amounts are unaudited). A delay in raising the statutory debt limit existed as of September 30, 2015. When delays in raising the statutory debt limit occur, the Department of the Treasury often must deviate from its normal debt management operations and take a number of extraordinary measures to meet the government's obligations as they come due without exceeding the debt limit. Extraordinary measures taken by Treasury during the period of March 16, 2015 through September 30, 2015 resulted in federal debt securities not being issued to certain federal government accounts. As reported in Note 16, as a result of Treasury securities not being issued to the TSP's G Fund, Treasury reported miscellaneous liabilities in the amount of $204.6 billion that represent uninvested principal and related interest for TSP's G Fund that would have been reported as federal debt securities had there not been a delay in raising the statutory debt limit as of September 30, 2015 and had the securities been issued. The most recent audited financial statements for the TSP are as of December 31, 2014, and 2013. As of December 31, 2014, and 2013, the TSP held $428.1 billion and $394.5 billion, respectively, in net assets, which included $191.3 billion and $172.7 billion, respectively, of U.S. Government Securities. These unaudited amounts above are included to enhance comparability of the TSP net assets with the remainder of the Government's fiduciary net assets as of September 30, 2015, and 2014.

DOI–Indian Trust Funds

As stated above, DOI has responsibility for the assets held in trust on behalf of American Indian Tribes and individuals, and these account for all of DOI's fiduciary net assets. DOI maintains accounts for Tribal and Other Trust Funds (including the Alaska Native Escrow Fund and Individual Indian Money Trust Funds) in accordance with the *American Indian Trust Fund Management Reform Act of 1994*. The fiduciary balances that have accumulated in these funds have resulted from land use agreements, royalties on natural resource depletion, other proceeds derived directly from trust resources, judgment awards, settlements of claims, and investment income. These funds are maintained for the benefit of individual Native Americans as well as for designated Indian tribes. DOI maintains separate financial statements for these trust funds which were prepared using the cash or modified cash basis of accounting, a comprehensive basis of accounting other than GAAP. The independent auditors' reports were qualified as it was not practical to extend audit procedures sufficiently to satisfy themselves as to the fairness of the trust fund balances. For further information related to these assets, please refer to the DOI website at http://www.doi.gov.

All Other Entities with Fiduciary Activities

The Government is responsible for the management of other fiduciary net assets on behalf of various non-federal entities. The component entities presented individually in the table on the previous page represent the vast majority of the Government's fiduciary net assets. All other component entities with fiduciary net assets are aggregated in accordance with SFFAS No. 31. As of September 30, 2015, and 2014, including FRTIB and DOI, there are a total of 17 and 15 federal entities, respectively, with fiduciary activities at a grand total of 65 and 50 fiduciary funds, respectively. SBA and LOC are the significant agencies relating to the fiduciary activities of the remaining component entities within the "all other" aggregate balance. As of September 30, 2015, "all other" fiduciary net assets were $2.8 billion, compared to $5.9 billion as of September 30, 2014.

Note 23. Social Insurance

The Statement of Social Insurance presents the projected actuarial present value of the estimated future revenue and estimated future expenditures of the Social Security, Medicare, Railroad Retirement, and Black Lung social insurance programs which are administered by the SSA, HHS, RRB, and DOL, respectively. These estimates are based on the economic as well as demographic assumptions presented later in this note as set forth in the relevant Social Security and Medicare trustees' reports and in the agency financial reports of HHS, SSA, and DOL as well as in the relevant agency performance and accountability report for RRB. The basis for the projections has changed since last year due to the enactment of the Medicare Access and Children's Health Insurance Program (CHIP) Reauthorization Act (MACRA) of 2015. This law repealed the sustainable growth rate (SGR) formula that set physician fee schedule payments, and replaced it with specified payment updates for physicians. In last year's report, the income, expenditures, and assets for Medicare Part B reflected the *projected baseline* scenario, which assumed an override of the SGR payment provisions and an increase in the physician fee schedule equal to the average of the most recent 10 years of SGR overrides (through March 2015) or 0.6 percent. Since the new legislation has replaced the SGR system with specified payment updates for physicians, the projections in this year's report are based on the continuation of program provisions contained in current law, with one exception in regard to payment reductions that would result from the projected depletion of the Social Security and Medicare Hospital Insurance (Part A) Trust Funds; under current law, payments would be reduced to levels that could be covered by incoming tax and premium revenues when the Social Security and Medicare Hospital Insurance (Part A) Trust Funds are depleted. The estimates in the consolidated SOSI of the open group measures are for persons who are participants or eventually will participate in the programs as contributors (workers) or beneficiaries (retired workers, survivors, and disabled) during the 75-year projection period. The Black Lung projection period ends September 30, 2040, because the primary purpose of the BLDTF is to compensate the victims of coal mine dust exposures which occurred prior to 1970. By the end of fiscal year 2040, not only the disabled miners and their widows in that class, but also virtually all of their eligible dependent disabled adult children will be deceased.

Contributions and dedicated taxes consist of: payroll taxes from employers, employees, and self-employed persons; revenue from federal income taxation of Old-Age Survivors and Disability Insurance (OASDI) and railroad retirement benefits; excise tax on the domestic sale of coal (Black Lung); premiums from, and state transfers on behalf of, participants in Medicare; and reimbursements from the General Fund to the OASDI Trust Funds to make up for reductions in payroll tax revenue due to temporary payroll tax rate reductions. Income for all programs is presented from a consolidated perspective. Future interest payments and other future intragovernmental transfers have been excluded upon consolidation. Expenditures include scheduled benefit payments and administrative expenses. Scheduled benefits are projected based on the benefit formulas under current law, with an exception in regard to payment reductions that would result from the projected depletion of the Social Security and Medicare Hospital Insurance (Part A) Trust Funds. Current Social Security and Medicare law also provides for full benefit payments only to the extent that there are sufficient balances in the trust funds. Expenditures reflect full benefit payments even after the point at which assets are projected to be depleted. As mentioned above, this methodology has changed since last year when, instead of current law, the Part B projections reflected the *projected baseline* scenario, which assumed an override of the SGR payment provisions used to set physician fee schedule payments.

Actuarial present values of estimated future income (excluding interest) and estimated future expenditures for the Social Security, Medicare, and Railroad Retirement social insurance programs are presented for three different groups of participants: (1) current participants who have not yet attained eligibility age; (2) current participants who have attained eligibility age; and (3) new entrants, who are expected to become participants in the future. Current participants in the Social Security and Medicare programs are the "closed group" of taxpayers and/or beneficiaries who are at least age 15 years at the start of the projection period. Since the projection period for the Social Security, Medicare, and Railroad Retirement social insurance programs consists of 75 years, the period covers virtually all of the current participants' working and retirement years, a period that could be greater than 75 years in a relatively small number of instances. Future participants for Social Security and Medicare include births during the projection period and individuals below age 15 as of January 1 of the valuation year. Railroad Retirement's future participants are the projected new entrants as of January 1 of the valuation year.

The present values of estimated future expenditures in excess of estimated future revenue are calculated by subtracting the actuarial present values of future scheduled contributions as well as dedicated tax income by and on behalf of current and future participants from the actuarial present value of the future scheduled benefit payments to them or on their behalf. To determine a program's funding shortfall over any given period of time, the starting trust fund balance is subtracted from the present value of expenditures in excess of revenues over the period.

The trust fund balances as of the valuation date for the respective programs, including interest earned, are shown in the table below. Substantially all of the Social Security (OASDI), Medicare Hospital Insurance (HI), and Supplementary Medical Insurance (SMI) Trust Fund balances consist of investments in special nonmarketable U.S. Treasury securities that are backed by the full faith and credit of the U.S. Government.

Social Insurance Programs Trust Fund Balances [1]

(In billions of dollars)	2015	2014	2013	2012	2011
Social Security	2,789	2,764	2,732	2,678	2,609
Medicare:					
HI	197	205	220	244	272
SMI Part B	68	74	66	80	71
SMI Part D	1	1	1	1	1
Railroad Retirement	28	28	26	24	26
Black Lung	(6)	(6)	(6)	(6)	(6)

[1] As of the valuation date of the respective programs.

Social Security

The Federal Old-Age and Survivors Insurance (OASI) program, created in 1935, and the Federal Disability Insurance (DI) program, created in 1956, collectively referred to as OASDI or "Social Security," provides cash benefits for eligible U.S. citizens and residents. Eligibility and benefit amounts are determined under the laws applicable for the period. Current law provides that the amount of the monthly benefit payments for workers, or their eligible dependents or survivors, is based on the workers' lifetime earnings histories.

The primary financing of the OASDI Trust Funds are taxes paid by workers, their employers, and individuals with self-employment income, based on work covered by the OASDI Program. Refer to the Unaudited Required Supplementary Information—Social Insurance section for additional information on Social Security program financing.

That portion of each trust fund not required to pay benefits and administrative costs is invested, on a daily basis, in interest-bearing obligations of the U.S. Government. The Social Security Act authorizes the issuance by the Treasury of special nonmarketable, intragovernmental debt obligations for purchase exclusively by the trust funds. Although the special issues cannot be bought or sold in the open market, they are redeemable at any time at face value and thus bear no risk of fluctuation in principal value due to changes in market yield rates. Interest on the bonds is credited to the trust funds and becomes an asset to the funds and a liability to the General Fund. These Treasury securities and related interest are eliminated in consolidation at the governmentwide level.

Medicare

The Medicare Program, created in 1965, has two separate trust funds: the HI (Medicare Part A) and SMI (Medicare Parts B and D) Trust Funds. HI pays for inpatient acute hospital services and major alternatives to hospitals (skilled nursing services, for example), and SMI pays for hospital outpatient services, physician services, and assorted other services and products through the Part B account and pays for prescription drugs through the Part D account. Though the events that trigger benefit payments are similar, HI and SMI have different dedicated financing structures. Similar to OASDI, HI is financed primarily by payroll contributions. Other income to the HI Trust Fund includes a small amount of premium income from voluntary enrollees, a portion of the federal income taxes that beneficiaries pay on Social Security benefits and interest credited on Treasury securities held in the HI Trust Fund. These Treasury securities and related interest are eliminated in the consolidation at the governmentwide level.

For SMI, transfers from the General Fund represent the largest source of income for both Parts B and D. Generally, beneficiaries finance the remainder of Parts B and D costs via monthly premiums to these programs. With the introduction of Part D drug coverage, Medicaid is no longer the primary payer for beneficiaries dually eligible for Medicare and Medicaid. For those beneficiaries, states must pay a portion of their estimated foregone drug costs into the Part D account (referred to as state transfers). As with HI, interest received on Treasury securities held in the SMI Trust Fund is credited to the fund and these Treasury securities as well as related interest are eliminated in consolidation at the governmentwide level. By accounting convention, the transfers of general revenues are eliminated in the consolidation of the SOSI at the governmentwide level and as such, the general revenues that are used to finance Medicare Parts B and D are not included in these calculations even though the expenditures on these programs are included. For the fiscal year 2015 and 2014 SOSI, the amounts eliminated totaled $24.8 trillion and $24.7 trillion, respectively. Refer to Unaudited Required Supplementary Information—Social Insurance section for additional information on Medicare program financing.

The *Medicare Prescription Drug, Improvement, and Modernization Act* (MMA), enacted on December 8, 2003, created the Part D account in the SMI Trust Fund to account for the prescription drug benefit that began in 2006. The MMA established within SMI two Part D accounts related to prescription drug benefits: the Medicare Prescription Drug Account and the Transitional Assistance Account. The Medicare Prescription Drug Account was used in conjunction with the broad, voluntary prescription drug benefits that commenced in 2006. The Transitional Assistance Account was used to provide transitional assistance benefits, beginning in 2004 and extending through 2005, for certain low-income beneficiaries prior to the start of the new prescription drug benefit.

Affordable Care Act (ACA)

In fiscal year 2010, President Barack Obama signed health insurance reform legislation giving Americans more control over their health care. The *Patient Protection and Affordable Care Act* and the *Health Care and Education Reconciliation Act* collectively referred to as the *Affordable Care Act* ensures that all Americans have access to quality, affordable health care, while helping to reduce health care costs.

The *Affordable Care Act* contains the most significant changes to health care coverage since the passing of the *Social Security Act*. The *Affordable Care Act* provided funding for the establishment by CMS of a Center for Medicare and Medicaid Innovation to test innovative payment and service delivery models to reduce program expenditures while preserving or enhancing the quality of care furnished to individuals. It also allowed for the establishment of a Center for Consumer Information and Insurance Oversight (CCIIO). The programs under CCIIO include the Marketplace and other programs listed below. A brief description of these programs and their impact on the financial statement is presented below.

Grants have been provided to the states to establish Affordable Insurance Marketplaces. The initial grants were made by the HHS to the states "not later than one year after the date of enactment." Thus, HHS made the initial grants by March 23, 2011. Subsequent grants were issued by CMS. All Marketplaces were launched on October 1, 2013.

To help make health insurance more affordable to consumers, HHS makes advance payments of the premium tax credits (APTC) and cost-sharing reductions (CSR) to health insurance issuers on behalf of consumers who are eligible for financial assistance. APTC and CSR payments (which are included in the IRS financial statements) are a critical component of the Marketplace, and $30.0 billion has been allocated for these payments. In addition to these payments on behalf of consumers, HHS collects Marketplace user fees from issuers participating in the Federally-Facilitated Marketplace (FFM).

The Basic Health Program (BHP) gives states the ability to provide more affordable coverage for low-income residents and improve continuity of care for people whose income fluctuates above and below Medicaid and CHIP levels. Through the BHP, states can provide coverage to individuals who do not qualify for Medicaid, CHIP, or other minimum essential coverage and have income between 133 percent and 200 percent of the federal poverty level (FPL). A state that operates a BHP will receive federal funding equal to 95 percent of the amount of the premium tax credits and the cost sharing reductions that would have otherwise been provided to (or on behalf of) eligible individuals if these individuals enrolled in Qualified Health Plans through the Marketplace. Similar to APTC and CSR payments, BHP payment amounts are included in the IRS financial statements.

The Consumer Operated and Oriented Plan (CO-OP) Program fosters qualified non-profit health insurance issuers created to offer qualified health plans to the individual and small group markets. Under this program, HHS provides assistance to organizations applying to become qualified non-profit health insurance issuers through loans to assist in meeting start-up costs and to assist the applicant meet state solvency requirements. In accordance with regulations as well as legislative requirements, start-up loans shall be repaid within five years and the solvency loans within 15 years after disbursement, considering state reserve requirements and solvency regulations.

The Transitional Reinsurance program was established in each state to help stabilize premiums for coverage in the individual market from 2014 through 2016. All health insurance issuers and third party administrators, on behalf of some self-insured group health plans, must make contributions to support reinsurance payments that cover high-cost individuals in non-grandfathered plans in the individual market, inside and outside the Marketplace. The Transitional Reinsurance program is a critical element in helping to ensure a stabilized individual market in the first years of the Exchange operation of the Marketplace.

The Risk Adjustment program is a permanent program. It applies to non-grandfathered individual market and small group market plans inside and outside the Marketplaces. It provides payments to health insurance issuers that disproportionately attract higher-risk populations (such as individuals with chronic conditions) and transfers funds from plans with relatively lower risk enrollees to plans with relatively higher risk enrollees to protect against risk selection and adverse selection. States may operate risk adjustment programs and CMS will operate a risk adjustment program for each state that does not operate its own. In 2014 and 2015, Massachusetts is the only state that operated its own risk adjustment program.

The temporary Risk Corridors program will operate during the years 2014 through 2016. This program applies to qualified health plans in the individual and small group markets, inside and outside the Marketplaces and protects against inaccurate rate-setting by sharing risk (gains and losses) on allowable costs between CMS and qualified health plans to help ensure stable health insurance premiums.

The financial projections for the Medicare program reflect substantial, but very uncertain, cost savings deriving from provisions of the ACA and the specified physician updates put in place by the MACRA. However, it is important to note that the improved results for HI and SMI Part B since 2010 depend in part on the long-range feasibility of the various cost-saving measures in the ACA–most importantly, the reductions in the annual payment rate updates for most categories of Medicare providers by the growth in economy-wide productivity. Under the ACA, the rate of increase of Medicare payment rates is equal to the prior law rate of increase (equal to the rate of increase in the prices of inputs used to produce Medicare services) less the rate of increase of total economy multifactor productivity. Without fundamental change in the current delivery system, these productivity-related adjustments to Medicare payment rates would probably not be viable indefinitely. However, this outcome is achievable if health care providers are able to realize productivity improvements at a faster rate than experienced historically. On the other hand, if the health sector cannot transition to more efficient models of care delivery and achieve productivity increases commensurate with economy-wide productivity, and if the provider reimbursement rates paid by commercial insurers continue to follow the same negotiated process used to date, then the availability and quality of health care received by Medicare beneficiaries would, under current law, fall over time relative to that received by those with private health insurance.

A transformation of health care in the United States, affecting both the means of delivery and the method of paying for care, is also a possibility. The ACA takes important steps in this direction by initiating programs of research into innovative payment and service delivery models, such as accountable care organizations, patient-centered medical homes, improvement in care coordination for individuals with multiple chronic health conditions, improvement in coordination of post-acute care, payment bundling, pay for performance, and assistance for individuals in making informed health choices. Such changes have the potential to reduce health care costs as well as cost growth rates and could, as a result, help lower Medicare cost growth rates to levels compatible with the lower price updates payable under current law.

The ability of new delivery and payment methods to significantly lower cost growth rates is uncertain at this time, since specific changes have not yet been designed, tested, or evaluated. Preliminary indications are that some of these delivery reforms have had modest levels of success in lowering costs, but at this time it is too early to tell if these reductions in spending will continue, or if they will grow to the magnitude needed to align with the statutory Medicare price updates. The ability of health care providers to sustain the price reductions for those providers impacted by the productivity adjustments and the specified updates to physician payments will be challenging, as the best available evidence indicates that most providers cannot improve their productivity to this degree for a prolonged period given the labor-intensive nature of these services and that physician costs will grow at a faster rate than the specified updates. As a result, actual Medicare expenditures are highly uncertain for reasons apart from the inherent difficulty in projecting health care cost growth over time.

The reduction in provider payment updates, if implemented for all future years as required under current law, could have secondary impacts on provider participation, beneficiary access to care; quality of services; and other factors. These possible impacts are very speculative and at present there is no consensus among experts as to their potential scope. Further research and analysis will help to better inform this issue and may enable the development of specific projections of secondary effects under current law in the future.

The SOSI projections are based on current law, with one exception in regard to payment reductions that would result from the projected depletion of the Medicare Hospital Insurance (Part A) Trust Fund; under current law, payments would be reduced to levels that could be covered by incoming tax and premium revenues when the Medicare Hospital Insurance (Part A) Trust Funds are depleted.

The extent to which actual future Part A and Part B costs exceed the projected amounts due to changes to the productivity adjustments and specified physician updates depends on what specific changes might be legislated and whether Congress would pass further provisions to help offset such costs. However, absent an unprecedented change in health care delivery systems and payment mechanisms, the prices paid by Medicare for health services will fall increasingly short of the cost of providing such services. If this issue is not addressed by subsequent legislation, it is likely that access to, and quality of, physicians' services would deteriorate over time for beneficiaries. By the end of the long-range projection period, Medicare prices for many services would be less than half of their level without consideration of the productivity price reductions and physician payments would be 30 percent lower than they would have been under the SGR. Before such an outcome would occur, lawmakers would likely intervene to prevent the withdrawal of providers from the Medicare market and the severe problems with beneficiary access to care that would result. Overriding the productivity adjustments and specified physician updates, as lawmakers have done repeatedly in the case of physician payment rates, would lead to substantially higher costs for Medicare in the long range than those projected in this report.

To help illustrate and quantify the potential magnitude of the cost understatement, the Trustees asked the Office of the Actuary at CMS to prepare an illustrative Medicare Trust Fund projection under a hypothetical alternative that assumes that, starting in 2020, the economy-wide productivity adjustments gradually phase down to 0.4 percent, and starting in 2024, physician payments transition from a payment update of 0.0 percent to an increase of 2.3 percent. In addition, the illustrative alternative also assumes that requirements for the Independent Payment Advisory Board would not be implemented.[5] This alternative was developed for illustrative purposes only; the calculations have not been audited; no endorsement of the policies underlying the illustrative alternative by the Trustees, CMS, or the Office of the Actuary should be inferred; and the examples do not attempt to portray likely or recommended future outcomes. Thus, the illustrations are useful only as general indicators of the substantial impacts that could result from future legislation affecting the productivity adjustments and physician updates under Medicare and of the broad range of uncertainty associated with such impacts. The table below contains a comparison of the Medicare 75-year present values of estimated future income and estimated future expenditures under current law with those under the illustrative alternative scenario.

---

[5] The illustrative alternative projections included changes to the productivity adjustments starting with the 2010 annual report, following enactment of the *Affordable Care Act*. The assumption regarding physician payments is being used because the SGR was replaced earlier this year.

Medicare Present Values (in billions) (Unaudited)

	2015 Consolidated SOSI Current Law	Illustrative Alternative Scenario [1,2]
Income:		
Part A	$17,902	$17,929
Part B [3]	$6,529	$8,065
Part D [4]	$2,869	$2,895
Total income	$27,300	$28,889
Expenditures:		
Part A	$21,089	$25,824
Part B	$23,995	$29,605
Part D	$10,156	$10,246
Total expenditures	$55,240	$65,675
Part A	$3,187	$7,895
Part B	$17,466	$21,540
Part D	$7,287	$7,352
Excess of expenditures over income	$27,940	$36,787

[1] These amounts are not presented in the 2015 Trustees' Report.

[2] At the request of the Trustees, the Office of the Actuary at CMS has prepared an illustrative set of Medicare Trust Fund projections that differ from current law. No endorsement of the illustrative alternative to current law by the Trustees, CMS, or the Office of the Actuary should be inferred.

[3] Excludes $17,466 billion and $21,540 billion of General Revenue Contributions from the 2015 Consolidated SOSI Current Law projection and the Illustrative Alternative Scenario's projection, respectively; i.e., to reflect Part B income on a consolidated governmentwide basis.

[4] Excludes $7,287 billion and $7,352 billion of General Revenue Contributions from the 2015 Consolidated SOSI Current Law projection and the Illustrative Alternative Scenario's projection, respectively; i.e., to reflect Part D income on a consolidated governmentwide basis.

Note: Amounts may not add up due to rounding.

The difference between the current law and illustrative alternative projections is substantial for Parts A and B. All Part A fee-for-service providers and roughly half of Part B fee-for-service providers are affected by the productivity adjustments, so the current-law projections reflect an estimated 1.1 percent reduction in annual cost growth each year for these providers. If the productivity adjustments were gradually phased out and physician updates transitioned to the Medicare Economic Index update of 2.3 percent, as illustrated under the alternative scenario, the estimated present value of Part A and Part B expenditures would be higher than the current law projections by roughly 22 percent and 23 percent, respectively. As indicated above, the present value of Part A income is basically unaffected under the alternative scenario.

The Part D values are similar under each projection because the services are not affected by the productivity adjustments or the physician updates. The very minor impact is the result of a slight change in the discount rates that are used to calculate the present values.

The extent to which actual future Part A and Part B costs exceed the projected amounts due to changes to the productivity adjustments and physician updates depends on what specific changes might be legislated and whether Congress would pass further provisions to help offset such costs. As noted, these examples reflect only hypothetical changes to provider payment rates.

Social Security and Medicare–Demographic and Economic Assumptions

The Boards of Trustees[6] of the OASDI and Medicare Trust Funds provide in their annual reports to Congress short-range (10-year) and long-range (75-year) actuarial estimates of each trust fund. Because of the inherent uncertainty in estimates for 75 years into the future, the Boards use three alternative sets of economic and demographic assumptions to show a range of possibilities. Assumptions are made about many economic and demographic factors, including Gross Domestic Product (GDP)[7], disability incidence and terminations, earnings, the Consumer Price Index (CPI), the unemployment rate, the fertility rate, immigration, mortality, and for the Medicare projections health care cost growth. The assumptions used for the most recent set of projections shown in Table 1A (Social Security) and Table 1B (Medicare) are generally referred to as the "intermediate assumptions," and reflect the trustees' reasonable estimate of expected future experience. For further information on Social Security and Medicare demographic and economic assumptions, refer to SSA's and HHS' Agency Financial Reports.

---

[6] There are six trustees: the Secretaries of the Treasury (managing trustee), Health and Human Services, and Labor, the Commissioner of the Social Security Administration, and two public trustees who are generally appointed by the President and confirmed by the Senate for a 4-year term. By law, the public trustees are members of two different political parties.
[7] In July 2013, the Bureau of Economic Analysis (BEA) revised upward the historical values for GDP beginning with estimates for 1929.

Table 1A
Social Security – Demographic and Economic Assumptions

Demographic Assumptions

Year	Total Fertility Rate[1]	Age-Sex Adjusted Death Rate (per 100,000)[2]	Net Annual Immigration (persons per year)[3]	Period Life Expectancy at Birth[4]	
				Male	Female
2015	1.91	771.3	1,465,000	76.9	81.5
2020	2.04	730.1	1,395,000	77.7	82.1
2030	2.00	667.6	1,190,000	78.9	83.1
2040	2.00	615.0	1,135,000	80.0	84.0
2050	2.00	568.9	1,110,000	81.0	84.8
2060	2.00	528.2	1,095,000	81.9	85.5
2070	2.00	492.2	1,085,000	82.8	86.2
2080	2.00	460.1	1,085,000	83.6	86.9

Economic Assumptions

Year	Real Wage Differential (percent)[5]	Average Annual Wage In Covered Employment (percent change)[6]	CPI (percent change)[7]	Real GDP (percent change)[8]	Total Employment (percent change)[9]	Average Annual Interest Rate (percent)[10]
2015	3.18	3.38	0.20	3.3	1.3	2.2
2020	1.73	4.43	2.70	2.7	1.0	5.3
2030	1.23	3.93	2.70	2.1	0.5	5.6
2040	1.20	3.90	2.70	2.2	0.6	5.6
2050	1.21	3.91	2.70	2.1	0.5	5.6
2060	1.16	3.86	2.70	2.0	0.4	5.6
2070	1.11	3.81	2.70	2.1	0.4	5.6
2080	1.13	3.83	2.70	2.1	0.4	5.6

[1]The total fertility rate for any year is the average number of children that would be born to a woman in her lifetime if she were to experience, at each age of her life, the birth rate observed in, or assumed for, the selected year, and if she were to survive the entire childbearing period.

[2]The age-sex-adjusted death rate is based on he enumerated total population as of April 1, 2010, if that population were to experience he death rates by age and sex observed in, or assumed for, the selected year. It is a summary measure and not a basic assumption; it summarizes the basic assumptions from which it is derived.

[3]Net annual immigration is the number of persons who enter during he year (both legally and otherwise) minus the number of persons who leave during the year. It is a summary measure and not a basic assumption; it summarizes the effects of the basic assumptions from which it is derived.

[4]The period life expectancy at a given age for a given year is the average remaining number of years expected prior to death for a person at that exact age, born on January 1, using the mortality rates for that year over the course of his or her remaining life. It is a summary measure and not a basic assumption; it summarizes the effects of the basic assumptions from which it is derived.

[5]The real-wage differential is the annual percentage change in the average annual wage in covered employment less the annual percentage change in the Consumer Price Index for Urban Wage Earners and Clerical Workers (CPI-W). Values are rounded after all computations.

[6]The average annual wage in covered employment is the total amount of wages and salaries for all employment covered by the OASDI program in a year, divided by the number of employees with any such earnings during the year. It is a summary measure and not a basic assump ion; it summarizes the basic assumptions from which it is derived.

[7]The CPI is the Consumer Price Index for Urban Wage Earners and Clerical Workers (CPI-W).

[8]The real GDP is the value of total output of goods and services in 2009 dollars. It is a summary measure and not a basic assumption; it summarizes the effects of the basic assump ions from which it is derived.

[9]Total employment is total U.S. military and civilian employment. It is a summary measure and not a basic assumption; it summarizes the basic assumptions from which it is derived.

[10]The average annual interest rate is the average of the nominal interest rates, which compound semiannually, for special public-debt obligations issuable to he OASI and DI Trust Funds in each of the 12 months of the year. It is a summary measure and not a basic assumption; it summarizes the basic assumptions from which it is derived.

Table 1B
Medicare – Demographic and Economic Assumptions

Demographic Assumptions

Year	Total Fertility Rate[1]	Age-Sex Adjusted Death Rate (per 100,000)[2]	Net Annual Immigration (persons per year)[3]
2015	1.91	771.3	1,465,000
2020	2.04	730.1	1,395,000
2030	2.00	667.6	1,190,000
2040	2.00	615.0	1,135,000
2050	2.00	568.9	1,110,000
2060	2.00	528.2	1,095,000
2070	2.00	492.2	1,085,000
2080	2.00	460.1	1,085,000

Economic Assumptions

Year	Real Wage Differential (percent)[4]	Average Annual Wage In Covered Employment (percent change)[5]	CPI (percent change)[6]	Real GDP (percent change)[7]	Per Beneficiary Cost[8] (percent change) HI	SMI Part B	SMI Part D	Real Interest Rate (percent)[9]
2015	3.18	3.38	0.20	3.3	(0.9)	2.2	2.5	2.1
2020	1.73	4.43	2.70	2.7	4.2	5.9	5.7	2.4
2030	1.23	3.93	2.70	2.1	4.4	4.9	5.1	2.9
2040	1.20	3.90	2.70	2.2	4.9	4.1	4.9	2.9
2050	1.21	3.91	2.70	2.1	3.9	3.7	4.8	2.9
2060	1.16	3.86	2.70	2.0	3.7	3.7	4.6	2.9
2070	1.11	3.81	2.70	2.1	3.9	3.7	4.5	2.9
2080	1.13	3.83	2.70	2.1	3.9	3.7	4.5	2.9

[1] The total fertility rate for any year is he average number of children that would be born to a woman in her lifetime if she were to experience, at each age of her life, the birth rate observed in, or assumed for, the selected year, and if she were to survive the entire childbearing period.

[2] The age-sex-adjusted death rate is based on the enumerated total population as of April 1, 2010, if hat population were to experience the death rates by age and sex observed in, or assumed for, the selected year. It is a summary measure and not a basic assumption; it summarizes the basic assumptions from which it is derived.

[3] Net annual immigration is the number of persons who enter during the year (both legally and otherwise) less the number of persons who leave during the year. It is a summary measure and not a basic assumption; it summarizes the effects of the basic assumptions from which it is derived.

[4] The real-wage differential is the annual percentage change in the average annual wage in covered employment less the annual percentage change in CPI. Values are rounded after computations.

[5] The average annual wage in covered employment is the total amount of wages and salaries for all employment covered by the OASDI program in a year, divided by the number of employees with any such earnings during the year. It is a summary measure and not a basic assumption; it summarizes the basic assumptions from which it is derived.

[6] The CPI is the Consumer Price Index for Urban Wage Earners and Clerical Workers (CPI-W).

[7] The real GDP is the value of total output of goods and services produced in the U.S. in 2009 dollars. It is a summary measure and not a basic assumption; it summarizes the effects of the basic assumptions from which it is derived.

[8] These increases reflect the overall impact of more detailed assumptions that are made for each of the different types of service provided by the Medicare program (for example, hospital care, physician services, and pharmaceutical costs). These assumptions include changes in the payment rates, utilization, and intensity of each type of service.

[9] The real interest rate is the average rate of interest earned on new trust fund securities, above and beyond the rate of inflation.

Railroad Retirement

The Railroad Retirement and Survivor Benefit program pays full retirement annuities at age 60 to railroad workers with 30 years of service. The program pays disability annuities based on total or occupational disability. It also pays annuities to spouses and divorced spouses of retired workers and to widow(er)s, surviving divorced spouses, partitioned surviving spouses, partitioned surviving divorced spouses, remarried widow(er)s, children, and parents of deceased railroad workers. Medicare covers qualified railroad retirement beneficiaries in the same way as it does Social Security beneficiaries.

The RRB and the SSA share jurisdiction over the payment of retirement and survivor benefits. The RRB has jurisdiction over the payment of retirement benefits if the employee has at least 10 years of railroad service, or 5 years if performed after 1995. For survivor benefits, RRB requires that the employee's last regular employment before retirement or death be in the railroad industry. If a railroad employee or his or her survivors do not qualify for railroad retirement benefits, the RRB transfers the employee's railroad retirement credits to SSA, where they are treated as social security credits.

Payroll taxes paid by railroad employers and their employees are a primary source of income for the Railroad Retirement and Survivor Benefit Program. By law, railroad retirement taxes are coordinated with Social Security taxes. Employees and employers pay Tier I taxes at the same rate as Social Security taxes and Tier II taxes to finance railroad retirement benefit payments that are higher than Social Security levels.

Other sources of program income include: financial transactions with the Social Security and Medicare Trust Funds, earnings on investments, federal income taxes on railroad retirement benefits, and appropriations (provided after 1974 as part of a phase out of certain vested dual benefits). The financial interchange between RRB's Social Security Equivalent Benefit (SSEB) Account, the Federal Old-Age and Survivors Insurance Trust Fund, the Disability Insurance Trust Fund, and the Federal Hospital Insurance Trust Fund is intended to put the latter three trust funds in the same position they would have been had railroad employment been covered under the Social Security Act. From a governmentwide perspective, these future financial interchanges and transactions are intragovernmental transfers and are eliminated in consolidation.

Railroad Retirement–Employment, Demographic, and Economic Assumptions

The most recent set of projections is prepared using employment, demographic, and economic assumptions reflecting the Board Members' reasonable estimate of expected future experience.

Three employment assumptions were used in preparing the projections and reflect optimistic, moderate, and pessimistic future passenger rail as well as freight employment. The average railroad employment is assumed to be 238,000 in 2015 under the moderate employment assumption. This employment assumption, based on a model developed by the Association of American Railroads, assumes that (1) passenger service employment will remain at the level of 46,000 and (2) the employment base, excluding passenger service employment, will decline at a constant 2.0 percent annual rate for 25 years, at a falling rate over the next 25 years, and remain level thereafter. All the projections are based on an open-group (i.e., future entrants) population.

The moderate (middle) economic assumptions include a long-term cost of living increase of 2.7 percent, an interest rate of 7.0 percent, and a wage increase of 3.7 percent. The cost of living assumption reflects the expected level of price inflation. The interest (or investment) rate assumption reflects the expected rate of return on NRRIT investments. The wage increase reflects the expected increase in railroad employee earnings.

Sources of the demographic assumptions (including mortality rates and total termination rates, remarriage rates for widow(er)s, retirement rates, and withdrawal rates) are listed in Table 2. For further details on the employment, demographic, economic and all other assumptions, refer to the 26th *Actuarial Valuation of the Assets and Liabilities under the Railroad Retirement Acts* (Valuation Report) as of December 31, 2013, with Technical Supplement.

Table 2
Railroad Retirement Demographic Actuarial Assumptions (Sources)

Mortality Rates [1]	Mortality after age retirement	2010 Base Year RRB Annuitants Mortality Table with 2013 RRB Mortality Improvement Scale
	Mortality after disability retirement	2010 Base Year RRB Disabled Mortality Table for Annuitants with Disability Freeze with 2013 RRB Mortality Improvement Scale
		2010 Base Year RRB Disabled Mortality Table for Annuitants without Disability Freeze with 2013 RRB Mortality Improvement Scale
	Mortality during active service	2009 RRB Active Service Mortality Table
	Mortality of widowed annuitants	2013 RRB Mortality Table for Widows
Total Termination Rates [2]	Termination for spouses	2010 Base Year RRB Spouse Total Termination Table with 2013 RRB Mortality Improvement Scale
	Termination for disabled children	2004 RRB Total Termination Table for Disabled Children
Widow(er) Remarriage Rates [3]		1997 RRB Remarriage Table
Retirement Rates [4]	Age retirement	See the Valuation Report.
	Disability retirement	See the Valuation Report.
Withdrawal Rates [5]		See the Valuation Report.

[1] These mortality tables are used to project the termination of eligible employee benefit payments within the population.

[2] Total termination rates are used to project the termination of dependent benefits to spouses and disabled children.

[3] This rate is used to project the termination of spousal survivor benefits.

[4] The retirement rates are used to determine the expected annuity to be paid based on age and years of service for both age and disability retirees.

[5] The withdrawal rates are used to project all withdrawals from the railroad industry and resultant effect on the population and accumulated benefits to be paid.

Black Lung–Disability Benefit Program

The Black Lung Disability Benefit Program provides for compensation, medical, and survivor benefits for eligible coal miners who are totally disabled due to pneumoconiosis (black lung disease) attributed to their coal mine employment. The same program also provides for survivor benefits for eligible survivors of coal miners who died due to pneumoconiosis. DOL operates the Black Lung Disability Benefit Program.

Black lung disability benefit payments are funded by excise taxes from coal mine operators based on the domestic sale of coal, as are the fund's administrative costs. These taxes are collected by the Internal Revenue Service (IRS) and transferred to the BLDTF, which was established under the authority of the Black Lung Benefits Revenue Act, and administered by the Treasury.

P.L. 110-343, *Division B-Energy Improvement and Extension Act of 2008*, enacted on October 3, 2008, among other things, restructured the BLDTF debt by refinancing the outstanding high interest rate repayable advances with low interest rate discounted debt instruments similar in form to zero-coupon bonds, plus a one-time appropriation. This Act also allowed that any subsequent debt issued by the BLDTF may be used to make benefit payments, other authorized expenditures, or to repay debt and interest from the initial refinancing.

Black Lung–Demographic and Economic Assumptions

The demographic assumptions used for the most recent set of projections are the number of beneficiaries and their life expectancy. The beneficiary population data is updated from information supplied by the program. The beneficiary population is a nearly closed universe in which attrition by death exceeds new entrants by a ratio of more than ten to one. SSA Life Tables are used to project the life expectancies of the beneficiary population.

The economic assumptions used for the most recent set of projections are coal excise tax revenue estimates, the tax rate structure, federal civilian pay raises, medical cost inflation, and the interest rates used to discount future cash flows.

Treasury's Office of Tax Analysis provides estimates of future receipts of the black lung excise tax. Its estimates are based on projections of future coal production and sale prices prepared by the Energy Information Administration (EIA) of DOE. In fiscal year 2015 EIA projections of future coal production and sale prices reflect, among other things, regulation pursuant to the Clean Power Plan. Treasury's Office of Tax Analysis provides the first 10 years of tax receipt estimates. In fiscal year 2015, DOL refined the approach for selecting the growth rate for tax receipt estimates for the remaining years to enhance consistency of future tax receipts over the projection period. For fiscal year 2015, the growth rate for the remaining years is based on the average EIA growth rates for future coal production that reflect regulation pursuant to the Clean Power Plan. For fiscal years 2011 through 2014, the remaining years of future tax receipts were estimated using a growth rate based on both historical tax receipts and Treasury's estimated tax receipts. The coal excise tax rate structure is $1.10 per ton of underground-mined coal and $0.55 per ton of surface-mined coal sold, with a cap of 4.4 percent of sales price until the earlier of December 31, 2018 (used in all presentations), or the first December 31, in which there exists no (1) balance of repayable debt described in section 9501 of the Internal Revenue Code and (2) unpaid interest on the debt. At that time, the tax rates revert to $0.50 per ton of underground-mined coal and $0.25 per ton of surface-mined coal sold, and a limit of 2.0 percent of sales price.

OMB supplies assumptions for future monthly benefit rate increases based on increases in the federal pay scale and future medical cost inflation based on increases in the CPIM, which are used to calculate future benefit costs. During the current projection period, the future benefit rate increases 3.03 percent in 2016, 3.25 percent in 2017, 3.02 percent in 2018, and 3.0 percent in each year thereafter, and medical cost increases 3.4 percent in 2016, 3.7 percent in 2017, 3.8 percent in 2018, and 3.9 percent in each year thereafter. Estimates for administrative costs for the first 10 years of the projection period are supplied by DOL's Budget Office, based on current year enacted amounts, while later years are based on the number of projected beneficiaries.

Statement of Changes in Social Insurance Amounts

The Statement of Changes in Social Insurance Amounts reconciles the change (between the current valuation and the prior valuation) in the present value of estimated future revenue less estimated future expenditures for current and future participants (the open group measure) over the next 75 years (except Black Lung which has a projection period through September 30, 2040). The reconciliation identifies several components of the changes that are significant and provides reasons for the changes. The following disclosures relate to the Statement of Changes in Social Insurance Amounts including the reasons for the components of the changes in the open group measure during the reporting period from the end of the previous reporting period for the Government's social insurance programs. The Statement of Changes in Social Insurance

Amounts shows two reconciliations: (1) changing from the period beginning on January 1, 2014, to the period beginning on January 1, 2015, and (2) changing from the period beginning on January 1, 2013, to the period beginning on January 1, 2014.

Social Security

All estimates relating to the Social Security Program in the Statement of Changes in Social Insurance Amounts represent values that are incremental to the prior change. As an example, the present values shown for economic data, assumptions, and methods represent the additional effect of these new data, assumptions, and methods after considering the effects from demography and the change in the valuation period. In general, an increase in the present value of net cash flows represents a positive change (improving financing), while a decrease in the present value of net cash flows represents a negative change (worsening financing).

Assumptions Used for the Components of the Changes for the Social Security Program

The present values included in the Statement of Changes in Social Insurance Amounts are for the current and prior years and are based on various economic as well as demographic assumptions used for the intermediate assumptions in the Social Security Trustees Reports for these years. Table 1A summarizes these assumptions for the current year.

Period Beginning on January 1, 2014, and Ending January 1, 2015

Present values as of January 1, 2014 are calculated using interest rates from the intermediate assumptions of the 2014 Social Security Trustees Report. All other present values in this part of the Statement of Changes in Social Insurance Amounts are calculated as a present value as of January 1, 2015. Estimates of the present value of changes in social insurance amounts due to changing the valuation period and changing demographic data, assumptions, and methods are presented using the interest rates under the intermediate assumptions of the 2014 Social Security Trustees Report. Because interest rates are an economic estimate and all estimates in the table are incremental to the prior change, all other present values in this part of the Statement of Changes in Social Insurance Amounts are calculated using the interest rates under the intermediate assumptions of the 2015 Social Security Trustees Report.

Period Beginning on January 1, 2013, and Ending January 1, 2014

Present values as of January 1, 2013, are calculated using interest rates from the intermediate assumptions of the 2013 Social Security Trustees Report. All other present values in this part of the Statement of Changes in Social Insurance Amounts are calculated as a present value as of January 1, 2014. Estimates of the present value of changes in social insurance amounts due to changing the valuation period and changing demographic data, assumptions, and methods are presented using the interest rates under the intermediate assumptions of the 2013 Social Security Trustees Report. Because interest rates are an economic estimate and all estimates in the table are incremental to the prior change, all other present values in this part of the Statement of Changes in Social Insurance Amounts are calculated using the interest rates under the intermediate assumptions of the 2014 Social Security Trustees Report.

Change in Valuation Period

Period Beginning on January 1, 2014, and Ending January 1, 2015

The effect on the 75-year present values of changing the valuation period from the prior valuation period (2014-2088) to the current valuation period (2015-2089) is measured by using the assumptions for the prior valuation and extending them to cover the current valuation. Changing the valuation period removes a small negative net cash flow for 2014, replaces it with a much larger negative net cash flow for 2089, and measures the present values as of January 1, 2015, one year later. Thus, the present value of estimated future net cash flows (excluding the combined OASI and DI Trust Fund asset reserves at the start of the period) decreased (became more negative) when the 75-year valuation period changed from 2014-2088 to 2015-2089. In addition, the effect on the level of asset reserves in the combined OASI and DI Trust Funds of changing the valuation period is measured by assuming all values projected in the prior valuation for the year 2014 are realized. The change in valuation period increased the starting level of asset reserves in the combined OASI and DI Trust Funds.

Period Beginning on January 1, 2013, and Ending January 1, 2014

The effect on the 75-year present values of changing the valuation period from the prior valuation period (2013-2087) to the current valuation period (2014-2088) is measured by using the assumptions for the prior valuation and extending them to cover the current valuation. Changing the valuation period removes a small negative net cash flow for 2013, replaces it with a much larger negative net cash flow for 2088, and measures the present values as of January 1, 2014, one year later. Thus, the present value of estimated future net cash flows (excluding the combined OASI and DI Trust Fund asset reserves at the start of the period) decreased (became more negative) when the 75-year valuation period changed from 2013-2087 to 2014-2088. In addition, the effect on the level of asset reserves in the combined OASI and DI Trust Funds of changing the valuation period is measured by assuming all values projected in the prior valuation for the year 2013 are realized. The change in valuation period increased the level of asset reserves in the combined OASI and DI Trust Funds.

Changes in Demographic Data, Assumptions, and Methods

Period Beginning on January 1, 2014, and Ending January 1, 2015

The ultimate demographic assumptions for the current valuation (beginning on January 1, 2015), with the exception of changes made due to the executive actions on immigration, are the same as those for the prior valuation. However, the starting demographic values and the way these values transition to the ultimate assumptions were changed.

- Final birth rate data for 2012 and preliminary data for 2013 indicated lower birth rates than were expected in the prior valuation. In this year's report the total fertility rate reaches the ultimate in 2027, which is eleven years earlier than in last year's report.
- Incorporating mortality data obtained from Medicare experience at ages 65 and older for 2012 resulted in slightly higher death rates for 2012 and a slightly slower rate of decline in mortality over the next 25 years than were projected in last year's report. Incorporating mortality data obtained from the National Centers for Health Statistics at ages under 65 for 2011 resulted in slightly lower death rates for 2011 and a slightly faster rate of decline in mortality over the next 25 years than were projected in last year's report.
- Historical legal immigration was revised to include single age data (rather than 5-year age groups); including more recent marriage, legal immigration, and other-than-legal immigration data; historical data since 2001 was revised to be more consistent with the most recent estimates from the Census Bureau.

The effect of including the new birth rate data and immigration data was a decrease in the present value of estimated future net cash flows, while the inclusion of the remaining data increased the present value of estimated future net cash flows.

Period Beginning on January 1, 2013, and Ending January 1, 2014

The ultimate demographic assumptions for the current valuation (beginning on January 1, 2014) are the same as those for the prior valuation. However, the starting demographic values, and the way these values transition to the ultimate assumptions, were changed.

- Preliminary birth rate data for 2012 indicated lower birth rates than were expected in the prior valuation. During the period of transition to their ultimate values, the birth rates in the current valuation are generally lower than they were in the prior valuation.
- New detailed historical divorce data along with revisions in the assumed path of the age-sex-adjusted divorce rate in the period of transition to the ultimate were used in the current valuation.
- New historical data since 2001 along with smoothing to the historical distribution of the married population by age of husband and wife was used in the current valuation period.

The effect of including the new birth rate data was a decrease in the present value of estimated future net cash flows, while the inclusion of the remaining data increased the present value of estimated future net cash flows.

There was one change in demographic methodology.

- The modeling of the other immigrant population was divided into three distinct groups for the current valuation: (1) those with temporary legal status; (2) those never authorized to be in the country; and (3) those that had temporary legal status previously but are no longer authorized to be in the country.

The effect of this new valuation methodology was an increase in the present value of estimated future net cash flows.

Changes in Economic Data, Assumptions, and Methods

Period Beginning on January 1, 2014, and Ending January 1, 2015

For the current valuation (beginning on January 1, 2015), there was one change to the ultimate economic assumptions.

- The ultimate real-wage differential is assumed to be 1.17 percent in the current valuation period, compared to 1.13 percent in the previous valuation period.

The higher real wage differential assumption is more consistent with recent experience and expectations of slower growth in employer sponsored group health insurance premiums from the Centers for Medicare and Medicaid Services. Because these premiums are not subject to the payroll tax, slower growth in these premiums means that a greater share of employee compensation will be in the form of wages that are subject to the payroll tax. This change to the real-wage assumption increased the present value of estimated future net cash flows.

Otherwise, the ultimate economic assumptions for the current valuation are the same as those for the prior valuation. However, the starting economic values and the way these values transition to the ultimate assumptions were changed.

- The ratio of average taxable earnings to the average wage averages about 0.6 percentage point higher during the long-range period, compared to the previous valuation period.
- The projected suspense file contains fewer wage items, which is consistent with having fewer workers (many of whom are undocumented immigrants) with wages on the suspense file and more of these workers with earnings in the underground economy, compared to the previous valuation.

The change to the ratio of average taxable earnings to the average wage index increased the present value of estimated future net cash flows while the change to the suspense file decreased the present value of estimated future net cash flows. Other, smaller changes in starting values and near term growth assumptions combined to increase the present value of estimated future net cash flows.

Period Beginning on January 1, 2013, and Ending January 1, 2014

For the current valuation (beginning on January 1, 2014), there was one change to the ultimate economic assumptions.

- The ultimate annual rate of change in the Consumer Price Index for Urban Wage Earners and Clerical Workers (CPI-W) is assumed to be 2.7 percent per year in the current valuation period, compared to 2.8 percent per year in the previous valuation period.

Lowering the ultimate average annual increase in the CPI-W makes it more comparable to recent historical annual increases. This change to the CPI-W assumption decreased the present value of estimated future cash flows.

Otherwise, the ultimate economic assumptions for the current valuation are the same as those for the prior valuation. However, the starting economic values, and the way these values transition to the ultimate assumptions, were changed.

- The ratio of average taxable earnings to the average wage index is lower by 1.9 percent in 2012 and 1.5 percent in 2013, compared to the previous valuation period.

This change to the ratio of average taxable earnings to the average wage index decreased the present value of estimated future cash flows.

There were two main changes in the economic methodology.

- Projected labor force participation rates for the older population are slightly lower for the current valuation in order to better reflect the difference in participation rates between never-married and married populations and the projected improvement in life expectancy.
- Different earnings levels are assigned to the three distinct groups of the other immigrant population supplied by demography. (This change decreased the present value of estimated future net cash flows by about the same amount as the related change in the demography methodology increased the present value of estimated future net cash flows.)

The effect of including these changes in methodology decreased the present value of estimated future net cash flows.

Changes in Law or Policy

Period Beginning on January 1, 2014, and Ending January 1, 2015

In the current valuation period (beginning on January 1, 2015), no laws were enacted that are expected to have significant effects on the long-range cost of the OASDI program. However, on November 20, 2014, the President announced a series of executive actions on immigration, which are expected to have a significant effect on the long-range income and cost of the OASDI program. Due to a federal court order, implementation of the actions affecting undocumented children and parents is on hold at the time of this report. However, the estimates in this report assume this court order will be temporary and that the executive actions will proceed by the end of 2015.

The effect of including these executive actions was an increase in the present value of estimated future net cash flows.

Period Beginning on January 1, 2013, and Ending January 1, 2014

In the current valuation period (beginning on January 1, 2014) no laws were enacted that are expected to have significant effects on the long-range cost of the OASDI program. However, the Supreme Court's decision in the *United States v. Windsor* repealed parts of the *Defense of Marriage Act*, which affects the payment of federal benefits based on same-sex marriages. The extent to which OASDI benefits based on marriage will be available to same-sex couples is still not completely clear. The agency has issued guidelines, approved by the Department of Justice, for certain benefits for same-sex couples who were legally married when the insured accountholder resided in a state or jurisdiction that recognized same-sex marriages at the time of application or death. For estimates in this valuation, it is assumed that the agency will expand its guidelines to recognize all auxiliary beneficiaries for such marriages and that same-sex marriage will eventually be recognized in all states.

This expected expansion of benefits decreased the present value of estimated future net cash flows.

Changes in Programmatic Data and Methods

Period Beginning on January 1, 2014, and Ending January 1, 2015

Several methodological improvements and updates of program-specific data are included in the current valuation (beginning on January 1, 2015). The most significant are identified below.

- The earnings histories of worker beneficiaries were changed to be more consistent with: (1) the projected employment and earnings by single year of age and gender used in estimating payroll tax revenue and (2) the projected distribution by single year of age and gender of newly entitled worker beneficiaries for each projection year.
- The projected relative earnings levels for those over age 65 were changed to those age 65 and younger. The projected insured rate for some immigrants was lowered. The affected group of immigrants includes those working in covered employment with a temporary visa that allows them to work and those working in covered employment without current legal work authorization.
- The ultimate projected ratio of income from taxation of benefits to total benefits was increased for this valuation period. There were also updates to programmatic data, changes in projections of beneficiaries and benefit levels over the first 10 years of the projection period, other small methodological improvements, and interactions.

All of these methodological improvements increased the present value of estimated future net cash flows.

Period Beginning on January 1, 2013, and Ending January 1, 2014

Several methodological improvements and updates of program-specific data are included in the current valuation (beginning on January 1, 2014). The most significant are identified below.

- The ultimate projected ratio of income from taxation of benefits to total benefits was increased for this valuation period.
- There were also updates to programmatic data, method changes for projecting beneficiaries and benefit levels over the first 10 years of the projection period, other small methodological improvements, and interactions.

The change to taxation of benefits increased the present value of estimated future net cash flows, while updates of program-specific data decreased the present value of estimated future net cash flows. Taken together, these changes decreased the present value of estimated future net cash flows.

Medicare

All estimates relating to the Medicare program in the Statement of Changes in Social Insurance Amounts represent values that are incremental to the prior change. As an example, the present values shown for demographic assumptions, represent the additional effect that these assumptions have, once the effects from the change in the valuation period and projection base have been considered.

Assumptions Used for the Components of the Changes for the Medicare Program

The present values included in the Statement of Changes in Social Insurance Amounts are for the current and prior years and are based on various economic and demographic assumptions used for the intermediate assumptions in the Medicare Trustees Reports for these years. Table 1B summarizes these assumptions for the current year.

Period Beginning on January 1, 2014, and Ending January 1, 2015
Present values as of January 1, 2014 are calculated using interest rates from the intermediate assumptions of the 2014 Medicare Trustees Report. All other present values in this part of the Statement of Changes in Social Insurance Amounts are calculated as a present value as of January 1, 2015. Estimates of the present value of changes in social insurance amounts due to changing the valuation period, projection base, demographic assumptions, and law are determined using the interest rates under the intermediate assumptions of the 2014 Medicare Trustees Report. Since interest rates are economic assumptions, the estimates of the present values of changes in economic and health care assumptions are presented using the interest rates under the intermediate assumptions of the 2015 Medicare Trustees Report.

Period Beginning on January 1, 2013, and Ending January 1, 2014
Present values as of January 1, 2013 are calculated using interest rates from the intermediate assumptions of the 2013 Medicare Trustees Report. All other present values in this part of the Statement of Changes in Social Insurance Amounts are calculated as a present value as of January 1, 2014. Estimates of the present value of changes in social insurance amounts due to changing the valuation period, projection base, demographic assumptions, and law are determined using the interest rates under the intermediate assumptions of the 2013 Medicare Trustees Report. Since interest rates are economic assumptions, the estimates of the present values of changes in economic and health care assumptions are presented using the interest rates under the intermediate assumptions of the 2014 Medicare Trustees Report.

Change in Valuation Period

Period Beginning on January 1, 2014, and Ending January 1, 2015
The effect on the 75-year present values of changing the valuation period from the prior valuation period (2014-88) to the current valuation period (2015-2089) is measured by using the assumptions for the prior valuation period and applying them, in the absence of any other changes, to the current valuation period. Changing the valuation period removes a small negative net cash flow for 2014 and replaces it with a much larger negative net cash flow for 2089. The present value of estimated future net cash flow (including or excluding the combined Medicare Trust Fund assets at the start of the period) was therefore decreased (made more negative) when the 75-year valuation period changed from 2014-2088 to 2015-2089. In addition, the effect on the level of assets in the combined Medicare Trust Funds of changing the valuation period is measured by assuming all values projected in the prior valuation for the year 2014 are realized. The change in valuation period decreased the level of assets in the combined Medicare Trust Funds.

Period Beginning on January 1, 2013, and Ending January 1, 2014
The effect on the 75-year present values of changing the valuation period from the prior valuation period (2013-2087) to the current valuation period (2014-2088) is measured by using the assumptions for the prior valuation period and applying them, in the absence of any other changes, to the current valuation period. Changing the valuation period removes a small negative net cash flow for 2013 and replaces it with a much larger negative net cash flow for 2088. The present value of estimated future net cash flow (including or excluding the combined Medicare Trust Fund assets at the start of the period) was therefore decreased (made more negative) when the 75-year valuation period changed from 2013-2087 to 2014-2088. In addition, the effect on the level of assets in the combined Medicare Trust Funds of changing the valuation period is measured by assuming all values projected in the prior valuation for the year 2013 are realized. The change in valuation period decreased the level of assets in the combined Medicare Trust Funds.

Changes in Demographic Assumptions

Period Beginning on January 1, 2014, and Ending January 1, 2015
The demographic assumptions used in the Medicare projections are the same as those used for the Old-Age Survivors and Disability Insurance (OASDI) and are prepared by the Office of the Chief Actuary at the SSA.
The ultimate demographic assumptions for the current valuation (beginning on January 1, 2015) are the same as those for the prior valuation. However, the starting demographic values, and the way these values transition to the ultimate assumptions, were changed.
- Final birth rate data for 2012 and preliminary data for 2013 indicated lower birth rates than were expected in the prior valuation. In this year's projections the total fertility rate reaches the ultimate in 2027, which is eleven

years earlier than in last year's projections.

- Incorporating mortality data obtained from Medicare experience at ages 65 and older for 2012 resulted in slightly higher death rates for 2012 and a slightly slower rate of decline in mortality over the next 25 years than were projected last year. Incorporating mortality data obtained from the National Centers for Health Statistics at ages under 65 for 2011 resulted in slightly lower death rates for 2011 and a slightly faster rate of decline in mortality over the next 25 years than were projected last year.
- Historical legal immigration was revised to include single age data (rather than 5-year age groups); including more recent marriage, legal immigration, and other-than-legal immigration data; historical data since 2001 was revised to be more consistent with the most recent estimates from the Census Bureau.

These changes slightly lowered overall Medicare enrollment for the current valuation period resulting in a decrease in the estimated future net cash flow, and had a very minor impact on the present value of estimated income and estimated expenditures for Part A, Part B, and Part D.

Period Beginning on January 1, 2013, and Ending January 1, 2014
The demographic assumptions used in the Medicare projections are the same as those used for the Old-Age Survivors and Disability Insurance (OASDI) and are prepared by the Office of the Chief Actuary at the SSA.
The ultimate demographic assumptions for the current valuation (beginning on January 1, 2014) are the same as those for the prior valuation. However, the starting demographic values, and the way these values transition to the ultimate assumptions, were changed.

- Preliminary birth rate data for 2012 indicated lower birth rates than were expected in the prior valuation. During the period of transition to their ultimate values, the birth rates in the current valuation are generally lower than they were in the prior valuation.

There was one change in demographic methodology:

- The modeling of the other immigrant population was divided into three distinct groups for the current valuation: (1) those with the temporary legal status; (2) those never authorized to be in the country; and (3) those who had temporary legal status previously but are no longer authorized to be in the country.

These changes slightly lowered overall Medicare enrollment for the current valuation period resulting in a decrease in the estimated future net cash flow, and had a very minor impact on the present value of estimated income and estimated expenditures for Part A, Part B, and Part D.
A further assumption change was made that resulted in higher Part D enrollment for the current valuation period. The participation rate represents the percentage of beneficiaries assumed to enroll in a Part D plan out of all eligible and, in prior years, was assumed to stay relatively constant at the same rate as the recent historical period. However, since actual participation has consistently been higher than expected, it was decided to increase the participation rate by 1 percent per year for the first three years of the projection period before leveling out. This results in an assumed 62.4 percent participation rate, prior to adjustments for beneficiaries who have retiree drug subsidy coverage and those who are assumed to drop out because they are required to pay an income-related premium, for 2017 and later, which is higher than the 57.2 percent that was assumed for all years in the prior valuation period. This assumption change resulted in an increase in the present value of estimated future income and estimated future expenditures for Part D, and had no impact on the Part A and Part B present values.

Changes in Economic and Health Care Assumptions

Period Beginning on January 1, 2014, and Ending January 1, 2015
The economic assumptions used in the Medicare projections are the same as those used for the OASDI and are prepared by the Office of the Chief Actuary at the SSA.
For the current valuation (beginning on January 1, 2015), there was one change to the ultimate economic assumptions:

- The ultimate real-wage differential is assumed to be 1.17 percent in the current valuation period, compared to 1.13 percent in the previous valuation period.

The higher real wage differential assumption is more consistent with recent experience and expectations of slower growth in employer sponsored group health insurance premiums from the Office of the Actuary at the CMS. Because these premiums are not subject to the payroll tax, slower growth in these premiums means that a greater share of employee compensation will be in the form of wages that are subject to the payroll tax.

Otherwise, the ultimate economic assumptions for the current valuation are the same as those for the prior valuation. However, the starting economic values, and the way these values transition to the ultimate assumptions, were changed.

- The ratio of average taxable earnings to the average wage averages about 0.6 percentage point higher during the long-range period, compared to the previous valuation period.
- The projected suspense file contains fewer wage items, which is consistent with having fewer workers (many of whom are undocumented immigrants) with wages on the suspense file and more of these workers with earnings in the underground economy, compared to the previous valuation.

The health care assumptions are specific to the Medicare projections. The following health care assumptions were changed in the current valuation.

- Lower long-range growth rate assumptions.
- Utilization rate assumptions for inpatient hospital services were decreased.
- Lower assumed hospice spending.
- Higher assumed enrollment in Medicare Advantage plans where benefits are more costly.
- Introduction of high-cost specialty drugs used to treat hepatitis C.

The net impact of these changes resulted in an increase in the estimated future net cash flow for total Medicare. For Part A, these changes resulted in an increase to the present value of estimated future expenditures and income, with an overall increase in the estimated future net cash flow. For Part B and Part D, these changes decreased the present value of estimated future expenditures (and also income).

Period Beginning on January 1, 2013, and Ending January 1, 2014

The economic assumptions used in the Medicare projections are the same as those used for the OASDI and are prepared by the Office of the Chief Actuary at the SSA.

For the current valuation (beginning on January 1, 2014), there was one change to the ultimate economic assumptions:

- The ultimate annual rate of change in the Consumer Price Index for Urban Wage Earners and Clerical Workers (CPI-W) is assumed to be 2.7 percent per year in the current valuation period, compared to 2.8 percent per year in the previous valuation period. Lowering the ultimate average annual increase in the CPI-W makes it more comparable to recent historical annual increases.

Otherwise, the ultimate economic assumptions for the current valuation are the same as those for the prior valuation. However, the starting economic values, and the way these values transition to the ultimate assumptions, were changed.

- The ratio of average taxable earnings to the average wage index is lower by 1.9 percent in 2012 and 1.5 percent in 2013, compared to the previous valuation period.

There were two main changes in the economic methodology.

- Projected labor force participation rates for the older population are slightly lower for the current valuation in order to better reflect the difference in participation rates between never-married and married populations and the projected improvement in life expectancy.
- Different earnings levels are assigned to the three distinct groups of the other immigrant population supplied by demography. (This change decreased the present value of estimated future cash flows by about the same amount as the related change in the demography methodology increased the present value of estimated future cash flows.)

The health care assumptions are specific to the Medicare projections. The following health care assumptions were changed in the current valuation.

- The projections emphasized in the 2014 Medicare Trustees Report were changed to reflect the projected baseline scenario. This scenario assumes that the physician payment updates required under current-law sustainable growth rate formula will be overridden by lawmakers. The use of these projections increases the present value of estimated future expenditures, compared to the current law projections, for Part B by roughly 11 percent, and for total Medicare by about 5 percent.
- Utilization rate assumptions for inpatient hospital services were decreased.
- Case mix increase assumptions for skilled nursing facilities and home health agencies were decreased.
- Market basket differential for skilled nursing facilities was lowered.

- Higher assumed enrollment in Medicare Advantage plans where benefits are generally more costly.
- Higher increases in productivity rates, resulting in lower payment updates.
- The methodology used to transition from the short-range projections to the long-range projections was refined, resulting in smaller increases during this transition period.
- Lower projected prescription drug trend rates.
- Higher assumed rebates from drug manufacturers.

The net impact of these changes resulted in an increase in the estimated future net cash flow for total Medicare. For Part A, these changes resulted in a decrease to the present value of estimated future expenditures and income, with an overall increase in the estimated future net cash flow. For Part B, these changes increased the present value of estimated future expenditures (and also income). On the other hand, the abovementioned changes lowered the present value of estimated future expenditures (and also income) for Part D.

Changes in Law

Period Beginning on January 1, 2014, and Ending January 1, 2015
Although Medicare legislation was enacted since the prior valuation date, some of the provisions have a negligible impact on the present value of the 75-year estimated future income, expenditures, and net cash flow. The *Veteran's Access, Choice, and Accountability Act of 2014* established a temporary program that allows eligible veterans to receive hospital care and medical services from eligible providers outside of the Department of Veterans Affairs (VA) system, rather than waiting for a VA appointment or traveling to a VA facility. The *Improving Medicare Post-Acute Care Transformation Act of 2014* standardized the collection of data for post-acute providers and aligned the inflation of the hospice aggregate cap with that of hospice reimbursement. The *Tax Increase Prevention Act of 2014* accelerated the start date for the payment adjustment of misvalued codes under the physician fee schedule from 2017 to 2016, and delayed inclusion of oral-only end-stage renal disease (ESRD)-related drugs into the ESRD bundled payment system from 2024 to 2025. MACRA included many provisions affecting Medicare spending, including the repeal of the SGR formula for determining payments under the physician fee schedule, the continuation of extensions for several provisions from prior legislation, a reduction in payment updates for most post-acute providers in 2018, the replacement of a 3.2 percent reduction to inpatient hospitals in 2018 with a 0.5 percent reduction in 2018 through 2023, and a revision to the income thresholds for determining the income-related monthly adjustment amounts under Part B and Part D.

Overall these provisions resulted in an increase in the estimated future net cash flow for total Medicare. For Part A, these changes resulted in a decrease to the present value of estimated future expenditures, with an overall increase in the estimated future net cash flow. For Part B, these changes increased the present value of estimated future expenditures (and also income). For Part D, the above-mentioned changes increased the present value of estimated future expenditures (and also income) only very slightly.

Period Beginning on January 1, 2013, and Ending January 1, 2014
Although Medicare legislation was enacted since the prior valuation date, many of the provisions have a negligible impact on the present value of the 75-year estimated future income, expenditures, and net cash flow. The *Continuing Appropriations Resolution of 2014* included several provisions that had an impact on the Medicare program, including a 0.5 percent physician payment update for January through March of 2014, extension of the Medicare sequester to fiscal year 2022 and 2023, and payment reform for long-term care hospitals. Further, sections 1 and 3 of Public Law 113-82 included a further extension of the Medicare sequester to fiscal year 2024. Lastly, the *Protecting Access to Medicare Act of 2014* extended the 0.5 percent physician update through December 2014, enacted a 0 percent update for January through March of 2015, improved payment policy for clinical diagnostic lab tests, made revisions to the ESRD prospective payment system and physician fee schedule, and realigned the Medicare sequester in fiscal year 2024. Overall these provisions resulted in an increase in the estimated future net cash flow for total Medicare. For Part A, these changes resulted in an increase to the present value of estimated future expenditures, with an overall increase in the estimated future net cash flow. For Part B, these changes lowered the present value of estimated future expenditures (and also income) only very slightly. For Part D, the above mentioned changes increased the present value of estimated future expenditures (and also income) also very slightly.

Change in Projection Base

Period Beginning on January 1, 2014, and Ending January 1, 2015

Actual income and expenditures in 2014 were different than what was anticipated when the 2014 Trustees Report projections were prepared. Part A income was slightly lower and expenditures were slightly higher than anticipated, based on actual experience. Part B total income and expenditures were also higher than estimated based on actual experience. For Part D, actual income and expenditures were both higher than prior estimates. The net impact of the Part A, B, and D projection base changes is a decrease in the estimated future net cash flow. Actual experience of the Medicare Trust Funds between January 1, 2014 and January 1, 2015 is incorporated in the current valuation and is slightly more than projected in the prior valuation.

Period Beginning on January 1, 2013, and Ending January 1, 2014

Actual income and expenditures in 2013 were different than what was anticipated when the 2013 Trustees Report projections were prepared. Part A income was slightly higher and expenditures were lower than anticipated, based on actual experience. Part B total income and expenditures were also lower than estimated based on actual experience. For Part D, actual income and expenditures were both slightly higher on an incurred basis than prior estimates. The net impact of the Part A, B, and D projection base changes is an increase in the estimated future net cash flow. Actual experience of the Medicare Trust Funds between January 1, 2013 and January 1, 2014 is incorporated in the current valuation and is slightly more than projected in the prior valuation.

Railroad Retirement

The present values included in the Statement of Changes in Social Insurance Amounts are for the current and prior years and are based on various employment, demographic, and economic assumptions that reflect the RRB's reasonable estimate of expected future financial and actuarial status of the trust funds. Some economic and demographic assumptions were updated in 2015 along with the following other components of changes in the open group measure.

Change in Valuation Period

Period Beginning on January 1, 2014, and Ending January 1, 2015

The effect on the 75-year present values of changing the valuation period from the prior valuation period (2014-2088) to the current valuation period (2015-2089) was a $1.6 billion decrease (became more negative) on the open group measure between January 1, 2014, and January 1, 2015.

Period Beginning on January 1, 2013, and Ending January 1, 2014

The effect on the 75-year present values of changing the valuation period from the prior valuation period (2013-2087) to the current valuation period (2014-2088) was a $1.7 billion decrease (became more negative) on the open group measure between January 1, 2013, and January 1, 2014.

Changes in Demographic Data, Assumptions, and Methods

Period Beginning on January 1, 2014, and Ending January 1, 2015
Some demographic assumptions, such as the Annuitants Mortality Table, the Disabled Mortality Table for Annuitants with Disability Freeze, the Disabled Mortality Table for Annuitants without Disability Freeze, the Active Service Mortality Table, the Spouse Total Termination Table, the Mortality Improvement Scale, the probability of an employee having an eligible spouse, the Mortality Table for Widows, the rates of immediate age retirement, the rates of immediate disability retirement, the rates of eligibility for disability freeze, service months, salary scales, and family characteristics, were changed between the Statement of Social Insurance as of January 1, 2014, and the Statement of Social Insurance as of January 1, 2015. Changes in demographic data, assumptions, and methods resulted in a decrease of $3.5 billion in the open group measure between January 1, 2014, and January 1, 2015.

Period Beginning on January 1, 2013, and Ending January 1, 2014
Demographic assumptions were not changed between the Statement of Social Insurance as of January 1, 2013, and the Statement of Social Insurance as of January 1, 2014. Changes in demographic data resulted in an increase of $2.3 billion in the open group measure between January 1, 2013, and January 1, 2014.

Changes in Economic Data, Assumptions, and Methods

Period Beginning on January 1, 2014, and Ending January 1, 2015
Both select and ultimate economic assumptions were changed between the Statement of Social Insurance as of January 1, 2014, and the Statement of Social Insurance as of January 1, 2015. A COLA of 0.5 percent was used for 2016 in place of the 2.2 percent COLA assumed for 2016 in the prior year's report. A 1.6 percent COLA was assumed for 2017 instead of a 2.8 percent COLA. An ultimate COLA of 2.7 percent for 2018 and the following years was used in place of the ultimate COLA of 2.8 percent used in the prior year's report. An ultimate wage increase assumption of 3.7 percent was used in place of the 3.8 percent wage increase assumption used in the prior year's report. Also, the actual 2014 investment return of 5.5 percent was lower than the assumed 7.0 percent investment return used for 2014 in the prior year's report. Changes in economic data, assumptions and methods resulted in a change of about $3.2 billion from January 1, 2014, to January 1, 2015.

Period Beginning on January 1, 2013, and Ending January 1, 2014
Ultimate economic assumptions were not changed between the Statement of Social Insurance as of January 1, 2013, and the Statement of Social Insurance as of January 1, 2014, but select economic assumptions were. The actual COLA of 1.5 percent was used for 2014 in place of the 1.8 percent COLA assumed for 2014 in the prior year's report. A 1.7 percent COLA was assumed for 2015 instead of a 2.3 percent COLA, and a 2.2 percent COLA was assumed for 2016 instead of a 2.8 percent COLA. Also, the actual 2013 investment return of 16.0 percent was higher than the assumed 7.0 percent investment return used for 2013 in the prior year's report. Changes in economic data, assumptions, and methods resulted in a change of about ($1.2) billion between January 1, 2013, and January 1, 2014.

Changes in Methodology and Programmatic Data

Period Beginning on January 1, 2014, and Ending January 1, 2015
There were no changes in methodology and programmatic data.

Period Beginning on January 1, 2013, and Ending January 1, 2014
There were no changes in methodology and programmatic data.

Changes in Law or Policy

Period Beginning on January 1, 2014, and Ending January 1, 2015
There were no changes in law or policy.

Period Beginning on January 1, 2013, and Ending January 1, 2014
There were no changes in law or policy.

Black Lung

The significant assumptions used in the projections of the Black Lung social insurance program presented in the Statement of Social Insurance are the coal excise tax revenue estimates, the tax rate structure, the number of beneficiaries, life expectancy, federal civilian pay raises, medical cost inflation, and the interest rates used to discount future cash flows. These assumptions also affect the amounts reported on the Statement of Changes in Social Insurance Amounts.

During fiscal year 2015, the decrease in the open and closed group measures of ($2,886.1) million was primarily due to projected lower coal excise tax revenues and higher administrative costs, offset in part due to lower beneficiary costs and the change in interest rates used to discount the cash flows from 2.5 percent and 2.63 percent in fiscal year 2014 to 2.25 percent for income payments, medical payments, administrative expenses, and coal excise tax collections in fiscal year 2015. In fiscal years 2015 and 2014, DOL's approach for selecting the interest rate assumptions used to discount projected annual cash flows enhanced matching between the timing of cash flows and interest rates and increased comparability; the approach had been refined in fiscal year 2014. For fiscal year 2015, projected annual cash flows were discounted to present value based on Treasury rates that reflect the average duration of cash flows between 10.3 and 11.2 years for income payments, medical payments, administrative expenses, and coal excise tax collections. The interest rate used to discount fiscal year 2015 projections is 2.25 percent for income payments, medical payments, administrative expenses, and coal excise tax collections.

During fiscal year 2014, the decrease in the open and closed group measures of ($137.5) million was primarily due to projected lower coal excise tax revenues, offset in part due to lower beneficiary costs, and the change in interest rates used to discount the cash flows from between 2.79 and 2.95 percent in fiscal year 2013 to 2.5 percent for income payments, and 2.63 percent for medical payments, administrative expenses, and coal excise tax collections in fiscal year 2014. For fiscal year 2014, projected annual cash flows were discounted to present value based on Treasury rates that reflect the average duration of cash flows between 10.4 and 12.2 years for income payments, medical payments, administrative expenses, and coal excise tax collections. The interest rates used to discount fiscal year 2014 projections were 2.5 percent for income payments, and 2.63 percent for medical payments, administrative expenses, and coal excise tax collections.

Note 24. Long-Term Fiscal Projections

The Statement of Long-Term Fiscal Projections is prepared pursuant to SFFAS No. 36, *Comprehensive Long-Term Projections for the U.S. Government,* as amended. The basic financial statement, Note 24, and related unaudited required supplementary information (RSI) provide information to aid users in assessing whether current policies for Federal spending and taxation can be sustained and the extent to which the cost of public services received by current taxpayers will be shifted to future taxpayers under sustainable policies. This assessment requires prospective information about receipts and spending, the resulting debt, and how these amounts relate to the economy. A sustainable policy is defined as one where the ratio of Federal debt held by the public to GDP (the debt-to-GDP ratio) is ultimately stable or declining. The *Financial Report* does not address the sustainability of State and local government fiscal policy.

The projections and analysis presented here are extrapolations based on an array of assumptions described in detail below. A fundamental assumption is that current Federal policy will not change. This assumption is made so as to inform the question of whether current fiscal policy is sustainable and, if it is not sustainable, the magnitude of needed reforms to make fiscal policy sustainable. The projections are therefore neither forecasts nor predictions. If policy changes are implemented, perhaps in response to projections like those presented here, then actual financial outcomes will of course be different than those projected. The methods and assumptions underlying the projections are subject to continuing refinement.

The projections focus on future cash flows, and do not reflect either the accrual basis or the modified-cash basis of accounting. These cash-based projections reflect receipts or spending at the time cash is received or when a payment is made by the Government. In contrast, accrual-based projections would reflect amounts in the time period in which income is earned or when an expense or obligation is incurred. The cash basis accounting underlying the long-term fiscal projections is consistent with methods used to prepare the Statements of Social Insurance (SOSI) and the generally cash-based Federal budget.

The basic financial statement, Long-Term Fiscal Projections for the U.S. Government, displays the present value of 75-year projections for various categories of the Federal Government's receipts and non-interest spending.[8] Unaudited fiscal year 2014 projections from last year's *Financial Report* are included for comparison. The projections for fiscal years 2015 and 2014 are expressed in present value dollars and as a percentage of the present value of Gross Domestic Product (GDP)[9] as of September 30, 2015 and September 30, 2014, respectively. The present value of a future amount, for example $1 billion in October 2090, is the amount of money that if invested on September 30, 2015 in an account earning the government borrowing rate would have a value of $1 billion in October 2090.[10]

The present value of a receipt or expenditure category over 75 years is the sum of the annual present value amounts. When expressing a receipt or expenditure category over 75 years as a percent of GDP, the present value dollar amount is divided by the present value of GDP over 75 years. Measuring receipts and expenditures as a percentage of GDP is a useful indicator of the economy's capacity to sustain Federal Government programs.

Fiscal Projections

Receipt categories in the long-term fiscal projections include individual income taxes, Social Security and Medicare payroll taxes, and residual remaining category of "other receipts." On the spending side, categories include: (1) discretionary spending that is funded through annual appropriations, such as spending for national security, and (2) mandatory (entitlement) spending that is generally financed with permanent or multi-year appropriations, such as spending for Social Security and Medicare. This year's projections for Social Security and Medicare are based on the same economic and demographic assumptions that underlie the 2015 Social Security and Medicare trustees' reports and the 2015 Statement of Social Insurance, while comparative information presented from last year's report is based on the 2014 Social Security and Medicare trustees' reports and the 2014 Statement of Social Insurance. Projections for the other categories of receipts and spending are consistent with the economic and demographic assumptions used from the trustees' reports. The projections assume the continuance of current policy which, as is explained below, can be different than current law in cases where lawmakers have in the past periodically changed the law in a consistent way.

---

[8] For the purposes of this analysis, spending is defined in terms of outlays. In the context of Federal budgeting, spending can either refer to budget authority – the authority to commit the government to make a payment; to obligations – binding agreements that will result in payments, either immediately or in the future; or to outlays – actual payments made.

[9] GDP is a standard measure of the overall size of the economy and represents the total market value of all final goods and services produced domestically during a given period of time. The components of GDP are: private sector consumption and investment, government consumption and investment, and net exports (exports less imports). Equivalently, GDP is a measure of the gross income generated from domestic production over the same time period.

[10] Present values recognize that a dollar paid or collected in the future is worth less than a dollar today because a dollar today could be invested and earn interest. To calculate a present value, future amounts are thus reduced using an assumed interest rate, and those reduced amounts are summed.

The projections shown in the basic statement are made over a 75-year time frame, consistent with the time frame featured in the Social Security and Medicare trustees' reports. However, these projections are for fiscal years starting on October 1, whereas the trustees' reports feature calendar-year projections. This difference allows the projections to start from the actual budget results from fiscal years 2015 and 2014.

Changes in Long-Term Fiscal Projections		
Present Value (PV) of 75-Year Projections	Trillions of $	Percent of 75-Year PV of GDP
Non-Interest Spending Less Receipts: as of September 30, 2014 (unaudited)...	4.7	0.4
Components of Change:		
Change due to Economic and Demographic Assumptions....................	(1.4)	(0.1)
Change due to Program-Specific Actuarial Assumptions	(6.8)	(0.6)
Change due to Enacted Legislation...	-	-
Change due to Updated Budget Data..	7.0	0.6
Change in Reporting Period..	0.1	0.0
Change in Model Technical Assumptions.......................................	0.4	0.0
Total...	(0.6)	(0.1)
Non-Interest Spending Less Receipts: as of September 30, 2015......	4.1	0.3

NOTE: Totals may not equal the sum of components due to rounding.

This year's estimate of the 75-year present value imbalance of non-interest spending over receipts expressed as a share of the 75-year present value of GDP is 0.3, compared to 0.4 as was projected in last year's *Financial Report*. The above table reports the effects of various factors on the updated projections. The largest such factor, increasing the imbalance by 0.6 percent of GDP ($7.0 trillion), is attributable to actual budget results for fiscal year 2015 and other budget data used in formulating the projection. The next largest change in the table – lowering the imbalance by 0.6 percent of GDP ($6.8 trillion) – is attributable to programmatic assumptions for Social Security, Medicare, and Medicaid that decrease the present value of outlays less payroll taxes for those programs. The final substantial change noted in the table – lowering the imbalance by 0.1 percent of GDP ($1.4 trillion) – is attributable to changes in economic and demographic assumptions.[11]

The last row in the basic financial statement shows that this year's estimate of the overall 75-year present value net excess of non-interest spending over receipts is 0.3 percent of the 75-year present value of GDP ($4.1 trillion, as compared to GDP of $1,196.3 trillion). This imbalance can be broken down by funding source. There is a surplus of receipts over spending of 1.1 percent of GDP ($13.2 trillion) among programs funded by the government's general revenues, but an imbalance of 1.4 percent of GDP ($17.3 trillion[12]) for the combination of Social Security (OASDI) and Medicare Part A,

---

[11] As the 2015 long-term fiscal projections represent current policy without change as of September 30, 2015, the 2015 projections do not include the effects of the *Bipartisan Budget Act of 2015 (BBA)* or the *Protecting Americans from Tax Hikes (PATH) Act of 2015*, both of which represent changes in policy after September 30, 2015. Among the important provisions included in the BBA are: (1) an increase in the statutory limits on discretionary spending in 2016 and 2017, (2) extension of Joint Committee mandatory sequestration by one year, to 2025, and (3) specific programmatic deficit reduction in Medicare, Social Security, the Pension Benefit Guaranty Corporation, and the Strategic Petroleum Reserve, among other programs. The PATH Act extended a large number of expiring tax provisions, with the largest effects on sources of revenues that the long-term fiscal projections based on historical averages rather than on particular provisions of tax law. Neither of these acts is expected to have a material effect on the projections included in this *Financial Report*.

[12] The 75-year present value imbalance for Social Security and Medicare Part A of $17.3 trillion is comprised of several line items from the long-term fiscal projections – Social Security outlays net of Social Security Payroll Taxes ($17.6 trillion) and Medicare Part A outlays net of Medicare Payroll Taxes ($6.6 trillion) – as well as subcomponents of these programs not presented separately in the table. These subcomponents include Social Security and Medicare Part A administrative costs that are classified as non-defense discretionary spending ($0.6 trillion) and Social Security and Medicare Part A revenue other than payroll taxes: taxation of benefits (-$3.5 trillion), Federal employer share (-$1.1 trillion), and other income (-$2.9 trillion).

which under current law are funded with payroll taxes and not in any material respect with general revenues.[13, 14] By comparison, the fiscal year 2014 projections showed that programs funded by the Government's general revenues had an excess of receipts over spending of 1.2 percent of GDP ($13.5 trillion) while the payroll tax-funded programs had an imbalance of spending over receipts of 1.6 percent of GDP ($18.2 trillion).

Sustainability and the Fiscal Gap

As discussed further in RSI, the projections in this report indicate that current policy is not sustainable. If current policy is left unchanged, the projections show the debt-to-GDP ratio will fall about 6 percentage points between 2015 and 2025 before commencing a steady rise, exceeding its 2015 level (74 percent) by 2031, exceeding 100 percent by 2043, and reaching 223 percent in 2090. Moreover, if the trends that underlie the 75-year projections were to continue, the debt-to-GDP ratio would continue to rise beyond the 75-year window.

The fiscal gap measures how much the primary surplus (receipts less non-interest spending) must increase in order for fiscal policy to achieve a target debt-to-GDP ratio in a particular future year. In these projections, the fiscal gap is estimated over a 75-year period, from 2016 to 2090, and the target debt-to-GDP ratio is equal to the ratio at the beginning of the projection period, in this case the debt-to-GDP ratio at the end of fiscal year 2015.

The 75-year fiscal gap under current policy is estimated at 1.2 percent of GDP, which is 6.1 percent of the 75-year present value of projected receipts and 6.0 percent of the 75-year present value of non-interest spending. This estimate of the fiscal gap is 0.9 percentage point smaller than was estimated in 2014 (2.1 percent of GDP).

The projections show that projected primary deficits average 0.3 percent of GDP over the next 75 years under current policies. If policies were put in place that would result in a zero fiscal gap, the average primary surplus over the next 75 years would be 0.9 percent of GDP, 1.2 percentage points higher than the projected present value net excess of non-interest spending over receipts shown in the basic financial statement. Closing the fiscal gap requires that primary surpluses be substantially positive because the projections assume that interest rates will exceed the growth rate of GDP, so merely achieving primary balance would result in debt growing faster than GDP.

Assumptions Used and Relationship to Other Financial Statements

A fundamental assumption underlying the projections is that current Federal policy (defined below) does not change. The projections are therefore neither forecasts nor predictions, and do not consider large infrequent events such as natural disasters, military engagements, or economic crises. If policy changes are enacted, perhaps in response to projections like those presented here, then actual fiscal outcomes will of course be different than those projected.

Even if policy does not change, actual expenditures and receipts could differ materially from those projected here. Long-range projections are inherently uncertain and are necessarily based on simplifying assumptions. For example, one key simplifying assumption is that interest rates paid on debt held by the public remain unchanged, regardless of the amount of debt outstanding. To the contrary, it is likely that future interest rates would increase if the debt-to-GDP ratio rises as in these projections. To help illustrate this uncertainty, projections that assume higher and lower interest rate scenarios are presented in the "Alternative Scenarios" discussion in the RSI section of this *Financial Report*.

As is true for prior fiscal year projections, the assumptions for GDP, interest rates, and other economic factors underlying this year's projections are the same assumptions that underlie the most recent Social Security and Medicare trustees' report projections. The use of discount factors consistent with the Social Security trustees' rate allows for consistent

---

[13] As an example of General Fund transfers to these programs, the OASDI trust fund received General Fund transfers, primarily in 2011 and 2012, to account for lost payroll taxes resulting from enactment of the temporary 2 percent reduction of the employee payroll taxes. Social Security and Medicare Part A expenditures can exceed payroll tax revenues in any given year to the extent that there are sufficient balances in the respective trust funds, balances that derive from past excesses of payroll tax revenues over expenditures and interest earned on those balances and represent the amount the General Fund owes the respective trust fund programs. When spending does exceed payroll tax revenues, as has occurred each year since 2008 for Medicare Part A and 2010 for Social Security, the excess spending is financed first with interest due from the General Fund and secondly with a drawdown of the General Fund's loan balance; in either case, the spending is ultimately supported by general revenues or borrowing. Under current law, benefits for Social Security and Medicare Part A can be paid only to the extent that there are sufficient balances in the respective trust funds. In order for the projections here to reflect the full size of these program's commitments to pay future benefits, the projections assume that all scheduled benefits will be financed with borrowing to the extent necessary after the trust funds are exhausted.

[14] The fiscal imbalances reported in the long-term fiscal projections are limited to future outlays and receipts. They do not include the initial level of publicly-held debt, which was $13.1 trillion in 2015 and $12.8 trillion in 2014, and therefore they do not by themselves answer the question of how large fiscal reforms must be to make fiscal policy sustainable, or how those reforms divide between reforms to Social Security and Medicare Part A and to other programs. Other things equal, past cash flows (primarily surpluses) for Social Security and Medicare Part A reduced Federal debt at the end of 2015 by $3.0 trillion (the trust fund balances at that time); the contribution of other programs to Federal debt at the end of 2015 was therefore $16.1 trillion. Because the $17.3 trillion imbalance between outlays and receipts over the next 75 years for Social Security and Medicare Part A does not take account of the Social Security and Medicare Part A trust fund balances, it overstates the magnitude of reforms necessary to make Social Security and Medicare Part A solvent over 75 years by $3.0 trillion. The $3.0 trillion combined Social Security and Medicare Part A trust fund balance represents a claim on future general revenues.

present value calculations over 75 years between the Statements of Long-Term Fiscal Projections and the Statements of Social Insurance. Present value calculations under higher and lower interest rate scenarios are presented in the "Alternative Scenarios" section in RSI.

The following bullets summarize the key assumptions used for the categories of receipts and spending presented in the basic financial statement and the disclosures:

- **Social Security:** Projected Social Security (OASDI) spending excludes administrative expenses, which are classified as discretionary spending, and is based on the projected expenditures in the 2015 Social Security trustees' report for benefits and for the Railroad Retirement interchange. The projections of Social Security payroll taxes and future Social Security spending begin with actual receipts and expenditures for FY 2015, and assume the same growth rates for future spending and for payroll taxes as are projected in the 2015 Social Security trustees' report. More information about the assumptions for Social Security cost growth can be found in Note 23 and the RSI discussion of Social Insurance.

- **Medicare:** Projected Medicare spending is also shown net of administrative expenses and is based on projected incurred expenditures from the 2015 Medicare trustees' report. The projections here make some adjustments to the trustees' report projections. Medicare Part B and D premiums, as well as State contributions to Part D, are subtracted from gross spending in measuring Part B and Part D outlays, just as they are subtracted from gross cost to yield net cost in the financial statements.[15] Here, as in the Federal budget, premiums are treated as "negative spending" rather than receipts since they represent payment for a service rather than payments obtained through the Government's sovereign power to tax. This is similar to the financial statement treatment of premiums as "earned" revenue as distinct from all other sources of revenue, such as taxes. The projections start with actual FY 2015 Medicare spending and assume spending growth accords with the growth rates projected in the Medicare trustees' report. Medicare Part A payroll taxes are projected similarly. More information about the assumptions for Medicare cost growth can be found in Note 23 and the Required Supplementary Information for Social Insurance. As discussed in Note 23, there is uncertainty about whether the reductions in health care cost growth projected in the Medicare trustees' report will be fully achieved. Note 23 illustrates this uncertainty by considering Medicare cost growth assumptions under varying policy assumptions.

- **Medicaid:** The Medicaid spending projections start with the projections from the *2014 Actuarial Report on the Financial Outlook for Medicaid* prepared by the Office of the Actuary, Centers for Medicare & Medicaid Services (CMS)[16]. These projections are based on recent trends in Medicaid spending, the demographic, economic, and health cost growth assumptions in the 2014 Medicare Trustees' Report, and projections of the effect of the *Affordable Care Act (ACA)* on Medicaid enrollment. The projections, which end in 2023, are adjusted to accord with the actual Medicaid expenditures in fiscal year 2015. After 2023, the projections assume no further expansion in State Medicaid coverage under the ACA, with the number of Medicaid beneficiaries expected to grow at the same rate as total population, and Medicaid costs per beneficiary assumed to grow at the same rate as Medicare benefits per beneficiary, as is generally consistent with the experience since 1987. Between 1987 and 2014, the average annual growth rate of outlays per beneficiary for Medicaid and Medicare were within 0.4 percentage point of each other. Projections of Medicaid spending are subject to added uncertainty related to: (1) assumed reductions in health care cost growth discussed above in the context of Medicare, and (2) the projected size of the Medicaid enrolled population, which depends on a variety of factors, including the future extent of the ACA Medicaid expansion.

- **Other Mandatory Spending:** Other mandatory spending, which includes means-tested entitlements other than Medicaid, Federal employee retirement, and veterans disability benefits, is projected in two steps. First, spending prior to the automatic spending cuts called for by the enforcement provisions of the *Budget Control Act (BCA)* is projected and, second, the effect of the BCA enforcement is projected throughout the projection period. With regard to pre-BCA spending: (a) Current mandatory spending components that are judged permanent under current policy are assumed to increase by the rate of growth in nominal GDP starting in 2016, implying that such spending will remain constant as a percentage of GDP[17]; and (b) Projected spending for insurance exchange subsidies starting in 2016 grows with growth in the non-elderly population and with the National Health Expenditure (NHE) projected per enrollee cost growth for other private health insurance for the NHE projection period (through 2024 for the fiscal year 2015 projections), and with growth in per enrollee health care costs as projected for the Medicare program after

---

[15] Medicare Part B and D premiums and State contributions to Part D are subtracted from the Part B and D spending displayed in the basic financial statement. The total 75-year present value of these subtractions is $10.8 trillion, or 0.9 percent of GDP.

[16] Christopher J. Truffer, Christian J. Wolfe, and Kathryn E. Rennie, *2014 Actuarial Report on the Financial Condition for Medicaid*, Office of the Actuary, Centers for Medicare and Medicaid Services, United States Department of Health and Human Services, December 2014.

[17] This assumed growth rate for other mandatory programs exceeds the growth rate in the most recent OMB and CBO 10-year budget baselines.

that period. Exchange subsidy spending is ultimately constrained as a percentage of GDP in accordance with the failsafe provision in the ACA holding this spending to 0.504 percent of GDP.

- **Defense and Non-defense Discretionary Spending:** Through 2021, discretionary spending other than for Overseas Contingency Operations (OCO) is dictated by the spending caps and automatic spending cuts called for by the BCA. After 2021, this spending is assumed to grow at the same rate as nominal GDP, and thus plateaus at a long-term level of 4.8 percent of GDP. The BCA is projected to reduce the present value of spending by $0.5 trillion through 2021, and by an additional $3.9 trillion between 2022 and 2090 because of the lower base spending in 2021. Projected OCO spending steadily declines and is fully phased out after 2025, and amounts to $0.2 trillion in present value. To illustrate uncertainty, present value calculations under alternative discretionary growth scenarios are presented in the "Alternative Scenarios" RSI section.

- **Receipts (Other than Social Security and Medicare):** It is assumed that individual income taxes will equal the same share of wages and salaries as in the Administration's latest Budget current law baseline projection. That baseline accords with current policy as defined above, and incorporates the effects of the economic recovery and bracket creep. After reaching about 22 percent of wages and salaries in 2023, individual income taxes increase gradually to 29 percent of wages and salaries in 2090 as real taxable incomes rise over time and an increasing share of total income is taxed in the higher tax brackets. The ratio of all other receipts combined to GDP is projected to remain at 3.6 percent of GDP, based on a long-run historical average. To illustrate uncertainty, present value calculations under higher and lower receipts growth scenarios are presented in the "Alternative Scenarios" section.

- **Debt and Interest Spending:** Interest spending is determined by projected interest rates and the level of outstanding debt held by the public. The long-run interest rate assumptions accord with those in the 2015 Social Security trustees' report.[18] The average interest rate over the projection period is 5.4 percent. These rates are also used to convert future cash flows to present values as of the start of fiscal year 2016. Debt at the end of each year is projected by adding that year's deficit and other financing requirements to the debt at the end of the previous year.

The methods described above include several refinements from those used to produce the fiscal year 2014 projections. First, insurance exchange subsidies are projected based on assumed growth in enrollment and health care cost growth starting with the first projection year, rather than using external projections for the first 10-year period, and explicitly account for the ACA's failsafe provision. Second, the magnitude of the effect of other means of financing on changes in debt is based on assumptions about the eventual level of financial assets implied by other means financing, rather than simply based on the most recent actual level for other means of financing. Third, BCA enforcement through 2024 is now adjusted to account for the fact that Medicare enforcement through 2024 is included in the Medicare actuarial projections and does not need to be accounted for separately.

Departures of Current Policy from Current Law

The long-term fiscal projections are made on the basis of current Federal policy, which in some cases is different from current law. The notable differences between current policy that underlies the projections and current law are: (1) projected spending and receipts imply violation of the current statutory limit on Federal debt, (2) continued discretionary appropriations are assumed throughout the projection period, (3) scheduled Social Security and Medicare benefit payments are assumed to occur beyond the projected point of trust fund exhaustion, (4) many mandatory programs with expiration dates prior to the end of the 75-year projection period are assumed to be reauthorized, and (5) mandatory sequestration is assumed to continue throughout the projection period, notwithstanding its statutory expiration in 2025. As is true in the Medicare trustees' report and in the Statement of Social Insurance, the projections incorporate programmatic changes already scheduled in law, such as the ACA productivity adjustment for non-physician Medicare services.[19]

---

[18] As indicated in the more detailed discussion of Social Insurance in Note 23 to the financial statements.

[19] In the 2014 projections, Medicare physician payments were assumed to increase throughout the projected period, rather than being reduced sharply in April 2015 as scheduled under current law at that time. However, a permanent reform to Medicare physician payments has been enacted, so there is no departure from current law in this area in the 2015 projections.

Note 25. Stewardship Land and Heritage Assets

Stewardship land is federally-owned land set aside for the use and enjoyment of present and future generations, and land on which military bases are located. Except for military bases, this land is not used or held for use in general government operations. Stewardship land is land that the government does not expect to use to meet its obligations, unlike the assets listed in the Balance Sheets. Stewardship land is measured in non-financial units such as acres of land and lakes, and the number of National Parks and National Marine Sanctuaries. Examples of stewardship land include national parks, national forests, wilderness areas, and land used to enhance ecosystems for the encouragement of animal and plant species, and nature conservation. This category excludes lands administered by the Bureau of Indian Affairs and held in trust.

The majority of public lands that are under the management of DOI were acquired by the government during the first century of the Nation's existence between 1781 and 1867.

Stewardship land is used and managed in accordance with the statutes authorizing acquisition or directing use and management. Additional detailed information concerning stewardship land, such as agency stewardship policies, physical units by major categories, and the condition of stewardship land, can be obtained from the financial statements of DOI, DOD, DOE, HHS, TVA, and USDA.

Heritage assets are government-owned assets that have one or more of the following characteristics:
- Historical or natural significance;
- Cultural, educational, or artistic importance; and/or
- Significant architectural characteristics

The cost of heritage assets often is not determinable or relevant to their significance. Like stewardship land, the government does not expect to use these assets to meet its obligations. The most relevant information about heritage assets is non-financial. The public entrusts the government with these assets and holds it accountable for their preservation. Examples of heritage assets include the Mount Rushmore National Memorial and Yosemite National Park. Other examples of heritage assets include the Declaration of Independence, the U.S. Constitution, and the Bill of Rights preserved by the National Archives. Also included are national monuments/structures such as the Vietnam Veterans Memorial, the Jefferson Memorial, and the Washington Monument, as well as the Library of Congress. Many other sites such as battlefields, historic structures, and national historic landmarks are placed in this category, as well.

Many laws and regulations govern the preservation and management of heritage assets. Established policies by individual federal agencies for heritage assets ensure the proper care and handling of the assets under their control and preserve these assets for the benefit of the American public.

Some heritage assets are used both to remind us of our heritage and for day-to-day operations. These assets are referred to as multi-use heritage assets. One typical example is the White House. The cost of acquisition, betterment, or reconstruction of all multi-use heritage assets is capitalized as general Property, Plant, and Equipment (PP&E) and is depreciated.

The government classifies heritage assets into two broad categories: collection type and non-collection type. Collection type heritage assets include objects gathered and maintained for museum and library collections. Non-collection type heritage assets include national wilderness areas, wild and scenic rivers, natural landmarks, forests, grasslands, historic places and structures, memorials and monuments, buildings, national cemeteries, and archeological sites.

This discussion of the government's heritage assets is not exhaustive. Rather, it highlights significant heritage assets reported by federal agencies. Please refer to the individual financial statements of the DOC, VA, DOT, State, DOD, as well as websites for the Library of Congress (http://loc.gov), the Smithsonian Institution (http://si.edu), and the Architect of the Capitol (http://aoc.gov) for additional information on multi-use heritage assets, agency stewardship policies, and physical units by major categories.

Note 26. Subsequent Events

Statutory Debt Limit

On November 2, 2015 Congress enacted the *Bipartisan Budget Act of 2015* (P.L. 114-74) which temporarily suspended the debt limit through March 15, 2017. This was following a delay in raising the statutory debt limit from March 16, 2015 to November 1, 2015. During the delay period, Treasury deviated from its normal debt management operations and took extraordinary measures to meet the government's obligations as they came due without exceeding the debt limit. As a result of Treasury securities not being issued to the Government Securities Investment Fund (G-Fund) of the Thrift Savings Plan, Treasury reported in Note 16— Other Liabilities miscellaneous liabilities in the amount of $204.6 billion, representing uninvested principal of and related interest for the G-fund that would have been reported in Note 11— Federal Debt Securities Held by the Public and Accrued Interest had there not been a delay in raising the statutory debt limit as of September 30, 2015, and had the securities been issued Also as a result of Treasury securities not being issued, uninvested principal and related interest of $146.1 billion was not included in intragovernmental debt holding balances for the Civil Service Retirement and Disability Fund and the Postal Service Retiree Health Benefits Fund as of September 30, 2015. As required by the relevant statutes, the Department of the Treasury restored these funds with the accumulated principal balance of Treasury debt securities that bears such interest rates and maturity dates necessary to replicate the investments the funds would have held had the delay not occurred (the uninvested principal). Also as required by the relevant statutes, Treasury paid these funds the related lost interest (foregone interest) on the uninvested principal. See Note 11– Federal Debt Securities Held by the Public and Accrued Interest and Note 16 – Other Liabilities for further information on the Statutory Debt Limit.

This page is intentionally blank.

United States Government Required Supplementary Information (Unaudited) For the Years Ended September 30, 2015, and 2014

The Sustainability of Fiscal Policy

One of the important purposes of the *Financial Report* is to help citizens and policymakers assess whether current fiscal policy is sustainable and, if it is not, the urgency and magnitude of policy reforms necessary to make fiscal policy sustainable. A sustainable policy is one where the ratio of debt held by the public to GDP (the debt-to-GDP ratio) is ultimately stable or declining.

As discussed below, the projections in this report indicate that current policy is not sustainable. If current policy is left unchanged, the projections show the debt-to-GDP ratio will fall about 6 percentage points between 2015 and 2025 before commencing a steady rise, exceeding its 2015 level (74 percent) by 2031, exceeding 100 percent by 2043, and reaching 223 percent in 2090.

These conclusions are rooted in the projected trends in receipts, spending, and surpluses/deficits in the context of current law and policy, although, as described in the following pages, there is considerable uncertainty surrounding these projections. The projections are on the basis of policies currently in place and are neither forecasts nor predictions. For comparison, under the 2014 projections, the debt-to-GDP ratio fell about 4 percentage points between 2014 and 2024 before commencing a steady rise, exceeding the 2014 level (74 percent) by 2028, exceeding 100 percent by 2039, and reaching 321 percent in 2089.

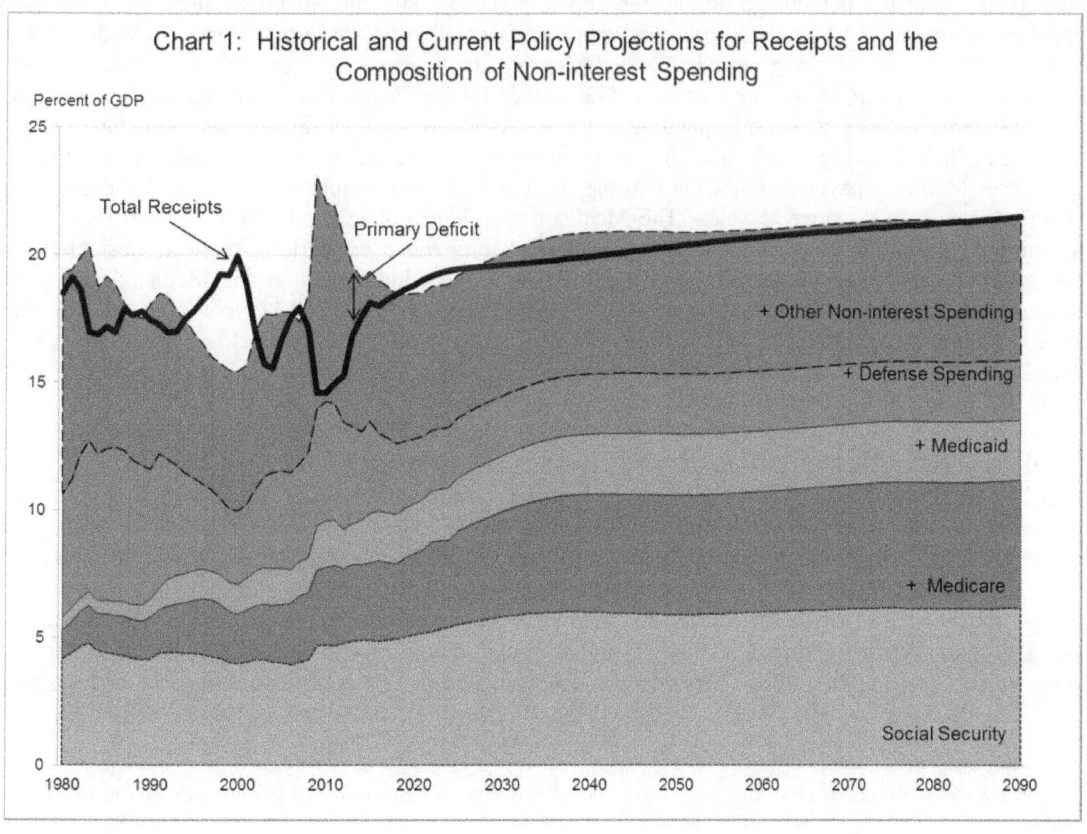

Chart 1: Historical and Current Policy Projections for Receipts and the Composition of Non-interest Spending

Current Policy Projections for Primary Deficits

A key determinant of growth in the debt-to-GDP ratio and hence fiscal sustainability is the primary deficit-to-GDP ratio. The primary deficit is the difference between non-interest spending and receipts, and the primary deficit-to-GDP ratio is the primary deficit expressed as a percent of GDP. As shown in Chart 1, the primary deficit-to-GDP ratio grew rapidly in 2009 due to the financial crisis and the recession and the policies pursued to combat both. The ratio remained high from 2010 to 2012 despite shrinking in each successive year, and fell significantly in 2013 and 2014. The primary deficit is projected to shrink in the next few years as the discretionary spending limits called for in the *Budget Control Act of 2011 (BCA)* remain in effect and the economy continues to recover. Starting in 2019, receipts are projected to exceed non-interest spending, and this primary surplus is projected to peak at 0.5 percent of GDP in 2024. After 2025, however, increased spending for Social Security and health programs due to the continued retirement of the baby boom generation is expected to cause the primary surplus to steadily deteriorate and become a primary deficit in 2028 that reaches 1.0 percent of GDP in 2038. The primary deficit gradually decreases beyond that point as the aging of the population continues at a slower pace, and becomes a primary surplus in 2085 that reaches 0.1 percent of GDP in 2090.

The receipt share of GDP fell substantially in 2009 and 2010 and remained low in 2011 and 2012 because of the recession and tax reductions enacted as part of the *2009 American Recovery and Reinvestment Act (ARRA)* and the *Tax Relief, Unemployment Insurance Reauthorization, and Job Creation Act of 2010*. The share rose to 18.1 percent in 2015, exceeding its 30-year average of 17.2 percent due to continued economic growth and the higher tax rates enacted under the *American Tax Relief Act (ATRA) of 2012*. Receipts are projected to grow slightly more rapidly than GDP as increases in real (i.e., inflation-adjusted) incomes cause more taxpayers and a larger share of income to fall into the higher individual income tax brackets. Other possible paths for the receipts-to-GDP ratio and the implications for projected debt are analyzed in the "Alternative Scenarios" section.

On the spending side, the non-interest spending share of GDP is projected to stay at or below its current level of about 19 percent until shortly before 2030, and to then rise gradually to 20.9 percent of GDP by 2040 and 21.4 percent of GDP by 2090. The reductions in the non-interest spending share of GDP over the next few years are mostly due to the expected reductions in spending for overseas contingency operations (OCO), caps on discretionary spending and the automatic spending cuts mandated by the BCA, and the subsequent increases are principally due to faster growth in Medicare, Medicaid, and Social Security spending (see Chart 1). The aging of the baby boom generation over the next 25 years is projected to increase the Social Security, Medicare, and Medicaid spending shares of GDP by about 1.1 percentage points, 1.6 percentage points, and 0.4 percentage points, respectively. After 2040, the Social Security spending share of GDP gradually declines, returns to 2040 levels in 2060 and then increases slightly, while the combined Medicare and Medicaid spending share of GDP continues to increase, albeit at a slower rate, due to projected increases in health care costs.

The *Patient Protection and Affordable Care Act*, as amended by the *Health Care and Education Reconciliation Act of 2010 (ACA)* significantly affects projected spending for both Medicare and Medicaid. That legislation expands health insurance coverage, including Medicaid, includes many measures designed to reduce health care cost growth, and significantly reduces Medicare payment rates. On net, the ACA is projected to substantially reduce the annual increases in Medicare payment rates over the next 75 years. The Medicare spending projections in the long-term fiscal projections are based on the projections in the 2015 Medicare trustees' report, and those projections show a substantial slowdown in Medicare cost growth. The projections assume that Medicaid enrollment increases and that Medicaid cost per beneficiary grows at the same reduced rate as Medicare cost growth per beneficiary. As discussed in Note 23 to the U.S. Government's Financial Statements, these projections are subject to much uncertainty about the ultimate effects of the ACA's provisions to reduce health care cost growth. Even if those provisions work as intended and as assumed in this projection, Chart 1 shows that there is still a long-term gap between projected receipts and projected total non-interest spending.

Current Policy Projections for Debt and Interest Payments

The primary deficit projections in Chart 1, along with projections for interest rates and GDP, determine the projections for the debt-to-GDP ratio that are shown in Chart 2 (right axis). That ratio was 74 percent at the end of fiscal year 2015, and under current policy is projected to be 67 percent in 2025, 106 percent in 2045, and 223 percent in 2090. The continuous rise of the debt-to-GDP ratio after 2025 indicates that current policy is unsustainable.

The change in debt held by the public from one year to the next is approximately equal to the unified budget deficit, the difference between total spending and total receipts.[1] Total spending is non-interest spending plus interest spending. Chart 2 (left axis) shows that the rapid rise in total spending and the unified deficit is almost entirely due to projected interest

---

[1] The change in debt each year is also affected by certain transactions not included in the unified budget deficit, such as changes in Treasury's cash balances and the non-budgetary activity of Federal credit financing accounts. These transactions are assumed to hold constant at about 0.4 percent of GDP each year, with the same effect on debt as if the primary deficit was higher by that amount.

payments on the debt. As a percent of GDP, interest spending was 1.2 percent in 2015, and under current policy is projected to reach 4.4 percent in 2035 and 12.0 percent in 2090.

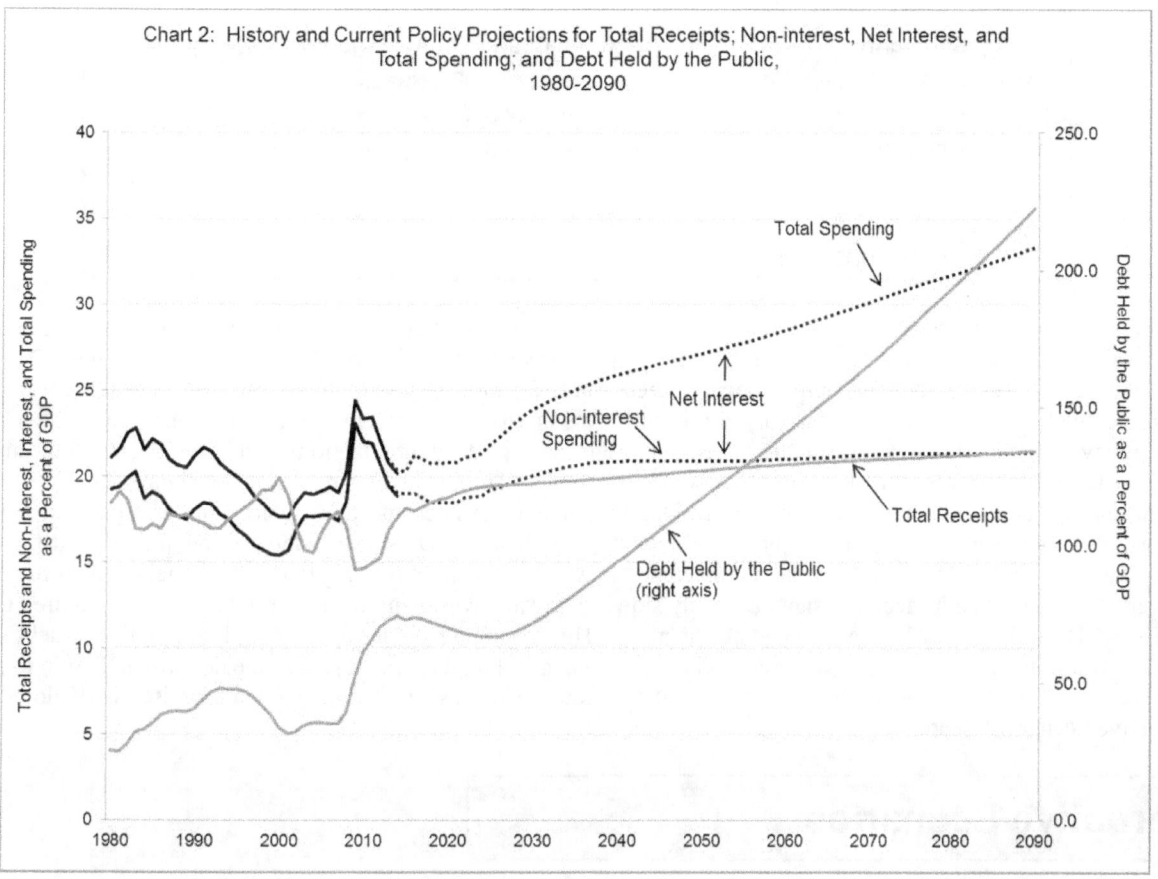

Chart 2: History and Current Policy Projections for Total Receipts; Non-interest, Net Interest, and Total Spending; and Debt Held by the Public, 1980-2090

Another way of viewing the change in the financial outlook in this year's report relative to previous years' reports is in terms of the projected debt-to-GDP ratio in 2088, the last year of the projection period in the FY 2013 report. This ratio is projected to reach 217 percent in the fiscal year 2015 projections, which compares with 315 percent projected in the fiscal year 2014 projections and 277 percent projected in the fiscal year 2013 projections.[2]

The Cost of Delay in Closing the 75-Year Fiscal Gap

The longer policy action to close the fiscal gap is delayed, the larger the post reform primary surpluses must be to achieve the target debt-to-GDP ratio at the end of the 75-year period. This can be illustrated by varying the years in which reforms closing the fiscal gap are initiated while holding the target ratio of debt to GDP in 2090 equal to the 2015 ratio (74 percent). Three reforms are considered, each one beginning in a different year, and each one increasing the primary surplus relative to current policy by a fixed percent of GDP starting in the reform year. The analysis shows that the longer policy action is delayed, the larger the post-reform primary surplus must be to bring the debt-to-GDP ratio to 74 percent of GDP in 2090. Future generations are harmed by delays in policy changes because delay necessitates higher primary surpluses during their lifetimes, and those higher primary surpluses must be achieved through some combination of lower spending and higher taxes and other receipts.

As previously shown in Chart 1, under current policy, primary deficits occur in much of the projection period. Table 1 shows primary surplus changes necessary to make the debt-to-GDP ratio in 2090 equal to its level in 2015 under each of the three policies. If reform begins in 2016, then it is sufficient to raise the primary surplus share of GDP by 1.2 percentage points in every year between 2016 and 2090 in order for the debt-to-GDP ratio in 2090 to equal its level in 2015 (74 percent). This policy raises the average 2016-2090 primary surplus-to-GDP ratio from -0.3 percent to +0.9 percent.

[2] For further information on changes from the 2013 projections, see the Required Supplementary Information in the 2014 *Financial Report*.

Table 1
Costs of Delaying Fiscal Reform

Timing of Reforms	Required Change in Average Primary Surplus
Reform in 2016 (No Delay)	1.2 percent of GDP between 2016 and 2090
Reform in 2026 (Ten-Year Delay)	1.5 percent of GDP between 2026 and 2090
Reform in 2036 (Twenty-Year Delay) ...	1.9 percent of GDP between 2036 and 2090

Note: Reforms taking place in 2015, 2025, and 2035 from the 2014 Financial Report were 2.1, 2.5, and 3.1 percent of GDP, respectively.

In contrast to a reform that begins immediately, if reform begins in 2026 or 2036, then the primary surpluses must be raised by 1.5 percent and 1.9 percent of GDP, respectively, in order for the debt-to-GDP ratio in 2090 to equal 74 percent. The difference between the primary surplus increase necessary if reform begins in 2026 and 2036 (1.5 and 1.9 percent of GDP, respectively) and the increase necessary if reform begins in 2016 (1.2 percent of GDP) is a measure of the additional burden policy delay would impose on future generations. The costs of delay are due to the additional debt that accumulates between 2015 and the year reform is initiated, in comparison to the scenario in which reform begins immediately.

These projections likely understate the cost of lengthy policy delays because they assume interest rates will not rise as the debt-to-GDP ratio grows. Under the current projections, the debt-to-GDP ratio is stable through 2030 and then grows rapidly. If a higher debt-to-GDP ratio causes the interest rate on government borrowing to rise, thus making it more costly for the government to service its debt and simultaneously slowing private investment, then the primary surplus required to return the debt-to-GDP ratio to its 2015 level would also increase. This dynamic may accelerate with higher ratios of debt to GDP, potentially resulting in there being no feasible level of taxes and spending that would reduce the debt-to-GDP ratio to its 2015 level. The potential impact on the projections of interest rates rising as the debt-to-GDP ratio rises is explored in the "Alternative Scenarios" section.

Alternative Scenarios

The long-run outlook for the budget is extremely uncertain. This section illustrates this inherent uncertainty by presenting alternative scenarios for the growth rate of health care costs, interest rates, discretionary spending, and receipts. (Not considered here are the effects of alternative assumptions for long-run trends in birth rates, mortality, and immigration.)

The population is aging rapidly and will continue to do so over the next several decades, which puts pressure on programs such as Social Security, Medicare, and Medicaid. A shift in projected fertility, mortality, or immigration rates could have important effects on the long-run projections. Higher-than-projected immigration, fertility, or mortality rates would improve the long-term fiscal outlook. Conversely, lower-than-projected immigration, fertility, or mortality rates would result in deterioration in the long-term fiscal outlook.

Effect of Changes in Health Care Cost Growth

One of the most important assumptions underlying the projections is the projected growth of health care costs. Enactment of the ACA in 2010 reduced the projected long-run growth rates of health care costs, but these growth rates are still highly uncertain. As an illustration of the dramatic effect of variations in health care cost growth rates, Table 2 shows the effect on the size of reforms necessary to close the fiscal gap of per capita health care cost growth rates that are one percentage point higher or two percentage points higher than the growth rates in the base projection, as well as the effect of delaying closure of the fiscal gap.[3] As indicated earlier, if reform is initiated in 2016, eliminating the fiscal gap requires that the 2016-2090 primary surplus increase by an average of 1.2 percent of GDP in the base case. However, that figure increases to 4.0 percent of GDP if per capita health cost growth is assumed to be 1 percentage point higher, and 8.5 percent of GDP if per capita health cost growth is 2 percentage points higher. The cost of delaying reform is also increased if health care cost growth is higher, due to the fact that debt accumulates more rapidly during the period of inaction. For example, the lower part of Table 2 shows that delaying reform initiation from 2016 to 2026 requires that 2026-2090 primary surpluses be higher by an average of 0.3 percent of GDP in the base case, 0.8 percent of GDP if per capita health cost growth is 1 percentage point

---

[3] The base case health cost growth rates are derived from the projections in the 2015 Medicare trustees' report. These projections are summarized and discussed in Note 23 (see Table 1B in particular) and the "Medicare Projections" section of the RSI for the SOSI.

higher, and 1.7 percent of GDP if per capita health cost growth is 2 percentage points higher. The dramatic deterioration of the long-run fiscal outlook caused by higher health care cost growth shows the critical importance of managing health care cost growth, including through effective implementation of the ACA.

Table 2

Impact of Alternative Health Cost Scenarios on Cost of Delaying Fiscal Reform

Scenario	Primary Surplus Increase (% of GDP) Starting in:		
	2016	2026	2036
Base Case...	1.2	1.5	1.9
1% pt. higher per person health cost growth................	4.0	4.8	6.1
2% pt. higher per person health cost growth................	8.5	10.2	12.8

	Change in Primary Surplus Increase if Reform is Delayed From 2016 to:	
	2026	2036
Base Case...	0.3	0.6
1% pt. higher per person health cost growth................	0.8	2.1
2% pt. higher per person health cost growth................	1.7	4.4

NOTE: Increments may not equal the subtracted difference of the components due to rounding.

Effects of Changes in Interest Rates

A higher debt-to-GDP ratio is likely to increase the interest rate on Government debt, making it more costly for the Government to service its debt. Table 3 displays the effect of several alternative scenarios using different nominal (and real) interest rates than assumed in the base case on the size of reforms to close the fiscal gap as well as the effect of delaying closure of the fiscal gap. If reform is initiated in 2016, eliminating the fiscal gap requires that the 2016-2090 primary surplus increase by an average of 1.2 percent of GDP in the base case, 1.5 percent of GDP if the interest rate is 0.5 percentage point higher in every year, and 0.9 percent of GDP if the interest rate is 0.5 percentage point lower in every year. The cost of delaying reform is also increased if interest rates are higher, due to the fact that interest paid on debt accumulates more rapidly during the period of inaction. For example, the lower part of Table 3 shows that delaying reform initiation from 2016 to 2026 requires that 2026-2090 primary surpluses be higher by an average of 0.3 percent of GDP in the base case, 0.4 percent of GDP if the interest rate is 0.5 percentage point higher in every year, and 0.2 percent of GDP if the interest rate is 0.5 percentage point lower in every year.

Table 3
Impact of Alternative Interest Rate Scenarios on Cost of Delaying Fiscal Reform

Scenario	Primary Surplus Increase (% of GDP) Starting in:		
	2016	2026	2036
Base Case: Average of 5.4 percent over 75 years............	1.2	1.5	1.9
0.5 percent higher interest rate in each year..................	1.5	1.9	2.5
0.5 percent lower interest rate in each year...................	0.9	1.1	1.4

	Change in Primary Surplus Increase if Reform is Delayed From 2016 to:	
	2026	2036
Base Case: Average of 5.4 percent over 75 years............	0.3	0.6
0.5 percent higher interest rate in each year..................	0.4	0.9
0.5 percent lower interest rate in each year...................	0.2	0.4

NOTE: Increments may not equal the subtracted difference of the components due to rounding.

Effects of Changes in Discretionary Spending Growth

The growth of discretionary spending has a large impact on long-term fiscal sustainability. The current base projection for discretionary spending assumes that after 2021, discretionary spending keeps pace with the economy and grows with GDP. The implications of two alternative scenarios are shown in Table 4. The first alternative scenario allows discretionary spending to grow with inflation and population after 2021 so as to hold discretionary spending constant on a real per capita basis. (This growth rate assumption is still larger than the standard 10-year budget baseline assumption, which assumes that discretionary spending grows with inflation but not with population.) The second alternative scenario sets discretionary spending in 2022 to levels consistent with the path established prior to the sequestration required by the failure of the Joint Select Committee on Deficit Reduction, and then grows discretionary spending with GDP from that point forward. As shown in Table 4, the fiscal gap decreases significantly if discretionary spending grows with inflation and population, from 1.2 percent of GDP to -0.3 percent of GDP. Conversely, if discretionary spending rises to the levels prior to Joint Committee sequestration in 2022 and then grows with GDP, the fiscal gap increases from 1.2 percent of GDP to 1.6 percent of GDP. The cost of delaying reform is greater when discretionary spending levels are higher. Initiating reforms in 2026 requires that the primary surplus increase by an average of 0.3 percent of GDP per year in the base case, and also increase by 0.3 percent of GDP if discretionary levels return to pre-Joint Committee sequestration levels. If delayed until 2036, the primary surplus must increase by an average of 0.6 percent of GDP in the base case, and increase by 0.8 percent of GDP at pre-sequestration levels.

Table 4

Impact of Alternative Discretionary Spending Growth Scenarios on Cost of Delaying Fiscal Reform

Scenario	Primary Surplus Increase (% of GDP) Starting in:		
	2016	2026	2036
Base Case: Discretionary spending growth with GDP after 2021............................	1.2	1.5	1.9
Growth with inflation and population after 2021..	(0.3)	(0.3)	(0.4)
Reversion in 2022 to pre-Joint Committee sequester levels and growth with GDP.....	1.6	1.9	2.4

	Change in Primary Surplus Increase if Reform is Delayed From 2016 to:	
	2026	2036
Base Case: Discretionary spending growth with GDP after 2021............................	0.3	0.6
Growth with inflation and population after 2021..	(0.1)	(0.1)
Reversion in 2022 to pre-Joint Committee sequester levels and growth with GDP.....	0.3	0.8

NOTE: Increments may not equal the subtracted difference of the components due to rounding.

Effects of Changes in Individual Income Receipt Growth

The growth rate of receipts, specifically individual income taxes, is another key determinant of long-term sustainability. The base projections assume growth in individual income taxes over time to account primarily for the slow shift of individuals into higher tax brackets due to real wage growth ("real bracket creep"). This assumption approximates the long-term historical growth in individual income taxes relative to wages and salaries and is consistent with current tax code policy without change, as future legislation would be required to prevent real bracket creep. As an illustration of the effect of variations in individual income tax growth, Table 5 shows the effect on the size of reforms necessary to close the fiscal gap and the effect of delaying closure of the fiscal gap if long-term receipt growth as a share of wages and salaries is 0.1 percentage point higher, than the base case, as well as 0.1 percentage point lower than the base case. If reform is initiated in 2016, eliminating the fiscal gap requires that the 2016-2090 primary surplus increase by an average of 1.2 percent of GDP in the base case, only 0.2 percent of GDP if receipt growth is higher, but 2.3 percent of GDP if receipt growth is lower. The cost of delaying reform is also affected if receipt growth assumptions change, much as was the case in the previous alternative scenarios.

Table 5
Impact of Alternative Revenue Growth Scenarios on Cost of Delaying Fiscal Reform

Scenario	Primary Surplus Increase (% of GDP) Starting in:		
	2016	2026	2036
Base Case: Individual income tax bracket creep of 0.1% of wages and salaries per year....	1.2	1.5	1.9
0.2% of wages and salaries per year after 2025...	0.2	0.2	0.3
0.0% of wages and salaries per year after 2025 (no bracket creep)..................................	2.3	2.7	3.5

	Change in Primary Surplus Increase if Reform is Delayed From 2016 to:	
	2026	2036
Base Case: Individual income tax bracket creep of 0.1% of wages and salaries per year....	0.3	0.6
0.2% of wages and salaries per year after 2025...	0.0	0.1
0.0% of wages and salaries per year after 2025 (no bracket creep)..................................	0.5	1.2

NOTE: Increments may not equal the subtracted difference of he components due to rounding.

Fiscal Projections in Context

In this report, a sustainable policy has been defined as one where the Federal debt-to-GDP ratio is stable or declining. However, this definition does not indicate what a sustainable debt-to-GDP ratio might be. Any particular debt ratio is not the ultimate goal of fiscal policy. Rather, the goals of fiscal policy are many, including: financing public goods, such as infrastructure and government services; a strong and growing economy; and managing the national debt so that it is not a burden to future generations. These goals are interrelated, and readers should consider how policies intended to affect one might depend on or affect another.

This report shows that current policy is not sustainable. In evaluating policies that could alter that trajectory, note that national debt may play roles in both facilitating and hindering a healthy economy. For example, Government deficit spending may support demand and allow economies to emerge from recessions more quickly. Debt may also be a cost-effective means of financing capital investment, promoting economic growth, which may in turn make debt levels more manageable in the future. However, economic theory also suggests that high levels of national debt may contribute to higher interest rates, leading to lower investment and a smaller capital stock which the economy can use to grow. Unfortunately, it is unclear what debt ratio would be sufficiently high to produce these negative outcomes, or whether the key concern is the level of debt per se, or a trend that shows debt increasing over time.

Whether the actual experience of countries supports a relationship between national debt and economic growth remains an open research question. It is not possible to perform randomized experiments on economies, and historical experience, while valuable, is filled with confounding events and circumstances. Some countries with high debt-to-GDP ratios have been observed to experience lower-than-average growth, while other countries with similarly high debt ratios continue to enjoy robust growth. Analogously, low debt-to-GDP ratios are no guarantee of strong economic growth. Moreover, the direction of causality is unclear. High debt may undermine growth; low growth may contribute to high debt.

Nevertheless, to put the current and projected debt-to-GDP ratios in context, it is instructive to examine the experiences of other countries as well as that of the United States. The United States Government's debt as a percentage of GDP is relatively large compared with central government debt of other countries, but far from the largest among developed countries. Based on historical data as reported by the International Monetary Fund (IMF) for 24 select countries, the debt-to-GDP ratio in 2013 ranged from 7 percent of GDP to 174 percent of GDP.[4] The United States is not included in this set of statistics, which underscores the difficulty in calculating debt ratios under consistent definitions, but the IMF does report a

---

[4] Government Finance Statistics Yearbook, Main Aggregates and Balances, available at http://data.imf.org. Data is for D1 debt liabilities for the central government, excluding social security funds.

similar debt statistic for the United States as 82 percent of GDP.[5] Despite using consistent definitions where available, these debt measures are not strictly comparable due to differences in the share of government debt that is debt of the central government, how government responsibilities are shared between central and local governments, how current policies compare with the past policies that determine the current level of debt, and how robustly each economy grows.

The historical experience of the U.S. may also provide some perspective. As Chart 3 shows, the debt-to-GDP ratio was highest in the 1940s, following the debt buildup during World War II. In the projections in this report, the U.S. would reach the previous peak debt ratio in 2045. However, the origins of current and future Federal debt are quite different from the wartime debt of the 1940s, which limits the pertinence of past experience.

As the cross-country and historical comparisons suggest, there is a very imperfect relationship between the current level of central government debt and the sustainability of overall government policy. Past accrual of debt is certainly important, but current policies and their implications for future debt accumulation are as well.

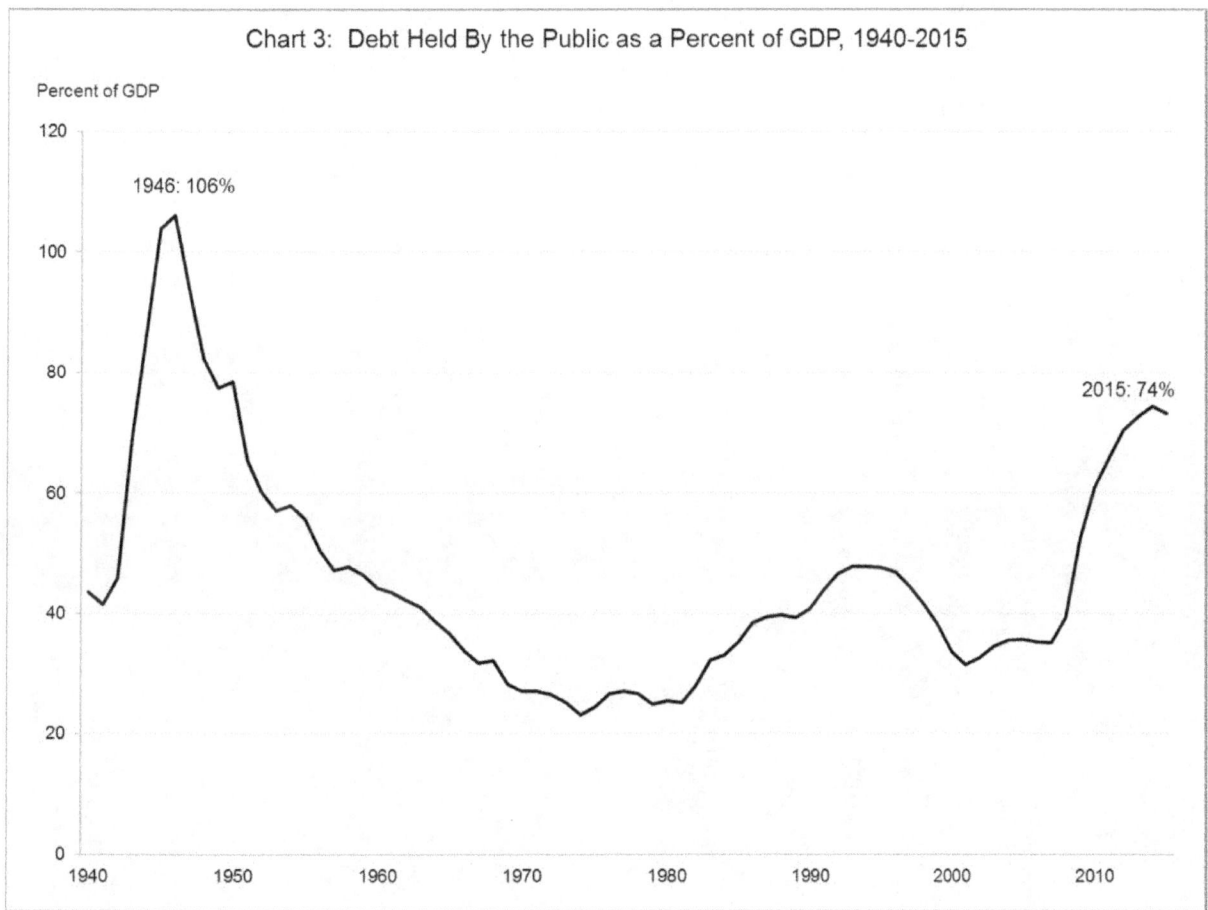

Chart 3: Debt Held By the Public as a Percent of GDP, 1940-2015

Conclusion

The United States took a potentially significant step towards fiscal sustainability in 2010 by reforming its system of health insurance through enactment of the ACA. The legislated changes for Medicare, Medicaid, and other health coverage hold the prospect of lowering the long-term growth trend for health care costs and significantly reducing the long-term fiscal gap. Furthermore, enactment of the BCA in August 2011 placed limits on future discretionary spending, while enactment of ATRA in January 2013 increased receipts under current policy. But even with these laws, the projections in this *Financial*

---

[5] Data is for D1 debt liabilities for the central government, including social security funds. For the few countries where both central government debt ratios (excluding and including social security funds) are reported, the values are similar.

Report indicate that if policy remains unchanged the debt-to-GDP ratio will continually increase over the next 75 years and beyond, which implies current policies are not sustainable and must ultimately change. Subject to the important caveat that policy changes are not so abrupt that they slow continued economic growth, the sooner policies are put in place to avert these trends, the smaller are the receipt increases and/or spending decreases necessary to return the Nation to a sustainable fiscal path, and the lower the burden of the national debt will be to future generations.

Social Insurance

The social insurance programs consisting of Social Security, Medicare, Railroad Retirement, and Black Lung were developed to provide income security and health care coverage to citizens under specific circumstances as a responsibility of the Government. Because taxpayers rely on these programs in their long-term planning, social insurance program information should indicate whether the current statutory provisions of the programs can be sustained, and more generally what effect these provisions likely have on the Government's financial condition. The resources needed to run these programs are raised through taxes and fees. Eligibility for benefits depends in part on earnings and time worked by the individuals. Social Security benefits are generally redistributed intentionally toward lower-wage workers (i.e., benefits are progressive). In addition, each social insurance program has a uniform set of eligibility events and schedules that apply to all participants.

Social Security and Medicare

Social Security

The OASI Trust Fund was established on January 1, 1940, as a separate account in the Treasury. The DI Trust Fund, another separate account in the Treasury, was established on August 1, 1956. OASI pays cash retirement benefits to eligible retirees and their eligible dependents and survivors, and the much smaller DI fund pays cash benefits to eligible individuals who are unable to work because of medical conditions and certain family members of such eligible individuals. Though the events that trigger benefit payments are quite different, both trust funds have the same dedicated financing structure: primarily payroll taxes and income taxes on benefits. All financial operations of the OASI and DI Programs are handled through these respective funds. The two funds are often referred to as the combined OASDI Trust Funds. At the end of calendar year 2014, OASDI benefits were paid to approximately 59 million beneficiaries.

The primary financing source for these two funds are taxes paid by workers, their employers, and individuals with self-employment income, based on work covered by the OASDI Program. Since 1990, with the exception of calendar years 2011 and 2012, employers and employees have each paid 6.2 percent of taxable earnings and the self-employed paid 12.4 percent of taxable earnings. In 2011 and 2012, payroll tax rates paid by employees and the self-employed were each reduced by 2 percentage points and the General Fund reimbursed the OASDI Trust Fund for the resulting reduction in payroll tax revenues. Payroll taxes are levied on wages and net earnings from self-employment up to a specified maximum annual amount, referred to as maximum taxable earnings ($118,500 in 2015), that increases each year with economy-wide average wages.

Legislation passed in 1984 subjected up to half of OASDI benefits to income tax and allocated the revenue to the OASDI Trust Funds. In 1993 legislation increased the potentially taxed portion of benefits to 85 percent and allocated the additional revenue to the Medicare's Hospital Insurance Trust Fund.

Medicare

The Medicare Program, created in 1965, has two separate trust funds: the Hospital Insurance (HI) Trust Fund (otherwise known as Medicare Part A) and the Supplementary Medical Insurance (SMI) Trust Funds (which consists of the Medicare Part B and Part D[6] accounts). HI pays for inpatient acute hospital services and major alternatives to hospitals (skilled nursing services, for example). SMI pays for hospital outpatient services, physician services, and assorted other services and products through the Part B account and for prescription drugs through the Part D account.

Though the events that trigger benefit payments are similar, HI and SMI have different dedicated financing structures. Similar to OASDI, HI is financed primarily by payroll contributions. Currently, employers and employees each pay 1.45 percent of earnings, while self-employed workers pay 2.9 percent of their net earnings. Beginning in 2013, employees and self-employed individuals with earnings above certain thresholds pay an additional HI tax of 0.9 percent on earnings above those thresholds. Other income to the HI Trust Fund includes a small amount of premium income from voluntary enrollees, a portion of the federal income taxes that beneficiaries pay on Social Security benefits (as explained above), and interest credited on Treasury securities held in the HI Trust Fund. As is explained in the next section, these Treasury securities and

---

[6] Medicare legislation in 2003 created the new Part D account in the SMI Trust Fund to track the finances of a new prescription drug benefit that began in 2006. As in the case of Medicare Part B, approximately three-quarters of revenues to the Part D account will come from future transfers from the General Fund. Consequently, the nature of the relationship between the SMI Trust Fund and the Federal Budget described below is largely unaffected by the presence of the Part D account though the magnitude will be greater.

related interest have no effect on the consolidated statement of governmentwide finances.

For SMI, direct transfers from the General Fund financed 75 percent of 2015 program costs for both Parts B and D. Premiums paid by beneficiaries and, for Part D state transfers, generally financed the remainder of expenditures. For beneficiaries dually eligible for Medicare and Medicaid, states must pay the Part D account a portion of their estimated foregone drug costs for this population (referred to as state transfers). As with HI, interest received on Treasury securities held in the SMI Trust Fund is credited to the fund. These Treasury securities and related interest have no effect on the consolidated statement of governmentwide finances. See Note 23—Social Insurance, for additional information on Medicare program financing.

Figure 1
Social Security, Medicare, and Governmentwide Finances

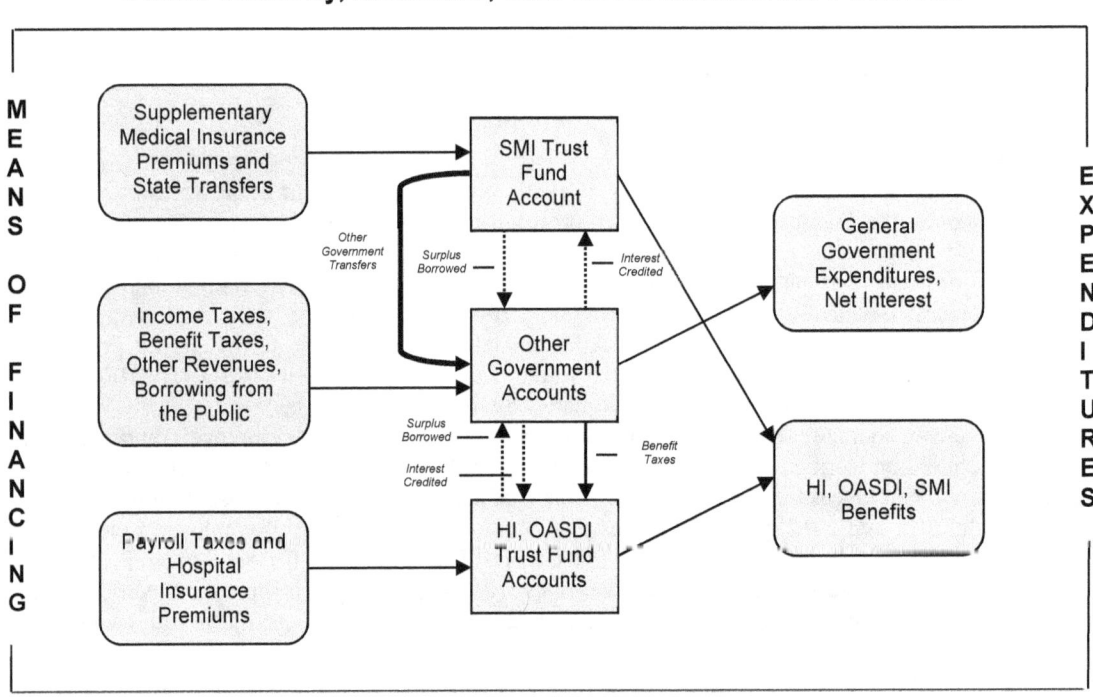

Social Security, Medicare, and Governmentwide Finances

The current and future financial status of the separate OASDI, HI, and SMI Trust Funds is the focus of the Social Security and Medicare Trustees' Reports, a focus that may appropriately be referred to as the "trust fund perspective." In contrast, the Government primarily uses the *unified budget* concept as the framework for budgetary analysis and presentation. It represents a comprehensive display of all federal activities, regardless of fund type or on- and off-budget status, and has a broader focus than the trust fund perspective that may appropriately be referred to as the "budget perspective" or the "governmentwide perspective." Social Security and Medicare are among the largest expenditure categories of the U.S. federal budget. Together, they now account for more than a third of all federal spending and the percentage is projected to rise dramatically for the reasons discussed below. This section describes in detail the important relationship between the trust fund perspective and the governmentwide perspective.

Figure 1 is a simplified depiction of the interaction of the Social Security and Medicare Trust Funds with the rest of the federal budget.[7] The boxes on the left show sources of funding, those in the middle represent the trust funds and other Government accounts, which include the General Fund into which that funding flows, and the boxes on the right show simplified expenditure categories. The figure is intended to illustrate how the various sources of program revenue flow through the budget to beneficiaries. The general approach is to group revenues and expenditures that are linked specifically to Social Security and/or Medicare separately from those for other government programs.

---

[7] The federal unified budget encompasses all Government financing and is synonymous with a governmentwide perspective.

Each of the trust funds has its own sources and types of revenue. With the exception of General Fund transfers to SMI, each of these revenue sources represents revenue from the public that is dedicated specifically for the respective trust fund and cannot be used for other purposes. In contrast, personal and corporate income taxes as well as other revenue go into the General Fund and are drawn down for any Government program for which Congress has approved spending.[8] The arrows from the boxes on the left represent the flow of the revenues into the trust funds and other Government accounts.

The heavy line between the top two boxes in the middle of Figure 1 represents intragovernmental transfers to the SMI Trust Fund from other Government accounts. The Medicare SMI Trust Fund is shown separately from the two Social Security Trust Funds (OASI and DI) and the Medicare HI Trust Fund to highlight the unique financing of SMI. Currently, SMI is only one of the programs that is funded through transfers from the General Fund, which is part of the other Government accounts (the SMI Part D account also receives transfers from the states). The direct transfers finance roughly three-fourths of SMI Program expenses. The transfers are automatic; their size depends on how much the program requires, not on how much revenue comes into the Treasury. If General Fund revenues become insufficient to cover both the mandated transfer to SMI and expenditures on other general Government programs, Treasury has to borrow to make up the difference. In the longer run, if transfers to SMI increase beyond growth in general revenues—and as shown in the Medicare Trustees Report and Chart 5 later in this section, they are projected to increase significantly in coming years—then Congress must either raise taxes, cut other Government spending, reduce SMI benefits, or borrow even more.

The dotted lines between the middle boxes of Figure 1 also represent intragovernmental transfers but those transfers arise in the form of "borrowing/lending" between the Government accounts. Interest credited to the trust funds arises when the excess of program income over expenses is loaned to the General Fund. The vertical lines labeled *Surplus Borrowed* represent these flows from the trust funds to the other Government accounts. These loans reduce the amount the General Fund has to borrow from the public to finance a deficit (or likewise increase the amount of debt paid off if there is a surplus). However, the General Fund has to credit interest on the loans from the trust fund programs, just as if it borrowed the money from the public. The credits lead to future obligations for the General Fund (which is part of the other Government accounts). These transactions are indicated in Figure 1 by the vertical arrows labeled *Interest Credited*. The credits increase trust fund income exactly as much as they increase credits (future obligations) in the General Fund. From the governmentwide standpoint, at least in an accounting sense, these interest credits are a wash.

When the trust funds get the receipts that they loan to the General Fund, these receipts provide additional authority to spend on benefits and other program expenses. The General Fund, in turn, has taken on the obligation of paying interest on these loans every year and repaying the principal when trust fund income from other sources falls below expenditures.

How loans from the trust funds to the General Fund and later repayments of those loans affect tax income and expenditures of the General Fund is uncertain. Two extreme cases encompass the possibilities. At one extreme, each dollar the trust funds loan to the General Fund might reduce borrowing from the public by a dollar at the time the loan is extended, in which case the General Fund could repay all trust fund loans by borrowing from the public without raising the level of public debt above the level that would have occurred in the absence of the loans. At the other extreme, each dollar the trust funds loan to the General Fund might result in some combination of higher General Fund spending and lower General Fund revenues amounting to one dollar at the time the loans are extended, in which case General Fund loan repayments to the trust funds might initially be financed with borrowing from the public but must at some point be financed with a combination of higher General Fund taxes and lower General Fund spending than would have occurred in the absence of the loans. In this latter extreme, trust fund loans result in additional largess (i.e., higher spending and/or lower taxes) in General Fund programs at the time the loans are extended, but ultimately that additional largess is financed with additional austerity (i.e., lower spending and/or higher taxes) in General Fund programs at later dates. The actual impact of trust fund loans to the General Fund and their repayment on General Fund programs is at one of these two extremes or somewhere in between.

Actual dollar amounts roughly corresponding to the flows presented in Figure 1 are shown in Table 1 for fiscal year 2015. In Table 1, revenues from the public (left side of Figure 1) and expenditures to the public (right side of Figure 1) are shown separately from transfers between Government accounts (middle of Figure 1). Note that the transfers ($264.8 billion) and interest credits ($107.1 billion) received by the trust funds appear as negative entries under "All Other" and are thus offsetting when summed for the total budget column. These two intragovernmental transfers are the key to the differences between the trust fund and budget perspectives.

From the governmentwide perspective, only revenues received from the public (and states in the case of Medicare, Part D) and expenditures made to the public are important for the final balance. Trust fund revenue from the public consists of

---

[8] Other programs also have dedicated revenues in the form of taxes and fees (and other forms of receipt) and there are a large number of dedicated trust funds in the federal budget. Total trust fund receipts account for about 40 percent of total Government receipts with the Social Security and Medicare Trust Funds accounting for about two-thirds of trust fund receipts. For further discussion, see the report issued by the Government Accountability Office, *Federal Trust and Other Earmarked Funds*, GAO-01-199SP, January 2001. In the figure and the discussion that follows, all other programs, including these other dedicated trust fund programs, are grouped under "Other Government Accounts" to simplify the description and maintain the focus on Social Security and Medicare.

payroll taxes, benefit taxes, and premiums. For HI, the difference between total expenditures made to the public ($278.7 billion) and revenues ($262.7 billion) was $16.0 billion in 2015, indicating that HI had a relatively small negative effect on the overall budget outcome *in that year*. For the SMI account, revenues from the public (premiums) were relatively small, representing about 25 percent of total expenditures made to the public in 2015. The difference ($267.9 billion) resulted in a net draw on the overall budget balance in that year. For OASDI, the difference between total expenditures made to the public ($887.7 billion) and revenues from the public ($817.1 billion) was $70.6 billion in 2015, indicating that OASDI had a negative effect on the overall budget outcome in that year. Combined OASDI payroll and benefit tax revenues were increased by $40.1 billion in fiscal year 2015.

The trust fund perspective is captured in the bottom section of each of the three trust fund columns. For HI, total expenditures exceeded total revenues by $6.4 billion in 2015, as shown at the bottom of the first column. This cash deficit was made up by calling in past loans made to the General Fund (i.e., by redeeming trust fund assets). For SMI, total expenditures exceeded total revenues by $1.9 billion. The total revenue for SMI is $357.5 billion ($91.5 + $266.0), which includes $266.0 billion transferred from other Government accounts (General Fund). Transfers to the SMI Program from other Government accounts (the General Fund), amounting to about 73.3 percent of program costs, are obligated under current law and, therefore, appropriately viewed as revenue from the trust fund perspective. For OASDI, total revenues of $913.4 billion ($817.1 + $96.3) exceeded total expenditures of $887.7 billion by $25.7 billion. Total revenues for OASDI included $96.3 billion in transfers from the General Fund, made up of interest credits of $96.0 billion and transfers of $0.3 billion called for by Public Laws 111-147, 111-312, 112-78, and 112-96 to make up for the reduction in payroll tax revenues attributable to the temporary payroll tax rate reductions.

Table 1

Revenues and Expenditures for Medicare and Social Security Trust Funds and the Total Federal Budget for the Fiscal Year ended September 30, 2015

(In billions of dollars)	Trust Funds					
	HI	SMI	OASDI	Total	All Other	Total[1]
Payroll taxes and other public revenues:						
Payroll and benefit taxes.........................	257.9	-	817.1	1,075.0	-	1,075.0
Premiums..	4.8	79.7	-	84.5	-	84.5
Other taxes and fees	-	11.8	-	11.8	2,077.4	2,089.2
Total...	262.7	91.5	817.1	1,171.3	2,077.4	3,248.7
Total expenditures to the public[2]	278.7	359.4	887.7	1,525.8	2,161.8	3,687.6
Net results for budget perspective[3]	(16.0)	(267.9)	(70.6)	(354.5)	(84.4)	(438.9)
Revenues from other Government accounts:						
Transfers	1.0	263.5	0.3	264.8	(264.8)	
Interest credits......................................	8.6	2.5	96.0	107.1	(107.1)	
Total...	9.6	266.0	96.3	371.9	(371.9)	
Net results for trust fund perspective[3]...	(6.4)	(1.9)	25.7	17.4	N/A	N/A

[1] This column is the sum of the preceding two columns and shows data for the total federal budget. The figure $438.9 was the total federal deficit in fiscal year 2015.

[2] The OASDI figure includes $4.7 billion transferred to the Railroad Retirement Board for benefit payments and is therefore an expenditure to the public.

[3] Net results are computed as revenues less expenditures.

Notes: Amounts may not add due to rounding.
　　"N/A" indicates not applicable.

Cash Flow Projections

Background

　　Economic and Demographic Assumptions. The Boards of Trustees[9] of the OASDI and Medicare Trust Funds provide in their annual reports to Congress short-range (10-year) and long-range (75-year) actuarial estimates of each trust fund. Because of the inherent uncertainty in estimates for 75 years into the future, the Boards use three alternative sets of economic and demographic assumptions to show a range of possibilities. The economic and demographic assumptions used for the most recent set of intermediate projections for Social Security and Medicare are shown in the "Social Security" and "Medicare" sections of Note 23—Social Insurance.

---

[9] There are six trustees: the Secretaries of the Treasury (managing trustee), Health and Human Services, and Labor; the Commissioner of the Social Security Administration; and two public trustees who are appointed by the President and confirmed by the Senate for a 4-year term. By law, the public trustees cannot both be members of the same political party.

Beneficiary-to-Worker Ratio. The expenditure projections for both the OASDI and Medicare Programs reflect the aging of the large baby-boom generation, born in the years 1946 to 1964, and its ultimate passing. Chart 1 shows that the number of OASDI beneficiaries per 100 covered workers is projected to grow rapidly from 36 in 2015 to 47 in 2035 as the baby boom generation enters their retirement years and receives benefits. After 2035 the baby boom's influence will have dissipated, and it is projected that the beneficiary-worker ratio will continue to rise but at a slower pace due to increasing longevity, reaching 51 beneficiaries per 100 workers by 2090. (In rough terms, the beneficiary-to-worker ratio at any point in time reflects the birth rates experienced by the generations who are retired; the birth rates of the baby boom generations' parents were much higher than those of the baby boomer generations and the generations to follow them.) A similar demographic pattern confronts the Medicare Program.

Chart 1—OASDI Beneficiaries per 100 Covered Workers
1970-2089

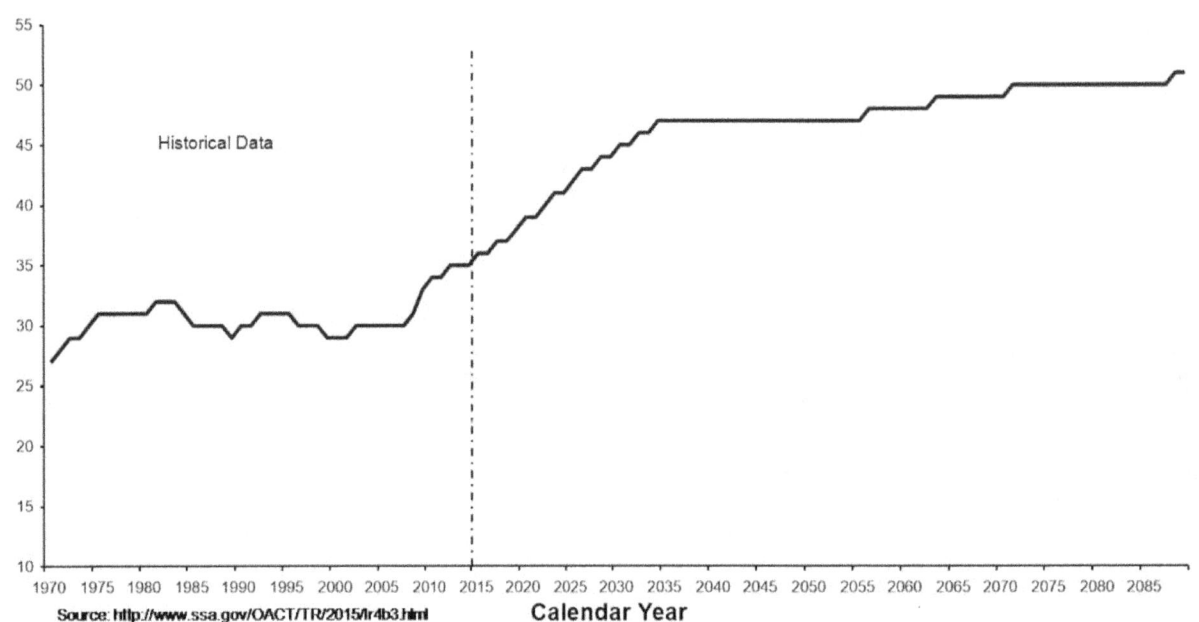

Source: http://www.ssa.gov/OACT/TR/2015/lr4b3.html

Calendar Year

Social Security Projections

Income and Expenditures. Chart 2 shows historical values and actuarial estimates of combined OASDI annual noninterest income and expenditures for 1970-2089. The estimates are for the open-group population of all workers and beneficiaries projected to be alive in each year. The expenditure projections in Chart 2 and all subsequent charts assume all scheduled benefits are paid regardless of whether the income and assets are available to finance them.

Chart 2—OASDI Income (Excluding Interest) and Expenditures
1970-2089

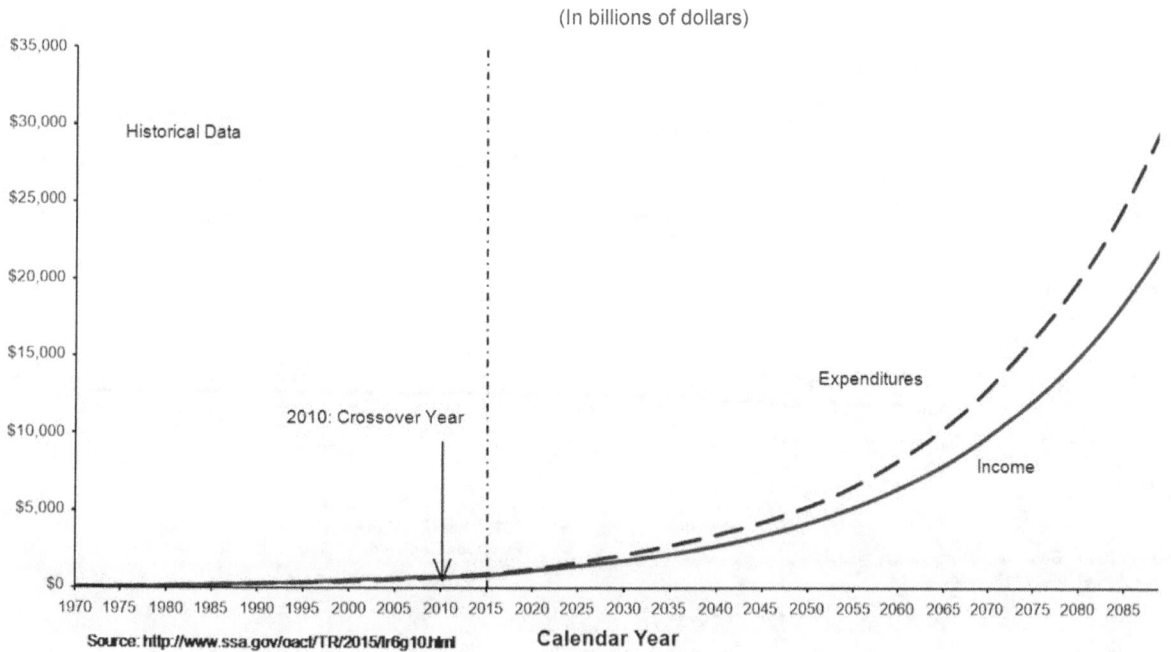

Source: http://www.ssa.gov/oact/TR/2015/lr6g10.html

Social Security's surplus of noninterest income over expenditures was positive every year between 1984 and 2009, became negative in 2010, and is projected to grow ever more negative over the next 75 years. This pattern reflects the aging of the population documented in Chart 1, as well as growth of the economy and growth in the price level. As described above, surpluses that occurred prior to 2010 were "loaned" to the General Fund and accumulated, with interest, increasing reserve spending authority for the trust fund. The reserve spending authority represents an obligation for the General Fund.

Income and Expenditures as a Percent of Taxable Payroll. Chart 3 shows annual noninterest income and expenditures expressed as percentages of taxable payroll, commonly referred to as the income rate and cost rate, respectively. Dividing noninterest income and expenditures by taxable payroll serves to isolate the effect of demographics on Social Security finances, and usefully gauges Social Security's financial imbalances against the size of the Social Security tax base. The time path of the cost rate in Chart 3 closely parallels that of the beneficiary-to-worker ratio in Chart 1. Social Security began using interest credits to meet full benefit obligations in 2010, and is projected to begin drawing down trust fund asset reserves starting in 2020 and to deplete those reserves in 2034. After trust fund asset reserves are depleted, noninterest income will continue to flow into the fund and will be sufficient to finance 79 percent of scheduled benefits in 2034 and 73 percent of scheduled benefits in 2089.

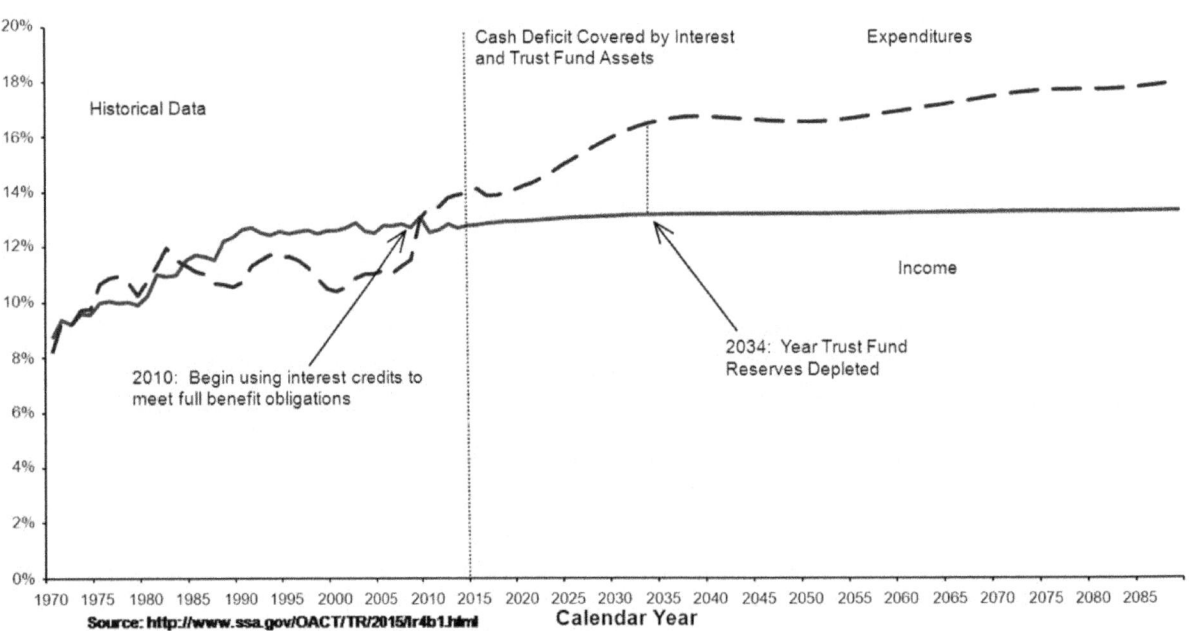

**Chart 3—OASDI Income (Excluding Interest) and Expenditures
as a Percent of Taxable Payroll
1970-2089**

Source: http://www.ssa.gov/OACT/TR/2015/lr4b1.html

Income and Expenditures as a Percent of GDP. Chart 4 shows estimated annual noninterest income and expenditures, expressed as percentages of GDP, which is the total value of goods and services produced in the United States. This alternative perspective shows the size of the OASDI Program in relation to the capacity of the national economy to sustain it. The gap between expenditures and income generally widens with expenditures generally growing as a share of GDP and income declining slightly relative to GDP. The cost of the program (based on current law) rises rapidly to 5.9 percent of GDP in 2030, hits a peak of 6.0 percent of GDP in 2037, declines to 5.9 percent by 2050, and generally increases to 6.2 percent of GDP by 2089. The rapid increase from 2016 to 2030 is projected to occur as baby boomers become eligible for OASDI benefits, lower birth rates result in fewer workers per beneficiary, and beneficiaries continue to live longer. In 2089, expenditures are projected to exceed income by 1.60 percent of GDP.

Chart 4—OASDI Income (Excluding Interest) and Expenditures as a Percent of GDP
1970-2089

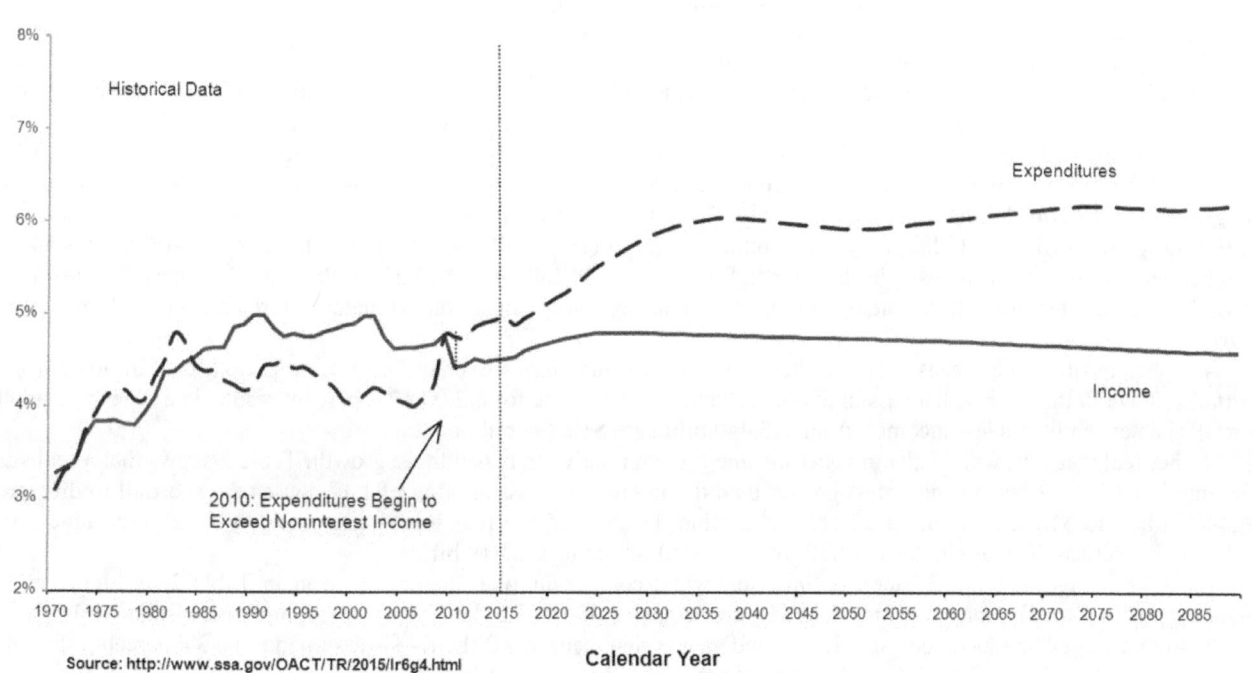

Source: http://www.ssa.gov/OACT/TR/2015/lr6g4.html

Sensitivity Analysis. Actual future income from OASDI payroll taxes and other sources and actual future expenditures for scheduled benefits and administrative expenses will depend upon a large number of factors: the size and composition of the population that is receiving benefits, the level of monthly benefit amounts, the size and characteristics of the work force covered under OASDI, and the level of workers' earnings. These factors will depend, in turn, upon future marriage and divorce rates, birth rates, death rates, migration rates, labor force participation and unemployment rates, disability incidence and termination rates, retirement age patterns, productivity gains, wage increases, cost-of-living increases, and many other economic as well as demographic factors.

This section presents estimates that illustrate the sensitivity of long-range expenditures and income for the OASDI Program to changes in *selected individual assumptions*. In this analysis, the intermediate assumption is used as the reference point, and one assumption at a time is varied. The variation used for each individual assumption reflects the levels used for that assumption in the low-cost (Alternative I) and high-cost (Alternative III) projections. For example, when analyzing sensitivity with respect to variation in real wages, income, and expenditure projections using the intermediate assumptions are compared to the outcome when projections are done by changing only the real wage assumption to either low-cost or high-cost alternatives.

The low-cost alternative is characterized by assumptions that improve the financial status of the program (relative to the intermediate assumption) such as slower improvement in mortality (beneficiaries die younger). In contrast, assumptions under the high-cost alternative worsen the financial outlook.

Table 2 shows the effects of changing individual assumptions on the present value of estimated OASDI expenditures in excess of income (the *shortfall* of income relative to expenditures in present value terms). The assumptions are shown in parentheses. For example, the intermediate assumption for the annual rate of *reduction in age-sex-adjusted death rates* is 0.78 percent. For the low-cost alternative, a slower reduction rate (0.41 percent) is assumed as it means that beneficiaries die at a younger age relative to the intermediate assumption, resulting in lower expenditures. Under the low-cost assumption, the shortfall drops from $13,440 billion to $11,467 billion, a 15 percent smaller shortfall. The high-cost death rate assumption (1.18 percent) results in an increase in the shortfall, from $13,440 billion to $15,511 billion, a 15 percent increase in the shortfall. Clearly, alternative death rate assumptions have a substantial impact on estimated future cash flows in the OASDI Program.

A higher fertility rate means more workers relative to beneficiaries over the projection period, thereby lowering the shortfall relative to the intermediate assumption. An increase in the rate from 2.0 to 2.2 percent results in a 9 percent smaller shortfall (i.e., expenditures less income), from $13,440 billion to $12,234 billion.

Higher real wage growth results in faster income growth relative to expenditure growth. Table 2 shows that a real wage differential that is 0.63 percentage points greater than the intermediate assumption of 1.17 causes the shortfall to drop from $13,440 billion to $10,457 billion, a 22 percent decline. Decreasing the real wage differential by 0.62 percentage points results in a 15 percent increase in the shortfall from $13,440 billion to $15,419 billion.

The CPI change assumption operates in a somewhat counterintuitive manner, as seen in Table 2. A higher rate of change results in a lower shortfall. This arises as a consequence of holding the real wage assumption constant while varying the CPI so that wages (the income base) are affected sooner than benefits. If the rate is assumed to be 3.4 percent rather than 2.7 percent, the shortfall decreases about 4 percent, from $13,440 billion to $12,930 billion.

The effect of net immigration is similar to fertility in that, over the 75-year projection period, higher immigration results in proportionately more workers (taxpayers) than beneficiaries. The low-cost assumption for net immigration results in a 4 percent drop in the shortfall, from $13,440 billion to $12,839 billion, relative to the intermediate case; and the high-cost assumption results in a 5 percent higher shortfall.

Finally, Table 2 shows the sensitivity of the shortfall to variations in the real interest rate or, in present value terminology, the sensitivity to alternative discount rates assuming a higher discount rate results in a lower present value. The shortfall is 15 percent lower, decreasing from $13,440 billion to $11,460 billion, when the real interest rate is 3.4 percent rather than 2.9 percent. The shortfall is 18 percent higher, increasing to $15,921 billion, when the real interest rate is 2.4 percent rather than 2.9 percent.

Table 2
Present Values of Estimated OASDI Expenditures in Excess of Income Under Various Assumptions, 2015-2089

(Dollar values in billions; values of assumptions shown in parentheses)

Assumption	Financing		
	Low	Intermediate	High
Average annual reduction in death rates	11,467 (0.41)	13,440 (0.78)	15,511 (1.18)
Total fertility rate	12,234 (2.2)	13,440 (2.0)	14,514 (1.8)
Real wage differential	10,457 (1.80)	13,440 (1.17)	15,419 (0.55)
CPI change	12,930 (3.4)	13,440 (2.7)	13,948 (2.0)
Net immigration	12,839 (1,465,000)[1]	13,440 (1,155,000)[1]	14,082 (850,000)[1]
Real interest rate	11,460 (3.4)	13,440 (2.9)	15,921 (2.4)

[1] Amounts represent the average annual net immigration over the 75-year projection period.

Source: 2015 OASDI Trustees Report and SSA.

Medicare Projections

Medicare Legislation. The *Affordable Care Act as amended by the Health Care and Education Reconciliation Act of 2010* (the "Affordable Care Act" or ACA) significantly improves projected Medicare finances. The most important cost saving provision in the ACA is a revision in payment rate updates for Parts A and B services other than for physicians' services. Relative to payment rates made under prior law that were generally based on the rate at which prices for inputs used to provide Medicare services increase, the ACA reduces those payment rate updates by the rate at which productive efficiency in the overall economy increases, which is projected to average 1.1 percent per year over the long range. The ACA also achieves substantial cost savings by benchmarking payment rates for private health plans providing Parts A and B services (Part C or Medicare Advantage) to more closely match per beneficiary costs. Partly offsetting these changes was an increase in prescription drug coverage. In addition, the ACA increases Part A revenues by: (a) taxing high-cost employer-provided health care plans and thereby giving employers incentives to increase the share of compensation paid as taxable earnings, and (b) imposing a new 0.9 percent surtax on earnings in excess of $200,000 (individual tax return filers) or $250,000 (joint tax return filers) starting in 2013.

The ACA substantially reduces the Medicare cost projections. Growth in Medicare cost per beneficiary in excess of growth in per capita GDP is referred to as "excess cost growth." In the 2009 *Financial Report*, the last report released prior to the passage of the ACA, excess cost growth was assumed to average one percentage point over the last 50 years of the 75-year projection period—that is, Medicare expenditures per beneficiary were assumed to grow, on average, about one percentage point faster than per capita GDP over the long range. That assumption for excess cost growth in Medicare was optimistic in the sense that it is smaller than in recent history; excess cost growth averaged 1.2 percentage points between 1990 and 2013.[10] In this year's *Financial Report*, as in the 2013 and 2014 reports, long-term excess cost growth is essentially zero. As a result, the long term projected Medicare spending share of GDP in this *Financial Report* is driven primarily by the same demographic trends that drive the OASDI spending share of GDP.

The 2015 Medicare Trustees' Report warns that the financial projections for the Medicare program reflect substantial, but very uncertain, cost savings deriving from provisions of the ACA and MACRA that lower increases in Medicare payment rates to most categories of health care providers. Without fundamental change in the current delivery system, these adjustments would probably not be viable indefinitely. In view of these issues with provider payment rates, actual future costs for Medicare could exceed those shown by the current-law projections that underlie both the Trustees' Report and this *Financial Report*.

Changes in Projection Methods. For 2015 the basis for the projections has changed since last year due to the enactment of the Medicare Access and CHIP Reauthorization Act (MACRA) of 2015. This law repealed the sustainable growth rate SGR formula that set physician fee schedule payments, which were usually modified. In the 2014 report, the income, expenditures, and assets for Part B reflected the *projected baseline* scenario, which assumed an override of the SGR payment provisions and an increase in the physician fee schedule equal to the average of the most recent 10 years of SGR overrides (through March 2015), or 0.6 percent. Since the new legislation has replaced the SGR system with specified payment updates for physicians, the projections in this year's report, with one exception related to Part A, are based on current law; that is, it is assumed that laws on the books will be implemented and adhered to with respect to scheduled taxes, premium revenues, and payments to providers and health plans. The one exception is that the projections disregard payment reductions that would result from the projected depletion of the Medicare Hospital Insurance (HI) Trust Fund. Under current law, payments would be reduced to levels that could be covered by incoming tax and premium revenues when the HI Trust Fund was depleted.

---

[10] Congressional Budget Office, the Long-Term Budget Outlook, June 2015.

Total Medicare. Chart 5 shows expenditures and current-law noninterest revenue sources for HI and SMI combined as a percentage of GDP. The total expenditure line shows Medicare costs rising to 6.02 percent of GDP by 2089. Revenues from taxes and premiums (including state transfers under Part D) are expected to increase from 1.98 percent of GDP in 2015 to 3.01 percent of GDP in 2089. Payroll tax income increases gradually as a percent of GDP because the new tax on earnings in excess of $250,000 for joint tax return filers and $200,000 for individual tax return filers applies to an increasing share of earnings because the $250,000 and $200,000 thresholds are not indexed for price changes. Premiums combined for Parts B and D of SMI are approximately fixed as a share of Parts B and D costs, so they also increase as a percent of GDP. General revenue contributions for SMI, as determined by current law, are projected to rise as a percent of GDP from 1.54 percent to 2.76 percent over the same period. Thus, revenues from taxes and premiums (including state transfers) will fall as a share of total noninterest Medicare income (from 56 percent in 2015 to 52 percent in 2089) while general revenues will rise (from 44 percent to 48 percent). The gap between total noninterest Medicare income (including general revenue contributions) and expenditures is expected to increase steadily beginning in about 2022, reaching roughly 0.25 percent of GDP by 2089.

**Chart 5—Total Medicare (HI and SMI) Expenditures and Noninterest Income
as a Percent of GDP
1970-2089**

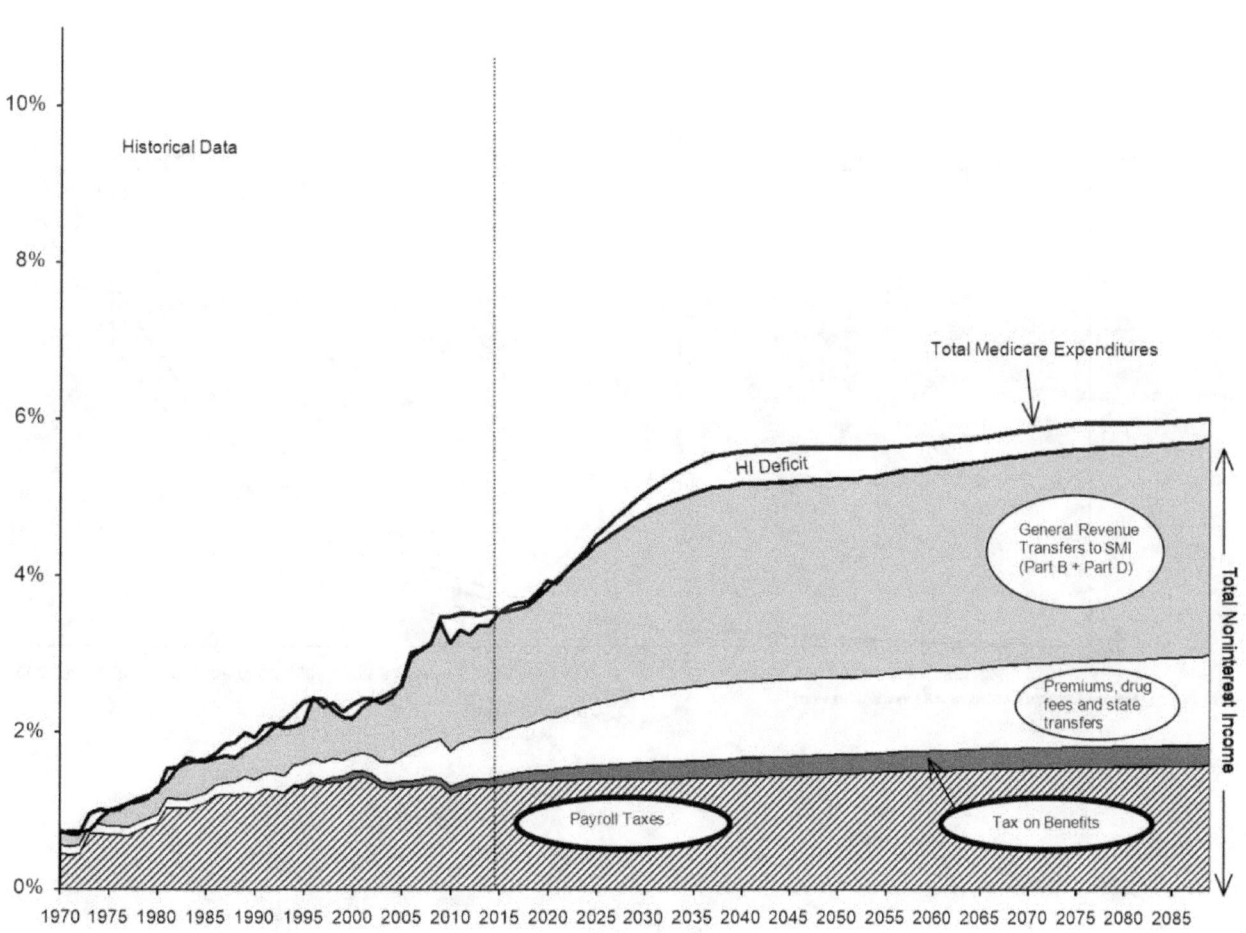

Source: http://www.ssa.gov/OACT/TRSUM/images/LD_ChartC.html

Medicare, Part A (Hospital Insurance)— Income and Expenditures. Chart 6 shows historical and actuarial estimates of HI annual income (excluding interest) and expenditures for 1970-2089 in nominal dollars. The estimates are for the open-group population.

Chart 6—Medicare Part A Income (Excluding Interest) and Expenditures
1970-2089

(In billions of dollars)

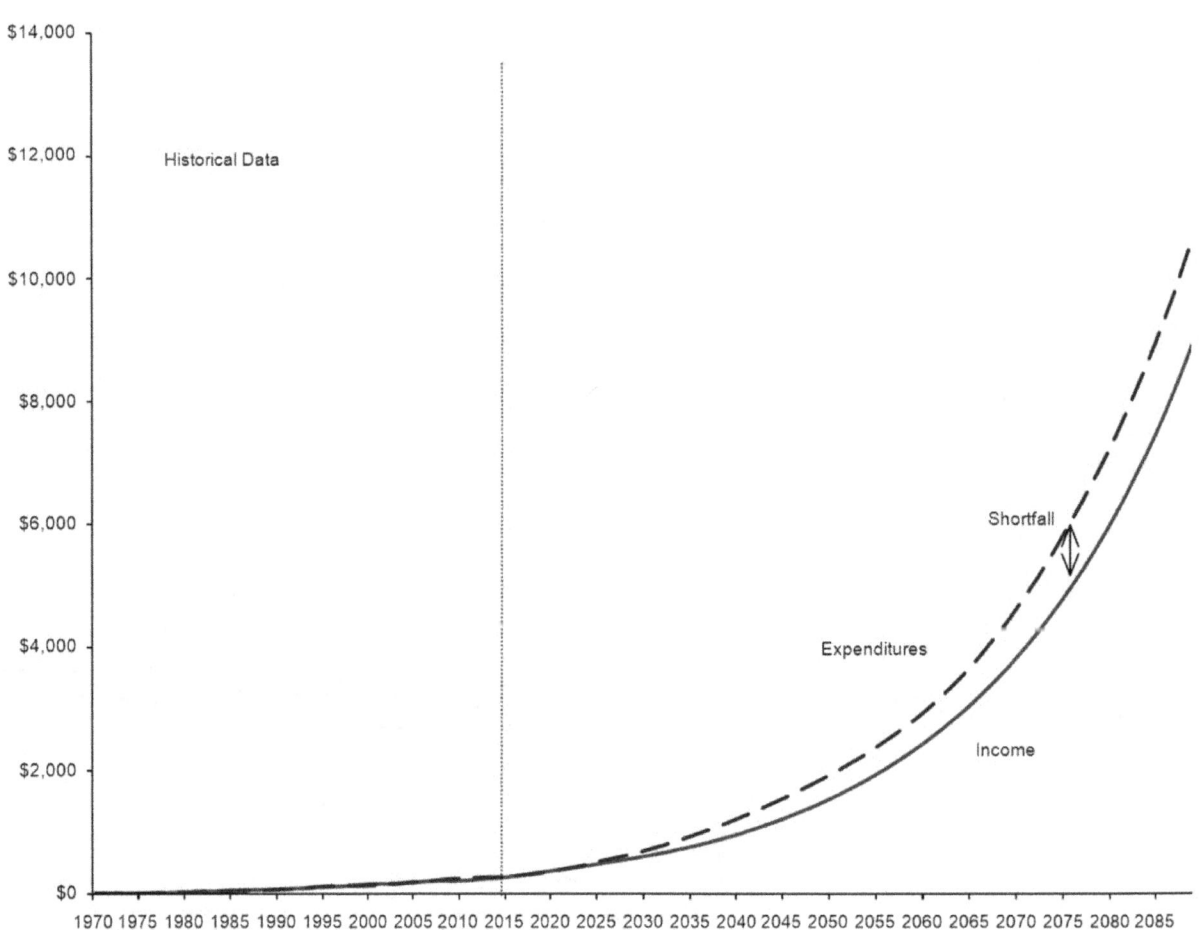

Source: Centers for Medicare & Medicaid Services

Calendar Year

Medicare, Part A Income and Expenditures as a Percent of Taxable Payroll. Chart 7 illustrates income (excluding interest) and expenditures as a percentage of taxable payroll over the next 75 years. The chart shows that beginning in 2022, the expenditure rate exceeds the income rate, and cash deficits continue thereafter. The cost rate declined from 2012 through 2014 and is projected to continue to decline through 2018, largely due to expenditure growth that was constrained in part by the sequester and low payment updates, as well as a rebound of taxable payroll growth from recession levels. Subsequent to 2018, the cost rate is projected to rise primarily due to retirements of those in the baby boom generation and partly due to a projected return to modest health services cost growth. This cost rate increase is moderated by the accumulating effect of the productivity adjustments to provider price updates, which are estimated to reduce annual HI per capita cost growth by an average 1.0 percent per year through 2024 and 1.1 percent per year thereafter. Trust fund interest earnings and assets provide enough resources to pay full benefit payments until 2030 with general revenues used to finance interest and loan repayments to make up the difference between cash income and expenditures during that period. Pressures on the federal budget will thus emerge well before 2030. Present tax rates would be sufficient to pay 86 percent of scheduled benefits after trust fund exhaustion in 2030 and 84 percent of scheduled benefits in 2089.

Chart 7—Medicare Part A Income (Excluding Interest) and Expenditures as a Percent of Taxable Payroll
1970-2089

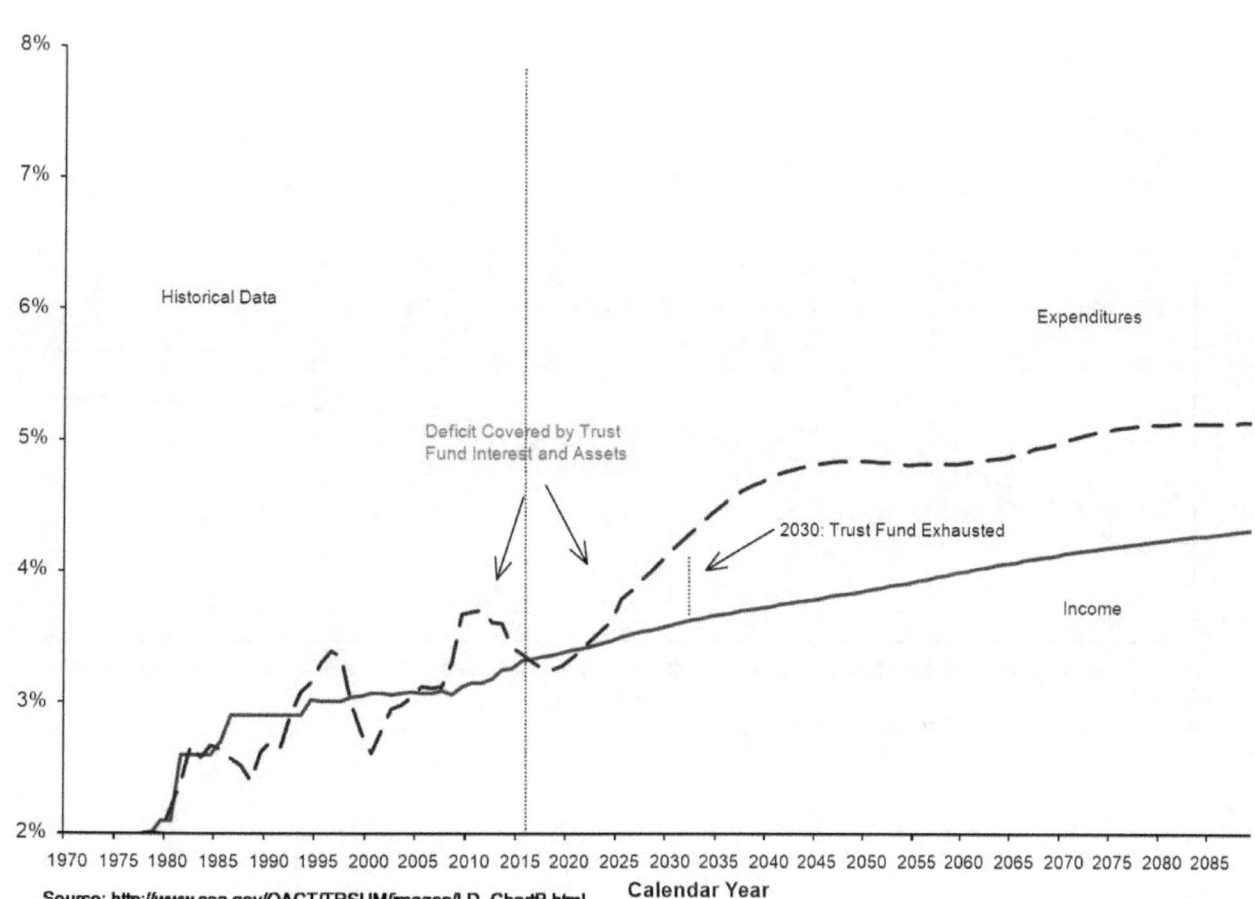

Source: http://www.ssa.gov/OACT/TRSUM/images/LD_ChartB.html

Medicare, Part A Income and Expenditures as a Percent of GDP. Chart 8 shows estimated annual noninterest income and expenditures, expressed as percentages of GDP, the total value of goods and services produced in the United States. This alternative perspective shows the size of the HI Program in relation to the capacity of the national economy to sustain it. Medicare Part A's expenditures as a percentage of GDP are expected to increase steadily until about 2045, and then remain fairly level throughout the rest of the 75-year period, as the accumulated effects of the price update reductions are realized. The gap between expenditure and income shares of GDP widens to 0.45 percent in 2042, remains fairly stable through 2047, and then commences a slight decline, reaching 0.35 percent of GDP in 2089.

Chart 8—Medicare Part A Income (Excluding Interest) and Expenditures as a Percent of GDP
1970-2089

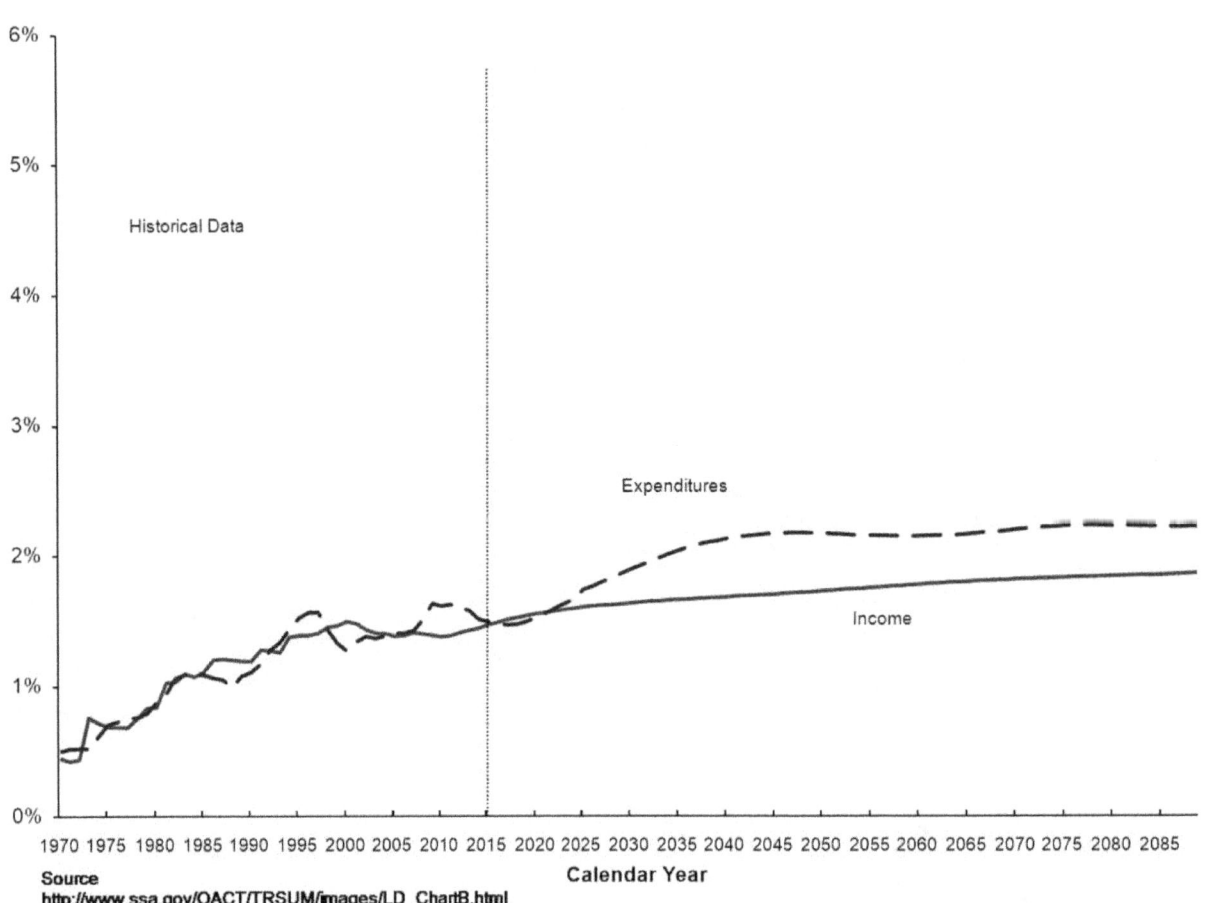

Source
http://www.ssa.gov/OACT/TRSUM/images/LD_Chart8.html

Medicare, Parts B and D (Supplementary Medical Insurance). Chart 9 shows historical and actuarial estimates of Medicare Part B and Part D premiums (and Part D state transfers) as well as expenditures for each of the next 75 years, in dollars. The gap between premiums, drug fees, and state transfer revenues plus program expenditures, a gap that will need to be filled with transfers from general revenues, grows throughout the projection period.

Chart 9—Medicare Part B and Part D Premium and State Transfer Income and Expenditures
1970-2089

(In billions of dollars)

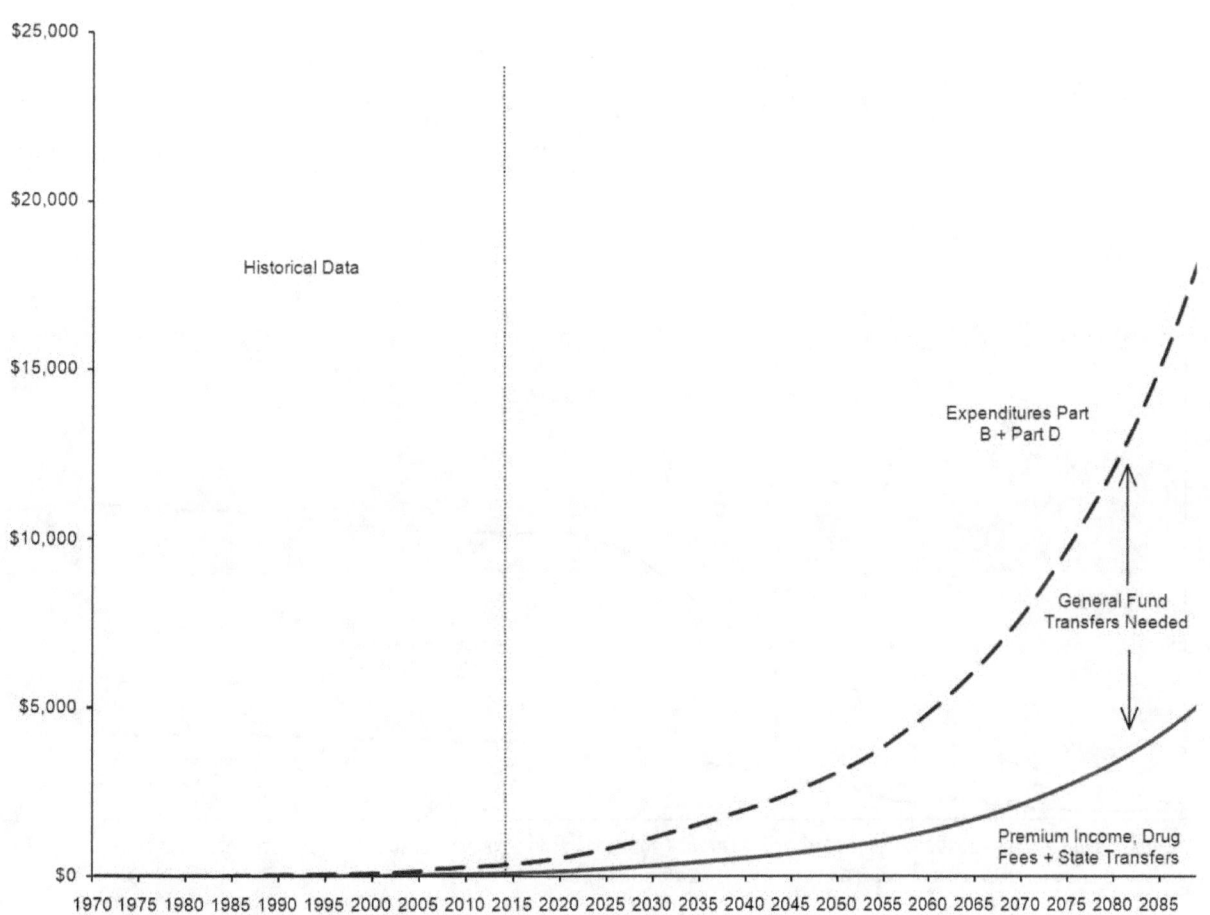

Source: Centers for Medicare & Medicaid Services

Medicare Part B and Part D Premium as well as State Transfer Income and Expenditures as a Percent of GDP. Chart 10 shows expenditures for the Supplementary Medical Insurance Program over the next 75 years expressed as a percentage of GDP, providing a perspective on the size of the SMI Program in relation to the capacity of the national economy to sustain it. SMI costs are projected to continue to outpace growth in GDP but at a slower rate compared to the last 10 years. SMI expenditures as a share of GDP are expected to grow rapidly from 2.04 percent in 2015 to 2.65 percent in 2024, and then grow more slowly reaching 3.80 percent in 2089. The relatively high growth during the period 2015-2024 is due to the continuing retirement of the baby boom generation, further economic recovery, and modest increases in cost trends. Growth rates are projected to decline during the 2025-2039 period primarily as a result of a deceleration in beneficiary population growth. For the last 50 years of the projection period, cost growth moderates further due to the continued deceleration in beneficiary population growth and lower ultimate growth rate assumptions. As a share of GDP, premium and state transfer income grows from about 0.52 percent in 2015 to 1.05 percent of GDP in 2089. The portion of SMI expenditures financed by General Fund transfers to SMI is projected to be about 72 percent throughout the projections period.

**Chart 10—Medicare Part B and Part D Premium and State Transfer
Income and Expenditures as a Percent of GDP
1970-2089**

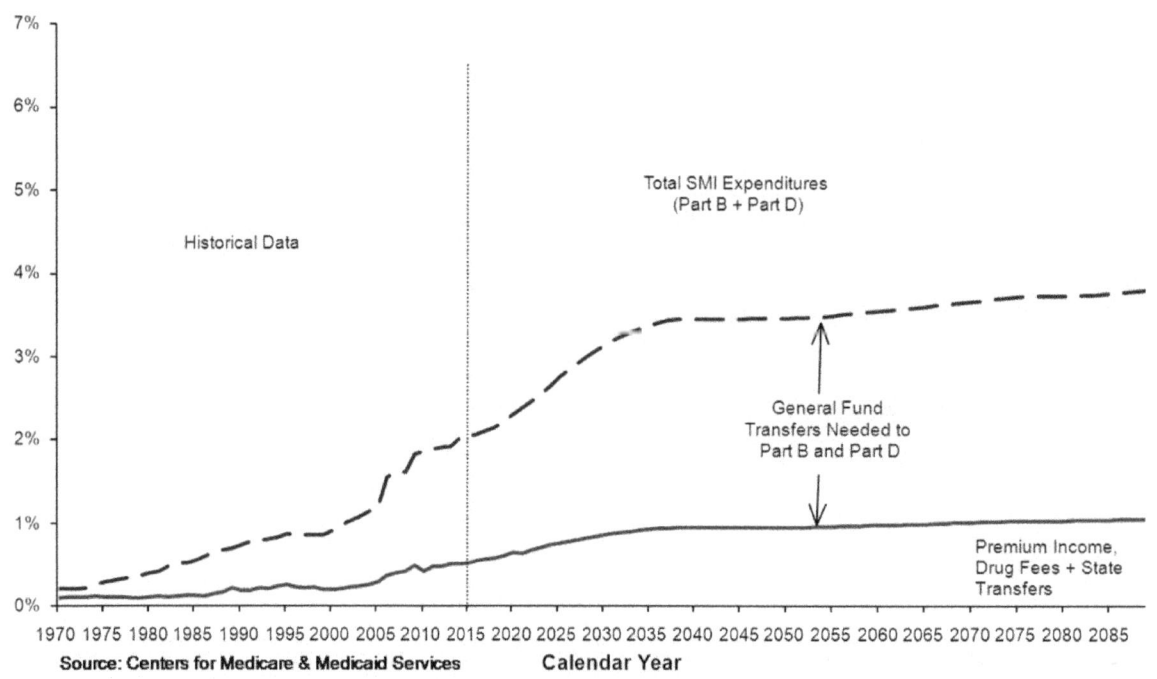

Source: Centers for Medicare & Medicaid Services   Calendar Year

Medicare Sensitivity Analysis. This section illustrates the sensitivity of long-range cost and income estimates for the Medicare Program to changes in *selected individual assumptions.* As with the OASDI analysis, the intermediate assumption is used as a reference point, and one assumption at a time is varied. The variation used for each individual assumption reflects the levels used for that assumption in the low-cost and high-cost projections (see description of sensitivity analysis for OASDI).

Table 3 shows the effects of changing various assumptions on the present value of estimated HI expenditures in excess of income (the *shortfall* of income relative to expenditures in present value terms). The assumptions are shown in parentheses. Clearly, net HI expenditures are extremely sensitive to alternative assumptions about the growth in health care cost. For the low-cost alternative, the slower growth in health costs causes the shortfall to drop from $3,187 billion to a surplus of $2,743 billion, a 186 percent change. The high-cost assumption results in more than tripling of the shortfall, from $3,187 billion to $12,594 billion.

The low and high real wage growth rate scenarios result in about a -58 and +37 percent, respectively, change in the shortfall relative to the intermediate case. Wages are a key cost factor in the provision of health care. Higher wages also result in greater payroll tax income. CPI inflation, fertility, and net immigration changes have very little effect on net HI expenditures. (When CPI inflation is varied, the real interest rate is held constant, which implies that the nominal interest changes one for one with the assumed rate of CPI inflation.) Higher immigration decreases the net shortfall modestly as the 75-year projection period captures a higher share of additional immigrants' tax payments than it does of their benefits.

Table 3 also shows that the present value of net HI expenditures is 15 percent lower if the real interest rate is 3.4 percent rather than 2.9 percent and 18 percent higher if the real interest rate is 2.4 percent rather than 2.9 percent.

Table 3
Present Values of Estimated Medicare Part A Expenditures in Excess of Income Under Various Assumptions, 2015-2089

(Dollar values in billions; values of assumptions shown in parentheses)

Assumption	Financing Shortfall Range		
	Low	Intermediate	High
Average annual growth in health costs	(2,743)	3,187	12,594
	(3.0)	(4.0)	(5.0)
Total fertility rate	2,793	3,187	3,547
	(2.2)	(2.0)	(1.8)
Real wage differential	1,326	3,187	4,365
	(1.8)	(1.2)	(0.6)
CPI change	2,386	3,187	4,221
	(3.4)	(2.7)	(2.0)
Net immigration	2,981	3,187	3,455
	(1,465,000)[4]	(1,155,000)[4]	(850,000)[4]
Real interest rate	2,704	3,187	3,774
	(3.4)	(2.9)	(2.4)

[1] The sensitivity of the projected HI net cash flow to variations in future mortality rates also is of interest. At this time, however, relatively little is known about the relationship between improvements in life expectancy and the associated changes in health status and per beneficiary health expenditures. As a result, it is not possible at present to prepare meaningful estimates of the Part A, mortality sensitivity.
[2] Annual growth rate is the aggregate cost of providing covered health care services to beneficiaries. The low-cost and high-cost alternatives assume that costs increase 1 percent slower or faster, respectively, than the intermediate assumption, relative to growth in taxable payroll.
[3] The total fertility rate for any year is the average number of children who would be born to a woman in her lifetime if she were to experience the birth rates by age observed in, or assumed for, the selected year and if she were to survive the entire childbearing period.
[4] Amount represents the average annual net immigration over the 75-year projection period.

Source: Center for Medicare & Medicaid Services.

Table 4 shows the effects of various assumptions about the growth in health care costs on the present value of estimated SMI (Medicare Parts B and D) expenditures in excess of income. As with HI, net SMI expenditures are very sensitive to changes in the health care cost growth assumption. For the low-cost alternative, the slower assumed growth in health costs reduces the governmentwide resources needed for Part B from $17,466 billion to $12,792 billion and in Part D from $7,287 billion to $5,190 billion, about a 27 percent and 29 percent difference for Part B and Part D, respectively. The high-cost assumption increases governmentwide resources needed to $24,693 billion for Part B and to $10,600 billion for Part D, about a 41 percent and a 45 percent difference for Part B and Part D, respectively.

Table 4
Present Values of Estimated Medicare Parts B and D Future Expenditures Less Premium Income and State Transfers Under Three Health Care Cost Growth Assumptions, 2015-2089

(In billions of dollars)

Medicare Program	Governmentwide Resources Needed		
	Low (3.3)	Intermediate (4.3)	High (5.3)
Part B	12,792	17,466	24,693
Part D	5,190	7,287	10,600

[1] Annual growth rate is the aggregate cost of providing covered health care services to beneficiaries The low and high scenarios assume that costs increase one percent slower or faster, respectively, than the intermediate assumption.

Source: Centers for Medicare & Medicaid Services.

Sustainability of Social Security and Medicare

75-Year Horizon

According to the 2015 Medicare Trustees Report, the HI Trust Fund is projected to remain solvent until 2030 and, according to the 2015 Social Security Trustees Report, the OASI and DI Trust Funds are projected to have asset reserves until 2035 and the fourth quarter of 2016, respectively. The impending depletion of the DI Trust Fund was temporarily circumvented, however, by the passing of the *Bipartisan Budget Act of 2015* by Congress and the President, which reallocated a portion of the payroll tax rate from the OASI Trust Fund to the DI Trust Fund. This reallocation is expected to ensure full payment of disability benefits into 2022. In each case, some general revenues must be used to satisfy the authorization of full benefit payments until the year of trust fund depletion. This occurs when the trust fund interest income and balances accumulated during prior years are needed to pay benefits, which leads to a transfer from general revenues to the trust funds. Moreover, under current law, General Fund transfers to the SMI Trust Fund will occur into the indefinite future and will continue to grow with the growth in health care expenditures.

The potential magnitude of future financial obligations under these three social insurance programs is, therefore, important from a unified budget perspective as well as for understanding generally the growing resource demands of the programs on the economy. A common way to present future cash flows is in terms of their *present value*. This approach recognizes that a dollar paid or collected next year is worth less than a dollar today because a dollar today could be saved and earn a year's worth of interest.

Table 5 shows the magnitudes of the primary expenditures and sources of financing for the three trust funds computed on an open-group basis for the next 75 years and expressed in present values. The data are consistent with the Statements of Social Insurance included in the principal financial statements. For HI, revenues from the public are projected to fall short of total expenditures by $3,187 billion in present value terms which is the additional amount needed in order to pay scheduled benefits over the next 75 years.[11] From the trust fund perspective, the amount needed is $2,990 billion in present value after subtracting the value of the existing trust fund balances (an asset to the trust fund account but an intragovernmental transfer to the overall budget). For SMI, revenues from the public for Part B and D combined are estimated to be $24,753 billion less than total expenditures for the two accounts, an amount that, from a budget perspective, will be needed to keep the SMI program solvent for the next 75 years. From the trust fund perspective, however, the present values of total revenues and total expenditures for the SMI Program are roughly equal due to the annual adjustment of revenue from other Government accounts to meet program costs.[12] For OASDI, projected revenues from the public fall short of total expenditures by $13,440 billion in present value dollars, and, from the trust fund perspective, by $10,651 billion.

From the governmentwide perspective, the present value of the total resources needed for the Social Security and Medicare Programs over and above current-law funding sources (payroll taxes, benefit taxes, and premium payments from the public) is $41,379 billion. From the trust fund perspective, which counts the trust funds ($3,055 billion in present value) and the general revenue transfers to the SMI Program ($24,753 billion in present value) as dedicated funding sources, additional resources needed to fund the programs are $13,571 billion in present value.

Table 5
Present Values of Costs Less Revenues of 75-Year Open Group Obligations
HI, SMI, and OASDI

(In billions of dollars, as of January 1, 2015)

	HI	SMI Part B	SMI Part D	OASDI	Total
Revenues from the public:					
Taxes	17,902	-	-	55,537	73,439
Premiums, State transfers	-	6,529	2,869	-	9,398
Total	17,902	6,529	2,869	55,537	82,837
Total costs to the public	21,089	23,995	10,156	68,976	124,216
Net results - budget perspective*	3,187	17,466	7,287	13,440	41,379
Revenues from other Government accounts	-	17,466	7,287	-	24,753
Trust fund balances as of 1/1/2015	197	68	1	2,789	3,055
Net results - trust fund perspective*	2,990	(68)	(1)	10,651	13,571

*Net results are computed as costs less revenues and trust fund balances. Negative values are indicative of surpluses.

Note: Details may not add to totals due to rounding.

Source: 2015 OASDI and Medicare Trustees' Report

Infinite Horizon

The 75-year horizon represented in Table 5 is consistent with the primary focus of the Social Security and Medicare Trustees' Reports. For the OASDI Program, for example, an additional $13.4 trillion in present value will be needed above currently scheduled taxes to pay for scheduled benefits ($10.7 trillion from the trust fund perspective). Yet, a 75-year projection can be a misleading indicator of all future financial flows. For example, when calculating unfunded obligations, a 75-year horizon includes revenue from some future workers but only a fraction of their future benefits. In order to provide a more complete estimate of the long-run unfunded obligations of the programs, estimates can be extended to the infinite horizon. The open-group infinite horizon net obligation is the present value of all expected future program outlays less the present value of all expected future program tax and premium revenues. Such a measure is provided in Table 6 for the three trust funds represented in Table 5.

---

[11] Interest income is not a factor in this table as dollar amounts are in present value terms.
[12] The SMI Trust Fund has $69 billion of existing assets.

From the budget or governmentwide perspective, the values in line 1 plus the values in line 4 of Table 6 represent the value of resources needed to finance each of the programs into the infinite future. The sums are shown in the last line of the table (also equivalent to adding the values in the second and fifth lines). The total resources needed for all the programs sums to $72.0 trillion in present value terms. This need can be satisfied only through increased borrowing, higher taxes, reduced program spending, or some combination.

The second line shows the value of the trust fund at the beginning of 2015. For the HI and OASDI Programs this represents, from the trust fund perspective, the extent to which the programs are funded. From that perspective, when the trust fund is subtracted, an additional $25.7 trillion is needed to sustain the OASDI program into the infinite future, while an additional $0.01 trillion is needed to sustain the HI program. However, looking just at present values ignores timing differences in the underlying projected cash flows; the HI Trust Fund is projected to remain solvent only until 2030. As described above, from the trust fund perspective, the SMI Program is fully funded, from a governmentwide basis, the substantial gap that exists between premiums, state transfer revenue, and program expenditures in the SMI Program ($28.2 trillion and $14.9 trillion for Parts B and D, respectively) represents future general revenue obligations of the federal budget.

In comparison to the analogous 75-year number in Table 5, extending the calculations beyond 2089, captures the full lifetime benefits, plus taxes and premiums of all current and future participants. The shorter horizon understates the total financial needs by capturing relatively more of the revenues from current and future workers and not capturing all of the benefits that are scheduled to be paid to them.

Table 6
Present Values of Costs Less Tax, Premium and State Transfer Revenue through the Infinite Horizon, HI, SMI, OASDI

(In trillions of dollars as of January 1, 2015)

	HI	SMI Part B	SMI Part D	OASDI	Total
Present value of future costs less future taxes, premiums, and state transfers for current participants	8.8	14.8	5.2	29.5	58.3
Less current trust fund balance	0.2	0.1	-	2.8	3.1
Equals net obligations for past and current participants	8.6	14.7	5.2	26.7	55.2
Plus net obligations for future participants	(8.5)	13.5	9.7	(1.0)	13.7
Equals net obligations through the infinite future for all participants	0.1	28.2	14.9	25.7	68.9
Present values of future costs less the present values of future income over the infinite horizon	0.3	28.3	14.9	28.5	72.0

Details may not add to totals due to rounding.

Source: 2015 OASDI and Medicare Trustees' Reports.

Railroad Retirement, Black Lung, and Unemployment Insurance

Railroad Retirement

The Railroad Retirement Board (RRB) was created in the 1930s to establish a retirement benefit program for the Nation's railroad workers. As the Social Security Program legislated in 1935 would not give railroad workers credit for service performed prior to 1937, legislation was enacted in 1934, 1935, and 1937 (collectively the Railroad Retirement Acts of the 1930s) to establish a railroad retirement program separate from the Social Security Program.

Railroad retirement pays full retirement annuities at age 60 to railroad workers with 30 years of service. The program pays disability annuities based on total or occupational disability. It also pays annuities to spouses, divorced spouses, widow(er)s, remarried widow(er)s, surviving divorced spouses, children, and parents of deceased railroad workers. Medicare covers qualified railroad retirement beneficiaries in the same way as it does Social Security beneficiaries.

Payroll taxes paid by railroad employers and their employees provide a primary source of income for the Railroad Retirement and Survivors' Benefit Program. By law, railroad retirement taxes are coordinated with Social Security taxes. Employees and employers pay Tier I taxes at the same rate as Social Security taxes. Tier II taxes finance railroad retirement benefit payments that are higher than Social Security levels.

Other sources of program income include: the RRB-SSA-CMS Financial Interchanges with the Social Security and Medicare Trust Funds, earnings on investments, federal income taxes on railroad retirement benefits, and appropriations (provided after 1974 as part of a phase out of certain vested dual benefits). See Note 23—Social Insurance, for additional information on railroad retirement program financing.

Amounts in the Railroad Retirement Account and the SSEB Account that are not needed to pay current benefits and administrative expenses may be transferred to the NRRIT or used to offset transfers from the NRRIT to the Railroad Retirement Account. The NRRIT's sole purpose is to manage and invest railroad retirement assets. NRRIT's Board of Trustees is empowered to invest trust assets in nongovernmental assets, such as equities and debt, as well as in Government securities.

Since its inception, NRRIT has received $21.3 billion from RRB (including $19.2 billion in fiscal year 2003, pursuant to RRSIA) and returned $17.8 billion. During fiscal year 2015, the NRRIT made net transfers of $1.2 billion to the RRB to pay retirement benefits. Administrative expenses of the trust are paid out of trust assets. The balance as of September 30, 2015, and 2014, of non-federal securities and investments of the NRRIT are disclosed in Note 7—Debt and Equity Securities.

Cash Flow Projections

Economic and Demographic Assumptions. The economic and demographic assumptions used for the most recent set of projections are shown in the "Railroad Retirement" section of Note 23—Social Insurance.

Income and Expenditures. Chart 11 shows, in dollars, estimated railroad retirement income (excluding interest and financial interchange income) and expenditures for the period 2015-2089 based on the intermediate set of assumptions used in the RRB's actuarial valuation of the program. The estimates are for the open-group population, which includes all persons projected to participate in the Railroad Retirement Program as railroad workers or beneficiaries during the period. Thus, the estimates include payments from, and on behalf of, those who are projected to be employed by the railroads during the period as well as those already employed at the beginning of the period. They also include expenditures made to, and on behalf of, such workers during that period.

Chart 11—Estimated Railroad Retirement Income
(Excluding Interest and Financial Interchange Income) and Expenditures
2015-2089

(In billions of dollars)

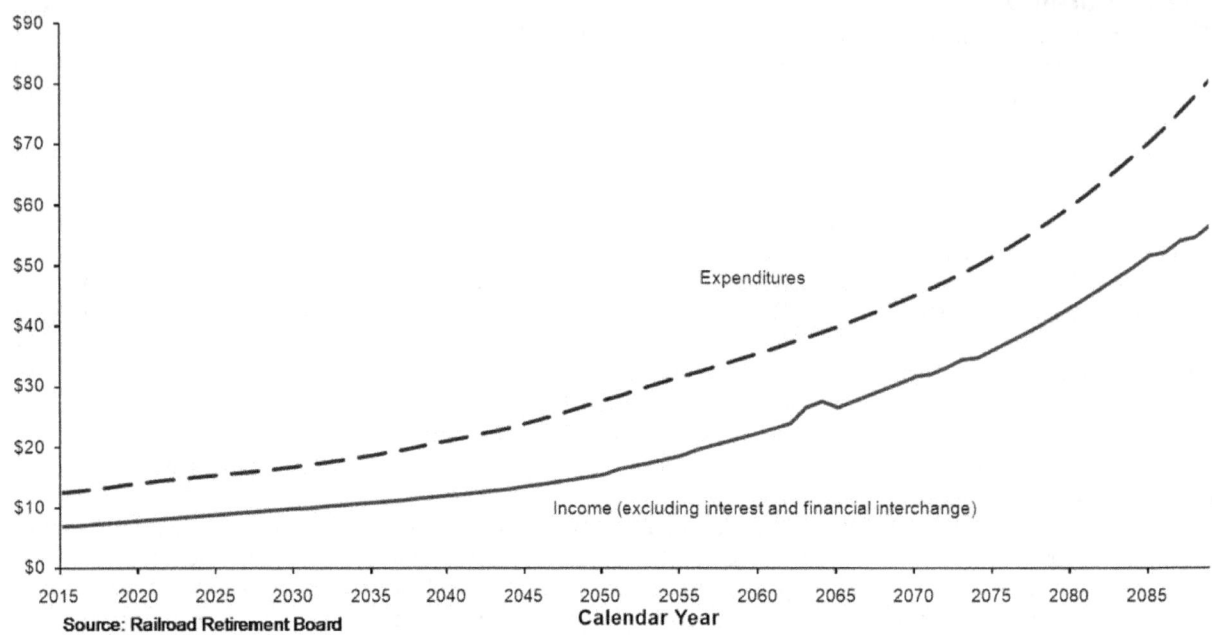

Source: Railroad Retirement Board

As Chart 11 shows, expenditures are expected to exceed tax income for the entire projection period. The imbalance generally grows at a moderate amount until about 2082 when it begins to grow a little more rapidly.

Income and Expenditures as a Percent of Taxable Payroll. Chart 12 shows estimated expenditures and income as a percent of Tier II taxable payroll. Expenditures as a percentage of payroll range between 67% and 71% until 2058, after which the percentage decreases from one year to the next. This is largely due to the anticipated decline in the number of annuitants per full-time employee.

**Chart 12—Estimated Railroad Retirement Income
(Excluding Interest and Financial Interchange Income) and Expenditures
as a Percent of Tier II Taxable Payroll
2015-2089**

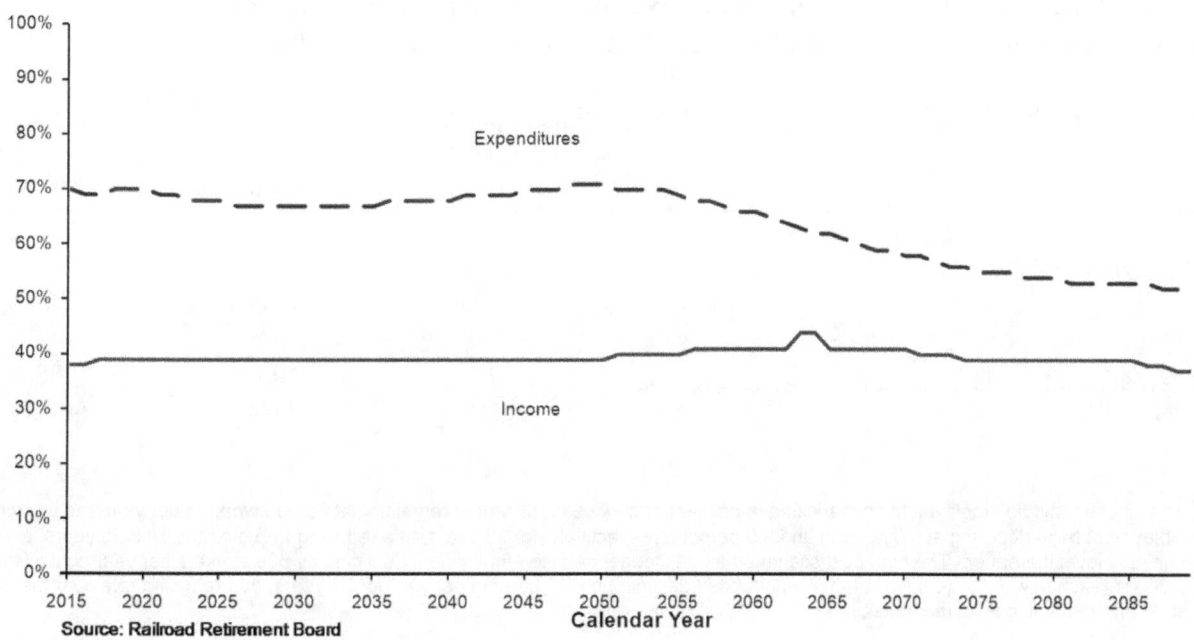

Source: Railroad Retirement Board

Sensitivity Analysis. Actual future income from railroad payroll taxes and other sources and actual future expenditures for scheduled benefits and administrative expenses will depend upon a large number of factors as mentioned above. Two crucial assumptions are employment growth and the interest rate. The interest rate assumption reflects the expected rate of return on NRRIT investments. Table 7 shows the sensitivity of the shortfall in the Railroad Retirement Program to variations in these two assumptions. The low-cost employment scenario has a 7.0 percent smaller shortfall of income to expenditures, and the high-cost scenario has a 6.9 percent higher shortfall. A higher discount rate reduces future values relative to a lower rate. As seen in the table, the shortfall is 27.8 percent lower if the interest rate is 10.0 percent rather than 7.0 percent and 71.5 percent higher when the interest rate is 4.0 percent rather than 7.0 percent.

Table 7
Present Values of Railroad Retirement Expenditures in Excess of Income Under Various Employment and Interest Rate Assumptions, 2015-2089

(Dollar values in billions; values of assumptions shown in parentheses)

Assumption	Low	Middle	High
Employment[1]	102.1	109.8	117.4
	(-0.5%)	(-2.0%)	(-3.5%)
Interest rate	79.3	109.8	188.3
	(10.0%)	(7.0%)	(4.0%)

[1] The low and middle employment scenarios have passenger service employment remaining at 46,000 workers per year and the remaining employment base declining at 0.5 percent and 2.0 percent, respectively, for 25 years, at a reducing rate over the next 25 years, and remaining level thereafter. The high-cost scenario has passenger service employment declining by 500 workers per year until a level of 35,000 is reached with the remaining employment base declining by 3.5 percent per year for 25 years, at a reducing rate over the next 25 years, and remaining level thereafter.

Source: Railroad Retirement Board

Sustainability of Railroad Retirement

Table 8 shows the magnitudes of the primary expenditures and sources of financing for the Railroad Retirement Program computed on an open-group basis for the next 75 years and expressed in present values as of January 1, 2015. The data are consistent with the Statements of Social Insurance.

From a governmentwide perspective, revenues are expected to fall short of expenditures by approximately $109.8 billion, which represents the present value of resources needed to sustain the Railroad Retirement Program. From a trust fund perspective, when the trust fund balance and the financial interchange and transfers are included, the combined balance of the NRRIT, the Railroad Retirement Account, and the SSEB Account show a slight surplus.

Table 8
Present Values of 75-Year Projections of Revenues and Expenditures for the Railroad Retirement Program[1,2]

(In billions of present-value dollars as of January 1, 2015)

Estimated future income (excluding interest) received from or on behalf of: [3]	
Current participants who have attained retirement age	8.0
Current participants not yet having attained retirement age	66.4
Those expected to become participants	78.5
All participants	152.9
Estimated future expenditures: [4]	
Current participants who have attained retirement age	130.6
Current participants not yet having attained retirement age	97.2
Those expected to become participants	34.9
All participants	262.7
Net obligations from budget perspective (expenditures less income)	109.8
Railroad retirement program assets (mostly investments stated at market) [5]	27.6
Financial interchange from Social Security Trust	83.7
Net obligations from trust fund perspective	(1.5)

[1] Represents combined values for the Railroad Retirement Account, SSEB Account, and NRRIT, based on middle employment assumption.

[2] The data used reflect the provisions of RRSIA of 2001.

[3] Future income (excluding interest) includes Tier I taxes, Tier II taxes, and income taxes on benefits.

[4] Future expenditures include benefits and administrative expenditures.

[5] The value of the fund reflects the 7.0 percent interest rate assumption. The RRB uses the relatively high rate due to investments in private securities.

Note: Detail may not add to totals due to rounding. Employee and beneficiary status are determined as of 1/1/2014, whereas present values are as of 1/1/2015.

Source: Railroad Retirement Board

Black Lung

The Federal Coal Mine Health and Safety Act of 1969 created the Black Lung Disability Benefit Program to provide compensation, medical, and survivor benefits for eligible coal miners who are totally disabled due to pneumoconiosis (black lung disease) arising out of their coal mine employment and to eligible survivors of coal miners who died due to pneumoconiosis. DOL operates the Black Lung Disability Benefit Program. The beneficiary population is a nearly closed universe in which attrition by death exceeds new entrants by a ratio of more than ten to one.

Excise taxes on coal mine operators, based on the domestic sale of coal, are the primary source of financing black lung disability payments and related administrative costs. The *Black Lung Benefits Revenue Act* provided for repayable advances to the BLDTF from the General Fund, in the event that BLDTF resources were not adequate to meet program obligations.

Prior to legislation enacted in 2008 that allowed for the restructuring of BLDTF debt, the trust fund had accumulated large liabilities from significant and growing shortfalls of excise taxes relative to benefit payments and interest expenses.

The *Energy Improvement and Extension Act of 2008* (Public Law 110-343), enacted on October 3, 2008, contained several provisions that significantly improved the BLDTF's financial position, including:

- Continuation of a previously-enacted increase in coal excise tax rates for an additional 5 years, through December 2018;

- Provision for the restructuring of BLDTF debt by refinancing the outstanding repayable advances with proceeds from issuing new debt instruments with lower interest rates; and

- Establishment of a one-time appropriation that significantly reduced the outstanding debt of the BLDTF.

This Act also allowed that any debt issued by the BLDTF subsequent to the refinancing may be used to make benefit payments, other authorized expenditures, or to repay debt and interest from the initial refinancing. All debt issued by the BLDTF was effected as borrowing from the Treasury's Bureau of the Fiscal Service.

On September 30, 2015, total liabilities of the BLDTF exceeded assets by $5.6 billion. Prior to the enactment of Public Law 110-343, this shortfall was funded by repayable advances to the BLDTF, which were repayable with interest. Pursuant to Public Law 110-343, these repayable advances were restructured as zero coupon bonds and any future shortfall is financed with one-year borrowing from Treasury.

From the budget or consolidated financial perspective, Chart 13 shows projected black lung expenditures (excluding interest) and excise tax collections for the period 2016-2040 in constant dollars. The significant assumptions used in the most recent set of projections, in constant dollars, are coal excise tax revenue estimates, the tax rate structure, the number of beneficiaries, life expectancy, federal civilian pay raises, medical cost inflation, the interest rate on new debt issued by the BLDTF, and the CPI-U for goods and services. The projected excise tax collections reflect, among other things, regulation pursuant to the Clean Power Plan. The projected decrease in cash inflows in the year 2019 and thereafter is the result of a scheduled reduction in the tax rate on the sale of coal. This rate reduction is projected to result in a 39.6 percent decrease in the amount of excise taxes collected between the years 2018 and 2019.

**Chart 13—Estimated Black Lung Disability Trust Fund Income and Expenditures (Excluding Interest)
In Constant (or Inflation-Adjusted) Dollars
2016-2040**

(In millions of dollars)

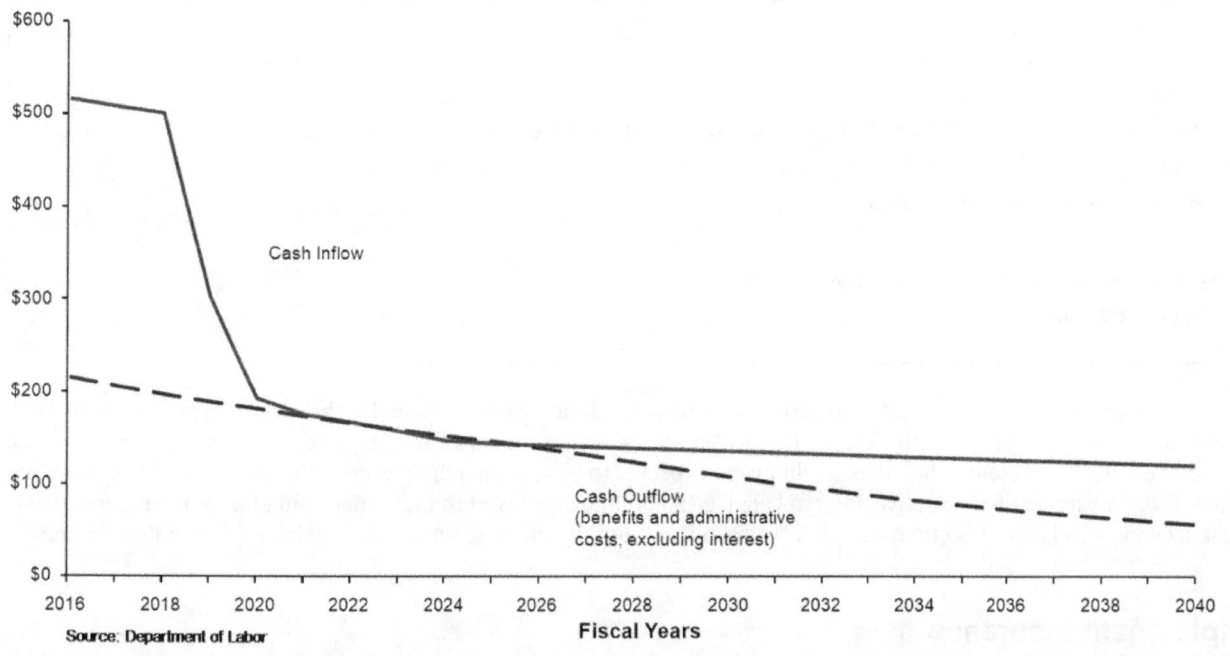

Source: Department of Labor

Table 9
Present Values of 25-Year Projections of Expenditures and Revenues for the Black Lung Disability Trust Fund

(in billions of present value dollars as of September 30, 2015)

Projected future expenditures	3.1
Projected future tax income	4.7
Net obligations from budget perspective (expenditures less income)	(1.6)
Accumulated balance due General Fund	5.6
Net obligations from trust fund perspective	4.0

Note: Detail may not add to totals due to rounding.
Source: Department of Labor

Table 9 shows present values of 25-year projections of expenditures and revenues for the Black Lung Disability Trust Fund computed as of September 30, 2015. Cash flows were discounted using a rate of 2.25 percent. From a governmentwide (budget) perspective, the present value of expenditures is expected to be less than the present value of income by $1.6 billion (a surplus). From a trust fund perspective, a large balance ($5.6 billion) is owed to the General Fund. From that perspective, when that accumulated balance is combined with the cash flow surplus, the program has a shortfall of $4.0 billion in present value dollars.

Unemployment Insurance

The Unemployment Insurance Program was created in 1935 to provide temporary partial wage replacement to workers who lost their jobs. The program is administered through a unique system of federal and state partnerships established in federal law but administered through conforming state laws by state agencies. The program includes the 50 states and Puerto Rico, U.S. Virgin Islands, and the District of Columbia. DOL interprets and enforces federal law requirements and provides broad policy guidance and program direction, while program details such as benefit eligibility, duration, and amount of benefits are established through individual state unemployment insurance statutes and administered through state unemployment insurance agencies.

The program is financed through the collection of federal and state unemployment taxes that are credited to the UTF and reported as federal tax revenue. The fund was established to account for the receipt, investment, and disbursement of unemployment taxes. Federal unemployment taxes are used to pay for federal and state administration of the Unemployment Insurance Program, veterans' employment services, state employment services, and the federal share of extended unemployment insurance benefits. Federal unemployment taxes also are used to maintain a loan account within the UTF, from which insolvent state accounts may borrow funds to pay unemployment insurance benefits.

Chart 14 shows the projected cash contributions and expenditures over the next 10 years under expected economic conditions (described below) in constant dollars. The significant assumptions used in the projections include total unemployment rates, civilian labor force levels, percent of unemployed receiving benefits, total wages, distribution of benefit payments by state, state tax rate structures, state taxable wage bases, interest rates on UTF investments, and the Consumer Price Index for goods and services. These projections, excluding interest earnings, indicate a positive net cash flow in fiscal year 2016 through fiscal year 2025.

The *Federal/State Extended Unemployment Compensation Act of 1970* provides for the extension of the duration of unemployment insurance benefits during periods of high unemployment to individuals who have exhausted their regular unemployment benefits. When the insured unemployment level within a state, or in some cases total unemployment, reaches certain specified levels, the state must extend benefit duration by 50 percent, up to a combined maximum of 39 weeks; certain states voluntarily extended the benefit duration up to a combined maximum of 46 weeks. These extended benefits are financed one-half by state unemployment taxes and one-half by federal unemployment taxes. However, the American Recovery and Reinvestment Act of 2009 (ARRA) began temporary 100 percent federal funding of extended benefits. Subsequent legislation, most recently P.L. 112-240, the *American Taxpayer Relief Act of 2012*, authorized continuing 100 percent federal funding of extended unemployment benefits to December 31, 2013.

During prolonged periods of high unemployment, Congress may authorize the payment of emergency unemployment benefits to supplement extended Unemployment Insurance (UI) benefit payments. Emergency benefits began in July 2008, authorized under the *Supplemental Appropriations Act, 2008*. This emergency program was temporarily extended and additionally funded by the ARRA of 2009 and has been subsequently modified several times, most recently by P.L. 112-240, the *American Taxpayer Relief Act of 2012*, which extended the emergency unemployment insurance program to January 1, 2014. The DOL's appropriations decreased $12.5 billion, or 21.1 percent, in fiscal year 2015 primarily due to decreases in transfers to the UTF for Emergency Unemployment Compensation due to decrease in benefit costs. DOL's borrowing authority also decreased $2.7 billion, or 100 percent. A $15.5 billion dollar decrease in benefit outlays from the prior year also resulted in part due to the discontinuance of the federally funded Emergency Unemployment Compensation program, as well as a decline in the number of new claims, and the absence of states meeting the trigger thresholds required to pay extended benefits.

Chart 14—Estimated Unemployment Trust Fund Cash Flow Using Expected Economic Conditions In Constant (or Inflation-Adjusted) Dollars 2016-2025

(In billions of dollars)

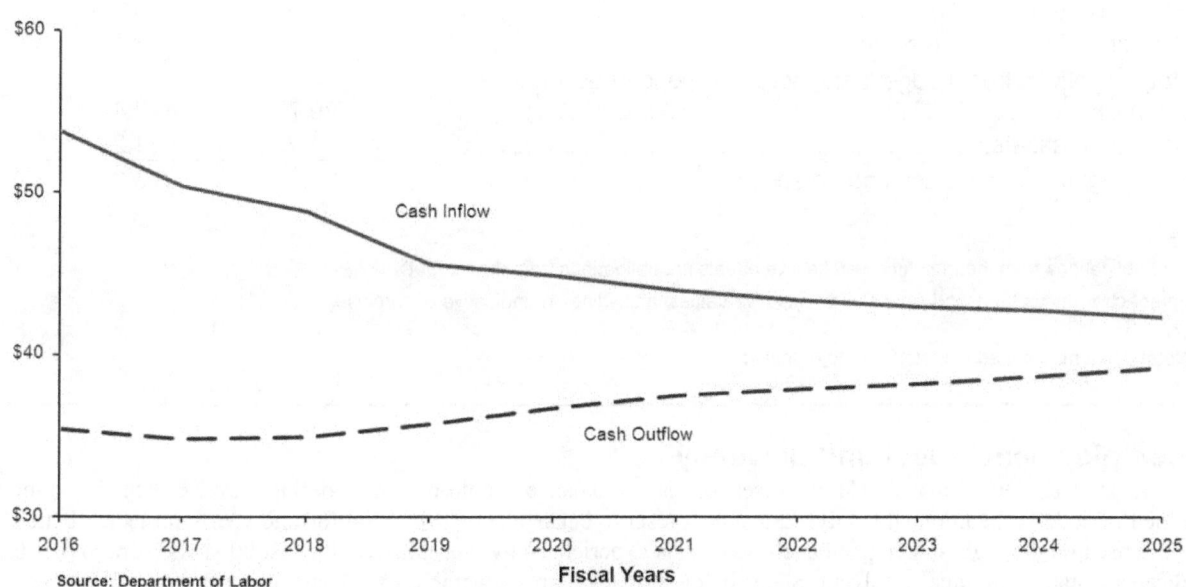

Source: Department of Labor

Fiscal Years

Table 10 shows 10-year projections of revenues and expenditures for the Unemployment Insurance Program in constant dollars. Three sets of numbers are presented in order to show the effects of varying economic conditions as reflected in different assumptions about the unemployment rate. For expected economic conditions, the estimates are based on an unemployment rate of 4.95 percent during fiscal year 2016, and remaining between 4.6 percent and 4.9 percent thereafter. Under Sensitivity Analysis I which utilizes a higher unemployment rate of 6.3 percent beginning in fiscal year 2016, net cash inflows are negative in fiscal years 2017 and 2018, but become positive in fiscal year 2019, and continue to be positive through 2025. Under Sensitivity Analysis II, which utilizes a higher unemployment rate of 6.36 percent in fiscal year 2016, net cash inflows including interest earnings and expenses, are projected in fiscal year 2016, but outflows exceed inflows in fiscal years 2017, 2018, and 2019 by $17.7 billion, $26.5 billion, and $8.4 billion, respectively. Net cash inflows are reestablished in fiscal year 2020 and peak in fiscal year 2025 with a drop in the unemployment rate to 7.32 percent in fiscal year 2020 and then steadily downward for fiscal years 2021 through 2025.

Each analysis uses an open group that includes current and future participants of the Unemployment Insurance Program. Table 10 shows the impact on the UTF projections of varying projected unemployment rates. For example, in Sensitivity Analysis II, while tax income is projected to increase as higher layoffs result in higher employer taxes, benefit outlays increase even more. From the Governmentwide (budget) perspective, under expected conditions, future cash income exceeds future expenditures by $89.7 billion. From the same perspective, under Sensitivity Analysis II, future cash income exceeds future expenditures by $2.5 billion. From a trust fund perspective, which takes into account the $31.2 billion trust fund balance, the program has a surplus of $73.6 billion under the economic conditions for Sensitivity Analysis I.

Table 10
10-Year Projections of Expenditures and Revenues for Unemployment Insurance in Constant (or Inflation-Adjusted) Dollars Under Three Alternative Analyses for Economic Conditions

(in billions as of September 30, 2015)

		Economic Conditions	
	Expected	Sensitivity Analysis I	Sensitivity Analysis II
Projected future expenditures	368.9	499.3	608.0
Projected future cash income	458.5	541.7	610.5
Net obligations from budget perspective (expenditures less income)	(89.7)	(42.4)	(2.5)
Trust fund assets	31.2	31.2	31.2
Net obligations from trust fund perspective [1]	(120.9)	(73.6)	(33.7)

[1]Net obligations from the trust fund perspective equals net obligations from the budget perspective minus trust fund assets. The negative values in this line are indicative of surpluses

Note: Data may not add to totals due to rounding.

Unemployment Trust Fund Solvency

Each state's accumulated UTF net assets or reserve balance should provide a defined level of benefit payments over a defined period. To be minimally solvent, a state's reserve balance should provide for one year's projected benefit payment needs based on the highest levels of benefit payments experienced by the state over the last 20 years. A ratio of 1.0 or greater indicates a state is minimally solvent. States below this level are vulnerable to exhausting their funds in a recession. States exhausting their reserve balance borrow funds from the Federal Unemployment Account (FUA) to make benefit payments. During fiscal year 2009, the balances in the FUA were depleted; the FUA borrowed from the General Fund and continued to do so through fiscal year 2015, although in fiscal year 2015 the FUA repaid all its outstanding borrowings.

Chart 15 presents the state by state results of this analysis as of September 30, 2015. As the chart illustrates, 32 state funds plus the fund of the Virgin Islands were below the minimal solvency ratio of 1.0 at September 30, 2015.

Chart 15—Unemployment Trust Fund Solvency as of September 30, 2015

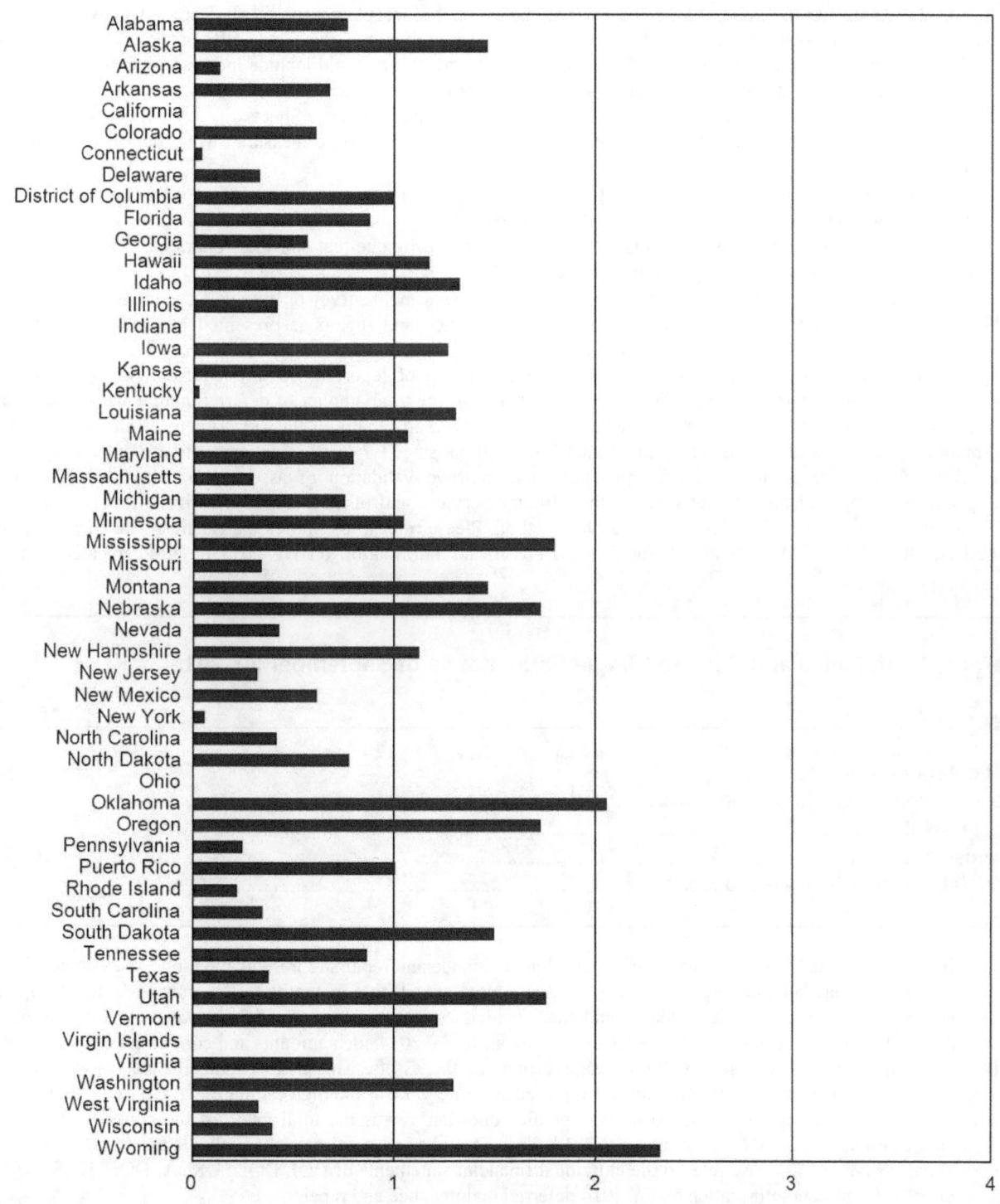

Years of average high benefit payments held in reserve

Deferred Maintenance and Repairs

Deferred maintenance and repairs result from maintenance not being performed on a timely basis and is the estimated cost to bring Government-owned property, plant, and equipment to an acceptable condition. Deferred maintenance and repairs exclude the cost of expanding the capacity of assets or upgrading them to serve needs different from those originally intended. The consequences of not performing regular maintenance and repairs could include increased safety hazards, poor service to the public, higher costs in the future, and inefficient operations. Estimated deferred maintenance and repairs costs are not accrued in the Statements of Net Cost or recognized as a liability on the Balance Sheets.

The amounts disclosed for deferred maintenance and repairs are allowed to be measured using one of the following three methods:

- Condition assessment surveys which are periodic inspections of Government-owned property to determine the current condition and estimated cost to bring the property to an acceptable condition.
- Life-cycle cost forecast that is an acquisition or procurement technique that considers operation, maintenance, and other costs in addition to the acquisition cost of assets.
- Any other method of choice that is similar to the condition assessment survey or life-cycle costing methods.

The table below for FY 2015 reporting of deferred maintenance and repairs is presented as a single estimate in accordance with SFFAS No. 42, *Deferred Maintenance and Repairs: Amending Statements of Federal Financial Accounting Standards 6, 14, 29, and 32.* The single estimate is presented instead of reporting condition information and low-high deferred maintenance and repairs estimates. The significant change in the total amount of deferred maintenance and repairs from FY 2014 is mainly due to the increase in deferred maintenance and repairs at the Department of Defense. DOD's deferred maintenance and repairs increased by more than $24.6 billion, since FY 2014. This is largely attributable to DOD's ongoing efforts to validate existence and completeness and improve validation of assets, and ensure consistency in accounting and reporting maintenance costs across the Military Services and other Defense organizations. These amounts were all measured using the condition assessment survey method. Please refer to the individual financial statements of DOI, DOD, USDA, DOE, HHS, NASA, and VA for detailed significant information on FY 2015 deferred maintenance and repairs.

Deferred Maintenance and Repairs (Single Estimate) as of September 30, 2015

(In billions of dollars)	2015
Asset category:	
General property, plant, and equipment	167.5
Heritage assets	15.6
Stewardship land	0.4
Total deferred maintenance and repairs	183.5

The following table for FY 2014 reporting of deferred maintenance and repairs represents the range of estimates for FY 2014. These amounts were all measured using the condition assessment survey method. The standards for acceptable operating condition, the changes in these standards, and changes in asset condition varied widely between federal entities.

Some deferred maintenance and repairs were deemed critical. In FY 2014 such amounts and conditions were defined by the individual agencies with responsibility for the safekeeping of the assets. The critical maintenance amount was not included in the low or high estimates amounts and was reported separately. Low and high estimates were based on materiality of the estimated cost of returning the asset to the acceptable condition versus the total value of the corresponding asset. Single figure cost estimates were not prepared for FY 2014. Therefore, the information is not available to compare directly to amounts reported for FY 2015. Please refer to the individual financial statements of DOI, DOD, USDA, DOE, HHS, NASA, and VA for detailed significant information on FY 2014 deferred maintenance and repairs.

Deferred Maintenance and Repairs as of September 30, 2014

(In billions of dollars)	Cost Range		Critical Maintenance 2014
	Low Estimate 2014	High Estimate 2014	
Asset category:			
Buildings, structures, and facilities...	27.4	31.2	103.7
Furniture, fixtures, and equipment...	0.2	0.2	1.8
Other general property, plant, and equipment......................................	7.7	7.7	0.9
Heritage assets..	6.2	8.6	5.0
Total deferred maintenance and repairs..	41.5	47.7	111.4

Other Claims for Refunds

Management has estimated amounts that may be paid out as other claims for tax refunds. This estimate represents an amount (principal and interest) that may be paid for claims pending judicial review by the federal courts or, internally, by appeals. The total estimated payout (including principal and interest) for claims pending judicial review by the federal courts is $2.1 billion and $3.1 billion for fiscal years 2015 and 2014, respectively. For those under appeal, the estimated payout is $2.7 billion and $4.7 billion for fiscal years 2015 and 2014, respectively. Although these refund claims have been deemed to be probable, they do not meet the criteria in SFFAS No. 5, *Accounting for Liabilities of the Federal Government*, for reporting the amounts in the balance sheets or for disclosure in the notes to the financial statements. However, they meet the criteria in SFFAS No. 7, *Accounting for Revenue and Other Financing Sources,* for inclusion as required supplementary information. To the extent judgments against the Government for these claims prompt other similarly situated taxpayers to file similar refund claims, these amounts could become significantly greater.

Tax Assessments

The Government is authorized and required to make inquiries, determinations, and assessments of all taxes that have not been duly paid. Unpaid assessments result from taxpayers filing returns without sufficient payment, as well as enforcement programs such as examination, under-reporter, substitute for return, and combined annual wage reporting. Under federal accounting standard, unpaid assessments are categorized as taxes receivable if taxpayers agree or a court has determined the assessments are owed. If neither of these conditions are met, the unpaid assessments are categorized as compliance assessments. Assessments with little or no future collection potential are called write-offs. Although compliance assessments and write-offs are not considered receivables under federal accounting standards, they represent legally enforceable claims of the Government. There is, however, a significant difference in the collection potential between compliance assessments and receivables.

Compliance assessments and pre-assessment work in process are $82.1 billion and $88.8 billion for fiscal years 2015 and 2014, respectively. The amount of allowance for uncollectible amounts pertaining to compliance assessments cannot be reasonably estimated, and thus the net realizable value of the value of the pre-assessment work-in-process cannot be determined. The amount of assessments that agencies have statutory authority to collect at the end of the period but that have been written off and excluded from accounts receivable are $138.0 billion for both fiscal years 2015 and 2014.

Risk Assumed

Risk assumed information is important for all federal insurance and guarantee programs (i.e., USDA-Federal Crop Insurance Corporation programs, DHS-National Flood Insurance Program, NCUA-Credit Unions), except social insurance, life insurance, and loan guarantee programs. Risk assumed is generally measured by the present value of unpaid losses net of associated premiums, based on the risk inherent in the insurance or guarantee coverage in force. In addition to the liability for unpaid insurance claims included in Note 15—Insurance and Guarantee Program Liabilities, for events that have already occurred, the Government also is required to report as supplementary information risk assumed amounts and the periodic changes in those amounts.

The assessments of losses using the risk assumed are made by actuarial or financial methods that include information and assumptions applicable to the economic, legal, and policy environment in force at the time the assessments are made. Management has estimated the loss amounts based on the risk assumed as well as the periodic changes.

Please refer to the individual financial statements of the USDA, DHS, and NCUA for further detailed information, including information as to the indicators of the range of uncertainty around expected estimates and the indicators of the sensitivity of the estimates to changes in major assumptions. The table does not include all federal insurance and guarantee programs.

Risk Assumed Information as of September 30, 2015, and 2014

(In billions of dollars)	2015	2014
Present value of unpaid losses, net of associated premiums:		
Department of Agriculture - Federal Crop Insurance Corporation programs	7.6	7.6
Department of Homeland Security - National Flood Insurance program	-	0.4
National Credit Union Administration - Credit Unions	0.2	0.2
Total	7.8	8.2
Period changes in risk assumed amounts:		
Department of Agriculture	-	2.7
Department of Homeland Security	(0.4)	(0.2)
Total	(0.4)	2.5

Federal Oil and Gas Resources

DOI plays an integral part in the implementation of the President's *Blueprint for a Clean and Secure Energy Future*, designed to build a safe, secure energy future by using cleaner, alternative fuels to power our homes and economy, producing more oil and gas domestically, and improving energy efficiency. The DOI is responsible for managing the nation's oil and natural gas resources and the mineral revenues on federal lands, both onshore and on the Outer Continental Shelf. This management process can be broken down into six essential analysis components: pre-leasing, post-leasing and pre-production, production and post-production, revenue collection, fund disbursement, and compliance.

Federal Oil and Gas Resources as of September 30, 2015, and 2014

(In billions of dollars)	Offshore		Onshore		Total	
	2015	2014	2015	2014	2015	2014
Oil and lease condensate.....................	31.6	39.6	14.8	15.5	46.4	55.1
Natural gas, wet after lease separation.................................	2.8	4.5	14.1	19.2	16.9	23.7
Total	34.4	44.1	28.9	34.7	63.3	78.8

The above table presents the estimated present value of future federal royalty receipts on estimated proved reserves[13] as of September 30, 2015 and 2014. The federal government's estimated petroleum royalties have as their basis the DOE's Energy Information Administration (EIA) estimates of proved reserves. The EIA provides such estimates directly for federal offshore areas and they are adjusted to extract the federal subset of onshore proved reserves. The federal proved reserves were then further adjusted to correspond with the effective date of the actual production for calendar year 2013, the most recently published EIA proved reserves report and then are projected, separately for oil and natural gas, over time to simulate a schedule of when the reserves would be produced. Future royalties are then calculated from these production streams by applying future price estimates by the OMB, and effective royalty rates, adjusted for transportation allowances and other allowable deductions. The valuation method used for gas captures royalties from three products–dry gas, wet gas, and natural gas liquids–which collectively are reported as natural gas, wet after lease separation. The present value of these royalties are then determined by discounting the revenue stream back to the effective date at a public discount rate assumed to be equal to the OMB's estimates of future 30-year Treasury bill rates. The 30-year rate was chosen because this maturity life most closely approximates the productive lives of the proved reserves estimates.

---

[13] Per the EIA, lease condensate is a mixture consisting primarily of pentanes and heavier hydrocarbons which is recovered as a liquid from natural gas in lease separation facilities. This category excludes natural gas plant liquids, such as butane and propane, which are recovered at downstream natural gas processing plants or facilities. Also per the EIA, natural gas, wet after lease separation, is the volume of natural gas remaining after removal of lease condensate in lease and/or field separation facilities, if any, and after exclusion of nonhydrocarbon gases where they occur in sufficient quantity to render the gas unmarketable. Natural gas liquids may be recovered from volume of natural gas, wet after lease separation, and at natural gas processing plants (http://www.eia.gov/naturalgas/data.cfm).

Estimated Federal Oil and Gas Petroleum Royalties (Proved Reserves)
As of September 30, 2015, and 2014

Petroleum Category	Quantity (in millions)		Average Purchase Price ($)		Average Royalty Rate (%)	
	2015	2014	2015	2014	2015	2014
Oil and lease condensate (Bbl):						
Offshore	4,623.6	4,917.4	56.45	99.17	13.42	13.60
Onshore	2,377.1	2,147.1	49.95	90.03	12.26	12.15
Total	7,000.7	7,064.5				
Natural gas, wet after lease separation (Mcf):						
Offshore	6,858.8	8,587.3	3.25	4.93	12.84	13.52
Onshore	46,310.8	48,098.6	3.14	4.80	10.11	10.63
Total	53,169.6	56,685.9				

Bbl = barrels
Mcf = 1,000 cubic feet

The table above provides the estimated quantity, a weighted average purchase price, and a weighted average royalty rate by category of estimated federal petroleum royalties at the end of fiscal year 2015 and 2014.[14] The estimated quantities, average purchase prices and royalty rates vary by region; the above table reflects an overall weighted average purchase price and royalty rate, and is not presented on a regional basis, but is instead calculated based on regional averages. The prices and royalty rates are based upon historical (or estimated) averages, excluding prior-period adjustments, if any, and are affected by such factors as accounting adjustments and transportation allowances, resulting in effective average prices and royalty rates. Prices are valued at the lease rather than at the market center, and differ from those used to compute the asset estimated present values, which are forecasted and discounted based upon OMB economic assumptions. For further details on federal oil and gas resources, refer to the financial statements of DOI. In addition to the oil and gas resources discussed above, the federal government also owns oil and gas resources that are not currently under lease.

---

[14] Gulf of Mexico proved reserves are royalty bearing volumes. In the Gulf of Mexico, an additional 879.0 million Bbl for fiscal year 2015 and 564.1 million Bbl for fiscal year 2014 of proved oil reserves, and 1,097.0 million Mcf for fiscal year 2015 and 728.0 million Mcf for fiscal year 2014 of proved gas reserves are not reflected in these totals as they are estimated to be producible royalty free under various royalty relief provisions. The net present value of the royalty value of the royalty free proved reserves volumes in the Gulf of Mexico is estimated to be $6.5 billion for fiscal year 2015 and $5.3 billion for fiscal year 2014.

Federal Natural Resources Other than Oil and Gas

Federal Natural Resources Other than Oil and Gas as of September 30, 2015, and 2014

(in billions of dollars)

Natural Resource Category	2015	2014
Coal royalties	10.5	12.0
Total	10.5	12.0

DOI plays an integral part in the implementation of the President's *Blueprint for a Clean and Secure Energy Future* which is designed to build a safe, secure energy future by using cleaner, alternative fuels to power our homes and economy, producing more oil and gas domestically and improving energy efficiency. DOI is responsible for managing the Nation's coal resources and revenues on federal lands.

The Office of Natural Resources Revenue (ONRR) within DOI is responsible for the management and collection of revenues associated with federal coal leases which are managed by the Bureau of Land Management (BLM) within DOI. The ONRR achieves optimal value by ensuring that all natural resource revenues are efficiently and accurately collected as well as disbursed to recipients in a timely manner by performing audit and revenue compliance activities.

The Mineral Leasing Act of 1920, as amended, and the *Mineral Leasing Act for Acquired Lands of 1947*, as amended, gives DOI the responsibility for coal leasing on approximately 700 million acres of federal mineral estate which includes 570 million of acres where coal development is allowed. The surface estate of these lands may be under the control of BLM, the U.S. Forest Service (within USDA), private or state land owners, or other federal agencies.

Public lands are available for coal leasing after the lands have been evaluated through a multiple-use planning process. *The Mineral Leasing Act,* as amended by the *Federal Coal Leasing Amendments Act of 1976*, generally requires that coal be leased competitively and that the federal government must receive a fair market value for land leased for coal development. Once a lease is issued, federal coal leasing laws and lease terms determine the federal government's share of production from coal leasing operations.

DOI receives coal leasing revenues from a bonus paid at the time of the lease, an annual rent payment of $3.00 per acre, and royalties paid on the value of the coal after it has been mined. A portion of the total federal coal royalties will be distributed to other non-federal entities. The royalty rate for surface-mining methods is 12.5 percent and is 8 percent for underground mining, and the BLM can approve reduced royalty rates based on maximum economic recovery. Regulations that govern BLM's coal leasing program are contained in Title 43, Groups 3000 and 3400 of the Code of Federal Regulations.

The above table presents the estimated present value of federal coal royalties under lease contract or other long-term arrangements as of September 30, 2015 and 2014. The federal government's estimated coal royalties have as their basis the DOI's BLM estimates of recoverable reserves. The federal recoverable reserves are then further adjusted to correspond with the effective date of the analysis and then are projected over time to simulate a schedule of when the reserves would be produced. Futures royalties are then calculated by applying future price estimates and effective royalty rates, adjusted for transportation allowances and other allowable deductions. The present value of these royalties are then determined by discounting the revenue stream back to the effective date at a public discount rate assumed to be equal to the OMB's estimates of future 30-year Treasury bill rates. The 30-year rate was chosen because this maturity life most closely approximates the productive lives of the recoverable reserves estimates.

In addition to the coal resources discussed above, the federal government has other natural resources under lease contract whereby the lessee is required to pay royalties on the sale of the natural resource. These natural resources include soda ash, potash muriates of potash and langbeinite phosphate, lead concentrate, copper concentrate, and zinc concentrate. Soda ash and potash have the largest estimated present value of future royalties. The federal government also owns coal resources and certain other natural resources that are not currently under lease. For further details on federal natural resources-other than oil and gas, refer to the financial statements of DOI.

This page is intentionally blank.

United States Government
Other Information (Unaudited) for the
Years Ended September 30, 2015, and 2014

Unexpended Balances of Budget Authority

The President's budget and the federal budget process largely use a distinct administrative process of accounting, through which federal agencies control, monitor, and report on the status of funds at their disposal. Government agencies can be granted authority to enter into obligations that result in immediate or future outlays by law; this authority is known as budget authority. Unexpended balances of budget authority consist of the unobligated and obligated, but unliquidated balances.

Unobligated balances, including amounts for trust funds, are the cumulative amount of budgeted balances that are not contractually committed or bound legally by the government and that remain available for obligation. At the end of each fiscal year, unobligated balances that are still available for new obligations are carried forward to the start of the next fiscal year. Unobligated balances that are expiring (i.e., are not available for new obligation) are canceled and not carried forward to the start of the next fiscal year. The total unobligated balances as of September 30, 2015, and 2014, are $896.0 billion and $871.6 billion, respectively.

Obligated balances refer to the balances where there have been legally binding action but for which payment has not yet been made; however, payment will be required in the future. By law, obligated balances are either no-year, or available to pay unpaid expenses (normally for five expired years, after which the obligated balances are canceled). In no-year accounts, the unobligated balance is carried forward until specifically rescinded by law, or the head of the agency concerned determines that the purposes for which it was provided have been accomplished and disbursements have not been made against the appropriation for two consecutive years. Therefore, the obligated balances that are still available are carried forward to the start of the next fiscal year. The total obligated balances as of September 30, 2015, and 2014, are $1,413.5 billion and $1,399.5 billion, respectively.

The President's Fiscal Year 2017 Budget (issued on February 9, 2016) is located at www.whitehouse.gov/omb and includes the actual unexpended balances of budget authority for fiscal year 2015 in the supplemental materials section under "Balances of Budget Authority."

Tax Burden

The Internal Revenue Code provides for progressive tax rates, whereby higher earned income is generally subject to higher tax rates. The following tables present the latest available information on income tax and related income, deductions, and credit: for individuals by income level, and for corporations by size of assets.

Individual Income Tax Liability for Tax Year 2013

Adjusted Gross Income (AGI)	Number of Taxable Returns (In thousands)	AGI (in millions of dollars)	Total Income Tax (in millions of dollars)	Average AGI Per Return (in whole dollars)	Average Income Tax per Return (in whole dollars)	Income Tax as a Percentage of AGI
Under $15,000	37,255	76,709	2,093	2,059	56	2.7%
$15,000 under $30,000	30,556	671,851	18,614	21,988	609	2.8%
$30,000 under $50,000	25,753	1,008,621	55,379	39,165	2,150	5.5%
$50,000 under $100,000	31,803	2,272,956	198,233	71,470	6,233	8.7%
$100,000 under $200,000	16,426	2,209,424	278,504	134,508	16,955	12.6%
$200,000 under $500,000	4,488	1,277,489	250,646	284,645	55,848	19.6%
$500,000 or more	1,070	1,576,579	431,571	1,473,438	403,337	27.4%
Total	147,351	9,093,629	1,235,040			

Corporation Income Tax Liability for Tax Year 2012

Total Assets (In thousands of dollars)	Income Subject to Tax (in millions of dollars)	Total Income Tax After Credits (in millions of dollars)	Percentage of Income Tax After Credits to Taxable Income
Zero Assets	16,712	4,788	28.7%
$1 under $500	7,196	1,433	19.9%
$500 under $1,000	3,521	785	22.3%
$1,000 under $5,000	11,870	3,433	28.9%
$5,000 under $10,000	7,557	2,438	32.3%
$10,000 under $25,000	12,705	4,107	32.3%
$25,000 under $50,000	11,352	3,690	32.5%
$50,000 under $100,000	14,208	4,595	32.3%
$100,000 under $250,000	25,864	8,190	31.7%
$250,000 under $500,000	29,767	9,297	31.2%
$500,000 under $2,500,000	122,526	36,757	30.0%
$2,500,000 or more	886,522	188,341	21.2%
Total	1,149,800	267,854	

Tax Gap

The tax gap is the difference between what taxpayers should pay and what they actually pay on time. The tax gap, about $450.0 billion based on updated fiscal year 2006 estimates, represents the amount of noncompliance with the tax laws. The IRS remains committed to finding ways to increase compliance and reduce the tax gap, while minimizing the burden on the vast majority of taxpayers who pay their taxes accurately and on time.

The tax gap is the aggregate amount of tax (excluding interest and penalties) that is imposed by the tax laws for any given tax year but is not paid voluntarily and timely. The tax gap arises from three types of noncompliance: not filing required tax returns on time or at all (the nonfiling gap), underreporting the correct amount of tax on timely filed returns (the underreporting gap), and not paying on time the full amount reported on timely filed returns (the underpayment gap). Underreporting of income tax, employment taxes, and other taxes represents 84 percent of the gross tax gap. Each instance of noncompliance by a taxpayer contributes to the tax gap, whether or not the IRS detects it, and whether or not the taxpayer is even aware of the noncompliance. Some of the tax gap arises from intentional (willful) noncompliance, and some of it arises from unintentional mistakes.

The collection gap is the cumulative amount of assessed tax, penalties, and interest that has been assessed over many years, but has not been paid by a certain point in time and which the IRS expects to remain uncollectible. In essence, it represents the difference between the total balance of unpaid assessments and the net taxes receivable reported on the IRS' balance sheet. The tax gap and the collection gap are related and overlapping concepts, but they have significant differences. The collection gap is a cumulative balance sheet concept for a particular point in time, while the tax gap is like an income statement item for a single year. Moreover, the tax gap estimates include all noncompliance, while the collection gap includes only amounts that have been assessed (a small portion of all noncompliance).

Unmatched Transactions and Balances

(in millions of dollars)	Fiscal Year 2015	Fiscal Year 2014
Change in intragovernmental unmatched balances:		
Debt/investment	(32.0)	25.2
Interest payable/receivable	1.8	0.7
Accounts payable/receivable capital transfers**	2.8	4,812.0
Loans payable/receivable	(1.6)	(8.7)
Benefit program contributions payable/receivable	33.7	106.3
Accounts payable/receivable	314.4	(318.6)
Advances from/to others & deferred credits/prepayments	(295.6)	209.4
Transfers payable/receivable	24.0	10.2
Other assets/liabilities**	(4,360.1)	2,405.6
Fund balance with Treasury	(11,961.6)	(5,980.5)
Asset for custodial and non-entity asset/liability**	(12,065.1)	279.0
	(28,339.3)	1,540.6
Unmatched intragovernmental transactions:		
Federal securities interest revenue/expense-investment exchange	4.0	73.5
Borrowings interest revenue/expense-exchange	(36.4)	(31.4)
Borrowings gains/losses	903.7	583.0
Nonexpenditure transfers-in/out	(99.8)	(1,473.1)
Expenditure transfers-In/oul	643.2	(131.4)
Nonexpenditure transfers-in/out capital transfers**	5.9	292.8
Transfers-in/out without reimbursement	157.0	127.2
Imputed financing source/cost	(55.7)	(18.7)
Benefit program revenue/cost	(938.6)	(1,277.7)
Nonreciprocating**	58,767.6	737,548.5
Appropriations used*	(28,928.3)	-
Appropriations received/warrants issued	5,835.6	55,219.0
Appropriations of unavailable special or trust fund receipts transferred out/in	(0.2)	0.9
Custodial and non-entity collections transferred out/in	(2,886.5)	(7,431.5)
Other taxes and receipts/trust fund warrants	(2,984.6)	(19,053.9)
Accrual amounts collected/transferred in**	(6,382.3)	126.5
Other**	(772.5)	(748,682.6)
	23,232.1	18,817.3
Unmatched transactions and balances, net	(5,107.2)	20,357.9

( ) Parentheses indicate a decrease to Net Position.

* The fiscal year 2014 amount for appropriations used is included under "Appropriations received/warrants issued."

** The fiscal year 2014 amounts were previously reported under "Other General Fund transactions."

The Statement of Operations and Changes in Net Position includes an amount for unmatched transactions and balances that result from the consolidation of federal reporting entities. Transactions between federal entities must be eliminated in consolidation to calculate the financial position of the government. Many of the amounts included in the table represent intragovernmental activity and balances that differed between federal agency trading partners and often totaled significantly more in the absolute than the net amounts shown. The table also reflects other consolidating adjustments and other adjustments that contributed to the unmatched transactions and balances amount. Prior to fiscal year 2015, unmatched transactions and balances related to the General Fund were reported in a separate section of the table. In fiscal year 2015, the presentation of the "Unmatched Transactions and Balances" table was modified to reflect two sections instead of three, incorporating the General Fund with the other intragovernmental activity and balances.

Unmatched transactions and balances between federal entities impact not only in the period in which differences originate but also in the periods where differences are reconciled. As a result, it would not be proper to conclude that increases or decreases in the unmatched amounts shown in the "Unmatched Transactions and Balances" table reflect improvements or deteriorations in the Government's ability to reconcile intragovernmental transactions. The federal community considers the identification and accurate reporting of intragovernmental activity a priority.

This page is intentionally blank.

United States Government Required Supplementary Stewardship Information (Unaudited) for the Years Ended September 30, 2015, and 2014

Stewardship Investments

Stewardship investments focus on government programs aimed at providing long-term benefits by improving the Nation's productivity and enhancing economic growth. These investments can be provided through direct federal spending or grants to state and local governments for certain education and training programs, research and development, and federally financed but not federally owned property, such as bridges and roads. When incurred, these investments are included as expenses in determining the net cost of operations. Stewardship investments for the current year and for the immediately preceding four years are shown in the table below.

**Stewardship Investments for the Years Ended
September 30, 2011, through 2015**

(In billions of dollars)	Fiscal Year 2015	Fiscal Year 2014	Fiscal Year 2013	Fiscal Year 2012	Fiscal Year 2011
Investments in non-federal physical property ..	64.8	65.6	66.1	68.1	69.9
Investments in human capital............................	97.8	108.5	58.7	87.1	91.9
Research and development:					
Investments in basic research........................	29.4	34.0	35.2	34.2	35.7
Investments in applied research	28.8	28.1	28.0	29.1	28.8
Investments in development............................	63.3	61.8	64.1	67.0	71.7
Total investments	284.1	298.0	252.1	285.5	298.0

Non-Federal Physical Property

The Government makes grants and provides funds for the purchase, construction, and/or major renovation of state and local government physical properties. Costs for non-federal physical property programs are included as expenses in the Statements of Net Cost and are reported as investments in the table. They are measured on the same accrual basis of accounting used in the *Financial Report* statements. DOT, EPA, and HUD had $55.2 billion (85 percent), $3.7 billion (6 percent), and $3.5 billion (5 percent), respectively, of the total non-federal physical property investments in fiscal year 2015 as shown in the table. Within DOT, the Federal Highway Administration invested $40.8 billion during fiscal year 2015, primarily via reimbursement from the Highway Trust Fund, for States' construction costs on projects related to the federal highway system. The main programs in which the States participate are the National Highway System, Interstate Systems, Surface Transportation, and Congestion Mitigation/Air Quality Improvement programs. The States' contribution is 10 percent for the Interstate System and 20 percent for most other programs.

Human Capital

The Government runs several programs that invest in human capital. Those investments go toward increasing and maintaining a healthy economy by educating and training the general public. Costs do not include training expenses for federal workers.

Education, VA, and DOL had $71.8 billion (73 percent), $14.0 billion (14 percent), and $6.2 billion (6 percent), respectively, of the total human capital investments in fiscal year 2015 as shown in the table. In comparison over the past five years, Education had an increase in human capital investments in fiscal year 2014 primarily due to the acquisition of the Health Education Assistance Loan Program (HEAL). Prior to that, Education had a decrease in human capital investments in fiscal years 2011 through 2013 due to a decrease in net cost for Perkins loans, grant programs, and other programs, including the *American Recovery and Reinvestment Act of 2009* and education jobs fund; while VA increased in fiscal years 2011 through 2014 due to implementation of the Post 9/11 GI Bill. Education administers a wide variety of programs related to general public education and training programs that are intended to increase or maintain national economic productive capacity. The Office of Federal Student Aid administers need-based financial assistance programs for students pursuing postsecondary education and makes available federal grants, direct loans, and work-study funding to eligible undergraduate and graduate students.

The significant human capital programs administered by DOL relate to grants for job training and employment programs. The significant human capital programs administered by VA include veterans rehabilitation and employment programs which are provided to service disabled veterans; they are designated to improve employability and promote independence for the disabled. They also include education and training programs intended to provide higher education to dependents that might not be able to participate otherwise.

Research and Development

Federal investments in research and development (R&D) comprise those expenses for basic research, applied research, and development that are intended to increase or maintain national economic productive capacity or yield other future benefits.

- Investments in basic research are for systematic studies to gain knowledge or understanding of the fundamental aspects of phenomena and of observable facts without specific applications toward processes or products in mind.
- Investments in applied research are for systematic studies to gain knowledge or understanding necessary for determining the means by which a recognized and specific need may be met.
- Investments in development are the systematic use of the knowledge and understanding gained from research for the production of useful materials, devices, systems, or methods, including the design and development of prototypes and processes.

With regard to basic and applied research, HHS had $17.1 billion (58 percent) and $11.8 billion (41 percent), of the total basic and applied research investments, respectively, in fiscal year 2015 as shown in the table. HHS also had similar R&D investment amounts (and percentage contributions) in each of the preceding four years.

Within HHS, the National Institutes of Health (NIH) conducts almost all (97 percent) of the Department's basic and applied research. The NIH research program includes all aspects of the medical research continuum, including basic and disease-oriented research, observational and population-based research, behavioral research, and clinical research, including research to understand both health and disease states, to move laboratory findings into medical applications, to assess new treatments or compare different treatment approaches; and health services research.

The NIH regards the expeditious transfer of the results of its medical research for further development and commercialization of products of immediate benefit to improved health as an important mandate.

With regard to development, the DOD and NASA had $53.3 billion (84 percent) and $6.2 billion (10 percent), respectively, of total development investments in fiscal year 2015, as shown in the table. Major outputs of DOD development are scientific studies, investigations, research papers, hardware components, software codes, or limited construction of a weapon system component, to include non-system-specific development efforts. Development takes what has been discovered or learned from basic research and uses it to establish technological feasibility, assessment of operability, and production capability. Development is comprised of five stages: 1) advanced technology development, 2) advanced component development and prototypes, 3) system development and demonstration, 4) research, development, test and evaluation management support, and 5) operational systems development.

NASA development includes activities to extend the knowledge of Earth, its space environment, and the universe, and to invest in new aeronautics and advanced space transportation technologies that support the development and application of technologies critical to the economic, scientific, and technical competitiveness of the United States.

This page is intentionally blank.

Appendix A: Reporting Entity

This appendix lists the organizations and agencies (entities) included in the U.S. Government's consolidated reporting entity for the *Financial Report,* as well as some entities not included in the reporting entity. Federal Accounting Standards Advisory Board's (FASAB) Statement of Federal Financial Accounting Concept (SFFAC) No. 2, *Entity and Display*, provides criteria for determining which entities are included in the reporting entity.

Under the first, conclusive criterion, any entity appearing in the "Federal Programs by Agency and Account" section of the federal budget is included in the consolidated reporting entity. Also, based on a consideration of the indicative criteria in the aggregate, certain entities not meeting the conclusive criteria are also included in the consolidated reporting entity, as the general purpose financial statements might be misleading or incomplete if the organization were not included therein. Indicative criteria are that an entity (1) exercises government sovereign power to carry out federal functions, (2) is owned by the federal government, particularly if the ownership is of the organization and not just the property, (3) is subject to the direct or continuing administrative control of the reporting entity, (4) carries out federal missions and objectives, (5) determines the outcome or disposition of matters affecting recipients of services that the federal government provides, and (6) has a fiduciary relationship with a reporting entity.

1. Entities included in the Reporting Entity for the Financial Report:

There are a total of 154 entities that met either the conclusive or indicative criteria, and as such are included in the *Financial Report*. The lists below describe three groups of entity types that comprise the reporting entity for the *Financial Report* and include entities from all three branches of government.

Twenty-Four Chief Financial Officer Act Agencies

Department of Agriculture
www.usda.gov
Department of Commerce
www.doc.gov
Department of Defense
www.defense.gov
Department of Education
www.ed.gov
Department of Energy
www.energy.gov
Department of Health and Human Services
www hhs.gov
Department of Homeland Security
www.dhs.gov
Department of Housing and Urban Development
www hud.gov
Department of the Interior
www.doi.gov
Department of Justice
www.usdoj.gov
Department of Labor
www.dol.gov
Department of State
www.state.gov

Department of Transportation
www.dot.gov
Department of the Treasury
www.treasury.gov
Department of Veterans Affairs
www.va.gov
Environmental Protection Agency
www.epa.gov
General Services Administration
www.gsa.gov
National Aeronautics and Space Administration
www nasa.gov
National Science Foundation
www.nsf.gov
Office of Personnel Management
www.opm.gov
Small Business Administration
www.sba.gov
Social Security Administration
www.ssa.gov
U.S. Agency for International Development
www.usaid.gov
U.S. Nuclear Regulatory Commission
www.nrc.gov

Fifteen Additional Significant Entities

Defense Security Cooperation Agency**
    www.dsca.mil
Export-Import Bank of the United States
    www.exim.gov
Farm Credit System Insurance Corporation
    www.fcsic.gov
Federal Communications Commission
    www.fcc.gov
Federal Deposit Insurance Corporation
    www.fdic.gov
General Fund of the U.S. Government
    www.treasury.gov
Millennium Challenge Corporation
    www.mcc.gov
National Credit Union Administration
    www.ncua.gov

Overseas Private Investment Corporation
    www.opic.gov
Pension Benefit Guaranty Corporation
    www.pbgc.gov
Railroad Retirement Board
    www rrb.gov
Securities and Exchange Commission
    www.sec.gov
Smithsonian Institution
    www.si.edu
Tennessee Valley Authority
    www.tva.gov
U.S. Postal Service
    www.usps.gov

One Hundred Fifteen Additional Entities/Funds

Abraham Lincoln Bicentennial Commission*
Administrative Conference of the United States
Advisory Council on Historic Preservation
African Development Foundation
American Battle Monuments Commission
Appalachian Regional Commission
Architect of the Capitol
Architectural and Transportation Barriers Compliance
  Board
Armed Forces Retirement Home
Barry Goldwater Scholarship and Excellence in
  Education Foundation
Broadcasting Board of Governors
Bureau of Consumer Financial Protection
Central Intelligence Agency
Chemical Safety Hazard Investigation Board
Christopher Columbus Fellowship Foundation
Commission for the Preservation of America's
  Heritage Abroad
Commission of Fine Arts
Commission of Civil Rights
Commission on International Religious Freedom
Commission on Security and Cooperation in Europe
Commission to Eliminate Child Abuse and Neglect
  Fatalities
Committee for Purchase from People Who Are Blind
  or Severely Disabled
Commodity Futures Trading Commission
Congressional Budget Office

Congressional-Executive Commission on the People's
  Republic of China
Consumer Product Safety Commission
Corporation for National and Community Service
Council of the Inspector General on Integrity and
  Efficiency
Court of Appeals for Veterans Claims
Court Services and Offender Supervision Agency for DC
DC Courts
DC Courts–Defender Services
Defense Nuclear Facilities Safety Board
Delta Regional Authority
Denali Commission
Dwight D. Eisenhower Memorial Commission
Election Assistance Commission
Environmental Dispute Resolution Fund
Equal Employment Opportunity Commission
Executive Office of the President
Farm Credit Administration
Federal Election Commission
Federal Financial Institutions Examination Council
  Appraisal Subcommittee
Federal Housing Finance Agency
Federal Labor Relations Authority
Federal Maritime Commission
Federal Mediation and Conciliation Service
Federal Mine Safety and Health Review Commission
Federal Retirement Thrift Investment Board
Federal Trade Commission

Financial Crisis Inquiry Commission*
Government Accountability Office
Government Printing Office
Gulf Coast Ecosystem Restoration Council
Harry S. Truman Scholarship Trust Fund
Indian Law and Order Commission
Institute of Museum and Library Services
Intelligence Community Management Account
Interagency Council on the Homeless
Inter-American Foundation
International Trade Commission
James Madison Memorial Fellowship Foundation
Japan-United States Friendship Commission
John C. Stennis Center
John F. Kennedy Center for the Performing Arts
Library of Congress
Marine Mammal Commission
Medicaid and Children's Health Insurance Program
  Payment and Access Commission
Medicare Payment Advisory Commission
Merit Systems Protection Board
Military Compensation and Retirement Modernization
  Commission
Morris K. Udall Scholarship Foundation
National Archives and Records Administration
National Capital Planning Commission
National Council on Disability
National Endowment for the Arts
National Endowment for the Humanities
National Gallery of Art
National Labor Relations Board
National Mediation Board
National Railroad Passenger Corporation, Office of the
  Inspector General

National Railroad Retirement Investment Trust
National Transportation Safety Board
Neighborhood Reinvestment Corporation
Northern Border Regional Commission
Nuclear Waste Technical Review Board
Occupational Safety and Health Review Commission
Office of Compliance
Office of Government Ethics
Office of Navajo and Hopi Indian Relocation
Office of Nuclear Waste Negotiator*
Office of Special Counsel
Office of the Federal Coordination for Alaska Natural
  Gas Transportation Projects
Open World Leadership Center
Patient Centered Outcomes Research Trust Fund
Peace Corps
Presidio Trust
Privacy and Civil Liberties Oversight Board
Public Defender Service
Recovery Act Accountability and Transparency Board
Ronald Reagan Centennial Commission*
Selective Service System
Senate Preservation Fund
St. Lawrence Seaway Development Corporation
State Justice Institute
U.S. Capitol Police
U.S. Capitol Preservation Commission
U.S. China Security Review Commission
U.S. Holocaust Memorial Museum
U.S. Institute of Peace
U.S. Tax Court
U.S. Trade and Development Agency
Vietnam Education Foundation
Woodrow Wilson International Center for Scholars
WWI Centennial Commission

*These entities are no longer active and have either returned all remaining fund balances to Treasury during fiscal year 2015 or have remaining fund balances pending final return to Treasury as of September 30, 2015.
**Foreign Military Financing Program and Foreign Military Sales Program were consolidated to create Defense Security Cooperation Agency.

Legislative and Judicial Branches

There are no legal or other requirements for the legislative or judicial branches to prepare consolidated audited financial statements or to provide accrual-based accounting data for inclusion in the governmentwide financial statements. However, a portion of legislative and judicial branch entities voluntarily prepare accrual-based financial statements (e.g., Government Accountability Office, Government Printing Office, and Library of Congress) and are included in the 154 entities listed above. The other entities of the legislative and judicial branch voluntarily provide accrual-based accounting data for inclusion in the governmentwide financial statements, except for the U.S. Senate and the U.S. House of Representatives which are included on a cash basis.

2. Entities not Included in the Reporting Entity of the Financial Report

The entities discussed below either do not meet the conclusive criteria or indicative criteria or were specifically excluded from the consolidated reporting entity in accordance with SFFAC No. 2. Information about the federal government's relationship with and investments in or liabilities to certain of these entities are disclosed in the notes to the financial statements.

Entities that Did not Meet the Conclusive or Indicative Criteria

The following entities are examples of entities with which the federal government has business relationships but did not meet the above mentioned conclusive or indicative criteria:
> Federal Home Loan Banks
> National Railroad Passenger Corporation (does business as Amtrak)
> Resolution Funding Corporation
> Student Loan Marketing Association
> The Financing Corporation
> Thrift Savings Plan

Entities Specifically Excluded From the Consolidated Reporting Entity

SFFAC 2 specifically excludes the Federal Reserve System—the Board of Governors of the Federal Reserve System and the Federal Reserve Banks. The Federal Reserve System could be considered as functioning consistent with the indicative criteria presented above since it establishes and monitors monetary policy. However, in the United States, the organization and functions pertaining to monetary policy are traditionally separated from and independent of the other central government organizations and functions in order to achieve more effective monetary and fiscal policies and economic results. Therefore, the Federal Reserve System is not considered part of the governmentwide reporting entity.

SFFAC 2 also excludes bailout entities. The Federal government may guarantee or pay debt for a privately owned entity whose failure could have an adverse impact on the nation's economy, commerce, national security, etc. As a condition of the bailout, the Federal government may obtain rights similar to the authorities associated with the indicative criteria presented above. However, the existence of these rights does not make the bailed out entity part of the governmentwide reporting entity.

Examples of bailout entities are:
> Federal Home Loan Mortgage Corporation (Freddie Mac)
> Federal National Mortgage Association (Fannie Mae)

Appendix B: Acronyms

This appendix lists the acronyms used in the Financial Statements and Notes to the Financial Statements section of this *Financial Report.*

ACA	Affordable Care Act
ACH	Automated Clearinghouse
AFR	Agency Financial Reports
AIG	American International Group, Inc.
AMT	Alternative Minimum Tax
ARRA	American Recovery and Reinvestment Act of 2009
ASC	Accounting Standards Codification
ATDA	Accountability of Tax Dollars Act of 2002
ATRA	American Taxpayer Relief Act of 2012
BBEDCA	Balanced Budget and Emergency Deficit Control Act
Bbl	Barrel
BCA	Budget Control Act
BLDTF	Black Lung Disability Trust Fund
BLM	Bureau of Land Management
Board	Federal Reserve Board of Governors
CCC	Commodity Credit Corporation
CDCI	Community Development Capital Initiative
CDFI	Community Development Financial Institutions
CERCLA	Comprehensive Environmental Response, Compensation, and Liability Act
CFO	Chief Financial Officers
CFO Act	Chief Financial Officers Act of 1990
CFPB	Bureau of Consumer Financial Protection
CMS	Centers for Medicare and Medicaid Services
COLA	Cost of Living Adjustments
CPI	Consumer Price Index
CPI-U	Consumer Price Index for All Urban Consumers
CPIM	Consumer Price Index–Medical
CPI-W	Consumer Price Index for Urban Wage Earners and Clerical Workers
CPP	Capital Purchase Program
CSRDF	Civil Service Retirement and Disability Fund
CSRS	Civil Service Retirement System
DACA	Deferred Action for Childhood Arrivals
DFAS	Defense Finance and Accounting Service
DHS	Department of Homeland Security
DI	Disability Insurance
DIF	Deposit Insurance Fund
DIP	Debtor in Possession

DOC	Department of Commerce
DOD	Department of Defense
DOE	Department of Energy
DOI	Department of the Interior
DOJ	Department of Justice
DOL	Department of Labor
DOT	Department of Transportation
DM&R	Deferred Maintenance and Repairs
Education	Department of Education
EESA	Emergency Economic Stabilization Act of 2008
EPA	Environmental Protection Agency
EOP	Executive Office of the President
ESF	Exchange Stabilization Fund
FAA	Federal Aviation Administration
Fannie Mae	Federal National Mortgage Association
FASAB	Federal Accounting Standards Advisory Board
FASB	Financial Accounting Standards Board
FCC	Federal Communications Commission
FCRA	Federal Credit Reform Act of 1991
FCSIC	Farm Credit System Insurance Corporation
FDIC	Federal Deposit Insurance Corporation
FECA	Federal Employees' Compensation Act
FEGLI	Federal Employees' Group Life Insurance
FEHB	Federal Employees Health Benefits Program
FERS	Federal Employees Retirement System
FERSA	Federal Employees' Retirement System Act of 1986
FFAS	Farm and Foreign Agricultural Services
FFEL	Federal Family Education Loan
FFMIA	Federal Financial Management Improvement Act of 1996
FHA	Federal Housing Administration
FHFA	Federal Housing Financing Agency
FHWA	Federal Highway Administration
FICA	Federal Insurance Contribution Act
FMFIA	Federal Managers' Financial Integrity Act
FOMC	Federal Open Market Committee
FR	Financial Report
FR System	Federal Reserve System
FRBNY	Federal Reserve Bank of New York
FRBs	Federal Reserve Banks
Freddie Mac	Federal Home Loan Mortgage Corporation
FRTIB	Federal Retirement Thrift Investment Board
FSA	Farm Service Agency

FUA	Federal Unemployment Account
FUTA	Federal Unemployment Tax Act
GAAP	U.S. Generally Accepted Accounting Principles
GAO	U.S. Government Accountability Office
GDP	Gross Domestic Product
General Fund	General Fund of the U.S. Government
Ginnie Mae	Government National Mortgage Association
GM	General Motors
GMRA	Government Management Reform Act of 1994
G-PP&E	General Property, Plant, and Equipment
GSA	General Services Administration
GSE	Government-Sponsored Enterprises
HBP	Health Benefits Program
HEA	Higher Education Act of 1965
HERA	Housing and Economic Recovery Act of 2008
HFA	Housing Financing Agencies
HHS	Department of Health and Human Services
HI	Hospital Insurance
HMO	Health Maintenance Organization
HUD	Department of Housing and Urban Development
IPERIA	Improper Payments Elimination and Recovery Improvement Act of 2012
IPIA	Improper Payments Information Act of 2002
IRS	Internal Revenue Service
LAC	Latest Acquisition Cost
LOC	Library of Congress
LPR	Legal Permanent Resident
MAC	Moving Average Cost
MBS	Mortgage-Backed Securities
MCC	Millennium Challenge Corporation
Mcf	The volume of 1,000 cubic feet of natural gas
MDBs	Multilateral Development Banks
MERHCF	Medicare Eligible Retiree Health Care Fund
MMA	Medicare Prescription Drug, Improvement, and Modernization Act
MRF	Military Retirement Fund
NAB	New Arrangement to Borrow
NASA	National Aeronautics and Space Administration
NCUA	National Credit Union Administration
NIH	National Institutes of Health
NRC	U.S. Nuclear Regulatory Commission
NRRIT	National Railroad Retirement Investment Trust
NSF	National Science Foundation
NSLI	National Service Life Insurance

NTIA	National Telecommunications and Information Administration
NYSE	New York Stock Exchange
OASDI	Old-Age, Survivors, and Disability Insurance
OASI	Old-Age and Survivors Insurance
OCO	Overseas Contingency Operations
OECD	Organization for Economic Co-operation and Development
OFS	Office of Financial Stability
OMB	Office of Management and Budget
ONRR	Office of Natural Resources Revenue
OPEB	Other Postemployment Benefits
OPIC	Overseas Private Investment Corporation
OPM	Office of Personnel Management
ORB	Other Retirement Benefits
PAR	Performance and Accountability Reports
PBGC	Pension Benefit Guaranty Corporation
PCF	Periodic Commitment Fee
PEFCO	Private Export Funding Corporation
PMAs	Power Marketing Authorities
PP&E	Property, Plant, and Equipment
PPACA	Patient Protection and Affordable Care Act
PPIF	Public Private Investment Funds
PPIP	Public Private Investment Program
PPO	Preferred Provider Organization
PSRHB	Postal Service Retiree Health Benefits
QFI	Qualified Financial Institution
R&D	Research and Development
RCRA	Resource Conservation and Recovery Act
RD	Rural Development
REDUX	Military Retirement Reform Act of 1986
RRB	Railroad Retirement Board
RRSIA	Railroad Retirement and Survivors Improvement Act
RSI	Required Supplementary Information
RSSI	Required Supplementary Stewardship Information
SAFETEA-LU	Safe, Accountable, Flexible, Efficient Transportation Equity Act: A Legacy for Users
SBA	Small Business Administration
SCSIA	Statement of Changes in Social Insurance Amounts
SDRs	Special Drawing Rights
SDRCs	SDR Certificates
SEC	Securities and Exchange Commission
SECA	Self-Employment Contributions Act
SFFAC	Statement of Federal Financial Accounting Concept
SFFAS	Statement of Federal Financial Accounting Standards

SFP	Supplementary Financing Program
SGR	Sustainable Growth Rate
SI	Smithsonian Institution
SLMA	Student Loan Marketing Association
SMI	Supplementary Medical Insurance
SOCNP	Statements of Operations and Changes in Net Position
SOMA	System Open Market Account
SOSI	Statement of Social Insurance
SPSPA	Senior Preferred Stock Purchase Agreements
SSA	Social Security Administration
SSEB	Social Security Equivalent Benefit
TARP	Troubled Asset Relief Program
TFL	TRICARE for Life
TIP	Targeted Investment Program
TIPS	Treasury Inflation-Protected Securities
TPTCCA	Temporary Payroll Tax Cut Continuation Act of 2011
Treasury	Department of the Treasury
TRIA	Terrorism Risk Insurance Act
TSP	Thrift Savings Plan
TVA	Tennessee Valley Authority
TVARS	Tennessee Valley Authority Retirement System
U.S.C.	United States Code
USAID	U.S. Agency for International Development
USDA	United States Department of Agriculture
U.S. GAAP	U.S. Generally Accepted Accounting Principles
USPS	United States Postal Service
UTF	Unemployment Trust Fund
VA	Department of Veterans Affairs
VRI	Veterans Reopened Insurance
VSLI	Veterans Special Life Insurance

This page is intentionally blank.

<u>U.S. GOVERNMENT ACCOUNTABILITY OFFICE</u>

441 G St. N.W.
Washington, DC 20548

Independent Auditor's Report

The President
The President of the Senate
The Speaker of the House of Representatives

In our audits of the U.S. government's consolidated financial statements as of and for the fiscal years ended September 30, 2015, and 2014, we found the following:

- Certain material weaknesses[1] in internal control over financial reporting and other limitations on the scope of our work resulted in conditions that continued to prevent us from expressing an opinion on the accompanying accrual-based consolidated financial statements as of and for the fiscal years ended September 30, 2015, and 2014.[2]

- Significant uncertainties (discussed in Note 23 to the consolidated financial statements), primarily related to the achievement of projected reductions in Medicare cost growth, and a material weakness in internal control over financial reporting, prevented us from expressing an opinion on the sustainability financial statements,[3] which consist of the 2015 Statement of Long-Term Fiscal Projections; the 2015, 2014, 2013, 2012, and 2011 Statements of Social Insurance; and the 2015 and 2014 Statements of Changes in Social Insurance Amounts.[4]

---

[1]A material weakness is a deficiency, or combination of deficiencies, in internal control over financial reporting, such that there is a reasonable possibility that a material misstatement of the entity's financial statements will not be prevented, or detected and corrected, on a timely basis. A deficiency in internal control exists when the design or operation of a control does not allow management or employees, in the normal course of performing their assigned functions, to prevent, or detect and correct, misstatements on a timely basis.

[2]The accrual-based consolidated financial statements as of and for the fiscal years ended September 30, 2015, and 2014, consist of the (1) Statements of Net Cost, (2) Statements of Operations and Changes in Net Position, (3) Reconciliations of Net Operating Cost and Unified Budget Deficit, (4) Statements of Changes in Cash Balance from Unified Budget and Other Activities, and (5) Balance Sheets, including the related notes to these financial statements. Most revenues are recorded on a modified cash basis. We previously reported that certain material weaknesses and, for some years, other limitations on the scope of our work prevented us from expressing an opinion on the accrual-based consolidated financial statements of the U.S. government for fiscal years 1997 through 2014.

[3]As required by the Statement of Federal Financial Accounting Standards (SFFAS) No. 36, "Reporting Comprehensive Long-Term Fiscal Projections for the U.S. Government," as amended, the federal government presents a new basic financial statement, the Statement of Long-Term Fiscal Projections, for fiscal year 2015, along with the related notes, as part of the consolidated financial statements. The Statement of Long-Term Fiscal Projections presents, for all the activities of the federal government, the present value of projected receipts and noninterest spending under current policy without change, the relationship of these amounts to projected gross domestic product (GDP), and changes in the present value of projected receipts and noninterest spending from the prior year. The unaudited statement of long-term fiscal projections for the year ended September 30, 2014, is presented for comparison purposes and was not subject to audit.

[4]Statements of Social Insurance are presented for the current year and each of the 4 preceding years in accordance with U.S. generally accepted accounting principles. Also, the sustainability financial statements do not interrelate with the accrual-based consolidated financial statements. In addition, the valuation date is January 1 for all social insurance programs except the Black Lung program, which has a valuation date of September 30. The valuation date for the Statement of Long-Term Fiscal Projections is September 30, 2015.

- Material weaknesses resulted in ineffective internal control over financial reporting for fiscal year 2015.

- Material weaknesses and other scope limitations discussed in this audit report limited our tests of compliance with selected provisions of applicable laws, regulations, contracts, and grant agreements for fiscal year 2015.

The following sections of this audit report discuss in more detail (1) our report on the accompanying consolidated financial statements, which includes (a) two emphasis of matters—equity investments, related to the federal government's actions to stabilize financial markets and to promote economic recovery, and long-term fiscal challenges, (b) required supplementary information (RSI),[5] required supplementary stewardship information (RSSI),[6] and other information[7] included with the consolidated financial statements in the *Fiscal Year 2015 Financial Report of the United States Government* (*2015 Financial Report*), and (c) information on Chief Financial Officers (CFO) Act agency financial management systems; (2) our report on internal control over financial reporting; (3) our report on compliance with laws, regulations, contracts, and grant agreements; and (4) the Department of the Treasury's (Treasury) and the Office of Management and Budget's (OMB) comments on a draft of this audit report. Appendix I discusses our audit objectives, scope, and methodology.

Report on the Consolidated Financial Statements

The Secretary of the Treasury, in coordination with the Director of OMB, is required to annually submit audited financial statements for the U.S. government to the President and Congress. GAO is required to audit these statements.[8] As noted above, the consolidated financial statements consist of the accrual-based consolidated financial statements as of and for the fiscal years ended September 30, 2015, and 2014, and the sustainability financial statements, consisting of the 2015 Statement of Long-Term Fiscal Projections; the 2015, 2014, 2013, 2012, and 2011 Statements of Social Insurance; the 2015 and 2014 Statements of Changes in Social Insurance Amounts; and the related notes to the financial statements.

We performed sufficient audit work to provide this report on the consolidated financial statements. We considered the limitations on the scope of our work regarding the accrual-based consolidated financial statements and the sustainability financial statements in forming our conclusions. Our work was performed in accordance with U.S. generally accepted government auditing standards.

---

[5]RSI consists of Management's Discussion and Analysis and information in the Required Supplementary Information section of the *Fiscal Year 2015 Financial Report of the United States Government*.
[6]RSSI consists of information on stewardship investments in the Required Supplementary Stewardship Information section of the *Fiscal Year 2015 Financial Report of the United States Government*.
[7]Other information consists of information in the *Fiscal Year 2015 Financial Report of the United States Government* other than the consolidated financial statements, RSI, RSSI, the auditor's report, and the Statement of the Comptroller General of the United States.
[8]The Government Management Reform Act of 1994 has required such reporting, covering the executive branch of government, beginning with financial statements prepared for fiscal year 1997. 31 U.S.C. § 331(e). Treasury and OMB have elected to include certain financial information on the legislative and judicial branches in the consolidated financial statements as well.

Management's Responsibility

Management of the federal government is responsible for (1) the preparation and fair presentation of annual consolidated financial statements of the U.S. government in accordance with U.S. generally accepted accounting principles; (2) preparing, measuring, and presenting the RSI and RSSI in accordance with U.S. generally accepted accounting principles; and (3) preparing and presenting other information included in documents containing the consolidated financial statements and auditor's report, and ensuring the consistency of that information with the consolidated financial statements, RSI, and RSSI. This includes maintaining effective internal control over financial reporting, including the design, implementation, and maintenance of internal control relevant to the preparation and fair presentation of financial statements that are free from material misstatement, whether due to fraud or error.

Auditor's Responsibility

Our responsibility is to express opinions on these consolidated financial statements based on conducting the audit in accordance with U.S. generally accepted government auditing standards. We are also responsible for applying certain limited procedures to the RSI, RSSI, and other information included with the consolidated financial statements. Because of the matters discussed below, we were unable to obtain sufficient appropriate evidence to provide a basis for audit opinions on the consolidated financial statements.

Basis for Disclaimers of Opinion on the Consolidated Financial Statements

Accrual-Based Consolidated Financial Statements

The federal government is not able to demonstrate the reliability of significant portions of the accompanying accrual-based consolidated financial statements as of and for the fiscal years ended September 30, 2015, and 2014, principally resulting from limitations related to certain material weaknesses in internal control over financial reporting and other limitations affecting the reliability of these financial statements and the scope of our work as discussed below. As a result of these limitations, readers are cautioned that amounts reported in the accrual-based consolidated financial statements and related notes may not be reliable.

The federal government did not maintain adequate systems or have sufficient appropriate evidence to support certain material information reported in the accompanying accrual-based consolidated financial statements. The underlying material weaknesses in internal control, which have existed for years, contributed to our disclaimer of opinion on the accrual-based consolidated financial statements. Specifically, these weaknesses concerned the federal government's inability to

- satisfactorily determine that property, plant, and equipment and inventories and related property, primarily held by the Department of Defense (DOD), were properly reported in the accrual-based consolidated financial statements;

- reasonably estimate or adequately support amounts reported for certain liabilities, such as environmental and disposal liabilities, or determine whether commitments and contingencies were complete and properly reported;

- support significant portions of the reported total net cost of operations, most notably related to DOD, and adequately reconcile disbursement activity at certain federal entities;

- adequately account for and reconcile intragovernmental activity and balances between federal entities;

- reasonably assure that the consolidated financial statements are (1) consistent with the underlying audited entities' financial statements, (2) properly balanced, and (3) in accordance with U.S. generally accepted accounting principles; and

- reasonably assure that the information in the (1) Reconciliations of Net Operating Cost and Unified Budget Deficit and (2) Statements of Changes in Cash Balance from Unified Budget and Other Activities is complete and consistent with the underlying information in the audited entities' financial statements and other financial data.

These material weaknesses continued to (1) hamper the federal government's ability to reliably report a significant portion of its assets, liabilities, costs, and other related information; (2) affect the federal government's ability to reliably measure the full cost, as well as the financial and nonfinancial performance, of certain programs and activities; (3) impair the federal government's ability to adequately safeguard significant assets and properly record various transactions; and (4) hinder the federal government from having reliable financial information to operate in an efficient and effective manner. Due to these material weaknesses and to other limitations on the scope of our work discussed below, additional issues may exist that could affect the accrual-based consolidated financial statements that were not identified. Appendix II describes these material weaknesses in more detail and highlights the primary effects of these material weaknesses on the accompanying accrual-based consolidated financial statements and on the management of federal government operations.

Sustainability Financial Statements

Significant uncertainties (discussed in Note 23 to the consolidated financial statements), which primarily relate to the achievement of projected reductions in Medicare cost growth, affect the sustainability financial statements. In addition, the material weakness related to the Reconciliations of Net Operating Cost and Unified Budget Deficit and the Statements of Changes in Cash Balance from Unified Budget and Other Activities, discussed above, hampers the federal government's ability to demonstrate the reliability of historical budget information used for certain key inputs to the 2015 Statement of Long-Term Fiscal Projections. As a result of these significant uncertainties and material weakness, readers are cautioned that amounts reported in the 2015 Statement of Long-Term Fiscal Projections; the 2015, 2014, 2013, 2012, and 2011 Statements of Social Insurance; the 2015 and 2014 Statements of Changes in Social Insurance Amounts; and the related notes to such financial statements may not fairly present, in all material respects, the sustainability information for those years in accordance with U.S. generally accepted accounting principles.

For 2015, these significant uncertainties primarily relate to the following.

- Medicare projections in the 2015 Statement of Long-Term Fiscal Projections and the 2015 Statement of Social Insurance were based on benefit formulas under current law and included a significant reduction in Medicare payment rates for productivity improvements relating to most categories of Medicare providers,[9] based on full implementation of the provisions of the Patient Protection and Affordable Care Act, as amended (ACA),[10] and physician payment updates specified by the Medicare Access and CHIP Reauthorization Act of 2015 (MACRA).[11]

- Management has noted that actual future costs for Medicare are likely to exceed those shown by the current law projections presented in the 2015 Statement of Social Insurance due, for example, to the likelihood of modifications to the scheduled reductions in Medicare payment rates for productivity adjustments relating to most categories of Medicare providers and to the specified physician payment updates. The extent to which actual future costs exceed the current law amounts due to changes to the scheduled reductions in Medicare payment rates for productivity adjustments and to specified physician payment updates depends on both the specific changes that might be legislated and whether such legislation would include further provisions to help offset such costs. Consequently, there are significant uncertainties concerning the achievement of these projected reductions in Medicare payment rates.

- Management has developed an illustrative alternative projection intended to provide additional context regarding the long-term sustainability of the Medicare program and to illustrate the uncertainties in the Statement of Social Insurance projections. The present value of future estimated expenditures in excess of future estimated revenue for Medicare, included in the illustrative alternative projection in Note 23, exceeds the $27.9 trillion estimate in the 2015 Statement of Social Insurance by $8.9 trillion.

- Management noted that these significant uncertainties about projected reductions in health care cost growth also affect the projected Medicare and Medicaid costs reported in the 2015 Statement of Long-Term Fiscal Projections.

The 2014, 2013, 2012, and 2011 Statements of Social Insurance were affected by significant uncertainties, primarily related to the achievement of projected reductions in Medicare payment rates for productivity improvements. The 2013, 2012, and 2011 Statements of Social Insurance were also affected by uncertainties related to projected reductions in Medicare payment rates for physician services. Specifically, the Medicare projections in the 2013, 2012, and 2011 Statements of Social Insurance were based on benefit formulas in current law and included significant reductions in Medicare payment rates for productivity improvements and physician services. The 2014 Statement of Social Insurance reflected a change from the assumption regarding scheduled reductions in Medicare payment rates for physician services that was used in the 2013, 2012, and 2011 Statements of Social Insurance. Specifically, the 2014 Statement of Social Insurance reflected a projected baseline that assumed that the physician payment rate reductions would not occur and that physician payment rates would annually increase at a rate equal to the average sustainable growth rate (SGR) override that occurred over the 10-year

---

[9]These categories include, but are not limited to, inpatient/outpatient hospital services, skilled nursing facilities, home health care, ambulance, ambulatory surgical centers, durable medical equipment, and prosthetics.
[10]ACA, Pub. L. No. 111-148, 124 Stat. 119 (Mar. 23, 2010), as amended by the Health Care and Education Reconciliation Act of 2010, Pub. L. No. 111-152, 124 Stat. 1029 (Mar. 30, 2010). In this report, references to ACA include any amendments made by the Health Care and Education Reconciliation Act of 2010.
[11]MACRA, Pub. L. No. 114-10, title I, § 101, 129 Stat. 87, 89 (Apr. 16, 2015). MACRA included many provisions that affect Medicare, including the repeal of the sustainable growth rate (SGR) formula for calculating annual updates to Medicare reimbursement payment rates to physicians and certain nonphysician medical providers and established an alternative set of annual updates.

period ending on March 31, 2015. For 2014, 2013, 2012, and 2011, management noted that actual future costs for Medicare were likely to exceed those shown by the current-law projections presented in the 2014, 2013, 2012, and 2011 Statements of Social Insurance due, for example, to the likelihood of modifications to the scheduled reductions in Medicare payment rates for productivity adjustments.

Projections of Medicare costs are sensitive to assumptions about future decisions by policymakers and about the behavioral responses of consumers, employers, and health care providers as policy, incentives, and the health care sector change over time. Such secondary impacts are not fully reflected in the sustainability financial statements but could be expected to influence the excess cost growth rate used in the projections.[12] Key drivers of uncertainty about the excess cost growth rate include the future development and deployment of medical technology, the evolution of personal income, and the cost and availability of insurance, as well as federal policy changes, such as the implementation of the ACA. The Required Supplementary Information section of the 2015 Financial Report includes unaudited information concerning how changes in various assumptions would change the present value of future estimated expenditures in excess of future estimated revenue. As discussed in that section, the projections are very sensitive to changes in the health care cost growth assumption.

As discussed in Notes 23 and 24 to the financial statements, the sustainability financial statements are based on management's assumptions. These sustainability financial statements present the present value of the U.S. government's estimated future receipts and future spending using a projection period sufficient to illustrate long-term sustainability.[13] The sustainability financial statements are intended to aid users in assessing whether future resources will likely be sufficient to sustain public services and to meet obligations as they come due. The Statements of Social Insurance and Changes in Social Insurance Amounts are based on income and benefit formulas in current law (except for the 2014 Medicare projections, which use the projected baseline) and assume that scheduled benefits will continue after any related trust funds are exhausted. The Statements of Long-Term Fiscal Projections are based on the continuation of current policy. The sustainability financial statements are not forecasts or predictions.

In preparing the sustainability financial statements, management considers and selects assumptions and data that it believes provide a reasonable basis to illustrate whether current policy or law is sustainable. Assumptions underlying such sustainability information do not consider changes in policy or all potential future events that could affect future receipts, future spending, and sustainability, for example, implementation of policy changes to avoid trust fund exhaustion or unsustainable debt levels.

As discussed in the unaudited Required Supplementary Information section of the 2015 Financial Report, the Social Security and Medicare Hospital Insurance (Part A) trust funds are, based on achievement of the cost reductions discussed above, projected to be exhausted in 2034 and 2030, respectively, at which time they would be unable to pay the full amount of scheduled future benefits.[14] For Social Security, future revenues were projected to be sufficient to pay 79 percent of scheduled benefits in 2034, the year of projected trust funds (combined)

---

[12] The excess cost growth rate is the increase in health care spending per person relative to the growth of gross domestic product per person after removing the effects of demographic changes on health care spending.

[13] The projection period used for the Social Security, Medicare, and Railroad Retirement social insurance programs is 75 years. For the Black Lung program, the projections are through September 30, 2040.

[14] The combined Social Security trust funds consist of the Federal Old-Age and Survivors Insurance trust fund and the Federal Disability Insurance trust fund, whose assets are projected to be exhausted in 2035 and 2022, respectively.

exhaustion, and decreasing to 73 percent of scheduled benefits in 2089. For Medicare Hospital Insurance (Part A), future revenues were projected to be sufficient to pay 86 percent of scheduled benefits in 2030, the year of projected trust fund exhaustion, and then decreasing to 84 percent of scheduled benefits in 2089.

Because of the large number of factors that affect the sustainability financial statements and the fact that future events and circumstances cannot be estimated with certainty, even if current policy is continued, there will be differences between the estimates in the sustainability financial statements and the actual results, and those differences may be material.

Other Limitations on the Scope of Our Work

For fiscal years 2015 and 2014, there were other limitations on the scope of our work, in addition to the material weaknesses and significant uncertainties noted above, that contributed to our disclaimers of opinion on the consolidated financial statements. Such limitations primarily relate to our ability to obtain adequate representations from management. Treasury and OMB depend on representations from certain federal entities to provide their representations to us regarding the U.S. government's consolidated financial statements. Treasury and OMB were unable to provide us with adequate representations regarding the U.S. government's accrual-based consolidated financial statements for fiscal years 2015 and 2014 primarily because of insufficient or no representations provided to them by certain federal entities, including DOD.

Disclaimers of Opinion on the Consolidated Financial Statements

Accrual-Based Consolidated Financial Statements

Because of the significance of the related matters described in the Basis for Disclaimer of Opinion paragraphs above, we were not able to obtain sufficient appropriate audit evidence to provide a basis for an audit opinion on the accrual-based consolidated financial statements. Accordingly, we do not express an opinion on the accrual-based consolidated financial statements as of and for the fiscal years ended September 30, 2015, and 2014.

Sustainability Financial Statements

Because of the significance of the related matters described in the Basis for Disclaimer of Opinion paragraphs above, we were not able to obtain sufficient appropriate audit evidence to provide a basis for an audit opinion on the Statement of Long-Term Fiscal Projections for 2015; the Statements of Social Insurance for 2015, 2014, 2013, 2012, and 2011; and the Statements of Changes in Social Insurance Amounts for 2015 and 2014. Accordingly, we do not express an opinion on these sustainability financial statements. The 2014 Statement of Long-Term Fiscal Projections was not subject to audit.

Emphasis of Matters

The following key items deserve emphasis in order to put the information contained in the consolidated financial statements and the Management's Discussion and Analysis section of the *2015 Financial Report* into context. However, our disclaimers of opinion noted above are not modified with respect to these matters.

Equity Investments Related to the Federal Government's Actions to Stabilize Financial Markets and to Promote Economic Recovery

In 2008, during the financial crisis, the federal government placed the Federal National Mortgage Association (Fannie Mae) and the Federal Home Loan Mortgage Corporation (Freddie Mac) under conservatorship and entered into preferred stock purchase agreements with these government-sponsored enterprises (GSE) to ensure their financial stability. The agreements with the GSEs could affect the federal government's financial position. As of September 30, 2015, the federal government continued to report about $106 billion of investments in the GSEs, which is net of about $88 billion in valuation losses.

In valuing these equity investments, management considered and selected assumptions and data that it believed provided a reasonable basis for the estimated values reported in the accrual-based consolidated financial statements. However, as discussed in Note 1 to the consolidated financial statements, there are many factors affecting these assumptions and estimates that are inherently subject to substantial uncertainty arising from the uniqueness of the transactions and the likelihood of future changes in general economic, regulatory, and market conditions. As such, there will be differences between the estimated values as of September 30, 2015, and the actual results, and such differences may be material. Also, as discussed in Note 1 to the consolidated financial statements, the financial statements do not include the assets, liabilities, or results of operations of entities in which Treasury holds either a direct, indirect, or beneficial equity interest. Treasury and OMB have determined that none of the entities meet the criteria for a federal entity.[15]

Long-Term Fiscal Challenges

While the near-term outlook has improved, the comprehensive long-term fiscal projections presented in the Statement of Long-Term Fiscal Projections, and related information in Note 24 and in the unaudited Required Supplementary Information section of the *2015 Financial Report* show that absent policy changes, the federal government continues to face an unsustainable long-term fiscal path. In the near term, the projections in the *2015 Financial Report* show the primary deficit continuing to decline from the recent historic highs. However, these projections do not reflect recent legislation enacted subsequent to September 30, 2015, which, in order to achieve certain national priorities and goals, causes deficits to increase in the near term.[16] Over the long term, the imbalance between spending and revenue that is built into current law and policy is projected to lead to continued growth of debt held by the public as a share of gross domestic product (GDP). This situation—in which debt grows faster than GDP—means the current federal fiscal path is unsustainable.

Under these projections, spending for the major health and retirement programs will increase in coming decades more rapidly than GDP as more members of the baby boom generation become eligible for benefits. These projections, with regard to Social Security and Medicare, are based on the same assumptions underlying the information presented in the Statement of

---

[15]For additional information on the criteria used to determine which federal entities are included in the reporting entity for the consolidated financial statements, as well as the reasons for not including certain entities, such as Fannie Mae and Freddie Mac, see Appendix A of the *2015 Financial Report*.

[16]The 2015 Statement of Long-Term Fiscal Projections is based on current policy as of September 30, 2015. This is prior to the enactment of the Bipartisan Budget Act of 2015 and the Consolidated Appropriations Act, 2016; therefore, the projections do not reflect the effects of these two statutes. Management notes that neither statute is expected to have a material effect on the long-term fiscal projections in its report.

Social Insurance and assume that the provisions enacted in the ACA designed to slow the growth of Medicare costs are sustained and remain effective throughout the projection period.[17] They also reflect the effects of the MACRA, which, among other things, revised the methodology for determining physician payment rates.[18] If, however, the Medicare cost containment measures and physician payment rate methodology are not sustained over the long term—concerns expressed by the Trustees of the Medicare trust funds, the Centers for Medicare & Medicaid Services' (CMS) Chief Actuary, the Congressional Budget Office, and others—spending on federal health care programs will grow more rapidly than assumed in the projections.

GAO also prepares long-term federal fiscal simulations, using different sets of assumptions, which continue to show debt held by the public rising as a share of GDP.[19] Under GAO's Alternative simulation,[20] using the CMS Office of the Actuary's alternative health care cost projections, future spending in excess of receipts would be greater and debt held by the public as a share of GDP would grow more quickly than the projections in the *2015 Financial Report*. Under the Alternative simulation, debt held by the public as a share of GDP will surpass its historical high (106 percent in 1946) by 2031.

Both the projections in the *2015 Financial Report* and our long-term simulations follow the spending limits enacted in the Balanced Budget and Emergency Deficit Control Act of 1985 (BBEDCA), as amended.[21] Under these limits, discretionary spending will continue to decline as a share of the economy and within the next 5 years will be lower as a share of GDP than any level seen in the last 50 years. At the same time, the projections in the *2015 Financial Report* show revenues rising in the near term as the economy continues to recover. Our long-term simulations show revenues rising in some years and declining in others in the near term.

Debt held by the public as a share of GDP, however, remains well above the post-war historical average of 43 percent since 1946. At the end of fiscal year 2015, debt held by the public reached about 74 percent of GDP—the second highest (after fiscal year 2014, when it was

---

[17]ACA, Pub. L. No. 111-148, 124 Stat. 119 (Mar. 23, 2010), as amended by the Health Care and Education Reconciliation Act of 2010, Pub. L. No. 111-152, 124 Stat. 1029 (Mar. 30, 2010).

[18]MACRA, Pub. L. No. 114-10, title I, § 101, 129 Stat. 87, 89 (Apr. 16, 2015), repealed the sustainable growth rate (SGR) formula for calculating annual updates to Medicare reimbursement payment rates to physicians and certain nonphysician medical providers and established an alternative set of annual updates.

[19]GAO, *Fiscal Outlook: Federal Fiscal Outlook* (2016) (Washington, D.C.: 2016), accessed February 17, 2016, http://www.gao.gov/fiscal_outlook/federal_fiscal_outlook/overview.

[20]Our 2016 Alternative simulation, the most recent one available as of the date of our audit report, incorporates the CMS Office of the Actuary's 2015 alternative projections for health care cost growth, which assume certain cost controls are not maintained over the long term. Our Alternative simulation also assumes that tax provisions that are scheduled to expire, such as the credit for construction of energy-efficient new homes, are extended. In the Alternative simulation, discretionary spending follows the caps established in the Balanced Budget and Emergency Deficit Control Act of 1985, as amended, but not the lower caps triggered by the automatic enforcement procedures.

[21]The Budget Control Act of 2011 (BCA) amended BBEDCA, imposing discretionary spending limits for fiscal years 2012 through 2021 to reduce projected spending by about $1 trillion. Pub. L. No. 112-25, 125 Stat. 240 (Aug. 2, 2011). The BCA also established the Joint Select Committee on Deficit Reduction (Joint Committee), which was tasked with proposing legislation to reduce the deficit by at least an additional $1.2 trillion through fiscal year 2021. The Joint Committee did not report a proposal, and Congress and the President did not enact legislation. This triggered the sequestration process in section 251A of BBEDCA. Section 251A, as amended by BCA, required (1) a sequestration for fiscal year 2013 and (2) annual downward adjustments to discretionary spending limits and sequestration of direct spending from fiscal years 2014 through 2021. BBEDCA has been amended several times since August 2011, most recently by the Bipartisan Budget Act (BBA) of 2015, which increased discretionary spending limits for fiscal years 2016 and 2017. The BBA of 2015 also extended the sequestration of direct spending through fiscal year 2025 and made other changes to direct spending and revenue. Pub. L. No. 114-74, §§ 101, 102, 129 Stat. 584, 585-87 (Nov. 2, 2015). GAO's long-term simulations reflect the effects of the BBA of 2015.

slightly higher) it has been as a share of GDP since 1950. Debt held by the public at these high levels could limit the federal government's flexibility to address emerging issues and unforeseen challenges, such as another economic downturn or large-scale disaster. Further, our past work has also identified a variety of fiscal exposures—responsibilities, programs, and activities that explicitly or implicitly expose the federal government to future spending.[22] Fiscal exposures vary widely as to source, extent of the government's legal commitment, and magnitude. Over the past decade, some fiscal exposures have grown because of events and trends and the government's response to them. Increased attention to these fiscal exposures will be important for understanding risks to the federal fiscal outlook and enhancing oversight of federal resources.

Other Matters

Required Supplementary Information and Required Supplementary Stewardship Information

U.S. generally accepted accounting principles issued by the Federal Accounting Standards Advisory Board (FASAB) require that RSI and RSSI be presented in the *2015 Financial Report* to supplement the financial statements. Although not a part of the financial statements, FASAB considers this information to be an essential part of financial reporting for placing the financial statements in appropriate operational, economic, or historical context. We were unable to apply certain limited procedures to the RSI and RSSI in accordance with U.S. generally accepted government auditing standards because of the material weaknesses and other scope limitations discussed in this audit report. We did not audit and do not express an opinion or provide any assurance on the RSI or RSSI.

Other Information

Other information included in the *2015 Financial Report* contains a wide range of information, some of which is not directly related to the consolidated financial statements. This information is presented for purposes of additional analysis and is not a required part of the consolidated financial statements, RSI, or RSSI. We read the other information included with the consolidated financial statements in order to identify material inconsistencies, if any, with the consolidated financial statements. We did not audit and do not express an opinion or provide any assurance on the other information in the *2015 Financial Report*.

Readers are cautioned that the material weaknesses, significant uncertainties, and other scope limitations discussed in this audit report may affect the reliability of certain information contained in the RSI, RSSI, and other information that is taken from the same data sources as the accrual-based consolidated financial statements and the sustainability financial statements.

CFO Act Agency Financial Management Systems

The federal government's ability to efficiently and effectively manage and oversee its day-to-day operations and programs relies heavily on the ability of entity financial management systems to produce complete, reliable, timely, and consistent financial information for use by executive

---

[22]GAO, *Fiscal Outlook: Federal Fiscal Outlook* (2016), accessed February 17, 2016, http://www.gao.gov/fiscal_outlook/federal_fiscal_outlook/overview#t=3, and *Fiscal Exposures: Improving Cost Recognition in the Federal Budget*, GAO-14-28 (Washington, D.C.: Oct. 29, 2013).

branch agencies and Congress.[23] The Federal Financial Management Improvement Act of 1996 (FFMIA) was designed to lead to system improvements that would result in CFO Act agency managers routinely having access to reliable, useful, and timely financial-related information with which to measure performance and increase accountability throughout the year.

The 24 CFO Act agencies are responsible for implementing and maintaining financial management systems that substantially comply with the requirements of FFMIA. FFMIA requires auditors, as part of the 24 CFO Act agencies' financial statement audits, to report whether those agencies' financial management systems substantially comply with (1) federal financial management systems requirements, (2) applicable federal accounting standards, and (3) the federal government's *U.S. Standard General Ledger* at the transaction level.

For fiscal years 2015 and 2014, auditors at 12 and 11 of the 24 CFO Act agencies, respectively, reported that the agencies' financial management systems did not substantially comply with one or more of the three FFMIA requirements. Agency management at the 24 CFO Act agencies also annually report on FFMIA compliance. For both fiscal years 2015 and 2014, agency management at 10 of the CFO Act agencies reported that their agencies' financial management systems were not in substantial compliance with one or more of the three FFMIA requirements. Based on agency financial reports, the differences in the assessments of substantial compliance between the auditors and agency management reflected differences in management's and auditors' views of the impact that reported deficiencies had on agencies' financial management systems.

Long-standing financial management systems weaknesses at several large CFO Act agencies, along with the size and complexity of the federal government, continue to present a formidable management challenge in providing accountability to the nation's taxpayers and have contributed significantly to certain of the material weaknesses and other limitations discussed in this audit report.

Report on Internal Control over Financial Reporting

Management's Responsibility

Management of the federal government is responsible for (1) maintaining effective internal control over financial reporting, including the design, implementation, and maintenance of internal control relevant to the preparation and fair presentation of financial statements that are free from material misstatement, whether due to fraud or error, and (2) evaluating the effectiveness of internal control over financial reporting, based on criteria established under the Federal Managers' Financial Integrity Act (FMFIA).[24]

---

[23]The Federal Financial Management Improvement Act of 1996, which is reprinted in 31 U.S.C. § 3512 note, defines "financial management systems" to include the financial systems and the financial portions of mixed systems necessary to support financial management, including automated and manual processes, procedures, controls, data, hardware, software, and support personnel dedicated to the operation and maintenance of system functions.
[24]31 U.S.C. § 3512 (c), (d) (commonly referred to as FMFIA). This act requires executive agency heads to evaluate and report annually to the President and Congress on the adequacy of their internal control and accounting systems and on actions to correct significant problems.

Auditor's Responsibility

The purpose of an audit of financial statements is to express an opinion on the financial statements. An audit of financial statements includes considering internal control over financial reporting to design audit procedures that are appropriate in the circumstances, but not for the purpose of expressing an opinion on the effectiveness of internal control over financial reporting. Accordingly, we do not express an opinion on the effectiveness of internal control over financial reporting. We did not consider all internal controls relevant to operating objectives as broadly established under FMFIA, such as those controls relevant to preparing performance information and ensuring efficient operations.

Our responsibility is to report any material weaknesses or significant deficiencies in internal control over financial reporting for fiscal year 2015 that come to our attention as a result of our audit. Based on the scope of our work and the effects of the other limitations on the scope of our audit noted throughout this audit report, our internal control work was not designed to, and would not necessarily, identify all deficiencies in internal control, including those that might be material weaknesses or significant deficiencies.[25] Therefore, additional material weaknesses or significant deficiencies may exist that were not identified. Our work was performed in accordance with U.S. generally accepted government auditing standards.

Definitions and Inherent Limitations of Internal Control over Financial Reporting

An entity's internal control over financial reporting is a process effected by those charged with governance, management, and other personnel, the objectives of which are to provide reasonable assurance that (1) transactions are properly recorded, processed, and summarized to permit the preparation of financial statements in accordance with U.S. generally accepted accounting principles, and assets are safeguarded against loss from unauthorized acquisition, use, or disposition, and (2) transactions are executed in accordance with provisions of applicable laws, including those governing the use of budget authority; regulations; contracts; and grant agreements, noncompliance with which could have a material effect on the financial statements.

Because of its inherent limitations, internal control over financial reporting may not prevent, or detect and correct, misstatements due to fraud or error.

Material Weaknesses Resulted in Ineffective Internal Control over Financial Reporting

The material weaknesses discussed in this audit report resulted in ineffective internal control over financial reporting. Consequently, the federal government's internal control did not provide reasonable assurance that a material misstatement of the consolidated financial statements would be prevented, or detected and corrected, on a timely basis.

In addition to the material weaknesses that contributed to our disclaimers of opinion on the accrual-based consolidated financial statements and the sustainability financial statements, which were discussed previously, we found the following three other material weaknesses in internal control. These other material weaknesses were the federal government's inability to

---

[25]A significant deficiency is a deficiency, or a combination of deficiencies, in internal control that is less severe than a material weakness, yet important enough to merit attention by those charged with governance.

- determine the full extent to which improper payments occur and reasonably assure that appropriate actions are taken to reduce them,

- identify and resolve information security control deficiencies and manage information security risks on an ongoing basis, and

- effectively manage its tax collection activities.

These material weaknesses are discussed in more detail in appendix III, including the primary effects of the material weaknesses on the accompanying accrual-based consolidated financial statements and on the management of federal government operations.

We also found a significant deficiency in the federal government's internal control related to implementing effective internal controls over management of federal grants at certain federal entities. This significant deficiency is discussed in more detail in appendix IV.

Further, individual federal entity financial statement audit reports identified additional control deficiencies that were reported by the entities' auditors as either material weaknesses or significant deficiencies at the individual entity level. We do not consider these additional deficiencies to represent material weaknesses or significant deficiencies with respect to the U.S. government's consolidated financial statements.

<u>Intended Purpose of Report on Internal Control over Financial Reporting</u>

The purpose of this report on internal control over financial reporting is solely to describe the scope of our consideration of internal control over financial reporting, and the results of our procedures, and not to provide an opinion on the effectiveness of internal control over financial reporting. This report on internal control over financial reporting is an integral part of an audit performed in accordance with U.S. generally accepted government auditing standards in considering internal control. Accordingly, this report on internal control over financial reporting is not suitable for any other purpose.

Report on Compliance with Laws, Regulations, Contracts, and Grant Agreements

<u>Management's Responsibility</u>

Management of the federal government is responsible for the federal government's compliance with laws, regulations, contracts, and grant agreements.

<u>Auditor's Responsibility</u>

An audit of federal financial statements includes testing compliance with selected provisions of applicable laws, regulations, contracts, and grant agreements that have a direct effect on the determination of material amounts and disclosures in the consolidated financial statements, and performing certain other limited procedures. Accordingly, we did not test the federal government's compliance with all laws, regulations, contracts, and grant agreements. Due to the limitations discussed below and the scope of our procedures, noncompliance may occur and not be detected by these tests.

Our objective was not to provide an opinion on the federal government's compliance with laws, regulations, contracts, and grant agreements. Accordingly, we do not express such an opinion.

Our work was performed in accordance with U.S. generally accepted government auditing standards.

<u>Results of Our Tests for Compliance with Laws, Regulations, Contracts, and Grant Agreements</u>

Our work to test compliance with selected provisions of applicable laws, regulations, contracts, and grant agreements was limited by certain of the material weaknesses and other scope limitations discussed in this audit report. U.S. generally accepted government auditing standards and OMB guidance require auditors to report on entities' compliance with selected provisions of applicable laws, regulations, contracts, and grant agreements. Certain component entity audit reports contain instances of noncompliance. None of these instances were deemed to be reportable noncompliance with regard to the accompanying U.S. government's consolidated financial statements.

<u>Intended Purpose of Report on Compliance with Laws, Regulations, Contracts, and Grant Agreements</u>

The purpose of this report on compliance with laws, regulations, contracts, and grant agreements is solely to describe the scope of our testing of compliance with selected provisions of applicable laws, regulations, contracts, and grant agreements, and the results of that testing, and not to provide an opinion on compliance. This report on compliance with laws, regulations, contracts, and grant agreements is an integral part of an audit performed in accordance with U.S. generally accepted government auditing standards in considering compliance. Accordingly, this report on compliance with laws, regulations, contracts, and grant agreements is not suitable for any other purpose.

Agency Comments

We provided a draft of this audit report to Treasury and OMB officials, who provided technical comments, which have been incorporated as appropriate. Treasury and OMB officials expressed their continuing commitment to addressing the problems this report outlines.

Robert F. Dacey
Chief Accountant
U.S. Government Accountability Office

February 17, 2016

Appendix I

Objectives, Scope, and Methodology

Our objectives were to audit the consolidated financial statements consisting of the (1) accrual-based consolidated financial statements as of and for the fiscal years ended September 30, 2015, and 2014, and (2) sustainability financial statements, which consist of the 2015 Statement of Long-Term Fiscal Projections; the 2015, 2014, 2013, 2012, and 2011 Statements of Social Insurance; and the 2015 and 2014 Statements of Changes in Social Insurance Amounts. Our objectives also included reporting on internal control over financial reporting and on compliance with selected provisions of applicable laws, regulations, contracts, and grant agreements.

The Chief Financial Officers (CFO) Act of 1990, as expanded by the Government Management Reform Act of 1994 (GMRA), requires the inspectors general of the 24 CFO Act agencies to be responsible for annual audits of agency-wide financial statements prepared by these agencies.[26] GMRA requires GAO to be responsible for the audit of the U.S. government's consolidated financial statements,[27] and the Accountability of Tax Dollars Act of 2002 (ATDA) requires most other executive branch entities to annually prepare financial statements and have them audited.[28] The Office of Management and Budget (OMB) and the Department of the Treasury (Treasury) have identified 39 federal entities that are significant to the U.S. government's fiscal year 2015 consolidated financial statements, including the 24 CFO Act agencies.[29] We consider these 39 entities to be significant component entities for purposes of our audit of the consolidated financial statements. Our work was performed in coordination and cooperation with the inspectors general and independent public accountants for these significant component entities to achieve our respective audit objectives.[30] Our audit approach regarding the accrual-based consolidated financial statements primarily focused on determining the current status of the material weaknesses that contributed to our disclaimer of opinion on the accrual-based consolidated financial statements and the other material weaknesses affecting internal control that we had reported in our report on the consolidated financial statements for fiscal year 2014.[31] We also separately audited the financial statements of certain component entities, and parts of a significant component entity, including the following.

- We audited and expressed an unmodified opinion on the Internal Revenue Service's (IRS) financial statements as of and for the fiscal years ended September 30, 2015, and 2014.[32] In fiscal years 2015 and 2014, IRS collected about $3.3 trillion and $3.1 trillion, respectively, in tax payments and paid about $403 billion and $374 billion, respectively, in refunds to taxpayers. For fiscal year 2015, we continued to report a material weakness in internal control over unpaid tax assessments that resulted in ineffective internal control over financial reporting. In addition, we continued to report a significant deficiency in IRS's internal control over financial reporting systems. We also reported that we found no reportable

---

[26]31 U.S.C. § 3521(e). GMRA authorized the Office of Management and Budget to designate agency components that also would receive financial statement audits. See 31 U.S.C. § 3515(c).

[27]GMRA, Pub. L. No. 103-356, § 405(c), 108 Stat. 3410, 3416-17 (Oct. 13, 1994), *codified at* 31 U.S.C. § 331(e)(2).

[28]ATDA, Pub. L. No. 107-289, 116 Stat. 2049 (Nov. 7, 2002), *codified at* 31 U.S.C. § 3515.

[29]See *Treasury Financial Manual*, vol. I, part 2, ch. 4700, for a listing of the 39 entities.

[30]For fiscal year 2015, the Defense Security Cooperation Agency and the General Fund of the U.S. Government were not audited.

[31]GAO, *Financial Audit: U.S. Government's Fiscal Years 2014 and 2013 Consolidated Financial Statements*, GAO-15-341R (Washington, D.C.: Feb. 26, 2015).

[32]GAO, *Financial Audit: IRS's Fiscal Years 2015 and 2014 Financial Statements*, GAO-16-146 (Washington, D.C.: Nov. 12, 2015).

noncompliance for fiscal year 2015 with provisions of applicable laws, regulations, contracts, and grant agreements we tested.

- We audited and expressed an unmodified opinion on the Schedules of Federal Debt managed by Treasury's Bureau of the Fiscal Service (Fiscal Service) for the fiscal years ended September 30, 2015, and 2014.[33] For these 2 fiscal years, the schedules reported (1) approximately $13.1 trillion (2015) and $12.8 trillion (2014) of federal debt held by the public;[34] (2) about $5.0 trillion (2015) and $5.0 trillion (2014) of intragovernmental debt holdings;[35] and (3) about $251 billion (2015) and $260 billion (2014) of interest on federal debt held by the public. We also reported that Fiscal Service maintained, in all material respects, effective internal control over financial reporting relevant to the Schedule of Federal Debt as of September 30, 2015. In addition, we reported that we found no reportable noncompliance for fiscal year 2015 with provisions of applicable laws, regulations, contracts, and grant agreements we tested related to the Schedule of Federal Debt.

- We audited and expressed unmodified opinions on the U.S. Securities and Exchange Commission's (SEC) and its Investor Protection Fund's (IPF) financial statements as of and for the fiscal years ended September 30, 2015, and 2014.[36] We also reported that SEC maintained, in all material respects, effective internal control over financial reporting for both the entity as a whole and the IPF as of September 30, 2015. In addition, we reported that we found no reportable noncompliance for either SEC or IPF for fiscal year 2015 with provisions of applicable laws, regulations, contracts, and grant agreements we tested.

- We audited and expressed an unmodified opinion on the Federal Housing Finance Agency's (FHFA) financial statements as of and for the fiscal years ended September 30, 2015, and 2014.[37] We also reported that FHFA maintained, in all material respects, effective internal control over financial reporting as of September 30, 2015. In addition, we reported that we found no reportable noncompliance for fiscal year 2015 with provisions of applicable laws, regulations, contracts, and grant agreements we tested.

- We audited and expressed an unmodified opinion on the Office of Financial Stability's (OFS) financial statements for the Troubled Asset Relief Program (TARP) as of and for the fiscal years ended September 30, 2015, and 2014.[38] We also reported that OFS maintained, in all material respects, effective internal control over financial reporting for TARP as of September 30, 2015. In addition, we reported that we found no reportable noncompliance for fiscal year 2015 with provisions of applicable laws, regulations, contracts, and grant agreements we tested.

---

[33]GAO, *Financial Audit: Bureau of the Fiscal Service's Fiscal Years 2015 and 2014 Schedules of Federal Debt*, GAO-16-160 (Washington, D.C.: Nov. 13, 2015).
[34]Debt held by the public on the Schedules of Federal Debt represents federal debt issued by Treasury and held by investors outside of the federal government, including individuals, corporations, state or local governments, the Federal Reserve, and foreign governments.
[35]Intragovernmental debt holdings represent federal debt owed by Treasury to federal government accounts, primarily federal trust funds, such as Social Security and Medicare.
[36]GAO, *Financial Audit: Securities and Exchange Commission's Fiscal Years 2015 and 2014 Financial Statements*, GAO-16-145R (Washington, D.C.: Nov. 16, 2015).
[37]GAO, *Financial Audit: Federal Housing Finance Agency's Fiscal Years 2015 and 2014 Financial Statements*, GAO-16-95R (Washington, D.C.: Nov. 16, 2015).
[38]GAO, *Financial Audit: Office of Financial Stability (Troubled Asset Relief Program) Fiscal Years 2015 and 2014 Financial Statements*, GAO-16-147R (Washington, D.C.: Nov. 10, 2015).

- We audited and expressed an unmodified opinion on the Bureau of Consumer Financial Protection's (CFPB) financial statements as of and for the fiscal years ended September 30, 2015, and 2014.[39] We also reported that although certain internal controls could be improved, CFPB maintained, in all material respects, effective internal control over financial reporting as of September 30, 2015. In addition, we reported that we found no reportable noncompliance for fiscal year 2015 with provisions of applicable laws, regulations, contracts, and grant agreements we tested.

In addition, we considered the CFO Act agencies' and certain other federal entities' fiscal years 2015 and 2014 financial statements and the related auditors' reports prepared by the inspectors general or contracted independent public accountants. Financial statements and audit reports for these entities provide information about the entities' operations. Each entity audit report also contains details regarding any identified material weaknesses or significant deficiencies and related recommendations for the respective entity. We did not audit, and we do not express an opinion on, any of these individual federal entity financial statements.

We considered the Department of Defense's (DOD) assertion in the *DOD Agency Financial Report for Fiscal Year 2015* regarding its noncompliant financial management systems and lack of reasonable assurance that internal controls over financial reporting were effective. In addition, in the DOD Inspector General's fiscal year 2015 report on internal control over financial reporting, the Inspector General cited material weaknesses in several areas, including (1) property, plant, and equipment; (2) inventory and operating material and supplies; (3) environmental liabilities; (4) intragovernmental eliminations; and (5) material amounts of unsupported accounting entries needed to prepare DOD's annual consolidated financial statements.

Our audit approach for the 2015 Statement of Long-Term Fiscal Projections focused primarily on assuring that the information relating to the Statements of Social Insurance is properly reflected therein and testing the methodology used as well as evaluating key assumptions. We also evaluated whether the internal control deficiencies concerning the accrual-based consolidated financial statements affected certain key inputs used in generating the projections.

Because of the significance of the amounts presented in the Statements of Social Insurance and Statements of Changes in Social Insurance Amounts related to the Social Security Administration (SSA) and the Department of Health and Human Services (HHS), our audit approach regarding these statements focused primarily on these two agencies. For each federal entity preparing a Statement of Social Insurance and Statement of Changes in Social Insurance Amounts,[40] we considered the entity's 2015, 2014, 2013, 2012, and 2011 Statements of Social Insurance and the 2015 and 2014 Statements of Changes in Social Insurance Amounts, as well as the related auditor's reports prepared by the inspectors general or contracted independent public accountants.

We performed sufficient audit work to provide our reports on (1) the consolidated financial statements; (2) internal control over financial reporting; and (3) compliance with selected provisions of applicable laws, regulations, contracts, and grant agreements.

---

[39]GAO, *Financial Audit: Bureau of Consumer Financial Protection's Fiscal Years 2015 and 2014 Financial Statements*, GAO-16-96R (Washington, D.C.: Nov. 16, 2015).
[40]These entities are SSA, HHS, the Railroad Retirement Board, and the Department of Labor.

We considered the limitations on the scope of our work regarding the accrual-based consolidated financial statements and the sustainability financial statements in forming our conclusions. Our work was performed in accordance with U.S. generally accepted government auditing standards.

Appendix II

Material Weaknesses Contributing to Our Disclaimer of Opinion on the Accrual-Based Consolidated Financial Statements

The continuing material weaknesses discussed below contributed to our disclaimer of opinion on the federal government's accrual-based consolidated financial statements.[41] The federal government did not maintain adequate systems or have sufficient appropriate evidence to support information reported in the accompanying accrual-based consolidated financial statements, as described below.

Property, Plant, and Equipment and Inventories and Related Property

The federal government could not satisfactorily determine that property, plant, and equipment (PP&E) and inventories and related property were properly reported in the accrual-based consolidated financial statements. Most of the PP&E and inventories and related property are the responsibility of the Department of Defense (DOD). As in past years, DOD did not maintain adequate systems or have sufficient records to provide reliable information on these assets. Certain other entities' auditors also reported continued deficiencies in internal control procedures and processes related to PP&E.

Deficiencies in internal control over such assets could affect the federal government's ability to fully know the assets it owns, including their location and condition, and its ability to effectively (1) safeguard assets from physical deterioration, theft, or loss; (2) account for acquisitions and disposals of such assets and reliably report asset balances; (3) ensure that the assets are available for use when needed; (4) prevent unnecessary storage and maintenance costs or purchase of assets already on hand; and (5) determine the full costs of programs that use these assets.

Liabilities and Commitments and Contingencies

The federal government could not reasonably estimate or adequately support amounts reported for certain liabilities. For example, DOD was not able to estimate with assurance key components of its environmental and disposal liabilities. In addition, DOD could not support a significant amount of its estimated military postretirement health benefits liabilities included in federal employee and veteran benefits payable. These unsupported amounts related to the cost of direct health care provided by DOD-managed military treatment facilities. Further, the federal government could not determine whether commitments and contingencies, including any related to treaties and other international agreements entered into to further the federal government's interests, were complete and properly reported.

Problems in accounting for liabilities affect the determination of the full cost of the federal government's current operations and the extent of its liabilities. Also, deficiencies in internal control supporting the process for estimating environmental and disposal liabilities could result in improperly stated liabilities, as well as adversely affect the federal government's ability to determine priorities for cleanup and disposal activities and to appropriately consider future budgetary resources needed to carry out these activities. In addition, to the extent disclosures of commitments and contingencies are incomplete or incorrect, reliable information is not available

---

[41]The material weakness related to the Reconciliations of Budget Deficit to Net Operating Cost and Changes in Cash Balance also contributed to our disclaimer on the 2015 Statement of Long-Term Fiscal Projections.

about the extent of the federal government's obligations.

Cost of Government Operations and Disbursement Activity

Reported net costs were affected by the previously discussed material weaknesses in reporting assets and liabilities; material weaknesses in financial statement preparation, as discussed below; and the lack of adequate disbursement reconciliations at certain federal entities. As a result, the federal government was unable to support significant portions of the reported total net cost of operations, most notably those related to DOD.

With respect to disbursements, auditors of DOD and certain other federal entities reported continued control deficiencies in reconciling disbursement activity. For fiscal years 2015 and 2014, inadequate reconciliations of disbursement activity included (1) unreconciled differences between federal entities' and the Department of the Treasury's (Treasury) records of disbursements and (2) unsupported federal entity adjustments, which could also affect the balance sheet.

Unreliable cost information affects the federal government's ability to control and reduce costs, assess performance, evaluate programs, and set fees to recover costs where required or authorized. If disbursements are improperly recorded, this could result in misstatements in the financial statements and in certain data provided by federal entities for inclusion in *The Budget of the United States Government* (President's Budget) concerning obligations and outlays.

Accounting for and Reconciliation of Intragovernmental Activity and Balances

Significant progress has been made over the past few years; however, the federal government continues to be unable to adequately account for and reconcile intragovernmental activity and balances between federal entitles. Federal entities are responsible for properly accounting for and reporting their intragovernmental activity and balances in their entity financial statements. When preparing the consolidated financial statements, intragovernmental activity and balances between federal entities should be in agreement and must be subtracted out, or eliminated, from the financial statements. If the two federal entities engaged in an intragovernmental transaction do not both record the same intragovernmental transaction in the same year and for the same amount, the intragovernmental transactions will not be in agreement, resulting in errors in the consolidated financial statements. The Office of Management and Budget (OMB) and Treasury require the chief financial officers (CFO) of the significant component entities to reconcile, on a quarterly basis, selected intragovernmental activity and balances with their trading partners. In addition, these entities are required to report to Treasury, their respective inspectors general, and GAO on the extent and results of intragovernmental activity and balance-reconciliation efforts as of the end of the fiscal year.

Treasury has continued to actively work with significant federal entities to resolve intragovernmental differences through its quarterly scorecard process.[42] This process highlights differences requiring the entities' attention, identifies differences that need to be resolved

---

[42]For each quarter, Treasury produces a scorecard for each significant entity that reports various aspects of the entity's intragovernmental differences with its trading partners, including the composition of the differences by trading partner and category. Entities are expected to resolve, with their respective trading partners, the differences identified in their scorecards.

through a formal dispute resolution process,[43] and reinforces the entities' responsibilities to resolve intragovernmental differences. Treasury also implemented the Governmentwide Treasury Account Symbol Adjusted Trial Balance System in fiscal year 2014, which among other things, provided more complete financial data from entities that are intended to improve the analysis of intragovernmental differences. In the third quarter of fiscal year 2015, Treasury began implementing a new initiative to identify and monitor systemic root causes of intragovernmental differences. As a result of these and other actions, a significant number of intragovernmental differences were identified and resolved. While progress was made, we continued to note that amounts reported by federal entity trading partners to Treasury were not in agreement by material amounts. Reasons for the differences cited by several CFOs included differing accounting methodologies, accounting errors, and timing differences. In addition, the auditor for DOD reported that DOD, which contributes significantly to the unreconciled amounts, could not accurately identify most of its intragovernmental transactions by customer and was unable to reconcile most intragovernmental transactions with trading partners, which resulted in adjustments that cannot be fully supported.

Further, a significant portion of intragovernmental differences are related to unreconciled transactions between the General Fund of the U.S. Government (General Fund)[44] and federal entity trading partners related to appropriations and other intragovernmental transactions, which amount to hundreds of billions of dollars. In fiscal year 2015, Treasury continued to make significant improvements to the processes used to identify and reconcile General Fund differences. For example, Treasury established more specific guidance regarding General Fund-related activity and balances and issued this guidance for federal entities to follow in reporting their financial data. Treasury also began developing policies and procedures over accounting for and reporting all significant General Fund activity and balances, and began reconciling the activity and balances between the General Fund and federal entity trading partners. In addition, Treasury implemented certain reconciliations for subcategories relevant to the General Fund, such as debt financing activities. However, the ability to effectively reconcile General Fund transactions will be hampered until General Fund-related activity and balances are properly accounted for, reported, and audited.

As a result of the above-noted circumstances, the federal government's ability to determine the impact of these differences on the amounts reported in the accrual-based consolidated financial statements is significantly impaired. Resolving the intragovernmental transactions problem remains a difficult challenge and will require a strong and sustained commitment by federal entities to timely resolve differences with their trading partners, as well as continued strong leadership by Treasury and OMB.

Preparation of Consolidated Financial Statements

Treasury, in coordination with OMB, has implemented several corrective actions during the past few years related to the preparation of the consolidated financial statements. Corrective actions included implementing new systems to collect certain additional data from entities and to compile the consolidated financial statements, and new or enhanced procedures to address

---

[43]When an entity and its respective trading partner cannot resolve an intragovernmental difference, the entity must request Treasury to resolve the dispute. Treasury will review the dispute and issue a decision on how to resolve the difference, which the entities must follow.
[44]The General Fund is a component of Treasury's central accounting function. It is a stand-alone reporting entity that comprises the activities fundamental to funding the federal government (e.g., issued budget authority, cash activity, and debt financing activities).

certain internal control deficiencies detailed in our previously issued report.[45] However, the federal government's systems, controls, and procedures were not adequate to reasonably assure that the consolidated financial statements are consistent with the underlying audited entity financial statements, properly balanced, and in accordance with U.S. generally accepted accounting principles (U.S. GAAP). During our fiscal year 2015 audit, we found the following.

- For fiscal year 2015, auditors reported internal control deficiencies at several entities regarding entities' financial reporting processes that could affect information in those entities' closing packages.[46] Further, Treasury had to record significant adjustments to correct errors found in federal entities' audited closing package information. These errors primarily related to intragovernmental activity and balances and totaled tens of billions of dollars. To reasonably assure consistency of underlying entity information and financial data with the U.S. government's consolidated financial statements, entity auditors are required to separately audit and report on the financial information that the significant component entities send to Treasury through closing packages.[47]

- Treasury is unable to properly balance the accrual-based consolidated financial statements. To make the fiscal years 2015 and 2014 consolidated financial statements balance, Treasury recorded a net decrease of $5.1 billion and a net increase of $20.4 billion, respectively, to net operating cost on the Statements of Operations and Changes in Net Position, which were identified as "Unmatched transactions and balances."[48] Treasury recorded an additional net $1.9 billion and $1.7 billion of unmatched transactions in the Statement of Net Cost for fiscal years 2015 and 2014, respectively. The material weakness in the federal government's ability to account for and reconcile intragovernmental activity and balances, discussed above, significantly contributes to the unmatched transactions and balances and consequently impairs Treasury's ability to fully eliminate such intragovernmental activity and balances.

- Over the past several years, Treasury has taken significant actions to assist in ensuring that financial information is reported or disclosed in the consolidated financial statements in accordance with U.S. GAAP. For example, Treasury has developed and implemented U.S. GAAP compliance operating procedures and checklists. However, Treasury's reporting of certain financial information required by U.S. GAAP continues to be impaired. Due to certain control deficiencies noted in this audit report—for example, commitments and contingencies related to treaties and other international agreements—Treasury is precluded from determining if additional disclosure is required by U.S. GAAP in the consolidated financial statements, and we are precluded from determining whether the omitted information is material. Further, Treasury's ability to report information in accordance with U.S. GAAP will also remain impaired until federal entities, such as DOD, can provide Treasury with

---

[45]Most of the issues we identified in fiscal year 2015 existed in fiscal year 2014, and many have existed for a number of years. Most recently, in July 2015, we reported the issues we identified to Treasury and OMB and provided recommendations for corrective action. See GAO, *Management Report: Improvements Needed in Controls over the Processes Used to Prepare the U.S. Consolidated Financial Statements*, GAO-15-630 (Washington, D.C.: July 30, 2015).

[46]The closing package methodology links federal entities' audited consolidated department-level financial statements to certain of the U.S. government's consolidated financial statements.

[47]There are 39 significant component entities, including the General Fund; however, the General Fund did not submit a closing package in fiscal year 2015.

[48]Although Treasury was unable to determine how much of the unmatched transactions and balances relates to net operating cost, it reported this amount as a component of net operating cost in the accompanying consolidated financial statements.

complete and reliable information required to be reported in the consolidated financial statements.

- The consolidated financial statements include financial information for the executive, legislative, and judicial branches, to the extent that federal entities within those branches have provided Treasury such information. However, while progress was made over the past few years, undetermined amounts of assets, liabilities, costs, and revenues are not included, and the federal government did not provide evidence that the excluded financial information was immaterial.

- In fiscal year 2015, Treasury continued to make progress with corrective actions intended to resolve internal control deficiencies in the processes used to prepare the consolidated financial statements. For example, Treasury enhanced its process for involving key federal entity personnel in the preparation of the consolidated financial statements. However, other internal control deficiencies existed in the processes used to prepare the consolidated financial statements, such as inadequate processes for monitoring and assessing internal controls over the preparation of the consolidated financial statements. As a result, we identified errors, such as unclear or incomplete disclosures, in draft consolidated financial statements that were subsequently corrected.

- In fiscal year 2015, Treasury and OMB made significant progress with respect to their corrective action plans by developing a remediation plan that focuses on corrective actions to be taken over the next 3 years to address the material weaknesses in internal control. Although improvements have been noted, the plans continued to lack certain key elements recommended in the *CFO Council's Implementation Guide for OMB Circular A-123, Management's Responsibilities for Internal Control—Appendix A, Internal Control over Financial Reporting*, such as (1) sufficient information on how progress on interim actions would be monitored and (2) outcome measures for assessing the effectiveness of the corrective actions. Without such elements, Treasury's and OMB's efforts to address internal control deficiencies involving the processes used to prepare the consolidated financial statements will be hampered.

- In fiscal year 2015, Treasury continued to improve its systems and processes for preparing the consolidated financial statements. For example, Treasury continued to enhance the automated tool used in the compilation process. However, challenges remain regarding systems and processes for certain central accounting functions related to accurately reporting, as well as obtaining audit assurance over, General Fund transactions and components of the budget deficit. It is important that Treasury (1) continues to improve its systems and continues to ensure it has a sufficient number of personnel with appropriate skills in order to implement the corrective action plans and (2) remain committed to maintaining the progress that has been made in this area and building on that progress to make needed improvements to fully address the magnitude of the financial reporting challenges it faces.

Until these internal control deficiencies have been fully addressed, the federal government's ability to reasonably assure that the consolidated financial statements are consistent with the underlying audited federal entities' financial statements, properly balanced, and in accordance with U.S. GAAP will be impaired. Resolving these internal control deficiencies remains a difficult challenge and will require a strong and sustained commitment from Treasury and OMB as they continue to execute and implement corrective actions.

Reconciliations of Budget Deficit to Net Operating Cost and Changes in Cash Balance

Over the past 2 years, Treasury has improved its process for preparing the (1) Reconciliations of Net Operating Cost and Unified Budget Deficit and (2) Statements of Changes in Cash Balance from Unified Budget and Other Activities (Reconciliation Statements). For example, during fiscal year 2015, Treasury began an initiative to ensure the consistency of reconciling items reported on the Reconciliation Statements to entity financial information that is processed through Treasury's records. However, the federal government has not established and implemented effective processes and procedures for (1) identifying and reporting all items needed to prepare the Reconciliation Statements and (2) reasonably assuring that the information in these statements was fully consistent with the underlying information in the significant component entities' audited financial statements and other financial data, including the cash activity processed through the central accounting function. Until Treasury develops and fully implements an effective process for reasonably assuring completeness and consistency of the information in the statements and is able to fully reconcile this information, the effect on the U.S. government's consolidated financial statements will continue to be unknown.

The Reconciliation Statements report unified budget deficits for fiscal years 2015 and 2014 of about $439 billion and $483 billion, respectively.[49] The budget deficit is calculated by subtracting actual budget outlays (outlays) from actual budget receipts (receipts). Also, such outlays and receipts are key inputs to the Statements of Long-Term Fiscal Projections. With respect to the reported budget deficit, Treasury and OMB continue to lack an effective process for reasonably assuring the consistency of (1) information Treasury uses to compute the budget deficit reported in the consolidated financial statements, (2) Treasury's records of cash transactions processed through its central accounting function, and (3) information reported in federal entity financial statements and underlying entity financial information and records. Over the past few years, Treasury has made progress by developing and implementing procedures to reconcile certain outlays and receipts between Treasury's records used to compute the budget deficit reported in the consolidated financial statements and underlying federal entity financial information and records.

In fiscal year 2015, we again noted that several entities' auditors reported internal control deficiencies related to monitoring, accounting, and reporting of budgetary transactions. These control deficiencies could affect the reporting and calculation of the net outlay amounts in the entities' Statements of Budgetary Resources. In addition, such deficiencies may also affect the entities' ability to report reliable budgetary information to Treasury and OMB and may affect the unified budget deficit reported in the accrual-based consolidated financial statements. Treasury also reports the unified budget deficit in its *Combined Statement of Receipts, Outlays, and Balances*,[50] and in other federal government publications.

---

[49]The budget deficit, receipts, and outlays amounts are reported in Treasury's *Monthly Treasury Statement* and the President's Budget.
[50]Treasury's *Combined Statement of Receipts, Outlays, and Balances* presents budget results and cash-related assets and liabilities of the federal government with supporting details. According to Treasury, this report is the official publication of receipts and outlays of the federal government based on entity reporting.

Appendix III

Other Material Weaknesses

Material weaknesses in internal control discussed in this audit report resulted in ineffective controls over financial reporting. In addition to the material weaknesses discussed in appendix II that contributed primarily to our disclaimer of opinion on the accrual-based consolidated financial statements, we found the following three other material weaknesses in internal control.

Improper Payments

The federal government is unable to determine the full extent to which improper payments occur and reasonably assure that appropriate actions are taken to reduce them. Reducing improper payments is critical to safeguarding federal funds.[51] The Improper Payments Information Act of 2002 (IPIA), as amended by the Improper Payments Elimination and Recovery Act of 2010 (IPERA) and the Improper Payments Elimination and Recovery Improvement Act of 2012 (IPERIA),[52] requires federal executive branch entities to (1) review all programs and activities, (2) identify those that may be susceptible to significant improper payments, (3) estimate the annual amount of improper payments for those programs and activities identified as risk-susceptible, (4) implement actions to reduce improper payments and set reduction targets with respect to the risk-susceptible programs and activities, and (5) report on the results of addressing the foregoing requirements.

The Office of Management and Budget (OMB) reported that the government-wide improper payment error rate increased to 4.4 percent of program outlays for programs and activities reporting estimates in fiscal year 2015 from 4.0 percent in fiscal year 2014 when including the Department of Defense's (DOD) Defense Finance and Accounting Service (DFAS) Commercial Pay program.[53] When excluding the DFAS Commercial Pay program, the reported government-wide error rate was 4.8 percent of program outlays in fiscal year 2015 compared to 4.5 percent in fiscal year 2014. In May 2013, we reported on major deficiencies in DOD's process for estimating fiscal year 2012 improper payments in the DFAS Commercial Pay program, including deficiencies in identifying a complete and accurate population of payments.[54] The foundation of reliable statistical sampling estimates is a complete, accurate, and valid population from which to sample. Because of DOD's lack of an auditable Statement of Budgetary Resources, the DOD Office of Inspector General reported in DOD's fiscal year 2015 agency financial report that the agency was unable to reconcile outlays and ensure that all required payments subject to improper payment estimation requirements were captured for review. Therefore, DOD's fiscal

---

[51]Under the Improper Payments Information Act of 2002, as amended, an improper payment is statutorily defined as any payment that should not have been made or that was made in an incorrect amount (including overpayments and underpayments) under statutory, contractual, administrative, or other legally applicable requirements. It includes any payment to an ineligible recipient, any payment for an ineligible good or service, any duplicate payment, any payment for a good or service not received (except for such payments where authorized by law), and any payment that does not account for credit for applicable discounts. Office of Management and Budget guidance also instructs agencies to report as improper payments any payments for which insufficient or no documentation was found.

[52]IPIA, Pub. L. No. 107-300, 116 Stat. 2350 (Nov. 26, 2002), as amended by IPERA, Pub. L. No. 111-204, 124 Stat. 2224 (July 22, 2010), and IPERIA, Pub. L. No. 112-248, 126 Stat. 2390 (Jan. 10, 2013), and reprinted in 31 U.S.C. § 3321 note.

[53]Reported error rates reflect the estimated improper payments as a percentage of total program outlays.

[54]GAO, *DOD Financial Management: Significant Improvements Needed in Efforts to Address Improper Payment Requirements*, GAO-13-227 (Washington, D.C.: May 13, 2013).

year 2015 improper payment estimates, including its estimate for the DFAS Commercial Pay program, may not be reliable.

Without the DFAS Commercial Pay program, federal entity improper payment estimates totaled $136.7 billion in fiscal year 2015, a significant increase from the revised prior year estimate of $124.6 billion.[55] The increase in estimated improper payments was mostly attributable to an increased error rate in the Department of Health and Human Services' (HHS) Medicaid program. It is important to note that pursuant to OMB implementing guidance, reported improper payment estimates include overpayments, underpayments, and payments for which adequate documentation was not found, and may also include amounts of payments for years prior to the current fiscal year.

While the specific programs included in the government-wide improper payment estimate may change from year to year, a net of four fewer programs were included when compared to fiscal year 2014. In addition, three federal entities did not report fiscal year 2015 estimated improper payment amounts for five risk-susceptible programs, including HHS's Temporary Assistance for Needy Families.[56] Further, various inspectors general reported deficiencies related to compliance with the criteria listed in IPERA for fiscal year 2014 at their respective federal entities,[57] including risk-susceptible programs that did not report improper payment estimates, estimation methodologies that may not produce reliable estimates, and risk assessments that may not accurately assess the risk of improper payment.

For fiscal year 2015, federal entities reported improper payment error rates that exceeded 10 percent for nine risk-susceptible programs, accounting for more than 50 percent of the government-wide improper payment estimate.[58] Under IPERA, an entity that is determined by its inspector general to not be in compliance with the criteria listed in IPERA, such as reporting an

---

[55]In their fiscal year 2015 performance and accountability reports (PAR) and agency financial reports (AFR), seven federal entities updated their fiscal year 2014 improper payment estimates to reflect changes since issuance of their fiscal year 2014 PARs and AFRs. These updates decreased the government-wide improper payment estimate for fiscal year 2014 from $124.7 billion to $124.6 billion.

[56]The remaining four programs were the Corporation for National and Community Services' Foster Grandparents, Retired and Senior Volunteer, and Senior Companion programs and the General Services Administration's Hurricane Sandy Disaster Relief Fund.

[57]IPERA established a requirement for entity inspectors general to report annually on entities' compliance with criteria listed in section 3 of IPERA. The six criteria are that the entity has (1) published an annual financial statement and accompanying materials in the form and content required by OMB for the most recent fiscal year and posted that report on the entity website; (2) conducted a risk assessment for each specific program or activity that conforms with IPIA, as amended; (3) published estimates of improper payments for all programs and activities identified as susceptible to significant improper payments under the entity's risk assessment; (4) published corrective action plans for programs and activities assessed to be at risk for significant improper payments; (5) published and met annual reduction targets for all programs and activities assessed to be at risk for significant improper payments; and (6) reported a gross improper payment rate of less than 10 percent for each program and activity for which an improper payment estimate was obtained and published. The most recent inspectors general reports on compliance with the criteria listed in IPERA were issued in 2015 for fiscal year 2014. Pursuant to the OMB implementing guidance in M-15-02, Appendix C to Circular No. A-123, *Requirements for Effective Estimation and Remediation of Improper Payments* (Oct. 20, 2014), each entity inspector general must complete its review of entity compliance under IPERA within 180 days of publication of the PAR or AFR. Therefore, inspector general reports on fiscal year 2015 compliance with the criteria listed in IPERA are generally expected to be issued by May 2016.

[58]The nine programs that reported improper payment estimates that exceeded 10 percent in fiscal year 2015 were (1) the Department of Veterans Affairs' (VA) VA Community Care, (2) VA's Purchased Long Term Services and Supports, (3) the Department of the Treasury's Earned Income Tax Credit, (4) the Department of Agriculture's (USDA) School Breakfast, (5) USDA's Farm Security and Rural Investment, (6) USDA's National School Lunch, (7) the Small Business Administration's Disbursement for Goods and Services, (8) HHS's Medicare Fee-for-Service, and (9) the Department of Labor's Unemployment Insurance programs.

improper payment rate of 10 percent or greater for any risk-susceptible program or activity, must submit a plan to Congress describing the actions that the entity will take to come into compliance.

Further, entity auditors continued to report internal control deficiencies over financial reporting in their fiscal year 2015 financial statement audit reports, such as financial system limitations and information system control weaknesses. Such deficiencies could significantly increase the risk that improper payments may occur and not be detected promptly.

The President's fiscal year 2016 and fiscal year 2017 budgets included program integrity proposals at multiple agencies aimed at reducing improper payments. Also, efforts continue to implement requirements established by IPERIA, which was enacted in January 2013 to intensify efforts to identify, prevent, and recover payment error, waste, fraud, and abuse within federal spending. Among other things, IPERIA enacted into law elements of the President's "Do Not Pay" initiative by requiring entities to review prepayment and pre-award procedures and ensure a thorough review of available databases to determine program or award eligibility before the release of any federal funds. IPERIA also directs OMB to annually identify a list of high-priority federal programs for greater levels of oversight and review and requires each entity responsible for administering one of these high-priority programs to annually submit a program report to its inspector general and make a report copy available to the public.

Until the federal government has implemented effective processes to determine the full extent to which improper payments occur and has taken appropriate actions across entities and programs to effectively reduce improper payments, it will not have reasonable assurance that the use of federal funds is adequately safeguarded.

Information Security

GAO has reported information security as a high-risk area across government since February 1997. During our fiscal year 2015 audit, we found that serious and widespread information security control deficiencies continued to place federal assets at risk of inadvertent or deliberate misuse, financial information at risk of unauthorized modification or destruction, sensitive information at risk of inappropriate disclosure, and critical operations at risk of disruption. Specifically, control deficiencies were identified related to (1) security management; (2) access to computer resources (data, equipment, and facilities); (3) changes to and configuration of information system resources; (4) segregation of incompatible duties; and (5) contingency planning.

Such information security control deficiencies unnecessarily increase the risk that data recorded in or transmitted by federal financial management systems are not reliable and available. A primary reason for these deficiencies is that federal entities generally have not yet fully institutionalized comprehensive security management programs, which are critical to identifying information security control deficiencies, resolving information security problems, and managing information security risks on an ongoing basis.

Although significant challenges remain, the federal government has taken actions toward improving information security. For example, Congress passed and the President signed the

Federal Information Security Modernization Act of 2014,[59] and the Federal Chief Information Officer launched a 30-day Cybersecurity Sprint intended to improve the protection of federal information and systems.[60] At the end of the Cybersecurity Sprint, according to OMB, federal agencies increased their use of strong authentication from 42 percent to 72 percent.[61] Further, the administration has issued a cybersecurity strategy and implementation plan for federal civilian agencies to guide efforts to improve the security over their information and systems. It also plans to continue to oversee agency security efforts by monitoring the implementation of cybersecurity capabilities, such as strong authentication, continuous monitoring, anti-phishing and malware defense, and developing or monitoring performance-based metrics to measure their success. However, until entities identify and resolve information security control deficiencies and manage information security risks on an ongoing basis, federal data and systems, including financial information, will remain at risk.

Tax Collection Activities

During fiscal year 2015, a material weakness continued to affect the federal government's ability to effectively manage its tax collection activities. Due to financial system limitations, as well as errors in taxpayers' accounts, the federal government's records did not always reflect the correct amount of taxes owed by the public to the federal government. Such errors may cause undue burden and frustration to taxpayers who either have already paid taxes owed or who owe significantly lower amounts.

Collectively, these deficiencies indicate that internal controls were not effective in (1) ensuring that reported amounts of taxes receivable and other tax assessments were accurate on an ongoing basis and could be relied upon by management as a tool to aid in making and supporting resource allocation decisions and (2) supporting timely and reliable financial statements, accompanying notes, and required supplementary information and other information without extensive supplemental procedures and adjustments.

---

[59]The Federal Information Security Management Act of 2002 was enacted as Title III of the E-Government Act of 2002, Pub. L. No. 107-347, 116 Stat. 2899, 2946 (Dec. 17, 2002). The Federal Information Security Modernization Act of 2014, which largely superseded the 2002 act, was enacted as Pub. L. No. 113-283, 128 Stat. 3073 (Dec. 18, 2014), and amended chapter 35 of Title 44, U.S. Code.

[60]In June 2015, the Federal Chief Information Officer launched the 30-day Cybersecurity Sprint, during which agencies were to take immediate actions to combat cyber threats within 30 days. Actions included patching critical vulnerabilities, tightening policies and practices for privileged users, and accelerating the implementation of multifactor or strong authentication.

[61]Authentication is the process a computer system uses to establish the validity of a user's claimed identity by requesting some kind of information, such as a password, that is known only by the user. Strong authentication involves the use of multiple factors to authenticate a user. These factors include something you know (password or personal identification number), something you have (smartcard or personal identity verification card), or something you are (biometric).

Appendix IV

Significant Deficiency

In addition to the material weaknesses discussed in appendixes II and III, we found a significant deficiency in the federal government's internal control related to implementing effective internal controls over management of federal grants at certain federal entities, as described below.

Federal Grants Management

In fiscal year 2015, several federal entities' auditors continued to identify internal control deficiencies related to grants management. Reported deficiencies primarily related to monitoring of grant activities and accounting for formula grants.[62] These internal control deficiencies could adversely affect the federal government's ability to provide reliable financial statements as well as reasonable assurance that grants are awarded properly, recipients are eligible, and federal grant funds are used as intended.

---

[62]Formula grants are awarded to all eligible grantees based on a statutory allocation formula, which may be based on a number of variables, including population, poverty rate in a given area, or tax effort. The grants are typically awarded to states, which often pass funds through to eligible local government agencies and nonprofit organizations.